SEAMUS HEANEY

Seamus Heaney

The Making of the Poet

Michael Parker

Senior Lecturer in English
Liverpool Institute of Higher Education

MACMILLAN

First edition 1993

Published by
MACMILLAN PRESS LTD
Houndmills, Basingstoke, Hampshire RG21 2XS
and London
Companies and representatives
throughout the world

ISBN 0–333–47181–4 hardcover
ISBN 0–333–61879–3 paperback

A catalogue record for this book is available
from the British Library.

Printed and bound in Great Britain by
Antony Rowe Ltd
Chippenham, Wiltshire

8   7   6   5   4   3
02 01 00 99 98 97

for Aleksandra,
Judith, Juliet and Catherine

Contents

List of Illustrations   viii

Acknowledgements   ix

Preface   x

Map   xi

1   A Good Anchor: Home and Education, 1939–61   1

2   Affinities, 1961–66   28

3   Pioneer, 1966–69   61
     Death of a Naturalist   61
     Door into the Dark   76

4   Exposure, 1969–75   89
     Wintering Out   89
     North   117

5   Quickenings, 1975–84   152
     Field Work   152
     Station Island   177

6   Space, 1984–91   211
     The Haw Lantern   211
     Seeing Things   217

Notes   222

Bibliography   277

Index of Poems, Collections and Essays   284

Index of General References   288

List of Illustrations

1   Barn, Mossbawn

2   The Pump from 'Changes', an *Omphalos*

3   The Eel Fisheries, Toome

4   St. Columb's College, Derry

5   Queen's University, Belfast

6   Michael Longley, Derek Mahon, John Hewitt, Seamus Heaney, Cushendall, 1969 (courtesy of Arts Council of Northern Ireland)

7   David Hammond (courtesy of David Hammond)

8   T. P. Flanagan

9   Seamus Heaney and Philip Hobsbaum, Glasgow, 1989

10a The Windeby girl, the subject of Heaney's 'Punishment'. He
/b   encountered this image in P. V. Glob's *The Bog People* (courtesy of Archaologisches Landesmuseum der Christian Albrechts Universität, Schloss Gottorf, Schleswig)

Acknowledgements

I would like to thank the Education Authorities of Cheshire and Bury, and the Liverpool Institute of Higher Education and the University of Liverpool for their financial support while I was at work on this book. Considerable support was given to me by Michael Jones, the English Adviser for Cheshire, Sister Mary Kelly of Holy Cross College, Bury, and by Patrick Swinden of the University of Manchester, my supervisor in the early stages of the project.

I am grateful for the generous help I received from those I interviewed, Michael Longley, Frank Ormsby, Sean O'Kelly, T. P. Flanagan, David Hammond, Seamus Deane, Ann and Hugh Heaney, Harry Chambers, Raymond Gallagher, George McWhirter, and Philip Hobsbaum, who has been consistently encouraging and supportive. Many of the above provided me with rare source material, as did Queen's University Library, Belfast.

My interests in literature and history were fostered by my parents, and by excellent teachers at school, John Foster, Brian Hayward, Marcus Baker and Doreen Wren, and at the University of Reading, where I was taught by Ian Fletcher, John Goode and Christopher Salvesen. Colleagues at Holy Cross College, especially Kate Doran and Sandra Cameron, gave invaluable advice.

An earlier version of the section on *Seeing Things* appeared as a review in *The Honest Ulsterman*, Belfast, whose editors, Frank Ormsby and Robert Johnstone, have been 'confirmatory presences' to me.

My editors at Macmillan, Frances Arnold and Margaret Cannon, have been extremely patient and helpful over the six years I have been researching and writing.

Finally, my thanks to Seamus Heaney for his kindness and courtesy in answering questions in person and by post, and for correcting factual errors. Quotations from the published and unpublished poems and other material by Seamus Heaney are reproduced by permission of Faber and Faber Ltd, the B.B.C., and by Seamus Heaney himself. (For a complete list of references and acknowledgments see Notes and Bibliography.)

Preface

"Poetry is a natural growth, having more than a superficial relation to roses and trees and hills. However airy and graceful it may be in foliage and flower, it has roots deep in a substantial past. It springs apparently from an occupation of the land, from long, busy and quiet tracts of time, wherein a man or nation may find its soul. To have a future, it must have had a past."

(Edward Thomas, quoted in Edna Longley's *A Language not to be Betrayed: Selected Prose of Edward Thomas*, Carcanet, Manchester, 1981, p. iv)

My aim in this book has been, as far as possible, to identify and analyse the biographical, literary, historical and political influences and experiences that have shaped the poetry of Seamus Heaney. I have endeavoured to provide a detailed account of the contexts from which the poems sprang, so that Heaney's Irish, Catholic background might be better understood by readers less familiar with Catholicism and Ireland. Since *Wintering Out*, each of his collections have been carefully structured and organised, and so I have attempted to pay close attention to the way each book unfolds, as well as offering close readings and critical evaluations of individual poems. Ultimately I am just another reader, but I hope that my readings will encourage others to go back to the poems, and to other commentators, to mine their own meanings.

MICHAEL PARKER
Bury

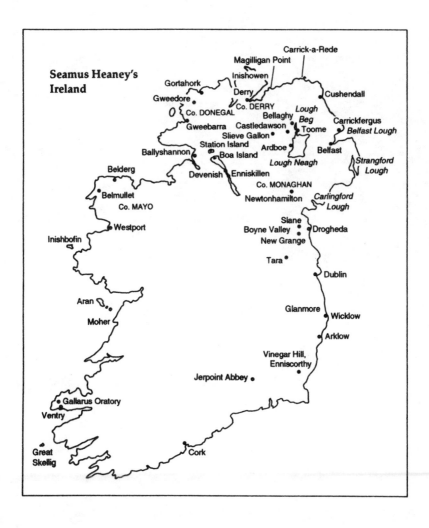

Seamus Heaney's Ireland

Gortahork
Gweedore
Co. DONEGAL
Inishowen
Magilligan Point
Carrick-a-Rede
Derry
Co. DERRY
Cushendall
Gweebarra
Bellaghy
Lough Beg
Carrickfergus
Castledawson
Toome
Belfast Lough
Slieve Gallon
Station Island
Ardboe
Belfast
Ballyshannon
Boa Island
Strangford Lough
Belderg
Devenish
Enniskillen
Lough Neagh
Belmullet
Co. MONAGHAN
Co. MAYO
Newtonhamilton
Carlingford Lough
Westport
Slane
Boyne Valley
Drogheda
Inishbofin
New Grange
Tara
Aran
Dublin
Moher
Glanmore
Wicklow
Arklow
Vinegar Hill, Enniscorthy
Jerpoint Abbey
Gallarus Oratory
Ventry
Great Skellig
Cork

xi

1

A Good Anchor: Home and Education, 1939–61

Is maith an t'ancoire an t-iarta.
The hearth is a good anchor.

(Gaelic Proverb)[1]

Whatever poetic success I've had has come from staying within the realm of my own imaginative country and my own voice.[2]

Seamus Justin Heaney was born on 13 April 1939, at Mossbawn, near Castledawson, County Derry. His father, Patrick, born at the end of the first decade of this century, was a cattle dealer, owning a forty-acre farm, an average size holding by Northern Irish standards. A yeoman farmer, who served as a member of the rural council, Patrick Heaney embodied solidity. The portrait in 'Ancestral Photographs' suggests a stocky, resolute individual, a skilled, successful bargainer, but also a figure from a lost world. With the passing of the cattle-fairs, something had been broken in him; parked behind the door, his ashplant, – a symbol of his 'office', – seemed like an abandoned wand.[3] Already in the earliest work of the young poet, his father had become an elegiac presence, a focus for his own mourning of change. As a child, Heaney had looked up to him as the possessor of a magical strength and skill; in 'Digging', at one point, he appears like some ancient hero, burying 'the bright edge deep'; presented first as the Titan Atlas in 'Follower', he is later praised as the complete master of his craft. The images and allusions are evidence of love and admiration, but are also the product of separation, a distance, born of time and education, which the young man half regrets.

Like many fathers of his, and every generation, Patrick Heaney seems to have found it difficult to communicate with his son, and to

1

treat him as an equal. In an uncollected poem of 1965, 'Boy driving his father to confession',[4] Heaney examines four moments when 'chinks' appeared 'in the paternal mail', when the silence between them eased and he discovered a man 'lost like me, quite vulnerable'. For his father to express his emotions might be to expose that vulnerability, something extremely difficult to do, especially in an area like South Derry, where the traditionalist codes of masculinity linger on. 'Tight-lipped silence', however, is typical of cattle-dealers, according to Estyn Evans,[5] and in considering the portraits of his father and the craftsmen who people his poetry, one should remember that taciturnity is a feature common to Northern Catholics and Protestants. "Some of the qualities that I recognise as typical of the Ulsterman," writes the poet, Michael Longley, "are a down-to-earth realism, a dislike of unnecessary frills, a distrust of verbiage. He doesn't speak for the sake of decoration, but prefers to search for the facts at the core of any matter."[6]

Initially in his work Heaney treated the 'famous/Northern reticence'[7] with a sympathetic understanding, for it was a quality – a rather disabling one for a writer! – he shared himself. Reluctance to acknowledge his own 'offspring', and a fear of appearing presumptuous lay behind his adoption of the pseudonym, 'Incertus', for his earliest poetic efforts. Even after the great success he had enjoyed in the 1970s, in an interview with John Haffenden, he admitted feeling something akin to guilt in writing:

> there is indeed some part of me that is entirely unimpressed by the activity, that doesn't dislike it, but it's the generations, I suppose of rural ancestors – not illiterate, but not literary. They in me, or through them, don't give a damn.[8]

In later volumes, he came to recognise that the 'gagging' in the North within both communities, and the unwillingness to confront and speak out against injustices within his own, had been major factors in the explosion of violence. Certain of the later poems indicate an impatience with his father's 'lifetime's speechlessness',[9] yet at the same time he is very conscious of the largeness of spirit passed on to him by his parents, and the richness of experience they provided which 'founded' and sustained him.

Heaney's mother, Margaret Kathleen McCann, was born in 1911, and died in 1984. The photograph of her that hangs above the stairs just outside Heaney's study in his Dublin home, and in his Bellaghy home, speaks of a warm, animated, imaginative personality. David Hammond, the poet's best friend since 1965, remarked on her sense of humour, which like her generosity and hospitality, seeped into her son. (On one occasion, Hammond asked after a frail young man of the locality, who led a cotton-wool existence, cossetted by two doting women in his family. Mrs Heaney replied wryly that he was "under new management now," and went on to explain how he had married a particularly imposing, handsome woman). Though not literary, she was fascinated by language and etymology, as the following passage from 'Feeling into Words' reveals. Heaney connects his awakening interest in words 'as bearers of history and mystery' with his mother's influence.

> Maybe it began early when my mother used to recite lists of affixes and suffixes, and Latin roots, with their English meanings, rhymes that formed part of her schooling in the early part of the century.[10]

Mrs Heaney bore nine children, Seamus, Sheena, Ann, Hugh, Patrick, Charles, Colum, Christopher, and Dan. The family she created was very close-knit, and according to her daughter-in-law, "utterly together, like an egg contained within the shell. They had confidence in the way they lived, a lovely impeccable confidence in their own style."[11] Margaret Heaney, along with her sister-in-law, Mary, who lived with the family, formed a special bond with the eldest child. Several poems in the sonnet sequence, 'Clearances', written after her death, capture beautifully the unspoken intimacy of mother and son, and how, in her company, humble, diurnal, domestic chores could become suffused with a precious radiance. In a poignant memory that re-surfaced as his mother lay on her deathbed, he recalls the gleam of the water as they dropped peeled potatoes in, one day while 'the others were away at Mass', and the joy of being united with her in 'fluent' labour.

> I remembered her head bent towards my head,
> Her breath in mine, our fluent dipping knives –
> Never closer the whole rest of our lives.[12]

The phrase 'Her breath in mine' reminds us that she breathed life into him, like the God of Genesis, and the poem repays the creative debt.[13] Perhaps the most important qualities Heaney received from his mother issued from her deeply religious sensibility, qualities such as patience, humility, awe, and reverence which permeate his personality and writing. In one interview, he speaks at some length of the heady, almost narcotic intensity of the religion of the home, and stresses the impact his mother made on his spiritual development, which far outweighed the clergy's influence.

> My sensibility was formed by the dolorous murmurings of the rosary, and the generally Marian quality of devotion. The reality that was addressed was maternal, and the posture was one of supplication. The attitude to life that was inculcated into me – not by priests, but by the active, lived thing of prayers and so on, in my house, *through my mother* – was really patience. At the bottom I think that probably patience is the best virtue. Irish Catholicism, until about ten years ago, had this Virgin Mary worship, almost worship. In practice, the shrines, the rosary beads, all the devotions, were centred towards a feminine presence, which I think was terrific for the sensibility. I think that the 'Hail Mary' is more of a poem than the 'Our Father'. 'Our Father' is between chaps, but there's something faintly amorous about the 'Hail Mary'.[14]

One finds the same, frank, humorous acknowledgement of the Mother-Virgin Mary-Lover axis occurs in the sixth sonnet of the 'Clearances' sequence,[15] which again sees son and mother together in communion, this time at Mass. The feelings of longing and grief embedded in the lines from Psalm 42, "*As the hind longs for the stream . . .*", "*Day and night my tears have been my bread*", serve to remind one that perhaps for Mrs Heaney, as for the mother figures of the *Door into the Dark* poems, 'The Wife's Tale' and 'Mother', being a wife and mother meant considerable sacrifice, exhaustion and frustration. Like his mother before him, Heaney employs ritual to help him take the strain, and offers up his experiences of pain, doubt and fear in the service of an art that assuages.

The 'sure and steadfast anchor'[16] of the poet's soul was forged by both his parents, therefore, and behind them stretched back generations of strength. In the Irish psyche, ancestry is a potent force, steadying the individual, and shaping his or her sense of identity. It is perhaps even more important in the North of Ireland where the Catholics are a minority 'in a province that insists that it is British', and where the notion was promoted that British and Protestant culture was superior. Though breaking with family tradition by working the field of literature, Heaney maintains his links with 'the energies of generation' in celebrating his forbears. Grandfather McCann, his mother's father, worked as a boiler man in the linen mill in Castledawson. His son, Margaret's brother, Matthew 'Sonny' McCann, was a famous Gaelic football player. Since the Church and the Gaelic football team were the two poles around which community life for the Catholics revolved,[17] this must have been a major source of pride to the family. From his father's side, he remembers a cousin who would "visit once a week and read and recite to the children in the family", perhaps another link in the chain joining the boy to his future craft. In an interview for *The Irish Times*, Heaney recalls

> listening to bits of local lore, the remnants of the oral tradition when his father's cousin came to visit the house. This rather fantastic figure on the poet's childhood landscape might be described as one of the surviving hedgerow schoolmasters whose wont it was, when he had had a few drinks, to recite a long poem in which Henry Joy McCracken figured.[18]

unconsciously taking in "the subculture of Nationalism/Catholicism which I suppose everybody in the minority imbibed." Ancestry, like history and myth, enabled Heaney to connect the currents of past and present, to be much more than a solitary Ego, to speak with *humilitas* and weight as an individual in a line stretching back to St Muredach O'Heney and earlier.[19] Even an Iron Age victim from the time of Christ, the Tollund Man, became 'like an ancestor almost' to him, like "one of my old uncles, one of those moustached archaic faces you used to meet all over the Irish countryside."[20] For a long time the bonds of loyalty to this extended family made him uneasy and guilty about his middle class life-style and literary success, almost as if he were a freed slave who could now afford to dine with the patricians.

The frequent tributes in poetry and prose to neighbours from his home ground reveal the debt he feels he owes to them, and his desire to fuse his achievements to theirs. In 'A Poet's Childhood' from 1971, we meet Joe Ward, a carpenter and 'a kind of poet too', since 'making a rhyme is like making a joint', and an unnamed young girl who came to darn old socks, whose needlework also provides a metaphor for the 'stitching and unstitching' of the poet's task.[21] In his earliest poems we meet Dan Taggart, Big Jim Evans, and Henry McWilliams, the Achilles, Ajax and Nestor of the local 'epic' world.[22] In the community in which Heaney grew up, Protestants and Catholics "lived in proximity and harmony with one another",[23] and generally showed tolerance and courtesy to each other, such as that displayed in 'The Other Side' in *Wintering Out* and 'Trial Runs' in *Stations*. In the latter, a demobbed Protestant neighbour returns from Italy with a particularly imposing set of rosary beads for his father. Behind the 'crack' and wisecracks sectarian tensions whisper:

> "Did they make a papish of you over there?
> "Oh damn the fear! I stole them for you, Paddy, off the pope's dresser when his back was turned."
> "You could harness a donkey with them."
> Their laughter sailed above my head, a hoarse clamour, two big nervous birds dipping and lifting, making trial runs over a territory.[24]

The fact that he was spared the overt prejudice and ghetto violence that many other Northern writers witnessed lends his poems of childhood an outward mellowness; underneath, though, a darker pattern veins the experiences.

The locations of his childhood prove to be almost as important to the later development of the poet as the human landscape. At the centre of his world was the thatched farmhouse at Mossbawn, the family home until 1953, a place which he has transformed 'into a country of the mind'.[25] In his search for myth and symbol, he has frequently returned to the Mossbawn pump as a source for his creative energy, its 'falling music' nourishing the inner ear and eye much as the Derwent did for the young Wordsworth. It is a recurring, fecund presence in several volumes.[26] With its phallic shape and life-giving water, it symbolises the creative union of his parents, the male and the female, the mysterious fusion of fixity and fluidity which gives the world and Art its shape; it is a South Derry equivalent of the Pierian spring. During Heaney's endless quest for self-definition, Mossbawn has proved an inexhaustible resource. Frequently it has been used to invoke images of Eden, with its beech and willow as trees of knowledge, feeding his 'appetite' for 'gravity'.[27] The serpentine tendrils of the pea-drill, where as a child he was lost, becomes a vehicle for his Fall into experience.[28] In

Preoccupations he recalls bathing in a moss-hole as a very young child, "treading the liver-thick mud", "unsettling a smoky muck off the bottom and coming out smeared and weedy and darkened."[29] A boy's hunger for dirt, danger, sensation, is fashioned in retrospect into a ritual baptism in nature, a sexual initiation, a love-act with the literal 'matter of Ireland', before political crisis forced him into a more bitter and lasting union. The very name of Mossbawn with its Scots/English/Gaelic etymology serves as an emblem of 'the split culture of Ulster', the Irish paradise seized and 'translated' by the alien Planters.

> Our farm was called Mossbawn. Moss, a Scots word probably carried to Ulster by the planters, and bawn, the name the English colonists gave to their fortified farmhouses . . . Yet in spite of the Ordnance Survey spelling, we pronounced it Moss bann, and ban is the Gaelic word for white. So might not the thing mean the white moss, the moss of bog-cotton?[30]

The childhood home itself becomes, therefore, an object for re-possession in several senses – imaginative, linguistic, political, and spiritual – its Gaelic naming a family gesture against four hundred years of colonisation, or theft. A simple glance at the place-names around Castledawson leads one to suspect that from his earliest years, Heaney must have had some consciousness of the racial and religious allegiances behind names such as Hill Head, Grove Park, Aughrim Hill on one hand and Broagh, Anahorish, Derrygarve on the other. Sandwiched between Moyola Park, a large estate belonging to James Chichester-Clarks, the former Unionist Prime Minister, and Toome, a village surrounded by bogland on the banks of the Bann, where Roddy McCorley, a young patriot was hung for his role in the 1798 rebellion, Mossbawn was situated on a ley line of Irish history. Although some critics have implied that Heaney expropriated the bog as a symbol after reading P. V. Glob's *The Bog People,* as if to accuse him of literary 'sharp practice', the truth is that, from childhood, bogland had been 'a genuine obsession', since it covered such a large area of his home territory. Its colours and smells were 'written into' his senses 'from the minute' he 'began to breathe',[31] just as surely as the heathland breathed in Hardy.

From his earliest days, he acquired the notion of places as mysterious and sacred, from the 'silky, fragrant' Sandy Loaning inhabited by wrens, rabbits, badgers and 'bogeys', to the awesome Church

Island in the centre of Lough Beg, where St Patrick was said to have 'fasted and prayed' fifteen centuries earlier. The mountain, Slieve Gallon, to the west, and Lough Beg to the East marked the distant borders of his territory, which had at its centre the Moyola River, to whose banks the boy could escape, to dream, to fish, to while away time listening to its music.

It would be a mistake, however, to view Heaney's infancy and early childhood as a succession of 'godlike hours'.[32] Though undoubtedly there were idyllic moments, like this Talbothays scene, when he "lay snug in a big soft pile of hay", "listening to the rich purring as the milk rose steadily in my aunt's pail",[33] there were also moments of menace such as that recorded in 'The Barn'. The first three *Stations* imply that, along with the epiphanies, there were moments of incommunicable grief; each of the three ends in sobbing. 'Hedge School', with its ironic allusion to the temple episode of Luke's Gospel (Chapter Two), would seem to indicate differences of sensibility between parent and child. Whereas the adult figures – his mother and aunt? – are trying to get to church for devotions, the boy, like young Oisin, holds back, entranced by the divine beauty of the natural world. "Pull them up for the May altar and hurry up", they urge him. Re-tracing their steps, they find him in tears, and ask him, not for the first time, "What are you crying about now, son? What is it next?"[34] His "closeness to the land, to the very pulse of it"[35] stirred in the child the deepest of feelings, to such an extent that the adult poet speaks of the home landscape as 'sacramental'.[36] Considering the significance given to place in the Celtic and Catholic and the Romantic imagination – the well, the tree, the fairy thorn, the standing stone, the hill – one should not be surprised by the fervour with which Heaney refers to his territory. The religious intensity with which Northern Catholics and Protestants view the land manifests itself not just in poetry, but also in the blood which they shed to sour the 'mother ground'.[37] The poet's concern, however, is with a pentecostal energy, the energy of the word generated by landscape;[38] his imagination, like Milton's Holy Spirit, broods 'dove-like' over the land, and makes it 'pregnant' with language, and each poem becomes 'a kind of love made to each acre'.[39]

From 1945–51 Heaney attended the local primary school at Anahorish, which catered for both Catholic and Protestant children, a mingling rarely found in Northern Ireland with its predominantly sectarian schooling. This experience made him gently conscious of religious differences, 'innocently' articulated in the playground rhymes. From simple antitheses – "Up the long ladder and down the short rope/To hell with King Billy and God bless the Pope", or, in the Protestant version, "Up with King William and down with the Pope" – the children graduated to more sophisticated verses, such as,

> Splitter splatter holy water
> Scatter the Papyshes every one
> If that won't do
> We'll cut them in two
> And give them a touch of the
> Red, white and blue.[40]

In an interview for *Les Lettres Nouvelles* in 1973, Heaney explains how these chants, 'semi-religieuses, semi-politiques', constituted an early layer in the formation of the two 'sub-cultures'.

> Nous savions aussi qu'elles symbolisaient des différences, mais très vaguement; tous les enfants connaissent des comptines qu'ils ne comprennent pas vraiment. Mais leur signification se précise à mesure qu'ils grandissent.[41]

Another feature of the 'primary' experience, which has probably taken on greater significance in retrospect, was his exposure to the 'attitudes and customs and habits of feeling' of the dominant culture. One symbol of this was the map of Ulster with its red border, that 'vestigially bloody marking' which 'halted the eye travelling south and west',[42] but permitted movement eastwards with its delicate, dotted lines reaching out towards Glasgow, Stranraer, Liverpool. In the Malone lecture he cites poems such as 'Oh to be in England' in the reading book, and 'The Lincolnshire Poacher' as illustrative of the school transmitting, albeit unconsciously, a culture 'at variance with the common hearth feelings of the pupils'. To be fair to the school, however, few publishers then, if any, would have had the foresight, or rather altruism, to produce educational material which reflected the cultural inheritance of either Ulster tradition; with such a small school population in the province, it would not have been economically viable. In such circumstances one might normally expect a government to be concerned, but

Stormont ministers would not have dreamt of 'acknowledging the validity of both traditions' in education by promoting such material, since such a concept would have constituted the blackest treachery. The cumulative result of the British bias in education in the North, though in part the product of economics, undoubtedly, was to fuel resentment in the minority, and to foster in both communities the debilitating and erroneous notion that English culture was inherently superior. Such a belief prompted many schools to teach only English history and literature, and encouraged many parents, like Tom Paulin's, to pack them off to elocution lessons to obliterate their 'ugly' regional accents. It could be argued that while Heaney's exposure to what he now regards as 'cultural colonialism'[43] may have bred feelings of inferiority and insecurity in the short term, in the long term it also honed his sense of identity, and provided him with sustenance from two rich traditions.

Certainly, at Anahorish School he was fortunate to be taught by a gifted teacher, Bernard Murphy. His appearance in the title sequence of *Station Island* gives the impression that teaching in the village school was not always spiritually rewarding.[44] 'Master Murphy' taught the young Seamus Latin, and was the first of many teachers to inspire a love of learning and to relish the success of his star pupil. 'The Wanderer'[45] in *Stations* portrays his pleasure in Heaney's scholarship to St Columb's College, but also shows the adult poet's recognition that it was a triumph which began his exile from Mossbawn.

> In a semi-circle we toed the line chalked around the master's desk . . . and he called me forward and crossed my palm with silver. "At the end of the holidays this man's going away to Derry, so this is for him for winning the scholarship . . . We all wish him good luck."

Sudden academic success had transformed the boy into 'a rich young man', a South Derry Philip Pirrip. In referring to himself with this phrase, Heaney is alluding to the character in the gospels (Matthew's, Mark's and Luke's) whose material security proves an encumbrance to his spiritual development. It also reminds one, however, of Wordsworth's positive self-definition in *The Prelude*, "I was most rich/ I had a world about me",[46] and Roethke's joyous description of himself, "Oh he was Fortune's child, a favourite son/ Upon whom every gift and thrill were showered."[47]

Even before winning his scholarship to St. Columb's College and departing from Mossbawn, his education almost certainly was beginning to prise open a gap between him and his parents. In *Preoccupations,* he recalls being interrupted in his reading one night by Hugh Bates, a neighbour. The passage hints at tensions in his father's teasing comment, which suggests a mixture of pride and unease.

'Boys but this Seamus fellow is a great scholar. What book are you in now, son?' And my father is likely wringing what he can from the moment with 'He's as bad as Pat McGuckin this minute.' Pat McGuckin was a notorious bachelor farmer – a cousin of ours – who was said to burn his scone like King Alfred every time he lifted a book.[48]

Like many parents whose children benefitted from the 1947 Northern Ireland Education Act – the equivalent of the 1944 Butler Act in England and Wales – the Heaneys were enthusiastic about their son's achievement, yet must have had mixed feelings about his separation from them.

Seamus Heaney began his secondary education at St. Columb's College, Derry in September 1951. The school was founded in 1879, on a site which originally belonged to the eighteenth century Protestant Bishop of Derry. Serving as a minor seminary, it prepared 'many of its best students for the priesthood', where they would pose no threat to 'Protestant commercial supremacy'.[49]

Until 1948 the college had stood aloof, physically and psychologically, from the squalid streets of the Bogside, but with the arrival of the first eleven-plus students it was forced to come to terms with the social deprivation all around it, since that was the background of many of its scholarship boys.[50]

These included the likes of Seamus Deane, Heaney's contemporary and a lifelong friend, and John Hume, who was two years senior. The school offered academic achievement as a passport to career success, and attempted to instil 'in one year what other schools would do in two.'[51] For a boarder, like Heaney, who was bright and willing, its rigorous, hothouse atmosphere must have been exhilarating at times. However, 'trim lawns and shady trees'[52] could hardly compensate for the loss of warmth and freedom the boy experienced. He was 'terribly homesick',[53] according to his sister, Ann, a fact confirmed by 'The Ministry of Fear' in *North*, where he records how in his first week he 'couldn't even eat/ The biscuits left to sweeten my exile'; instead he 'threw them over the fence one night' in a guilty – and angry? – 'act of stealth'.[54] One suspects he never repeated this dramatic gesture, and came to accept his confinement with a good grace. The weekly parcel from home of black cake, biscuits and Creamola foam – which was used to make an orangy fizzy drink – would reassure him that he was not forgotten.[55]

The intensive routine at the school would have allowed little time for the luxury of self-pity. The students rose at 7.30 a.m., and attended Mass, which was followed by breakfast and classes till lunch-time at midday. Afternoon lessons continued till 4 p.m. Private study from 5 to 7.30 p.m., and from 8.30 till 10 p.m., was interrupted for an hour by supper. The day would end with night prayers, and lights out was at 10.30 p.m. Classes were held every Saturday morning, and confessions heard on Saturday nights, appropriately preceded by showers.[56] The 'treats' consisted of a film once every three weeks, and an opportunity for the boarders, like Heaney, to visit town every third Saturday. Ordinarily much of the boys' leisure time was spent 'on a treadmill of walks inside the college walls, looking out at the streets and forward to the holidays'. There was an old joke about 'the appropriate siting of the gaol on the same street as the school'[57] which must have owed some its freshness to this timetable. Although the school was concerned with the preparation of young men for the religious life and encouraging all the students through Mass and devotions to commit themselves to Christ, St Columb's, like many other schools of this era, contained some staff who abused their power and position to 'herod' it, to make the little children suffer, to instruct their charges in the brutality that one might associate with a penal institution. According to one contemporary of Heaney's, there was considerable use of physical punishment, and he recalled how one boy was struck so hard by a priest that his eardrum burst. The victim in due course became a priest himself.[58] In his biography of John Hume, Barry White cites one teacher 'legendary for his arbitrary punishments'.

'It's raining today, so I'll give you a smack. If it's sunny tomorrow, you'll get another.' and 'I see Seamus at the back of the class not paying attention, but I'm too tired to walk down there, so I'll punish you instead and you can take it up with him after class.'[59]

David Hammond commented to me that when Heaney and Seamus Deane meet together, their conversation often turns to the jealousies and tensions of the school, and to some of the vengeful, vindictive teachers who 'were themselves victims of oppression, yet took revenge on the children.'[60] As a boy from a poor Bogside family, Seamus Deane suffered acutely from the snobbery and class distinctions rife in the college, another form of violence on the 'hidden curriculum'. Although Heaney may not have been victimised himself, he must have observed with horror the co-existence of faith and cruelty at St Columb's. 'Ministry of Fear' shows his shame at being a silent witness, 'bowed' in submission to an authority which at times seemed to have 'gone rancid'.[61]

In his early teens while at St Columb's, two incidents connected with home must have had a huge impact on him. One year, after returning from the happy reunion with his family the Christmas holiday afforded him, he was suddenly summoned back home for an unexpected, unwished-for 'Mid-Term Break'. His four-year-old brother, Christopher, had been killed in a car accident. Heaney's early poem recording this event accurately and vividly records the bewilderment he had felt as a child in the face of death. Less tragic, but almost equally momentous, was his parents' decision to move from his childhood home and birthplace, Mossbawn, to Bellaghy. Christopher's death must have been a factor in the decision; for the young Seamus, it must have constituted another physical and symbolic break with innocence.

St Columb's had its happier moments, fortunately, and as he moved up the school, distinction and academic success followed. One teacher, Raymond Gallagher, who took him for extra English in the third year, described him as 'a Renaissance type of boy',[62] a gifted all-rounder. He was a fine actor, with a rich speaking voice and impeccable timing. His natural talents developed under the influence of Jack 'Rusty' Gallagher, a former primary school headmaster, whose love of literature and drama, along with his good humour, made hislessons a pleasure. According to Barry White's *John Hume: Statesman of the Troubles*, Gallagher 'recalled giving Heaney . . . 100 out of 100 in an English exam, which some said was an impossible mark in the subject',[63] but Heaney firmly denied this when I mentioned it to him. (Certainly such generous marking would have been out of keeping with the general ethos of the school with its emphasis on the students striving after success, rather than having it recognised.) Heaney shone in school productions – his performance as the butler in *The Admirable Crichton* was referred to by both Raymond Gallagher and Ann Heaney as being particularly memorable – and he was very involved in the Gaelic Society which met every Friday evening. After leaving school, Heaney often performed the role of *fear a' tigh* at the local *ceilidh*, announcing the dances in Gaelic and then English, and acted as a blacksmith in *Betsy Grey* for the Bellaghy Dramatic Society, a play which dealt with the 1798 rebellion.[64] One summer holiday was spent in the Gaeltacht region, in County Donegal, where he was further initiated into 'the dialect of the tribe', where 'visionaries' would 'urge the mind to aftersight'.[65] 'Listening through the wall to fluent Irish' on his first night, the adolescent felt inadequate, but his Gaelic masters persevered "mixed the dust of croppies' graves with the fasting spittle of our creed and anointed my lips. Ephete, they urged. I blushed but only managed a few words."[66] Gradually he became acclimatised, happy and 'at home' under "the branchy shade/ Of an alphabet with letters named for trees", as can be seen from the Mossbawn-like imagery in 'Alphabets'.[67] Together his teachers at St Columb's and in the Gaeltacht did much to deepen his sense of his Irish Catholic identity. Retrospectively, however, he has lamented their lack of 'foresight', and the Church's and Nationalist leadership's failure to give social and political leadership. The attitudes voiced in 'From the Canton of Expectation' would seem to have a lot in common with those expressed by John Hume in his *Irish Times* articles of May 1964.

> Weak opposition leads to corrupt government. Nationalists in opposition have been in no way constructive . . . leadership has been the comfortable leadership of flags and slogans. Easy no doubt, but irresponsible. There has been no attempt to be positive, to encourage the Catholic community to develop the resources which they have in plenty[68]

Heaney's poem similarly rejects the Catholic defeatism of this period, living under 'high, banked clouds of resignation', with its obsessive poring over past wounds rather than tackling present injustices, a response which allowed the initiative to pass back to the 'men of violence'.[69] His fifth and lower sixth years at St Columb's coincided with the beginnings of fresh Republican 'activity', the I.R.A. border campaign of 1956–1962. On 26 November 1955, a mine was detonated at Roslea R.U.C. Barracks in Co. Fermanagh, by a Republican splinter group, Saor Uladh (Free Ulster), led by Liam Kelly. In July 1956 the I.R.A. held a battle school in the Wicklow Mountains. This lasted a fortnight, and though it involved considerable noise, "there was no interference from either the special branch or the regular army . . . The only complaint received was from traders in a nearby town who objected that the I.R.A. had not bought supplies locally"![70] In November 1956, Liam Kelly and Joseph Christle, who had also broken away from the main body of the I.R.A., organised twelve attacks on a 150-mile stretch of the border, "blowing up customs huts, telephone exchanges, bridges, B special drill halls, and demolishing the lough gates at Newry",[71] while December saw the outset of a six-year I.R.A. campaign which cost the lives of six young R.U.C. men and eleven Republicans. It was during this period that Heaney locates his coming to political consciousness. He describes himself at this time as 'plutôt papiste que républicain',[72] but, along with the whole Catholic community, he became infuriated by the activities of B Specials. They exploited the opportunity afforded to them to remind the minority where power really lay.

> A lot of fellows I knew during the day were out at night as Specials manning road blocks, and pretending they didn't know my name. I knew that if I had been an equally innocent Protestant I would have been allowed to pass without any bother.[73]

His interview for *Les Lettres Nouvelles* in March 1973 contains a more detailed account of the harassment Catholics suffered, and refers to a sadly typical incident of intimidation and brutality involving one of his brothers.

> Par exemple, vos voisins, armés, vous arrêtaient, vous fouilliaient; moi-même j'ai été fouillé en revenant des vêpres. Or il était très facile de se reconnaître. Le dimanche, ils arrêtaient tous ceux qui revenaient de la messe et les fouillaient. On a fouillé mon portefeuille, on a lu mes lettres. Tout ceci accompli par des hommes presque illetrés. Je le dis sans amertume. Des hommes assez ignorants et qui, orangistes, devaient se joindre à ces

manifestations: étant le centre de l'Etat, ils défendaient l'Etat. Mon frère se trouvait par hasard à un meeting républicain le jour de Pâques. Le lendemain, on l'a fait sortir du lit à six heures du matin; ce n'est que dix ans plus tard qu'il ma dit qu'on l'avait battu au commisariat, parce qu'il faisait, paraît-il, partie de l'I.R.A. A ce moment-là on n'était pas surpris par des tels faits, tout cela paraissait dans l'ordre des choses.[74]

During his lower sixth year Heaney's friendship with Seamus Deane crystallised, and he developed a fine rapport with a gifted English teacher, who was to prove an important mentor. The relationship with Deane deepened his insight into the fate of working-class Catholics in the Derry ghetto – 'I gazed into new worlds'[75] – where there was twenty per cent unemployment even then. There 'your first instinct was to throw a stone if you saw a policeman. If you met a priest, you kept your head down'.[76] They studied together under an excellent Latin teacher, Father McGlinchey, and in an English 'A' level class of twenty-eight students, taught by the Head of Senior English, J. B. S. O'Kelly. Born in Claudy, Co. Derry, O'Kelly was educated at St Columb's himself, and returned to teach there from 1948–1966. He had studied English at University College, Dublin, where his M.A. thesis was written on Thomas Hardy, an author for whom Heaney clearly has a lot of affection. 'Sean B.' was an inspired and inspiring teacher, motivated by the Leavisite faith in the 'civilizing influence of literature' and its potency in promoting spiritual development. For him literature was and is the core of English teaching, its function being to give pleasure and "to help young people to grow as human beings and critical beings. This is a faith to which I have remained true."[77] Although he encouraged students to read widely amongst the set authors, in retrospect he accuses himself of succumbing to the pressure of the examination, describing his teaching as far too narrow, and regretting in particular the absence of creative writing from the course. "I taught them to be critics, not creators," he remarked to me, apologetically. In fact the apprenticeship Heaney served with O'Kelly was doubly critical, since it deepened the young man's innate perceptiveness, and introduced him to writers whose creative processes would continue to intrigue him and stimulate his own desire to write.[78]

Deane and Heaney both passed their Senior Certificate in the Lower Sixth with the highest grades. Heaney gained the equivalent of Advanced Level grade A in English Language and Literature, Latin, Irish, French and Mathematics, and won one of twelve state bursaries for Northern Ireland of a thousand pounds to study at Queen's University, Belfast. As Heaney was only seventeen, it was proposed that his entry to Queen's should be deferred for a year, so that he could return to St Columb's for a final year. A letter of 30 August 1956, from the university, addressed inappropriately to 'Mr Shames Heaney', agreed to this proposal.[79] In their final year at the college, the two Seamuses were taught again by Sean O'Kelly in a class of four. O'Kelly remembers the pleasure he derived handing them essays on literary topics to see what they would make of them, and watching them surge ahead of him. With characteristic modesty, he commented, "I was teaching pupils at that stage who were already passing me out".[80] There developed a warm, fond, easy relationship between master and student, and though O'Kelly denies that he was a major influence on the young Heaney, the evidence that he was an important 'confidant and mentor' weighs against him. As both possess gentle, earnest, modest natures, there was a natural affinity of spirit between the two, which was compounded by a shared love of Wordsworth, Keats, Hazlitt and, above all, Hopkins. From the besieged faith of home to the lonely idealism of the Romantic poets was a natural progression; a melancholy longing for the eternal married to a sensual attachment to person, place, and object, perhaps characterises both of these 'voices of my education'.[81] Heaney, no doubt, observed the contours of his own home area and his own childhood in Wordsworth's rural settings.

> Fair seed time had my soul, and I grew up
> Fostered alike by beauty and by fear;
> Much favoured in my birthplace, and no less
> In that beloved Vale to which, erelong,
> I was transplanted.[82]

Cognizance of 'beauty' and 'fear', and the tensions they generate, animate so much of Heaney's poetry, from early poems such as 'Death of a Naturalist' and 'Personal Helicon' onward. With 'sympathy', 'propagated by pleasure',[83] Heaney must have read Wordsworth's celebrations of the lives of shepherds, ploughmen, quarrymen, fishermen. The older poet's admiration, suffused with awe, kindled kindred feelings in Heaney as he contemplated the 'expert' craftsmen who peopled his life, father, mother, grandfather,

diviner, thatcher, smith. Witnessing the grace, dignity and creative energy embodied in such figures, both poets humbly sought
an 'objective correlative' for their own artistic purposes, spiritual
endeavours. The Shepherd, like the poet, is 'wedded' to 'hope/ And
hazard', is alternately master and mastered in 'his own domain'.[84]

For both the role of poet is akin to that of priest. In *Preoccupations*,
Heaney describes poetry in terms which could equally apply to the
Mass or any other sacred ritual; it is a species of 'divination', a
'revelation of the self to the self', a 'restoration of the culture
to itself'; and poems themselves are 'elements of continuity'.[85]
Seamus Deane, in his fine essay, 'Seamus Heaney: the Timorous
and the Bold', accurately defines Heaney's poetry as an 'enfolding
and unfolding',[86] a phrase which neatly conveys the dual role
of poet and priest. A source of integration and love within the
community, he is simultaneously a man apart, a teacher. Before
Nature and 'the mind of man', like Wordsworth, Heaney exhibits
"the reverence of an acolyte before a mystery of which he is also
the celebrant",[87] as he attempts to reproduce within his poetry a
faithful echo of 'the ghostly language of the ancient earth'.[88] For both
poets early hopes and enthusiasm for liberating political change
left them with a taste of ash. In the aftermath of the massacres
of September 1792 and January 1972, which left the ideals of the
French Revolution and Civil Rights campaign smeared with blood,
Wordsworth and Heaney found in poetry a healing, an assuaging,
an enabling influence which could still 'confer dignity on what
might otherwise be derelict and distressing'.[89] Reading *The Prelude*,
Book VIII, one might be tempted to subscribe to the Eliot view of
history, the conviction that

> The same things happen again and again.
> Men learn little from others' experience.[90]

observing in the 1790s and 1970s a similar

> reservoir of guilt
> And ignorance, fill'd up from age to age,
> That could no longer hold its loathsome charge,
> But burst and spread in deluge through the land.[91]

Rather than surrendering their energies to anger or despair, both
placed their trust in the 'future restoration' that Art might achieve,
through patience, through a 'wise passiveness'.[92]

For Wordsworth, 'the joy, the consolation and the hope . . . great poetry gives' came only after an 'astringent and energising realisation of solitude.'[93] This last phrase calls to mind the other major influence on Heaney at St Columb's and for many years after, Gerard Manley Hopkins.[94] Sean O'Kelly and Heaney's next key literary father, Michael McLaverty, were equally passionate admirers of Hopkins' work, but there would have been many points of affinity between the Jesuit poet and the student of St Columb's anyway. The fervour of Hopkins' faith would have struck a chord in Heaney, with its emphasis on the male (Christ) and the female (the Virgin Mary), and its mixture of gladness and guilt.[95]

Hopkins' methods for composition, which were influenced by his daily reading of Ignatius Loyola's *Spiritual Exercises*, bear some resemblance to Heaney's procedures, albeit a coincidental one. The *Exercises* begin affirmatively stating that 'Man was created to praise, 'reverence, and serve God, and by so doing to save his soul', and then go on to outline three stages of meditation.[96] Firstly, the priest should 'compose the place', to recreate in his imagination in as vivid detail as possible the subject of his meditation. Secondly, he should employ 'the three powers' of memory (to recall the subject), understanding (to reflect on and analyse it), and will, (to turn his reflection into virtuous action.) The third stage involved entering upon a colloquy with God on the chosen subject. The first two stages are certainly similar to Heaney's characteristic method in his early poems, establishing in vivid, sensual detail a sense of place, retrieving a moment of innocence from memory, before turning the poem towards some philosophic or lyric reflection.

Equally important to Hopkins' development as a poet was the writing of the Franciscan philosopher, Duns Scotus (1266–1308). Through the medium of Hopkins' verse his influence has certainly percolated into the poetry of Ted Hughes and Seamus Heaney. What distinguished Scotus' thought from that of traditional Jesuit theologians was his belief in the 'principle of individuation'.

All medieval philosophers were concerned with how human beings could come to know the universal; Scotus believed that they could do so by apprehending an individual object's essence, which he named its 'this-ness' (*haecceitas*); and that such apprehensions and intuitions ultimately reveal God. By directing such intuitions of nature towards God man can perfect his own *haecceitas*, his will.[97]

Hopkins' poetry, like Wordsworth's and Heaney's, is illuminated by his intense consciousness of nature and landscape, which are, for both, expressions of the beauty and individuality with which God has invested the world.[98] Though Heaney has praised the Cumbrian poet for his capacity to transform "an external scene into a country of the mind", "to be flooded by the durable and sustaining influences of rock, stream, hill, wind and cloud",[99] the same might be said of Hopkins, and of Heaney himself. Reviewing *Station Island*, John Carey has written of its author, "More than any other poet since Wordsworth he can make us understand that the outside world is not outside but what we are made of. Our feelings are echoes of what we touch and see. "Nature", as Cézanne said, "is on the inside."[100] In the poems of Wordsworth and Hopkins, of Heaney and Hughes, the *haecceitas* of the natural world is made flesh, and dwells within us. The poems record a 'discharge' of energy within the poet's mind, a burst of 'lightning and love'[101] which then becomes re-incarnate feeling in words.

Hopkins' influence on the early verse of Heaney is most obviously present in the vigorous thrust of his rhythm, the force of his diction, the stress generated by the 'heavily accented consonantal noise'[102] which embodies in sound the energy of the subject. His *Preoccupations* essay, 'Feeling into Words', draws attention to the connections between the 'staccato' consonantal qualities of the Ulster accent and Hopkins' poetic voice. In 'The Fire i' the Flint',[103] from the same volume, Heaney also lays stress on the 'masculinity' of his subject's verse, its manly vigour and muscularity, and reveals the way 'the artist's idea of the artistic act, conscious or unconscious, affected certain intrinsic qualities of the artefact'. For Hopkins, the act of creation occurs when Christ sires thought upon the 'mothering' imagination. Hopkins' longing to surrender to the irresistible force of Christ's will, the 'fire that strikes', perhaps had its counterpart in the adolescent Heaney, who was attempting to reconcile the conflicting 'male' and 'female' elements within his own nature. His comparison between the assertive, authoritative voice of Hopkins and the evocative, luxuriant music of Keats provides us with an insight into the two poetic modes to which he was originally attracted. At university he was to employ the pseudonym, *Incertus*, 'uncertain, a shy soul fretting and all that',[104] but ultimately he freed himself from the burden of 'feminine' submissiveness and the oppression of 'Lord I am not worthy' by donning a 'male' robustness from English and Anglo-Welsh influences such as Hopkins and Hughes, Dylan Thomas and R. S. Thomas. Though he learnt his craft from them, his technique and full poetic voice were achieved, I believe, as a result of his relationship with the 'feminine', Celtic influences.

Seamus Heaney began his-four year course at Queen's University, Belfast, in October 1957. The 1947 Education Act, which had provided him with the scholarship to St Columb's and the State bursary at Queen's, played an important part in the political and literary upsurge of the late 1960s since it enabled bright children from the urban working class and rural small-farmer class of both communities to emerge 'from a hidden, buried life' and enter 'the realm of education'.[105] Beneficiaries of the Act included, along with Heaney and Deane, writers such as Derek Mahon, who studied Classics at Trinity College, Dublin, and George McWhirter, both from Protestant Belfast working-class backgrounds. (McWhirter, who was in the same year as Heaney, recalls one bright friend, Peter Mullin, whose father was 'a spade-in-hand day labourer'.)[106] According to Philip Hobsbaum, the sectarian divisions of school were maintained in the first year at university. Groups of Catholics from the same school would bunch together at lectures and in dining halls, and would tend to mix with Protestants only at the Saturday night dances and at the popular Drama Society functions run by Gamini Salgado.

Through his membership of the Catholic Sodality[107] which involved evening devotions and, for some members, social work, and his renewed friendship with Seamus Deane during their second year at Queen's, Heaney maintained his loyalty to the culture from which he sprang. The institution of which he was a part, however, lay stress on 'official British culture', including the great traditions of the sherry party and *English* literature. In the John Malone Memorial lecture of 1983, he wryly highlights the conflict of cultures and worlds:

> I was studying English . . . considering the tradition of courtly love, learning to find my way among the ironies and niceties of Jane Austen's vicarages, discussing Tennyson's loss of faith and Lawrence's phallic consciousness, learning the rituals of club life in India by reading E. M. Forster . . . . Far from discussing the Victorian loss of faith, I was driving my mother to evening devotions in the 'chapel' or looking for my name in a list of 'adorers' at the exposition of the Blessed Sacrament. Far from the

melodies of courtly love, I was acting as *fear a' tigh* at the G.A.A.
[Gaelic Athletic Association] *ceilidh* . . . and trying to master a
way of coaxing a training college student into the back of our
Austin Sixteen. And far, far from Lawrence's phallic candour,
finding myself subsequently confessing sins of immodest and
immoderate embraces.[108]

The literary experiences which would eventually enable him to 'fill
the gap between the parish and the academy' and 'realigned my
sense of belonging to a place with the attendant sense of displacement',[109] he informs us, were his re-reading of Daniel Corkery's *The
Hidden Ireland* and Joyce's *Portrait of the Artist as a Young Man*.

However, despite this later criticism of the overwhelmingly British ethos at Queen's, he did derive enormous benefit from his
university English syllabus, as he himself admits. He recalls in
the first weeks discovering the 'moody energies'[110] of Webster,
his imagery with its 'dark brooding violence',[111] producing 'a kind
of aural gooseflesh'; Jacobean drama with its sadistic brutality and
political intrigue was perhaps offering a premonition of what was to
come. He delighted in the almost tactile pleasures of Anglo-Saxon
poetry, and in the 1970s would return to the world of the Dark
Ages, with its austere vision of human fate, embodied in flint-like,
craggy sound.[112] The alliterative thrust of Middle English literature
and the 'sensuous brunt'[113] of Marlowe's language charmed the ear
and mind with their 'thrilling physical texture'. As important at this
time was the intellectual stimulus of the teaching of Laurence Lerner
and his encouragement, which, like that of J. B. S. O'Kelly, proved
'confirmatory'. Heaney writes that "Lerner gave me pleasure in the
practice of practical criticism, praised an essay of mine in my first
year at Queen's, which 'corroborated' me, albeit it early on and
anonymously."[114] The result was that "A great deal that was latent
and inarticulate" within him "began to emerge in this first encounter with the world of letters."[115] No doubt this solid grounding in
'conventional English literature' helped to make Heaney's early
poetry so accessible to English audiences, its rural world exquisitely
evoked, its young author a potential successor to Clare, Hardy or
Edward Thomas. More importantly his familiarity with the figures,
forms and language of the English tradition supplied him with a
critical perspective from which he could assess the Celtic writers to
whom he was drawn after leaving Queen's, and his own attempts
to explore the rich hoard of his personal experience.

Surprisingly, given the choice of studying Hemingway or Joyce, Frost or Yeats, Heaney selected the lesser, American writers. It may have been that he was daunted at the thought of the Irish colossi, and opted to come to terms with them in his own good time. However, like so many intuitive decisions made in the course of his literary career, the choice of Frost was an inspired one. Here was a poet whose subject matter echoed the young man's experience, whose poetic voice captured the rhythms of natural speech, 'the language really spoken by men'.[116] Frost set contemporary language and characters within the framework of traditionalist verse forms, reconciling past and present in a way that appealed to the liberal and conservative in Heaney. Re-reading Frost in the light of our knowledge of Heaney's formative years, it is not too difficult to identify more specific points of affinity. The *North of Boston* collection from 1914 contains several poems 'which for some reason keep close to me',[117] poems such as 'Home Burial', which reveals how deeply sensitive autobiographical material can be transmuted into the finest 'public' art. Like 'Mid Term Break', it centres upon antithetical reactions to infant death. The painful integrity with which Frost dramatises his recognition of guilt and failure to console may have coloured Heaney's own attitude to poetic disclosure and exposure. 'Death of the Hired Man', from the same volume, similarly revolves around conflicting male and female responses, in the persons of the callous, pragmatic Warren and the sympathetic, grace-full Mary. During their dispute over what to do with an exhausted old farm worker, Silas, we learn how the old man is obsessed with memories of Harold Wilson, whose 'young college boy's assurance piqued him.' In the meeting together of Silas's rustic skills ("He said he couldn't make the boy believe/ He could find water with a hazel prong") and Harold's intellectual and cultural aspirations ("He studied Latin, like the violin/ Because he liked it" Heaney witnessed the tension between ancient craft and modern education which was part of his home experience. Like Frost, he valued the creative skills of both worlds, with their 'divine' symbols of hazel rod and violin, and strove to reconcile them in his own poem of discontinuity within continuity, 'Digging', where the spade is superseded by the pen.

'The Most of it' from *The Witness Tree*, published in 1942, contains the same instinctual and spiritual bedrock Blake dug, which Hughes and Plath expose in poems such as 'Jaguar', 'Pike' and 'Hardcastle Crags', into which Heaney himself would drill in 'Death of a

Naturalist', 'The Barn', and 'Personal Helicon'. It depicts a solitary figure's shocked apprehension that he shares the earth with a potent Force, which awes and dwarfs him with its beauty, its sexual energy, its magnificent otherness. One can imagine the relish with which Heaney would have responded to the poem, with its delight in the unknowable, its vigorous rhythm and virile imagery.[118] His encounter with such epiphanies acted as a confirmation of the legitimacy of his own experience, and excited and alerted him to the possibilities his own poetry might realise. Heaney was at a stage when he was tentatively seeking out non-English models, and in Frost he discovered an emotional immediacy, an accessibility of language and feeling, a cherishing of the rural and the indigenous, which were to become hallmarks of his own writing. Although Robert Buttel asserts that Frost was 'a pivotal figure'[119] in Heaney's development, I would suggest that he was one of a succession of major prophets, who prepared the way for 'one greater Man', or influence rather, Patrick Kavanagh.

Though at first he was inhibited by the weight of the literary canon, during his third year at university his poems began to appear in the Queen's literary magazines, *Q* and *Gorgon*. The Autumn 1959 edition of *Q* contains 'Reaping in Heat' and 'October Thought'. The former is an impressionistic piece, timeless, but unrealised. Within it Heaney 'innovated a South Derry rhyme/ With *hushed* and *lulled* full chimes for *pushed* and *pulled*'.[120] 'October Thought' is a light dance to the alliterative music of Hopkins, set in Mossbawn with its 'roof of black-oak, bog-sod and rods of willow' and Arcadia with its 'twittering flirtings in the eaves' and 'trickling tinkle of bells'. The stylistic influence of Hopkins has overwhelmed any personal impulse to communicate, and fittingly the poem ends with a phrase implying cosy constriction, 'well in the fold'. A month later 'Nostalgia in the Afternoon' appeared in *Gorgon*, number three, a paean, in sprung verse, to pre-lapsarian clouds, which reminds one of Hopkins' descriptions of sky in his Journal entries for August 30, 1867, March 12, 1870, and April 22, 1871. 'I live times distilled from times past', he writes, but makes no attempt to incarnate the physical, sensual reality he knew. George McWhirter writes:

> Seamus wrapped himself in a label, which was a true disguise. He went round calling himself a 'parnassian'. Maybe he should have called his poetry 'proto-parnassian: there was a notion of

fine style and in that (implied) the feeling that the fine style was yet to find its substance.[121]

The next edition of *Gorgon* from February 1960 contains 'Aran' by 'Seamus J. Heaney', which brings us down to earth after the clouds, larks and cuckoos of the earlier poems. It opens with a shock image, and a rhythm which cannot quite sustain itself – 'The rock breaks out like bone from a skinned elbow' – before the young author forces upon us a rapid succession of disconnected images. The island is personified – 'it coughs itself into high cliffs' – but by line three is inexplicably surrounded by 'goose-flesh waves'. The authentic Heaney voice is present in the image of 'the islander's spade' which 'spangs off rock', but soon the metaphorical muddle returns with 'the muscular, swallowing acres of sea' and the 'knifing wind' which 'shivers'. The final poem of his university days that I have been able to trace, which is 'all craft and not much technique', is 'Song of my man-alive', from the Hilary Term of 1961. Although Hopkins is still present in the curious image of the 'anvil-ding/ of your kiss',[122] the predominant voice is that Dylan Thomas, whose heady style, along with love, has clearly left the poet intoxicated with words.

> . . . . it was all tune-tumbling
>   Hill-happy and wine-wonderful.
> . . . .
> It was life leaping wild in the womb
>   of my young spring
> And bursting headlong from the dead belly of twenty-one
>   years
> I suddenly found myself, chestnut-ripe-round, pitched
>   new and naked
> Upon the open roadside of time.

This is Heaney's first poem dealing with a personal relationship, and its Lawrentian sexual imagery, 'golden life/ Pumped through dark pulses', though safely and 'catholically' channelled into 'trees and houses and clouds', marks perhaps an inching away from the inhibitions and guilt unhappily fostered by 'the Faith'. In the same edition of *Gorgon*, a short story by Incertus appears entitled 'There's Rosemary'. Una, the wife of a young teacher, Sean, decides to book a holiday in Galway, unaware that it was the location many years previously of a lightning affair between Sean and a local girl, Grainne. Subsequently, while working on the Isle of Man, Una had got to know Grainne, who 'was always talking about the fellows from Queen's she had met during that year'. The ironic twist at the end, when the cock crows, comes after Sean has denied having encountered anyone called Grainne on his wild week on the Aran Islands. His wife smugly informs him, 'Well, that's one consolation . . . She came to the Isle of Man to have an abortion!' Although the short story broaches 'risky' territory, Catholic morality is still in evidence. The 'swollen corpse of a mangy grey dog floating by the harbour wall' gives an ominous forewarning that the young couple's sin will find them out.

In the summer of 1961 Heaney was awarded a First Class Honours degree in English Language and Literature. In his letter to me, George McWhirter recalls Graduation Day, and how Patrick Heaney loaned his son the Humber. "That his father had a Humber to loan him was part of a chain of revelations to me at that time (to have a farm and a Humber . . .). So there was that sense that Seamus Heaney was of some substance." [123] He was also presented with the McMullen medal for academic achievement. (H. M. McMullen was Professor of English at Queen's at the turn of the century.) With the book token he received for the latter award, he bought himself the *Collected Poems of Louis MacNeice*, and volumes of plays by Synge and Wilde, which indicates his growing interest in Anglo-Irish literature, after his prolonged exposure to the English tradition. Professor Peter Butter of the English Department at Queen's urged him to accept the offer of a scholarship to Oxford University, but self-doubt and loyalty to his parents led him to decline. After such a long period of studying first at St Columb's and then at Queen's, he wanted to start earning some money and pay his parents back for the support they have given him throughout his education.

I always had this notion that I was going to be a secondary school teacher, living the generic life of the newly upwardly mobile eleven-plus Catholic; it was a very passive, conveyor-belt sense of things. But Peter Butter, who was chairman of the English Department then, suggested a studentship at Balliol, or certainly some graduate work at Oxford, and I remember just being bewildered, and my father and mother had absolutely no sense of that. They wouldn't have stopped me, I'm not saying that but the world I was moving in didn't have any direction for them, the

compass needle just *wobbled*. Butter was very encouraging . . .
but I suppose there was just some lack of confidence, and lack of
nous.[124]

In October, he began a P.G.C.E. course at St Joseph's College of
Education. Like many young men with a social conscience and
a desire to communicate something of the pleasure they have
experienced in learning, he decided to teach. That he eventually
chose a position in a Belfast secondary modern school, is further
indicative of his altruistic, generous nature.

At the age of twenty two, his formal critical apprenticeship
was completed. The next five years would witness a rapid movement towards creative maturity, as new friendships and literary
discoveries confirmed and corroborated him.

2

Affinities, 1961–66

The wise man who sits at home, travels a bit in his heart, while the wise man who goes away sits at home to some extent.[1]

An Irish poet has access to all this (English literary tradition) through his use of the English language, but he is unlikely to feel at home in it.

Thomas Kinsella[2]

References to 'home' and 'exile' abound in discussions of Heaney's work, and when the poet talks about his own writing. Although he broke with familial tradition in becoming a writer, a city-dweller, a member of the middle class, his poetry to the present bears witness to a continuity of spirit with his parents and a fidelity to his origins, of race and place. In a 1979 interview with John Haffenden, he suggests that reports that he has become a 'déraciné' are greatly exaggerated:

I'm very close to home. I've two homes: this house and the house where I was brought up. When I go back, my father and mother are still alive, my brothers and sisters still around the place, I merge into it. One deracinates oneself, and I'm not sure I have done so.[3]

Despite the prolonged periods of time spent away at boarding school and university, and a subsequent lifetime of physical and spiritual journeying over huge distances and times, the area around his parents' home in the North and his home bases in Dublin and Glanmore have remained fixed points of reference. 'Playing with' actual, remembered or imagined states of loss has been a characteristic poetic strategy, a 'game' in which intense feeling is liberated which the author then seeks to channel and master in language and form.

28

The 'exile' of the poet is symbolical and always represents, paradoxically, a 'homecoming', because the journey he undertakes is
one whereby he comes into his own ground, where he reaches
'the first circle' of himself.[4]

During the years from 1961–66, Celtic and Catholic influences in
his personal life – such as Michael McLaverty, Marie Devlin, and
T. P. Flanagan – and in his literary 'discoveries' – such as Patrick
Kavanagh, John Montague, Daniel Corkery, James Joyce – helped
him find and 'found' his sense of himself as an Irish poet, but did
not prevent him from drawing water from English and American
wells. To return to the initial image of the previous chapter, these
personalities and literary experiences furnished Heaney with a second anchor, strengthened his craft, and enabled him to undertake
ever more ambitious and testing voyages into himself.

For part of his postgraduate education course, early in 1962,
Seamus Heaney was sent for his teaching practice to St Thomas
Intermediate School, Ballymurphy, the school where he would
eventually take up his first appointment. He regarded himself
later as 'very fortunate in my school and in my Principal',[5] for
the headmaster was Michael McLaverty, a distinguished, but much
underrated, writer of short stories. His work had received critical
approval from Edwin Muir and John Middleton Murry. Reviewing
a book of his for *The Irish Press* in 1976, the late Sean O'Faolain
admitted to being mystified as to 'why it could happen that so
good a writer is not celebrated as he deserves at home'.[6] Born in
1907 in Co. Monaghan, the homeground of Patrick Kavanagh, and
slightly older than Heaney's own father, McLaverty was to become
another key literary mentor and spiritual guide. His importance in
Heaney's development may be gauged from the title of the section
in 'Singing School' dedicated to him, 'Fosterage'. While the *Oxford
English Dictionary* definition of a 'fosterer' as "one who cherishes,
favours, or promotes the growth of (anything)" accurately describes
the role McLaverty filled, more specifically the term 'fosterage'
refers to an ancient custom among the Celtic nobility of sending a
son to live with another family for the entire course of his childhood,
its aim being 'to reproduce the closeness of the family on a larger
scale'.[7]

In his introduction to the *Collected Short Stories of Michael
McLaverty*, Heaney speaks with deep affection of his former
boss:

> He would come into the English class to conduct, for the benefit
> of a less than literary 4B, elaborate and humorous conversations
> about the efficacy of poetry. "Did you ever remark, Mr Heaney,"
> he would enquire, "how when you see the photograph of a rugby
> team you can always pick out the boys who studied poetry by the
> look on their faces?" Faithfully and fallaciously, I would reply,
> "Yes, Mr McLaverty," and "There you are now," he would say to
> them, closing the case triumphantly, then leaving the room with
> a warning: "Work hard and when you leave school, don't end up
> measuring your spits on some street corner!"[8]

and his enthusiasm to 'educate the taste of this young graduate'
teacher:

> "Look for the intimate thing," he would say, and go on to praise
> the 'note of exile' in Chekhov, or to exhort me to read Tolstoy's
> *Death of Ivan Ilych*, one of his sacred texts.[9]

In an article greeting his poetic debut, lyrically entitled 'Turkeys made him a poet'(!), Heaney remembered with gratitude
how McLaverty "got me reading more than I had previously."[10]
Though regarded as an 'ineffectual dreamer' by some of his staff,
McLaverty's generosity with his books and his time, and his long
experience of and deep commitment to literature clearly made their
mark on the apprentice writer. Like Sean B. O'Kelly, McLaverty was
an ardent admirer of Gerard Manley Hopkins. He gave Heaney
his own copy of the *Journals*, which, like his own stories, realise
a 'love of the inscape of things, the freshness that lives deep down
in them,' and recognise 'the central place of suffering and sacrifice
in the life of the spirit'.[11] McLaverty's most significant 'gift' to the
future poet, perhaps, was the loan of a book by another Catholic
'master' – Patrick Kavanagh. The book was *A Soul for Sale*.

As Kavanagh's work has received scant attention in this country,
it may be appropriate to provide a brief outline of his career and
work.[12] Born in 1904 in Co. Monaghan – one of the three Catholic
counties of Ulster excluded from the northern state on partition –
Patrick Kavanagh was the son of a farmer and cobbler. At the age
of twenty-seven, in December 1931 he left his widowed mother
and the farm at Inniskeen and walked the fifty miles to Dublin,
fancying that the literary world would instantly embrace him. His
reception at the National Library should have warned him that the

capital was not yet fully attuned to contemporary poetry. "I asked for *The Waste Land*. The man with the goatee beard wanted to know if it was a book on drainage." [13] In 1939 he settled permanently in Dublin, and in the course of the 1950s edited his own periodical, *Kavanagh's Weekly*, along with his brother, Peter. The numerous articles and autobiographical essays produced during these years are gathered in his *Collected Pruse*, but he is best known for his long poem, *The Great Hunger* (1942), his autobiography, *The Green Fool* (1938) and his novel, *Tarry Flynn* (1948). Each of these articulate feelings of spiritual and sexual claustrophobia, and dramatise his own 'contradictory awarenesses'. [14]

Although Kavanagh later came to reject *The Great Hunger* as lacking the discipline and detachment of great Art, less censorious commentators, Heaney amongst them, have recognised its significance in modern Irish literature, and valued its linguistic and technical richness, and its honest, passionate portrayal of a contemporary hunger. It tells the story of Maguire, a farmer struggling to survive on a diet of 'labour and lethargy', [15] burdened with a soul that 'is never born'. [16] Maguire is a crippled pilgrim, emasculated by his upbringing and conditioning by mother and Church. Like Galton and Simpson's comic-tragic creation, Harold Steptoe, he is 'faithful to death' [17] to his clinging, ungrateful parent, having been married off to the family business at an early age. A perpetual adolescent, his sexuality is 'dammed' by his sense of sin – 'Written in letters larger than John Bunyan dreamt of' [18] – or 'leaked' [19] over the ashes at the end of each futile day. Although those who governed him acted 'out of love', their attempts to preserve him as a Christ-like infant, have bred only despair. In a marvellously simple, poignant, ironic image, he cries out against his fate, "O Christ! I am locked in a stable with pigs and cows for ever." [20]

Heaney had already come across *The Great Hunger* while at university, perhaps while still 'scalding with lust inside my daunting visor', [21] but his renewed acquaintance with Kavanagh's poetry and prose at this time made a huge impact on his early poetic development. In the later of his two essays on Kavanagh, 'The Placeless Heaven', he stresses how reading *The Great Hunger* was both a culturally and politically liberating experience. "Kavanagh gave you permission to dwell without cultural anxiety among the usual landmarks of your life", he writes. "Whether he wanted it or not, his achievement was inevitably co-opted, north and south, into the general current of feeling which flowed from and sustained ideas of

national identity, cultural otherness from Britain."[22] When someone
questioned Heaney in the 1960s as to why he had not dedicated
a poem to the older man, he replied, "I had no need to write a
poem to Patrick Kavanagh; I wrote *Death of a Naturalist*."[23] Even
a cursory examination of Kavanagh's poetry and prose would
throw up innumerable points of affinity between the two writers. For both men, poetry is a 'mystical thing',[24] demanding a
religious commitment from its practitioners. A primary task for
both is to bridge the physical world of the farm and the sacred
world of literature. Whereas Kavanagh frequently spiritualizes his
landscape with biblical metaphors, and celebrates a renewal of
the Word being made Flesh on the land and in the imagination,

> The maiden of Spring is with child / By the Holy Ghost.
>
> > ('April')
>
> O cut for me life's bread, for me pour wine.
>
> > ('Worship')
>
> Forget the worm's opinion too
> Of hooves and pointed harrow-pins,
> For you are driving your horses through
> The mist where Genesis begins'
>
> > ('To the man after the harrow')
>
> These men know God the Father in a tree:
> The Holy Spirit is the rising sap,
> And Christ will be the green leaves that will come
> At Easter from the sealed and guarded tomb.
>
> > (*The Great Hunger*)[25]

the young Heaney, belonging to a more secular age, quietly connects
his 'divining' with traditional images of rural craft and labour.
Writing in the early 1960s in Northern Ireland for a 'mixed' audience, at a time when Protestant and Catholic writers were coming
into closer and more creative contact with each other than ever
before, Heaney's first poetry does not display the intensive Catholic
allusion one finds in Kavanagh, since it might exclude, if not alienate
some readers.[26]

Originating from non-literary, small farming communities, both
were at first inhibited by feelings of inadequacy, awkwardness,

unworthiness before the Muse, and sought to protect themselves
from ridicule and mockery with masks such as 'the Green Fool'
and *Incertus*. Happily, in both writers provincial self- consciousness
about 'the clay of wet fields' clinging to 'feet' and to 'trouser
bottoms'[27] eventually would give way to a pride and confidence
in the local, the parochial. In an important statement, which 'cleared
a space'[28] for those who would follow him, Kavanagh distinguishes
between parochialism and provincialism:

> Parochialism and provincialism are direct opposites. A provincial
> is always trying to live by other people's loves, but a parochial
> is self-sufficient. A great deal of this parochialism with all its
> intended intensities and courage continued in rural Ireland up
> till a few years ago and possibly will continue in some form
> forever . . .
>
> My idea of a cultural parochial entitywas the distance a man
> could walk in a day in any direction. The centre was usually the
> place where oneself lived though not always.
>
> For me, my cultural parish was certain hills that I could see
> from my own hills. The ordinary bicycle did not change these
> dimensions, for though one seldom explored the full extent of
> one's parish on foot, one could and did so on the bicycle. And
> those bicycle journeys that I made to the limits of my kingdom
> were the greatest adventures of my life.[29]

Kavanagh's faith in 'the worn grain of unspectacular experience',[30]
that 'God is in the bits and pieces of Everyday',[31] that the local
could articulate the universal – a view Michael McLaverty shared
– assured Heaney of the validity and sufficiency of the Mossbawn
experience as a resource. Reading a poem today like 'A Christmas
Childhood' from *A Soul for Sale*, one can almost hear the twenty-
three-year-old Heaney's sigh of assent:

> Now and then
> I can remember something of the gay
> Garden that was childhood's. Again
>
> The tracks of cattle to a drinking-place,
> A green stone lying sideways in a ditch
> Or any common sight the transfigured face
> Of a beauty that the world did not touch.[32]

Cherishing the *haecceitas* of humble cattle tracks and stones, Kavanagh reveals himself to be in the Hopkins' mould, like Heaney's other mentors.[33]

Many of the themes and images of Kavanagh's poetry, autobiography and fiction – and some of the characters – re-surface in Heaney's first volumes, as we shall see. Although, generally, Kavanagh seems to make much more of the deprivation and poverty within the Catholic subculture than his 'disciple' – at least until *Wintering Out* – it is interesting to note that in two unpublished poems from the winter of 1963, Heaney does deal with these issues through the persona of MacKenna.[34] Clay-based and uncouth, like Patrick Maguire or R. S. Thomas's Iago Prytherch,

> MacKenna, his dungarees
> Stiff and stinking of sour pigmeal,
> Husks up warm phlegm and spits

MacKenna blazes with a cocky, pugnacious resilience which one does not find in his 'forebears'. Heaney's indecision over his creation makes him appear one minute as a kind of rustic equivalent of Hughes's retired colonel, repelling 'The age's neat civility', the next as a stout-inspired windbag, an aggressive and thought-less old fox, whose wife and children can presumably look forward to a beating when he finally staggers home.

Kavanagh's treatment of childhood, his success in transmuting the simplest of recollections into something magical and enduring, made a more lasting impression. Heaney's reading of *The Green Fool* in the reference section of Belfast Public Library, no doubt strengthened his feelings of affinity, and may even have set off a few stray sparks of memory that 'caught' in poems. In Chapter 3, 'Schooldays', he would have read how Kavanagh's love of poetry was kindled by a Marian hymn, 'Hail, Queen of Heaven/ The ocean star/ Guide of the wanderer/ Here below',[35] and recalled his own pleasure in 'the litany of the Blessed Virgin', 'part of the enforced poetry in our household'.[36] Chapter 7 contains a fine description of blackberry-picking, in which cheery greed and sensuous delight combine as they do in Heaney's poem.

> Up here the blackberries grew in wonderful abundance, good ones the size of big plums. I filled my can to the brim in a short time. I was raking in the money ... My bare legs

were raw with briar scratches . . . My hands were blue with berry-dye and my face as well – we used to stain our faces with the first blackberry . . . . We lived long and happy days in that blackberry time. The world that was Rocksavage was boundless and uncharted as the broad places of the imagination. Time had no say in that place, a day could be as long as a dream. We were in the Beginning, before common men had driven the fairies underground.[37]

The picture of the children staining their faces might just have prompted the Heaney image of Bluebeard. In eager or despondent phrases, like 'good ones the size of big plums', and 'It wasn't fair', both writers show their capacity to inject the authentic voice of childhood into what is essentially an adult perception of Time's treachery. Whereas Kavanagh sustains the idyll in his last three sentences, Heaney's poem concludes on the huge rift in the child's and adult's world between desire and disappointment. In Chapter 21, describing the aftermath of an old man's death, we find the common Ulster saying, 'Am sorry for yer trouble', which, of course, appears in Heaney's 'Mid Term Break'. Reading Kavanagh's account of the sadistic John Gorman might have reminded Heaney of the cruelty which he observed or in which he participated, feeding into 'The Early Purges' or 'Dawn Shoot'. 'A naturalist in his fashion', Gorman boiled a pigeon's eggs, and then over several months watched the mother bird try to hatch them 'till she died'.[38]

Many features of Kavanagh's style – his use of traditional forms adapted to suit the modulations of his individual poetic voice, his anecdotal tones and colloquialisms alongside the heightening effects of classical and biblical allusion, his proud use of Ulster dialect words – seeped naturally into Heaney's work, as he began to turn his feeling into words. The poetic process, writes Thomas Kinsella,

begins with the ingestion of experience and continues as the imagination . . . sieves that experience for its significance. The significant experience, so ingested, spends a period in the depths of the mind forming relationships with other material similarly collected and stored. And then it lies ready, in a kind of ever-saturating solution, to be 'crystallised out' at the moment of inspiration.[39]

Certainly the young poet's encounter with the work of Patrick Kavanagh at this time was crucial to his development, and encouraged him to

> be reposed and praise, praise, praise
> The way it happened and the way it is.[40]

During this critical period between Spring 1962 and Autumn 1963, several other Celtic voices helped in the 'bedding'[41] of the poet's ear. As part of his P.G.C.E. course at St Joseph's College of Education, Andersontown, Belfast, in 1962 he wrote an extended essay on 'Ulster literary magazines', which brought him into contact with writers such as W. R. Rodgers and John Hewitt,[42] who had also, like Kavanagh, "created a poetry out of their local and native background."[43] In the same year an anthology entitled *Six Irish Poets* was published, containing a selection from the work of Austin Clarke, Richard Kell, Thomas Kinsella, John Montague, Richard Murphy, and Richard Weber. Edited by Robin Skelton, the book supplied Heaney with more exemplars. Reading the introduction in itself must have been an act of confirmation for Heaney, as Skelton praised the way

> Irish poetry can still base itself firmly upon what might be described as 'natural resources'. It is interesting because in England there appear very few poets indeed with this kind of awareness of their nationality, this sense of belonging, however rebelliously, to a social or ethnic group.

Although a regionalist vision could be limiting, he wrote, "it can, however, lead to real vitality. The sense of belonging is, I believe, important to poetry. It gives it a firm foundation upon which to build. It gives it roots."[44] In the poetry of John Montague,[45] in particular, Heaney identified a duality of rootedness and exile which corresponded to his own, a maturity of feeling and expression to emulate. Significantly, Montague was a fellow admirer of the poetry of Patrick Kavanagh. Writing an introduction to the revised *Poisoned Lands* in 1976, Montague describes Kavanagh as "a man flailing between two faded worlds, the country he had left and the literary Dublin he never found",[46] yet his own poetry exhibits the tensions of a man pulled in diverse directions, labouring to find a sense of 'home'. A peregrine spirit, 'on the wing'[47] over Europe and America, past and present, rural and urban locales, his wanderings are reflected in *Poisoned Lands*, which Heaney acquired at the beginning of August 1963. Opening *parochially* in Co. Tyrone with spring water, fairies and the smell of flax, it shifts ground to take in urban wasteland in the Spender-like 'Slum Clearance', Audenesque perspectives on Ireland in 'Incantation in time of peace', American landscapes in 'Cultural Center' and 'Bus Stop, Nevada', and Paris in 'Walking the Dog'. His larger, cosmopolitan vision is evident in one of the finest poems in the collection, 'A Welcoming Party', where parochial Irish innocence is forced to face the larger tragic world. The 'party' of the title are children from the concentration camps, filmed for the last newsreel of the war and their contemporaries in Armagh. "Can these bones live?" the watchers ask in disbelief, after seeing children "conjugating the verb 'to die'." Prophetically Montague warns his home audience in the penultimate stanza,

> doves of mercy, as doves of air
> Can falter here as anywhere.[48]

The Montague selection from *Six Irish Poets* and, later, *Poisoned Lands*, presented Heaney with themes with which he could easily identify, and a variety of forms and styles he could utilise. A celebration of passionate transitoriness, 'Like Dolmens round my Childhood' prefigures Heaney's elegies to ancestors and neighbours, but lacks the affection that one finds in the younger man's poems. Brought up during a bleaker phase in contemporary Irish history, Montague did not enjoy the same degree of stability and integration Heaney experienced in childhood. Nevertheless, in retrieving figures such as Jamie McCrystal, Mary Moore, and Billy Harbison from the anonymity of death, the poet keeps faith with his people, victims of poverty, superstition and blindness of various kinds. The ending seems to imply that an exorcism is taking place of these shadows who 'trespassed on my dreams'; in fact Montague summons these presences from his psychic cast so that they may achieve the 'dark permanence of ancient forms', and remain. Acknowledging his role as one of the North's most important pioneers, Frank Ormsby writes that Montague

> was the first poet from north of the border to write in depth about the rural community in which he grew up. He identifies with

the people he describes, but is also sufficiently distanced from
them by education to see them not only as individuals but also
as representatives of a dying culture.[49]

If not a source for 'Digging', then at least an interesting parallel,
'The Country Fiddler'[50] reveals a poet re-establishing a line of
succession between himself and his family. Employing his 'craft' to
praise the 'rural art' of his forebears, Montague reconciles intellect
and instinct, the worlds of literature and the small farm, in a style
which combines poetic and colloquial diction, sympathy and gentle
self-mockery. Like Heaney in his poem, he engages in an act of
restoration, mending the 'bridge' between past familial tradition
and present discontinuity, 'keeping time'.[51]

A significant number of poems in *Poisoned Lands* begin with
scenes of childhood, which prompt the author to reflections on
his adult role as a poet, and the continuities of experience. 'Nursery
Story', like 'The Barn' and 'Death of a Naturalist' from Heaney's
first collection, portrays the dark underside of childhood, how
"Children learn the first lesson of fear in the night." As well as
supplying the form for Heaney's second published poem, 'Mid
Term Break',[52] 'The Water Carrier' may well have been a source
for 'Personal Helicon'. In both poems, a simple childhood chore,
collecting the water, becomes transformed first into a dramatic
experience, enlisting all the senses, and then into a metaphor for
the creative act. Each begins quietly, factually.

> Twice daily I carried water from the spring,
> Morning before leaving school, and evening.
>
> ('The Water Carrier')

> As a child, they could not keep me from wells
> And old pumps with buckets and windlasses.
>
> ('Personal Helicon')

Montague's image of himself as 'Balanced as a fulcrum between
two buckets' conveys a recognition of the dual sources sustaining
the artist's imagination, which draws living water from the 'half-
imagined', 'half-real' past. (Heaney may well have recalled this
image in 'Terminus', from *The Haw Lantern*, where he asserts "Two
buckets were easier carried than one/ I grew up in between.")[53]
Although Montague is very effective in his evocation of place and
rural ritual,

One stood until the bucket brimmed
Inhaling the musty smell of unpicked berries,
That heavy greenness fostered by water

he cannot immerse himself in the original experience or re-create it
as totally and vividly as Heaney – compare the effect of his formal
use of 'one' with Heaney's familiar 'you's in 'Personal Helicon' –
and at times makes us too conscious of his artifice. Both poems deal
with renewal, but whereas Montague offers us the status of observ-
ers, privileged to witness what is an elegant reflection, Heaney
creates an 'objective correlative' which sets 'the darkness echoing'
within the reader. Part of Montague's considerable achievement,
however, has been to point the way for Irish poets since the Sixties
to reconcile the claims of the parochial and the international, and
to explore identity through a personal and racial quest into dark
origins, like the Theseus of his poem:

Layer after layer of darkness
He stripped

And came at last, with harsh surprise
To where in breathing darkness lay
A lonely monster with almost human terror
In its lilac eyes.[54]

In the course of this same period which saw his aspirations
to become a poet quickened by his contact with Kavanagh and
Montague, his reading of Daniel Corkery's *The Hidden Ireland* and
James Joyce's *Portrait of the Artist as a Young Man* fortified his trust
in his linguistic and cultural inheritance. He had been introduced
to *The Hidden Ireland* while at St Columb's, but he re-read it in
the early sixties, and gave a brief lecture on Corkery as part
of the Belfast Festival of 1965. Corkery's passionate account of
the fate of Gaelic culture in eighteenth century Ireland deepened
Heaney's awareness of and pride in a tradition leading back far
beyond the Anglo-Irish 'Celtic' Twilight. Though not political by
nature, he could not but recognise how the contemptuous attitudes
of the Protestant Parliament of Dublin in the early eighteenth
century, which habitually referred to Catholics as 'the common
enemy', survived and thrived in the Stormont ruled over by Lord
Brookeborough for most of Heaney's lifetime. Prime Minister from

1943–63, Brookeborough "boasted that he would never employ a Catholic on his staff" since for him it would have been 'exactly like the British Government during the last war having a German in the Admiralty and a German in the War Office'.[55] The Penal Laws which denied Catholics the vote, education, ownership and the opportunity to enter the professions had been largely repealed by the 1790s, yet in the state of Northern Ireland their spirit was kept alive in the rank discrimination in the political sphere, by means of gerrymandering and the disenfranchisement of Catholics, and in jobs and in housing. 'National Trust', one of Heaney's earliest unpublished poems, read to the Group in late 1963 or early 1964, along with 'Docker', illustrates how some of Heaney's 'first attempts to speak, to make verse'[56] sprang from wounded political and religious sensibilities, rather than rural nostalgia. Emanating from a trip to Carrickfergus Castle, surrendered to William III in 1689, the poem concludes with a picture of contemporary English visitors mystified by the triumphalist symbols of Protestant supremacy which their forbears established. The masonic marks of the victors are contrasted with the ancient, holy and humble prints cherished by the vanquished. The sign proclaiming 'King William's Landing Stone'

> Sends English tourists to the crumbling wharf where
> Wind worries sporting headscarves. The basalt block
> Is imprinted with no saint's knee: they stare
> Instead at puzzling symbols hacked into the rock –
> A horse-shoe, LOL, a three runged ladder –
> Their king thus honoured by our conquered stock.[57]

Although sweet Edmund Spenser might deplore the 'barbarous rudeness' of 'that savage nation' and condemn the Irish for their 'ignorance in matters of learning',[58] Corkery's book drew attention to the achievements of Gaelic civilization, preserved in the bardic schools, the big houses and the works of major lyric poets such as Aodhagan O Raithaille, Eoghan Ruadh O Suilleabhain, and Brian Merriman. While these men must have appeared to the Planters as nobodies, mere peasants, their art and their classical learning – like that of Jimmy Jack Cassie in Brian Friel's *Translations* – made them pre-eminent amongst the people who sustained them, and whom they sustained. With delight, Heaney must have read Corkery's account of how O Suilleabhain wrote to his friend Seamas Mac Gerailt asking him to put a new handle on his spade.

> At the close of day, should my limbs be tired or sore,
> And the steward gibe that my spade-work is nothing worth,
> Gently I'll speak of Death's adventurous ways
> Or of Grecian battles in Troy, where princes fell!

"Labharfad féin go séimh" ('I myself will gently speak') – as if he said: "I will put off the *spailpin*, the earth delver, and assume my own self, the poet"! [59]

We hear that assertive, resolved note at the end of 'Digging', whose key images of spade and pen may well have been influenced by another Gaelic poem in *The Hidden Ireland*, 'An Scolaire', 'The Scholar':

> Great the harvest of his plough
> Coming in the front of Spring:
> And the yoke of his plough team,
> A handful of pens.[60]

It would have been surprising if Heaney had not identified with these poets, who treasured equally dialect and classical allusion, who attempted to create memorable phrases "that touch the life of the folk (so) intimately", who "shared their people's life and, indeed, their thoughts",[61] and 'named' their parishes. The accessibility and popularity of Heaney's own writing bears witness to his assimilation of these traditional virtues of Irish poetry.

His reading of Joyce at this time was also instrumental in enabling Heaney to free himself of his 'linguistic inferiority complex',[62] and to assert the legitimacy of his own language, place and voice. Though cherishing his Irish Catholic background, one suspects that part of him identified with Stephen Daedalus's longing to escape the 'nets' of 'nationality, language, religion'[63] which, according to Joyce, restrict the growth of the Irish soul. In *Among Schoolchildren*, he cites a small, Joycean 'experience which ratified my sense of relationship to a hidden Ulster in a memorable and intimate way, and ratified Corkery's notion of loss and deprivation'. He discovered that the word 'lachtar', meaning a flock of young chickens, which he had assumed to be English, was in fact Gaelic in origin, and peculiar to County Derry. He comments:

> The word had survived in our district as a common and as far as I had known until then, an English word, but now I realized that it lived upon our tongues like a capillary stretching back to a time when Irish was the lingua franca of the whole place.[64]

Although his sense of identity as a poet, as we have seen, was nourished by the native soil of his personal and Irish literary experience, he was not unresponsive to other influences in this formative phase from 1962–63. R. S. Thomas, Norman MacCaig and Ted Hughes were natural mentors for him to adopt, since, like Kavanagh and Montague, they were 'delineators of a rural parish', writers fired with a strong sense of place, who dwelt upon the intimacy of Man's relationship with Nature. R. S. Thomas's collection *Song at the Year's Turning*, published in 1955, contains many poems and attitudes with which Heaney could identify. In a little known review of Thomas's 1963 collection, *The Bread of Truth*, published in *Trench* in June 1964, Heaney's enthusiastic response to 'the poet and the pastor' embraces references to Wordsworth, Keats, Hardy, *Lear* and *Godot*, and highlights qualities of theme and style which one has come to associate with his own poetry. The characteristic strengths of the poetry of Thomas, Heaney and the early Hughes derive from their acute apprehension of the physical world, sustained as they are by 'a mouthful of earth, my staple'.[65] Hughes's image from 'Fire-eater' is perhaps recalled in the first line of Heaney's review. (For 'Welsh', substitute 'Irish'.)

> His nationality emerges as the staple of his poetry. Welsh religion, Welsh landscape, Welsh characters are the thongs tightening his imagination and intelligence . . . words common as broken glass are suddenly burnished into a self-illuminating mosaic . . . The physical features of the Welsh hill country and its inhabitants are presented in pungent detail, so that a self-contained world gradually evolves in the imagination . . . The sensibility that informs this work is instinctive, fermented in the dank valleys of a country imagination . . . Poems that could easily have ended as graphic presentation of environment go on to interpret and transform it . . . To regard this poet as regional . . . is to blind oneself to the blush of the universal on his gaunt Welsh features . . . One

critic has summarized his achievement admirably: the conclusion reached by R. George Thomas in a study of his namesake is that "the chronicler of the parish has become the bard of a raised hearth".[66]

Iago Prytherch, the strong, silent farmer in 'A Peasant', certainly prompted Heaney's McKenna poems, and the picture of him churning the crude earth 'To a stiff sea of clods that glint in the wind'[67] presages perhaps the sea-images of 'Follower'. The farmer in Thomas's 'Soil', who 'never looks up/ His gaze is deep in the soil', equally reminds one of the young poet's father, "His eye/ Narrowed and angled at the ground". Thomas's 'Welsh Landscape', with its bleak evocation of a tragic history which penetrates the present, has perhaps its counterpart in Heaney's 'At a Potato Digging', while 'Song for Gwydion', in which a father gives his son freshly caught trout to eat, shares some affinity with 'Blackberry Picking'; both articulate the doomed delights of pre-lapsarian innocence:

> They were the first sweet sacrifice I tasted,
> A young god, ignorant of the blood's stain.

Like R. S. Thomas, Norman MacCaig employs traditionalist forms in his poetry dwelling upon sacred places, people and landscapes, which offer opportunities for what Edna Longley calls 'prospecting of the mind'.[68] The first MacCaig ever to 'commit' an act of poetry, he seeks self-definition by establishing Man's familial relationship with Nature

> Parishes dwindle. But my parish is
> This stone, that tuft, this stone
> And the cramped quarters of my flesh and bone.[69]

Poems such as 'Byre', 'Spraying Sheep' and 'Water Tap' exude that warm and sensuous pleasuring in word and experience one associates with Heaney, with their opulent descriptions of cows as "Swagbellied Aphrodites, swinging/ A silver slaver from each chin", of sheep with 'golden fleeces every one' after spraying, of a 'rope' of water transformed miraculously, after it had 'frayed down' into a bucket, born again as it is "Hoisted up a plate/ Of flashing light." Illumined by the blessed commonplace

> Sheep wander haloed, birds at their plainsong shed
> Pure benedictions on water's painted glass.[70]

No doubt MacCaig's world with its epiphanies spilling easily from local, parochial experience, gave confidence to Heaney as he allowed his bucket to plummet into the well.

Seamus Heaney's most significant non-Irish 'find' during his poetic novitiate was his discovery of the work of Ted Hughes, when in November 1962 he borrowed *Lupercal* from Belfast Public Library. Hughes's work contained many of the 'masculine' features Heaney had admired in Hopkins; a preoccupation with energy and identity; an ability to capture the *haecceitas* of the animal and physical world and to express that 'thisness' by means of vigorous and vivid diction, which 'snicks through the air like an efficient blade, marking and carving out fast definite shapes',[71] and by charging his poems with powerful rhythms which achieve their thrust through the clash of consonants, a skilled use of assonance (vowel play?) and a subtle use of full and half-rhymes. Although their visions of the controlling Force or forces in the universe differ profoundly, Hopkins and Hughes share an intense reverence for creation, making words and worlds blaze with a religious awe. The celebration of sublime power in poems such as 'Wind', 'October Dawn', 'Crow Hill' and 'Pennines in April', in which Nature's ancient technology triumphs over the 'little world of Man', must have had a tremendous appeal for Heaney, whose upbringing had stressed humility and awe. Hughes's writing revealed an imagination tunnelling back before Christianity, conjuring a *Lear*-like universe in which endless repetitions of human guilt and brutality are set against the 'innocence' and permanence of elemental power.

In his *Preoccupations* essay, 'Englands of the Mind', Heaney connects the currents running through *The Hawk in the Rain* and *Lupercal* with King Lear's heath, where 'unaccommodated man' learns that he is but 'a poor bare forked animal',[72] 'kinned not in a chain but on a plane of being with the animals themselves.'[73] (Shakespeare's image is alluded to in the very Hughesian 'Turkeys Observed', Heaney's first major publication.) Accurately Heaney defines Hughes's sensibility as 'pagan', asserting that 'he is a haunter of the *pagus*, a heath-dweller, a heathen'.[74] Perhaps after twenty three years of intense exposure and devotion to Irish Catholicism, the 'primeval' feel of Hughes's world appealed to the Oisin in him, with its ancient landscapes and its magical beasts, like the old Celtic gods, defiant and doomed. With its cast of outcasts, beggars, scavengers, perpetual refugees, *Lupercal* may have actually become 'celticised' in Heaney's imagination; its displaced souls resemble the deities of Irish mythology, and recall the impoverished geniuses of Corkery's lost world.

Another common denominator between the Yorkshire poet and the Derry poet lay in their fascination for and ambiguous attitude towards the animal world. As young men both were keen hunters and fishers, pursuits which honed their powers of concentration and prepared them for 'capturing animals' in words.[75] Analysing the connections in *Poetry in the Making*, Hughes comments:

> It was years before I wrote what you could call an animal poem, and several more years before it occurred to me that my writing poems might be partly a continuation of my earlier pursuit. Now I have no doubt. The special kind of excitement, the slightly mesmerized and quite involuntary concentration with which you make out the stirrings of a new poem in your mind, then the outline, the mass and colour and clean final form of it, the unique living reality of it in the midst of the general lifelessness, all that is too familiar to mistake.[76]

While many Hughes and early Heaney poems may be said to exhibit traces of a boyish relish for violence because of their 'macho' imagery – a pen/ gun analogy opens 'Digging'; 'Trout' begins as 'a fat gun-barrel', 'gets bull's eye', and darts 'like a tracer-bullet'; 'Dawn Shoot' also boasts a 'bull's-eye', along with a corncrake 'sentry', a snipe which 'rocketed away', and two 'parachutists', one of whom 'emptied two barrels/ And got him' – equally evident in their works is a huntsman's respect, and an adult's empathy.

Although an affinity of feeling and feeling for language clearly links, for example, Heaney's 'Death of a Naturalist' with Hughes's 'Pike',[77] from the outset of his career Heaney has shown his capacity to 'overcome' rather than succumb to his influences. Published only two years previously, *Lupercal* quickened something instinctual in the young Heaney and set him off on a quest of self-discovery and re-discovery, like the otter, "Seeking/ Some world lost when first he dived that he cannot come at since".[78] It convinced him that poetry was a vocation, right and fitting, reinforcing his acute sense of the sacred, derived first from his mother, and subsequently affirmed by early literary influences such as Wordsworth and Hopkins.

The winter of 1962 and spring of 1963 marked a major turning point in his career. Feeling that he was not 'triumphing as a teacher',[79] he began to seek fresh outlets for his untapped talents. Heaney decided to register for a part-time postgraduate degree at Queen's, with 'a thesis on Wordsworth's educational ideas in mind.'[80] This academic study, like the poetry to come, may well have been a kind of compensation for not having seized the opportunity of going to Oxford. At this very time when, by his own admission he was adrift – "I was just floundering really"[81] – three new enabling figures entered his life, Terry Flanagan, Marie Devlin and Philip Hobsbaum. Their warmth, friendship and belief in him helped him to 'anchor'.

While he was at St Thomas's, Michael McLaverty had introduced Heaney to T. P. Flanagan, one of Ireland's most distinguished painters, at a lecture Flanagan was giving. As Head of Art at St Mary's College, he had taught Marie Devlin, the future Marie Heaney, on her subsidiary Art course. Another of his roles involved inspecting student teachers, and on one visit, Michael McLaverty told him he should meet "a young new teacher at my school, because I feel you would have a great deal in common."[82] Here was another Ulster maker 'living out – and living in – a vocation',[83] whose delight in creating images through his visual eye was to be matched by his young friend's accomplishment with his 'visual ear'. Born in 1929 at Enniskillen, by the shores of Lough Erne, T. P. Flanagan spent much of his childhood at Lissadell, where he was acquainted with Maeve Markiewicz, Constance's daughter. The lough and Lissadell were two of the sacred places of Flanagan's imagination, to which he frequently returned in his paintings of the early 1960s, exploring what Kenneth Jamison refers to as 'his childhood awareness of the peculiar gravity of light'.[84] The nostalgic, the elegiac, the melancholic note within his work – the Celtic-Catholic note? – appealed to Heaney, along with his capacity to capture the fundamentals of Irish landscape, suffused with a sense of its 'still sad music'. His landscapes seem a fulfilment of Hardy's vision of the future's sparer sense of the sublime:

The new Vale of Tempe may be a gaunt waste in Thule: human souls may find themselves in closer and closer harmony with external things wearing a sombreness distasteful to our race when it was young. The time seems near, if it has not actually arrived, when the chastened sublimity of a moor, a sea or mountain will be all of nature that is absolutely in keeping with the moods of the more thinking among mankind.[85]

With his long uninterrupted vistas in which sky shapes take on a dramatic force, where a thorn or a turf-stack can suddenly take on a 'monumentalquality',[86] Flanagan might be said to express in colour the diurnal wonder that Hopkins and Kavanagh caught in verse. It is not until the late 1960s, however, in *Door into the Dark* and *Wintering Out*, that Heaney achieves a verbal equivalent to the simplicity and austere lyricism permeating Flanagan's art.

One Tuesday in October of 1962 Heaney met Marie Devlin at a party at Queen's University Chaplaincy in Fitzwilliam Street, Belfast, held for the retiring chaplain. He lent her his copy of A. Alvarez's anthology, *The New Poetry*, and asked her to return it by the next Thursday. Born on 14 September 1940, from Ardboe in Co. Tyrone, on the shores of Lough Neagh, Marie was the second of seven children. Her mother was a schoolmistress from a middle-class family in Warrenpoint, while her father was 'the owner of the only public house in the district', and something of an athlete, 'the county high-jump champion before his marriage'.[87] Polly Devlin, her sister, in her book, *All of us There*, describes Marie as 'a true Celt with her thin skin and fine features, her shining hair high-lighted with red gleams' and speaks of her 'frisky athletic body', inherited from her father, whose charm and 'memorably good looks' she also shares. The Devlins lived in a substantial Edwardian house, surrounded by a large garden, lawns and orchards. This was built by Marie's grandfather, who had been a local Justice of the Peace, and had "battled his way above the crippling lack of expectation" in his district.[88] Its frontage figures in an important family photograph, in which Grandfather Devlin stands alongside a young politician, for whom he acted as Northern agent. This was Eamon de Valera, who was spared the death penalty after the Easter Rising after his counsel assured the authorities of his future 'good conduct'; later de Valera would become President of the Dail. Marie's father appears in this photograph, along with his brother, who became a doctor, and two sisters, who went to university and then abroad. This was a family, therefore, which had a history of ambition and academic achievement, and a strong sense of their Irish Catholic identity.

Within the Devlin family, there was a long tradition of religious tolerance. Marie's grandfather, on her father's side, John Sinnamond

Devlin, had married a Miss Walsh from Waterford, who was of
Scottish Presbyterian descent, and her maternal grandmother was
of French Huguenot extraction, with the maiden name Cadeau.
The home was, therefore, free from the taint of religious bigotry and prejudice "which so poisoned and continues to poison
much of life in Northern Ireland".[89] In her sister's book, Marie
Devlin recalls their initiation into the violence of prejudice, when
a coach full of Protestant children visited Ardboe. It was 'a most
significant moment for me', the equivalent perhaps of the road-
block interrogations Seamus Heaney experienced in his teenage
years.

> I remember that scene so well. Their bus was parked upon
> the New Road – and we had never seen a bus down there
> before . . . That rector in his grey suit. When they arrived where
> we were playing, and had always played, they spread themselves
> out and we shied away apologetically. We, who had spent all the
> days of our living memory on that shore, crept off . . . . We went
> further along the lough shore and went on playing and paddling
> and one girl followed us, pursued us. She said, "C'mere you two,
> are you two papishes?" . . . "Say the Lord's Prayer. Go on say it,
> at once."
> "Our Father Who art in Heaven," I said . . . when she heard
> 'Who art in Heaven' instead of 'which art' which is how they
> said it, she said, "You dirty wee papishes, you wee bitches, get
> on home."[90]

Like Heaney, Marie Devlin was a beneficiary of the 1947 Education
Act, and had studied English, Speech and Drama at a teacher
training college, St Mary's, Belfast, from 1958–1962. (Until the
late 1960s she taught at St Columcille's at Crossgar, Co Down.).
The substantial quotations in *All of us There* convey the impression
of a strong sensual and instinctual nature, like her husband's, and
a gift with language which once manifested itself in writing poetry
during her student days. Affinities of experience, interests and
nature – "She's entirely instinctive and usually, therefore, exactly
right"[91] – made her an ideal partner. Despite a certain Catholic
coyness about the union to which it refers, male 'rock' embracing
'yielding' water, in a poem like 'Lovers on Aran' Heaney writes
beautifully of the sense of completeness he achieved through their
relationship.

Did sea define the land or land the sea?
Each drew new meaning from the waves' cóllision.
Sea broke on land to full identity.

In November 1962, shortly after meeting Marie, and discovering *Lupercal*, Heaney's poem, 'Tractors', appeared in the *Belfast Telegraph*. It was followed the next month by 'Turkeys Observed', which was inspired by seeing a row of Christmas turkeys in a butcher's shop. These acceptances he describes as moments of 'confirmation'. When, in Spring 1963, 'almost by return of post' the *Kilkenny Magazine* took 'Mid-Term Break', "written very quickly one evening in early February, when Christopher's anniversary was coming up",[92] and 'An Advancement of Learning' appeared on March 9 in *The Irish Times*, he felt 'launched'.[93] May 1963 saw the publication of 'Essences' and 'Welfare State', neither of which has been reprinted. The latter prefigures such poems as 'Follower', 'Digging' and 'Ancestral Photograph', but offers a generalised picture, rather than an individualised portrait of the pathos of old age. Attuned to the 'subterraneous music' of the wind on the hills, Heaney's archetypal old men remind one of Wordsworth's Michael. The vigour of the diction, ('fierce', 'ravishing', 'relish', 'flash', 'Swivelled', 'probed'), the sense of scale, taking in 'horizon' and 'the heavens', and the rhythmic, alliterative thrust, echo the Hughes of *The Hawk in the Rain* and *Lupercal*. The poem strains too hard with its over-insistent adjectives, and turns too suddenly from celebration to sardonic lament. Nevertheless it looks forward to the 'contradictory awarenesses' of later poems, with their ambivalent attitudes towards his father and the Church Fathers, who, 'stumbling/ Behind me', refuse to 'go away'.[94]

'Welfare State' appeared in *Interest*, a Queen's University magazine, edited by Alan Gabbey. According to Neil Corcoran's book, it was Gabbey who "first told Heaney about Philip Hobsbaum, a lecturer who had recently joined the English Department".[95] Like J. B. S. O'Kelly and Michael McLaverty, Hobsbaum was to become an immensely important figure in Heaney's development as a poet, acting as another literary 'father', as well as being a loyal and generous friend. Philip Dennis Hobsbaum was born in 1932, and educated at Downing College, Cambridge, where he studied under F. R. Leavis, and at Sheffield University, where his supervisor was William Empson. He had edited *Delta* in Cambridge in the 1950s, publishing some of the earliest poems of Ted Hughes, and was a co-founder of the London 'Group' along with Edward Lucie-Smith, which boasted amongst its members Peter Redgrove, Peter Porter, George MacBeth, and Alan Brownjohn.

> At their weekly meetings, members of the Group listen to a fellow member read a number of his poems which have been previously circulated on cyclostyled sheets. They then discuss the verse very thoroughly, frankly, informally – and the poet is there to counteract, resent, and/or benefit from the criticism.[96]

The success of the London Group, which resulted in a major anthology, made Hobsbaum determined to start a Group in Belfast. He arrived there in July 1962, looking for accommodation, and when he started lecturing at Queen's in the October, he started immediately 'sussing the place' for likely talent.[97] In the Spring of 1963, when he was searching for a nucleus for a Group, he came across some of Heaney's poems, and wrote to him. He recalls how one sunny Saturday morning, a 'gangling youth' turned up, 'smiling and keen'. "He seemed incredibly pleased to be noticed, taken up and spoken to. He kept grinning, a trait I didn't quite understand at the time, but I think it was in pleasure at being recognised."[98] No doubt, Heaney's initial awe at the range of Hobsbaum's literary acquaintance and air of dogmatic certainty quickly turned to affection as he sensed the passionate commitment to literature and to his students which motivated the older man.

The 'gangling youth' had recently completed his review of *A Group Anthology*, probably in the March of 1963. Although he had not yet met Hobsbaum, he was very aware of the likely impact of his presence.[99] The piece, which appeared in *Hibernia* in September 1963, is mature and authoritative, and even risks a cheeky dig at the editor. "In 'The Place's Fault' it is clear that Mr Hobsbaum's parents 'Kept him from children who were rough'." He concludes the review asserting that the anthology is 'a must for all those interested in progress (and process) of poetry', and throughout shows how attracted he is to the 'Group' method of weekly meetings of readings and collective criticism.

> Mr. Hobsbaum, who is at present lecturing in the English Department at Queen's, has this to say:
> "I do not see why the approach adopted here should not work, with suitable amendments, in other places and times . . . I

should like to see similar enterprises started up and down the country and in the universities."

One can only hope his suggestion is taken up. If there was a Group in Belfast, Dublin, Cork and Galway, our young poets would find it easier to meet an audience; beginners would have the benefit of criticism from the established and above all, interest should increase. Which might not be a bad thing.[100]

In October 1963, prior to the inaugural meeting of the Group, Heaney enjoyed a beneficial change of job, which gave fresh impetus to his writing ambitions, moving from St Thomas's Secondary School to St Joseph's College of Education, where he had completed his Certificate in Education. Lecturing on Shakespeare, Wordsworth and the Romantics was a great pleasure to him, though an unpublished poem, 'Young Bachelor', implies that his duties ate up 'Five nights a week and much of the weekend'.[101] However, the greater intellectual stimulus of the College, despite its demands, must have been infinitely preferable to the slog of poring through endless exercise books.

The Belfast Group held its first meeting in the sitting room of Hobsbaum's house, 5 Fitzwilliam Street, in November 1963. Philip Hobsbaum's first wife, Hannah, performed an invaluable role in the proceedings, one of her most onerous tasks being to type out the cyclostyled stories, play extracts or poems, which were then posted in advance to the sixteen individuals on the mailing list. (Most sessions, however, had an attendance of ten writers.) At each weekly Monday meeting, Hobsbaum would invite someone to read their latest work during the first half of the evening, then, after a coffee break, others members would read and have their work scrutinised. While the contributors to the 1976 *Honest Ulsterman* 'The Belfast Group: A Symposium' may differ in their evaluations of the Group's impact on any individual's literary development, all pay tribute to Hobsbaum's role as a catalyst, bringing together from outside as well as within the University an outstanding gathering of talent. Between November 1963 and July 1966, Hobsbaum supplied an exciting and controversial environment in which writers, critics, and translators from very different backgrounds – such as Michael and Edna Longley, Stewart Parker, Harry Chambers, James Simmons, Michael Allen, Hugh Bredin, Arthur Terry, Joan Newman (neé Watton), Norman Dugdale, Bernard Mac Laverty, as well as Seamus and Marie Heaney – could meet together, test their work, and find confirmation, and at times, perhaps, consolation in the friendships formed. In his own contribution to the symposium, Heaney applauds Hobsbaum's "energy, generosity, belief in the community, trust in the parochial, the inept, the unprinted" and describes his time with the Group as "one of the most, sociable, and satisfying that I have experienced."[102]

On the 'neutral' ground of the Fitzwilliam Street sitting room, friendships and healthy rivalries developed across the sectarian divide. Born into a Protestant middle-class family in south Belfast in 1939, educated at the Royal Belfast Academical Institution, and Trinity College, Dublin, where Catholics feared to tread, Michael Longley told me that he had had no Catholic friends until meeting the Heaneys. As far as I am aware, before 1964, Heaney had no close confidants from within the Protestant community, yet during that year he developed important 'Protestant' relationships, with Michael Longley, and his future wife, Edna, and with David Hammond, whom Heaney's family describes as his closest friend. Centuries of distrust and years of 'separate development' in segregated schools and divided villages could be temporarily forgotten as the individuals in the Group fought over aesthetic issues. "From the beginning Hobsbaum made it clear that his stars were Seamus Heaney and Stewart Parker",[103] writes Michael Longley. After being 'pressurised' to join the Group in Spring 1964 – his fiancée, Edna, was a colleague of Hobsbaum's – he claims to have felt shocked 'at the ferocity of Hobsbaum's attacks' on his poems, which were condemned for their 'elegance'. In the 1976 symposium, he contrasts his notions of poetry then with 'the Group aesthetic', and provides one account of Hobsbaum's tastes, "I believed that poetry should be polished, metrical and rhymed; oblique rather than head-on; imagistic and symbolic rather than rawly factual; rhetorical rather than documentary."[104] Though perhaps initially unimpressed by the kind of poetry Longley produced, Hobsbaum certainly later acted generously towards him, persuading Macmillan to overturn their initial decision to reject his first volume, *No Continuing City*.

In conversation with me, the Belfast poet recalled how impressed he was with Heaney on their first meeting, as the latter approached him enthusiastically, saying "Are you Michael Longley?", then going on to praise the poems he had liked, 'Graffiti' and 'Circe'. Longley regarded the early Heaney poems, such as 'Death of a Naturalist', as 'basic', having greater respect for the sophistication and wit of his fellow-poet from Trinity College, Derek Mahon. Heaney, Mahon and Longley were to become close competitors and friends. Their poetry was characterised by greater variety and elegance of forms, by a rhetorical grace and verbal eloquence, a balance between urban and rural, classical and contemporary subject matter, a reflection of their different roots and poetic influences. Heaney greatly admired their poetry, telling them on one occasion, "I'd like to write like you boys, but I have to do my own thing."[105]

Heaney's important friendship with the singer and broadcaster, David Hammond, stems from late 1963. (Like Longley's and Mahon's, his family were from the Protestant community). Hammond, who had already a considerable reputation as a result of concerts, radio and television, received an invitation from Heaney to sing one afternoon to the students at St Joseph's, and after the session they went off for a few drinks. When in 1964, Hammmond was seconded from his post as a teacher at Orange Field Secondary School to join the B.B.C. as a temporary producer, he heard of an earlier abortive attempt by Heaney to work on a programme for the B.B.C., but was not then in a position to help. (While on a routine visit to St Thomas's, the education officer, Leslie Davidson, had met Heaney, and had suggested that he might offer a series of radio programmes for schools on the lines of Ted Hughes's *Poetry in the Making*. Davidson duly mentioned the idea to James Hawthorne, who was in charge of schools programmes. When Heaney called to meet Hawthorne at the B.B.C. to discuss his proposal, the latter decided not to continue with it since he felt that such a series would require 'a big name'.) However, when at the end of 1965, Hammond was given a permanent post with B.B.C. Radio Belfast, he approached Heaney, and asked him to contribute some radio scripts. The result was *Over to You*, a series for E.S.N. pupils throughout Britain. Although back in London objections were lodged about the number of regional accents and Irish references in the programmes, they became increasingly popular with teachers and pupils, because they dealt with powerful themes and did not talk down to their listeners. This was the first of many highly successful collaborations between the two men, whose friendship grew because of affinities of character and spirit.

David Hammond was born in 1928, and reared in Belfast. His parents, who came from a country area outside Belfast, always felt they were only temporarily resident in the city, and retained a distrust of townspeople. His father's family originated from

South Derry, Heaney's county, while his mother came from near Ballymoney in North Antrim. It was from his mother that he acquired his love of song, and, a feeling the majority of Ulster Protestants would be loath to acknowledge as legitimate – a sense of Irishness. Her family had been Home Rulers, and her father was so anti-English that he delighted in British setbacks in the Second World War. Hammond recalls that one of the largest tomes in the house was a biography of 'the Liberator', Daniel O'Connell. From an early age, the young David was very conscious of his parents' feelings of exile within the city, since in the home they spoke a language "no longer in currency", a dialect form of English. Like Heaney's, his parents felt a "reverence for learning",[106] a deep love for words and language, and regarded education both as an end in itself and as a means towards social mobility. After enjoying immensely the elementary schooling he received, in 1941 he won a scholarship to a Methodist College, where much of his motivation quickly disappeared. The college was full of teachers from England, "probably there to avoid conscription" and "nobody in the school seemed to respect learning much."[107] On moving to Stranmillis Teacher Training College, he did even less. Though he rejected the formal education proffered, Hammond, in traditional Nonconformist style, had striven to develop a strong sense of identity through a long process of self-education.[108]

His first post as a primary school teacher gave him a new lease of life, and he took pleasure in the responsibility of devising his own syllabus, in writing plays and organising field trips for local studies. He was fortunate in his first headmaster, as Heaney was with Michael McLaverty, since Dick Taylor gave him a free hand and considerable support, and in his colleagues many of whom were exiles from the Free State, and shared his love for Irish writers. After eight years in primary school, he went to the United States on a travel scholarship for one year, singing, making records and broadcasting. The exhilaration of this experience unsettled him, and on his return to Ireland in 1957, he found it difficult – just as Heaney would after his time at Berkeley – to sink back into the familiar routine. Instead in 1958 he took up a secondary teaching position at Orangefield School, under John Malone, a legendary headmaster in Northern Ireland, who ran his school with 'missionary fervour' and 'monastic dedication'.[109] Heaney's memorial lecture to John Malone in 1983 praises his 'pioneering and inspirational work', his belief in the writer's social and moral role, and in the 'good force of the imagination'.[110]

David Hammond, therefore, shared Heaney's profound love for Irish literature and consciousness of its neglect within the North, a passion for 'the hidden Ulster', for the folk customs and culture of their forebears, and sought through teaching and learning to sensitise their countrymen and themselves to their past and present inheritance.

Although it is generally easier to identify literary influences than to evaluate the impact of key relationships upon a writer's development, both help determine and shape that development. It would be foolish to underestimate the importance of such confirmatory presences and supportive voices as those of Marie Devlin, Michael McLaverty, T. P. Flanagan, Philip Hobsbaum, Michael Longley and David Hammond, who assisted Heaney in the process of establishing a firm sense of his own identity from which he could create, and freeing himself from his *Incertus* past. Any examination of Heaney's output during the period November 1963 to late April 1965 reveals the powerful stimulus the Group and these relationships gave to his creative development, as at last he enjoyed the benefit of a critically responsive audience. The first Heaney Groupsheet contains 'Oh Brave New Bull', which appeared as 'The Outlaw' in his second book, along with the published 'Mid Term Break' and 'Turkeys Observed', and the MacKenna poems referred to earlier. The second displays a more public voice, that of the 'aggravated young Catholic male',[111] and opens with 'Docker' and 'National Trust', both illustrating Heaney's resentment against the status quo which still treated Catholics as 'conquered stock'. His subsequent 'suppression' of that angry Catholic voice may be partly attributable to his new friendships with the Longleys and Hammond, who were both of Protestant stock, and by that spirit of communality generated by the Group.

In the third Groupsheet, from Spring/Summer of 1964, the voice of the 'private Derry childhood' asserts itself in 'The Early Purges'. Uncertainties about the future linger somewhat lugubriously in 'Taking Stock 5/4/64',

> Just one year older, with no child, no poem
> That will endure, no shape in paint or stone
> Shored up against the ruins. The diary
> Makes depressing reading

while in 'Ex-champ', he bobs and weaves with boxing metaphors. In its content, it echoes Hughes's 'Famous Poet'; in its search for analogies for the poetic process it parallels 'The Thought-Fox', and prepares the ground for 'Digging':

> At first there were short bouts
> With people and old poems
> For sparring partners.
> He hit language rough clouts
> But lacked style which only comes
> Many hard scraps later.

'Men's confessions' shifts from a general description of 'Subdued and tight-lipped farmers', awaiting the sacrament of absolution, to a particular centre of focus, the MacKenna persona.

> His turn comes round, confess he must;
> Within the hoarse dark of the box
> He catalogues his lies, booze, lust
> And noses out grace like an old fox.

This poem is clearly a precursor of the autobiographical 'Boy driving his father to confession', which was read to the Group on 27 April 1965. Gradually Heaney was developing the confidence to write directly from his childhood experience, and consequently fewer poems rely on personae and distancing effects. The fourth of the Groupsheets from late 1964 opens with 'Digging' and 'Death of a Naturalist', Groupsheets Five and Six from early 1965 contain 'Boy driving his father to confession', 'Blackberry Picking', 'The Diviner', 'Ancestral Photograph' and 'Personal Helicon'. His desire to explore his own past – first quickened by Wordsworth, Kavanagh, Montague and Hughes – was further 'corroborated'[112] during this period by his reading of Theodore Roethke's *The Far Field*. Within this and Roethke's earlier collections, one finds preoccupations and elements of style which would naturally appeal to Heaney. There are many celebrated and celebratory evocations of childhood, such as the 'Greenhouse' poems, in which a father's figure looms large. There is also the American's fine eye for detail, and his keen sense of both the menace and sensual delights of nature. Many poems exhibit his love of water and watery places, conceived of in fecund and feminine terms. In 'Cuttings', which bears affinities of theme with

Sylvia Plath's 'Mushrooms' and Ted Hughes's 'Snowdrop', Roethke examines first the delicacy, then the determination within these 'slips' of male nature. They long for and can only be sustained 'by the confirming touch of female water. The universality of this truth would be immediately acknowledged by the poet from Mossbawn on the verge of marriage:

> In my veins, in my bones I feel it, –
> The small waters seeping upward,
> The tight grains parting at last . . .
> I quail, lean to beginnings, sheath-wet.[113]

'Death of a Naturalist', in its sensual evocation of humanity's violation of Nature, may owe something to Roethke's 'Moss Gathering', also from *The Lost Son and Other Poems* (1948). Describing how 'something went out of me' after plunging 'to my elbows in the spongy yellowish moss', Roethke continues:

> afterwards I always felt mean, jogging back over the
>   logging road
> As if I had broken the natural order of things in that swamp-
>   land,
> Disturbed some rhythm, old and of vast importance,
> By pulling off flesh from the living planet;
> As if I had committed, against the whole scheme of life, a
>   desecration.[114]

Whether Heaney was actually 'influenced' or not, his poems from late 1964 to 1969 certainly articulate an equal commitment to the 'repossession of the childhood Eden'[115] which one finds in Roethke.

> The things I liked were 'Meditation at Oyster River' and those long sectioned late Whitmanesque things. I don't know that I was influenced: corroborated in a sense that the charges in a place could be a proper inspiration for poems, helped to trust a frank celebratory kind of writing, made to feel that illiterate, inchoate memory-place-feeling stuff was as important as 'thought'.[116]

His confidence was also fed by his increasing success during 1964. *Interest* had published in May 'Such men are dangerous' and 'Fisher' – the latter, like 'Ex-Champ', a Hughesian poem about writing poems – and in November 'Writer and Teacher', 'Young Bachelor' and 'Soliloquy for an Old Resident', which also appeared in a volume entitled *Young Commonwealth Writers of 1963*. Along with Stewart Parker, Hugh Bredin, Joan Watton and John Bond, he read at the Irish P.E.N. meeting, chaired by Philip Hobsbaum, held at the International Hotel, Belfast, on 7 May 1964. The major coup of that year, however, occurred as a result of Hobsbaum's London 'connections'. Hobsbaum introduced Seamus and Marie Heaney to Edward Lucie-Smith at a dinner party at the Fitzwilliam Street house – attended also by Peter and Bridget Butter – and, on returning to London, Lucie-Smith sent some of Heaney's poems to Karl Miller, who accepted three for the *New Statesman*. 'Digging', 'Scaffolding' and 'Storm on the Island' appeared on 4 December 1964. Then in January 1965 he received a letter from Charles Monteith of Faber & Faber, asking him for a manuscript.

> I just couldn't believe it, it was like getting a letter from God the Father . . . I sent them what I had and they didn't think there was a book there but they would like first refusal if ever I thought I had a book.[117]

After this very encouraging reply, Hobsbaum urged him "to get his name into the periodicals Charles Monteith would see",[118] such as the *Times Literary Supplement*. In the subsequent four months Heaney "wrote a hell of a lot", and sent them a fresh manuscript in the Summer of 1965, which they accepted. Philip Hobsbaum recalls Heaney turning up at Fitzwilliam Street to announce the news, with 'a big grin' on his face, and a half bottle of whiskey, which showed Heaney's 'incredible judgment'. Had it been a whole bottle, they would have got drunk.

One triumph was succeeded by another, and another. In August 1965 his marriage to Marie Devlin took place, followed by a honeymoon in London. Then in November, his *Eleven Poems* were published to coincide with the Belfast Festival of the Arts. In the 1964 Belfast Festival, Heaney had given a lecture on Daniel Corkery, 'a small scale affair',[119] he told me. The 1965 Festival, which was organised like its predecessor by Michael Emmerson, and lasted from November 12–27, was a much more impressive affair. Emmerson promoted Ulster's new poets by publishing a series of pamphlets each month, 'to be sold in Dublin, London and in the British University towns',[120] beginning with Michael Longley's

Ten Poems in October, Heaney's *Eleven Poems* in November, and a selection of Derek Mahon's poems in December. (Longley and Mahon had both won Gregory Awards earlier that year.) These three also received coverage and recognition in the London press in the form of Mary Holland's *Observer* article, which celebrated the 'cultural efflorescence in the city.'[121]

However, while the years which preceded the publication of Heaney's first volume witnessed a major upsurge in the cultural life of the province, and a creative coming together of Catholic and Protestant, sadly there was little real progress in the political sphere. In February 1962 the I.R.A. terminated their six-year long campaign, which had partly faltered due to lack of public support. In the Irish general election of 1961, Sinn Fein lost all its four seats and its share of the vote dropped by 50 per cent. Meanwhile in the North, the twenty-year reign as Prime Minister of Lord Brookeborough came to an end. He was replaced by Captain Terence O'Neill, an Old Etonian, and Irish Guards officer during World War II, who at least risked some tentative, though largely cosmetic changes in an attempt 'to adjust Northern Ireland to the world of the 1960s'.[122] Though in January and February 1965, he took part in the first meetings ever between the Prime Ministers of the North and South, and visited various Catholic girls' grammar schools in gestures of goodwill, his conciliatory behaviour provoked a sceptical response from Catholics, who felt they were the objects of condescension, and outrage from many Protestants, who regarded the giving of an inch as the first step to Rome (and Dublin) rule. The O'Neillite rapprochement certainly assisted the rise of the Reverend Ian Paisley, whose 'church militant' did so much to exarcerbate the political situation in the late sixties, and whose supporters were responsible for the stoning of Civil Rights marchers at Burntollet Bridge in 1969.

On his arrival in July 1962, Philip Hobsbaum had felt that Northern Ireland would explode sooner or later, for 'there was a rumble in the air'.[123] In his July 1966 *New Statesman* article 'Out of London: Ulster's Troubles', Heaney identified the threat to stability posed by Paisley

a man who has been described variously as a 'fascist' and 'a bloated bullfrog, whose recent prominence is regarded by many as the death throes of the ignorant and ugly bigotry that has numbed the social life of the community for years. Others tend to feel that he is a phoenix figure, stirring the embers of old feuds into a new conflagration.[124]

Although the Ulster Hall in Belfast was not permitted to be used for religious or political meetings, Paisley preached from there each Sunday. The aim of his extremist movement was to destroy

> any bridges that might exist between Catholic and Protestant; it would create its own Troubles and set the political and religious question back forty years. The atmosphere of the Troubles has been growing: there have been stabbings, shootings and bomb throwings. A month ago it was still possible to say 'hooliganism', but with the shooting down of three youths on Sunday, and the death of one of them nobody can ignore the threat to public safety. The government has since proscribed the Ulster Volunteers. Life goes on, yet people are reluctant to dismiss the possibility of an explosion.[125]

At the foot of his article, a brief poem by Roy McFadden, 'I Won't Dance', appeared, as it to underline Heaney's scepticism about the political future of the 'rotten' state. It is a Northern riposte to the famous medieval Irish lyric, 'I am of Ireland'. Twenty years later, it retains its grim topicality.

> I am of Northern Ireland, born
> Behind a mattressed window, when
> The crossfire between love and hate
> Jerked a corpse across our wooden gate.
> Where introverted streets reflect
> Pains from a shattered past: where all
> My constitutionals end with
> The dead man on the gate and in the myth.[126]

3

Pioneer, 1966–69

Our pioneers keep striking
Inwards and downwards,

Every layer they strip
Seems camped on before.
The bogholes might be Atlantic seepage,
The wet centre is bottomless.[1]

1. *Mil.* One of a body of footsoldiers who march with or in advance
of an army or regiment, having spades, pickaxes, etc, to dig trenches,
and clear and prepare the way for the main body. 2. *gen.* A digger,
an excavator: a miner –1640. 3. *fig.* One who goes before to prepare
the way: one who begins some enterprise, course of action, etc.: an
original investigator, explorer or worker; an initiator (of) 1605.[2]

DEATH OF A NATURALIST

Heaney's second volume, *Door into the Dark*, concludes with
'Bogland', a poem which embodies what had gone before and
anticipates the future direction of his poetry, looking forward to
the place-name and bog poems of *Wintering Out* and *North*. Like
so much of his first book, it asserts the author's sense of affinity
and continuity with his cultural forbears. It takes pleasure in the
particularity of the Irish landscape, which seems full of resilience
and fecundity, and transmutes Ireland's richest resource in economic
terms into a symbol for the imagination's potential.

In *Death of A Naturalist* and *Door into the Dark*, the young poet
overcomes his unease at abandoning the 'slane' for the pen, by
affirming his kinship with the humble diggers of ancestral turf
within his own family, and within Gaelic and Irish literature.
His use of the word 'pioneer' invokes memories of the spade-
carrying poets of Corkery's *The Hidden Ireland*, such as Eoghan

61

Ruadh O Suilleabhain, but also of his most important precursor, Patrick Kavanagh, whose work, like Heaney's, raised "the inhibited energies of a subculture to the power of a cultural resource".[3] From the outset, Heaney's poetic career began with acts of reclamation, as purposefully he dug 'inwards and downwards', reccying the border areas of the conscious and subconscious. While at first imitative of earlier explorers, even within his first volume he has begun to develop his own ways of saying, established his own 'patterns of perception'.[4] Through them, with them, in them, he is able to achieve a poetic resolution to inner tensions as he confronts the familial, parochial and national past. Moving into these regions, in poems such as 'Docker', 'At a Potato Digging', and 'Requiem for the Croppies', he stumbles upon mines and myths left over from previous conflicts, which would prove impossible to defuse by literary devices.

Death of a Naturalist opens with 'Digging', the first of three poems in which Patrick Heaney is a dominant presence. Along with the unpublished poem, 'Boy driving his father to confession', these poems reveal the creative importance within his early career of the 'state of negotiation' between Heaney and his idea of Father.[5] Although he has spoken deprecatingly of 'Digging', referring to it as 'a big coarse-grained navvy of a poem',[6] he has also described it as 'seminal', in that it "opened up a vein of experience which I afterwards explored."[7] Like its kindred pieces, 'Follower' and 'Ancestral Photograph', it is a poem about blood, ancestry, roots, growing up and away, and expresses a deeply felt need to reconcile his new identity as a poet with that of his former boyish self. To switch metaphors, it reveals the poet putting down his foundations, building upon many layers of literary and personal experience. In an early article, Heaney recalls how he would tarry on the way to school talking to old men, like the road-surface man. "Leaning on his spade, this man once said to me, "The pen's easily handled. Aye, boy, it's a lot lighter than the spade, I'm telling you."[8] Although the roadman may have supplied the antithetical images of the poem's beginning and ending, it is the figures of his father and grandfather who loom over the bulk of the poem. As in early Hughes poems such as 'Six Young Men', 'The Retired Colonel' or 'Dick Straightup', a tame domestic present is contrasted with an heroic, 'mightier-than-a-man' past.[9] His memory swiftly carries him from the present tense and a picture of his now ungainly father, pottering with 'straining rump' amongst the flowerbeds, to a past perfected, in which Patrick Heaney and *his* father wield their weapons like Byrhtnoth or Cuchulain, burying 'the bright edge deep'. The physical power and assuredness of these diggers is conveyed by means of vigorous verbs, alliteration, enjambed lines, and assertive diction, strategically placed at the end of lines. The poet's continuing sense of awe is conveyed by means of the heartfelt exclamation, 'By God', the rather stagey, colloquial repetition of the phrase, 'the old man', and the proud, but calmly factual assertion that

> My grandfather cut more turf in a day
> Than any other man on Toner's bog.

Scenes emphasising the child's dependence on and subservience to adult action, such as where the children gratefully gather the scattered potatoes, or when the young Heaney acts as a rustic Ganymede,[10] serve to reinforce the adults' heroic status. The poem strives to minimise change by attempting to marry the traditional labour of his forefathers with his newly discovered vocation, a reconciliation embodied in the image of the 'living roots' which 'awaken in my head'. However, in what will prove to be characteristically Heaneyesque dénouement, the poem ends commingling feelings of *humilitas* and regret with resolution and independence, the '*non serviam* of his original personality'.[11]

Two other poems, 'Churning Day' and 'Follower', also lay stress on the huge expenditure of physical energy involved in his parents' creative enterprises. In 'Churning Day', the magic, miraculous moment of change, when suddenly 'yellow curd' is transformed into 'heavy and rich, coagulated sunlight', is only achieved after an extended, exhausting 'bout', which leaves them 'bloodied'. The analogy between boxing and writing from 'Ex-Champ' reappears, as Heaney tells us how his mother 'slugged and thumped for hours'. The poem succeeds admirably marrying word to action in depicting a process with which few readers would be familiar, though it does suffer in places from Hughesian hyperbole.[12] Despite the mixed metaphors of its opening, in which Patrick Heaney's globed shoulders simultaneously resemble those of the Titan, Atlas, and a ship in 'full sail', 'Follower' constitutes an evocative record of his father's prowess as a ploughman, and a poignant record of the changing relationship between father and son. These initial images may be derived from Breughel's 'Icarus',[13] which depicts a bowed ploughman, preoccupied with his work, and a ship with rounded, billowing sails, which similarly ignores the fate of the fallen high flyer. Heaney's poem begins paying homage to a master craftsman, to a man able to control powerful horses merely by means of a 'clicking tongue' and 'a single pluck/ Of reins'. Surveying the land with mathematical precision, he is a Daedalus of the fields. Into this picture of integration and unity, Heaney introduces his boy self, a clumsy disciple, stumbling, 'tripping', 'yapping' like a puppy. Though at first the child's ambition is 'to grow up and plough' like his father, gradually he feels too conscious of his father's superiority, and living in a state of eclipse.

> All I ever did was follow
> In his broad shadow round the farm.[14]

Ultimately, as in so many father-son relationships, the hero of yesterday becomes tomorrow's encumbrance, a ghost, like Hamlet's father's, who can never be wholly exorcised. As so often in his work, Heaney reveals his capacity to transmute personal intuitions into universal insights.

Both 'Churning Day' and 'Follower' bear a sub-text of guilt over his rift with tradition, his less physically exacting labour as writer and teacher. Though in *Preoccupations*, he attempts an etymological reconciliation, pointing out how

> 'Verse' comes from the Latin *versus* which could mean a line of poetry but could also mean the turn that a ploughman made at the head of a field as he finished one furrow and faced back into another.[15]

some five years later, he acknowledged the reality of the break, recalling a conversation he had had with Dan Jacobson,

> who said to me once, "You feel bloody well guilty about writing" and indeed there is indeed some part of me that is entirely unimpressed by the activity, that doesn't dislike it, but it's the generations of rural ancestors – not illiterate, but not literary. They in me, or I through them, don't give a damn.[16]

These initial acts of 'piety to the terrain of his childhood'[17] and its giants are followed by many others incarnating archetypal experiences from the Mossbawn world, that 'green valley' and 'golden world'[18] which can only be repossessed imaginatively. In digging back into the past, however, he also uncovers layers of fear and dejection, recovering moments which exhibit what Lawrence calls 'the terrified helplessness of childhood'.[19]

The title poem begins with a fall from innocence into experience, a movement repeated in 'Blackberry Picking', 'The Early Purges', and 'Mid Term Break', and opens in a setting familiar only to Irish readers, a flax dam. In *Irish Folk Ways*, E. Estyn Evans vividly describes the harvesting of flax:

> When grown for fibre, flax is harvested after the pale blue flowers have fallen, but before the seed ripens, and because it is the stalk that is being harvested it is not cut, but pulled up by the roots. . . . The beets (sheaves) are carried as soon as possible to be steeped (drowned or dubbed) in the flax dam or 'lint hole' where soft peaty water has been standing for some days to warm up . . . The process of retting (rotting) takes from seven to twelve days and is soon advertised by a foul and penetrating odour as the core or 'bone' of the stalk decays.[20]

Close to Heaney's first home just such a dam was located, and his maternal grandfather was employed as a boiler man in a nearby linen works.[21] From the poem's outset, the reader is subjected to a rapid succession of images of decay, 'festered', 'rotted', 'weighted', 'sweltered'. The claustrophobic oppressiveness is compounded by a burdened rhythm, in which monosyllables predominate, and by the accretions of alliteration and assonance. From out a clot of sights, sounds and smells, images of tentative beauty briefly emerge

> Bubbles gargled delicately, bluebottles
> Wove a strong gauze of sound around the smell.

and the pace quickens, "There were dragon-flies, spotted butter-flies", anticipating the climactic description of the frogspawn's "warm thick slobber". By means of that delightfully repulsive phrase, references to Miss Walls, to 'the daddy frog' and 'the mammy frog', and the information that "you could tell the weather by frogs", Heaney cleverly conveys a child's psyche, and the pleasure of his initiation into the mysteries of Nature. In the poem's second half, fosterage in beauty gives way to fosterage in fear, when the easy, cosy domesticity of Mossbawn and Anahorish is displaced forever. The innocence of childhood is 'invaded' by the violent outer world, and penetrated from within by the emergence of a darker, daemonic self. Many critics have pointed to the Hughesian 'shock' diction and war imagery. P. R. King is surely correct in identifying the 'submerged sexual associations'[22] within the description of the frogs, a *'bass'*, *'gross-bellied'* chorus, *'cocked/* On *sods'*, whose *'slap and plop* were *obscene* threats', whose *blunt* heads seemed to be *'farting'*. Though on one level 'Death of a Naturalist', like Hughes's 'Pike', articulates a recognition of what Camus has called "the primitive hostility of the world . . . . facing us across the millenia",[23] at another it exposes the adolescent's "revulsion at his own sexuality", his "smutty embarrassment at his body."[24] Innocent delight at the 'warm thick slobber' has been replaced by disgust at his body's 'spawn'.

Several other poems, 'The Barn', 'An Advancement in Learning' and 'The Early Purges', similarly explore the child's initiation into fear, tapping into awful/awe-full memories from his earliest experiences. In 'A Poet's Childhood', after celebrating the snugness and security of the byre, he acknowledges the draw of the dreadful.

> The byre was not the only outhouse on the farm that I hung about. There was the barn, but the barn was not as safe a place, somehow. I was always afraid in its dark heat that something was going to jump out of its corners – a rat, an owl, anything. And sometimes at night I'd be afraid too, if I remembered that place.[25]

The Gothic menace of 'The Barn' is conveyed through its sounds – 's', 'p', 'c', , 'g', 'b', 'sh' feature prominently – and its imagery. His hot and cold shivers are recreated by the references to the oppressive atmosphere inside the barn, one minute like an oven, the next a place of 'chilly concrete'. It was a space in which sharp objects and frightening creatures conspired together, the 'scythe's edge' and the devilish 'pitch-fork's prongs' ganging up with cobwebs, bats and unknown, staring, fierce 'bright eyes'. The nightmare ends with the metamorphosis of harmless 'two-lugged' sacks into 'great blind rats'. Only in later life, as 'An Advancement of Learning' shows, was he able to overcome his revulsion at the sight of rats, and learn to outstare and outface the enemy.

'The Early Purges' again sees Heaney contrasting the bewilderment and terror of childhood with adult knowledge and 'sophistication', but contains a much more questionable, disturbing outcome. It begins baldly with the statement, 'I was six when I first saw kittens drown'. When Heaney goes on to describe their fate, he maintains a detached, hard-bitten, boyish tone, recalling how Dan Taggart 'pitched' and 'slung' them, how he heard 'Soft paws scraping like mad', how he watched the bodies turn 'crisp' and 'mealy'. Though sensing something wrong has happened, as the adverb 'sadly' and the adjective 'sickening' reveal, he remains 'dumb'.[26] Since most reader's sympathies throughout will have been with Dan Taggart's victims, Heaney's 'practical', countryman's conclusion comes as an affront to legitimate 'liberal' sensibilities.[27] By dismissing these as 'false sentiments', he appears to be collaborating in cruelty, unless one is meant to take the poem's ending ironically. The Stalinist associations of the title word, 'purges', might lead one to suspect a political dimension in the poem, and to expect a refutation of any argument in support of 'justifiable violence'. One suspects that the young, relatively unpolitical Heaney of this time did not consider sufficiently the freight borne by some of his images. If he had, he might have thought twice about that flat final line, with its reference to 'pests' and 'well-run farms', and its sentiments worthy of Beria, Himmler, or Orwell's Squealer.

Far more successful and sensitive in their use of language are two very different poems, 'Blackberry Picking' and 'Mid Term Break'. Each presents early intimations of mortality, and the incomprehension of a child confronted by injustice and grief. For the autumnal custom of 'Blackberry Picking', Heaney employs traditionalist forms, decasyllabic lines, arranged in half-rhymed couplets. Initially the poem forages, like a child, for sensual delight, relishing Nature for its sights ('glossy purple clot', 'red ones inked up', 'wet grass bleached our boots'), sounds ('the tinkling bottom'), tastes ('its flesh was sweet/ Like thickened wine'), and touch ('briars scratched', "our hands were peppered/ With thorn pricks"). The authentic voice and world of childhood are cleverly recreated through the use of the second person plural pronoun ('*You* ate that first one'), the deceitful trick of covering the bottom of the can with 'green ones', the melodramatic allusion to Bluebeard, the lamenting cry, 'It wasn't fair'. Although the motive for these expeditions was principally pecuniary, the poet dramatises and elevates the activity so that it takes on a sacramental significance. Allusions to 'flesh', 'wine', 'summer's blood', look forward to the fusion of religious and sexual imagery in depicting landscape which one finds in subsequent volumes. Whereas the first sixteen lines rejoice in 'what Nature is willing to give'[28] of her abundance, the final eight articulate the child's unhappy recognition of the laws of mutability. Change and loss arrive in the shape of a 'rat-grey' fungus, and the missing fifth sense, smell, makes its appearance ('The juice was stinking too.') The poem concludes on a cruel rhyme ('not'/'rot'), anticipating the longings and disappointments of adult life, and the future struggle between faith and a consciousness of 'the large brutal scheme of things'.[29]

> I always felt like crying. It wasn't fair
> That all the lovely canfuls smelt of rot.
> Each year I hoped they'd keep, knew they would not.

Though one of his first published poems, 'Mid Term Break' shows a remarkable degree of poetic maturity and control, dealing as it does with the death of one of his younger brothers, Christopher. Isolated from the rest of the school 'in the college sick bay' – as if death itself might be contagious – the boy narrator waits for neighbours to take him home, and listens to the 'bells knelling'. The familiarity, predictability of home, however, is immediately violated when by the sight of his crying father and the sound of his mother's 'angry tearless sighs'. Once more Heaney is deft and delicate in handling the double perspective, the reader being simultaneously aware of the child's embarrassment in suddenly becoming the focus of strangers' sympathy, and the adult writer's irony describing how 'The baby cooed and laughed and rocked the pram', and how Big Jim Evans referred 'a hard blow'. After the inadequate stock phrases proffered by the community – understatements that cannot bear grief – the poet chooses apposite images to move us. The snowdrops and the candle imply innocence and fragile beauty, qualities reiterated when Heaney talks of the 'poppy bruise on his left temple', and how how the child still slept in a 'cot'. The mathematical preciseness, the tragic equation within the final line – "A four foot box, a foot for every year" – deepen the pathos of the poem's ending. After the alliterative density of 'Death of a Naturalist', 'The Barn', 'Blackberry Picking', 'Churning Day', the decasyllabic tercets of 'Mid Term Break' seem fittingly austere and spare in sound, while vivid in image. Though the form is derived from Montague,[30] the voice is clearly Heaney's.

These autobiographical poems dealing with childhood may in part represent an attempt to assuage those feelings of guilt identified in 'Digging'. *Death of a Naturalist* includes also 'public' poems of considerable merit – 'At a Potato Digging', 'For the Commander of the *Eliza*' and 'Docker' – which reveal the burgeoning confidence of the young poet, addressing himself to national as well as personal history, serving his community by preserving its sense of the past. The first of these, 'At a Potato Digging', is a particularly ambitious piece, recalling as it does the Great Hunger of 1845–49. While from *Door into the Dark* onwards Heaney was to elevate the bog into a symbol of Irish identity, this poem renews a received symbol, the humble potato, as an emblem for his race's suffering. In the years which were to follow the 1798 Rebellion and the 1800 Act of Union, the impoverished and rapidly increasing Irish population were totally dependent on the potato crop. In Estyn Evans's *Irish Folk Ways*, Heaney would have read how each member of an Irish family would have consumed on average eight pounds of potatoes per day. Corkery quotes a poem written out of despair at the monotony of this diet of potatoes and buttermilk.

Prátai istoidhe,	Potatoes by night,
Prátai um ló	Potatoes by day,
Agus dá n-eireóchainn	And should I rise at midnight
i meadhon oidhche	Potatoes still I'd get.[31]
Prátai gheóbhainn!	

The killer fungus, *phytophthora infestans*, struck in September 1845, and by February of the next year three-quarters of the crop had been destroyed and typhus raged in twenty-five of the thirty-two counties. The inadequate and inept responses of the British Government to the crisis are well documented in Cecil Woodham Smith's book of 1962, *The Great Hunger*.[32] The famine left the Irish psyche permanently scarred. Approximately one million people died as a direct result of its ravages, and one and a half million emigrated. In the years after the famine, Gaelic language and folk customs fell into disuse and decline, and "the once proverbial gaiety and lightheartedness of the peasant people seemed to have vanished completely."[33] No wonder that Heaney comments that wherever "potato diggers are/ you still smell the running sore."

In the opening quatrains of 'At a Potato Digging' one detects significant echoes of Patrick Kavanagh's *The Great Hunger*. Both poets describe the potato gatherers in reductive terms; Heaney pictures them first as insects ('swarm'), then as 'crows' preying off the field, while Kavanagh compares them to 'mechanised scarecrows', an image perhaps picked up in Heaney's use of the word 'higgledy', and his later reference to 'higgledy skeletons'.[34] Writing some twenty years later, Heaney sets his poem in the mechanised present, and observes the destructive might of the latest agricultural technology, a far remove from Paddy Maguire, Patrick Heaney and their spades. His use of the present participle in the phrase 'attacking crow-black fields' implies that the earlier intimacy and interdependence between Man and his environment of the pre-Famine era have been lost forever. In the third and fourth stanzas, however, the poet draws a parallel between this contemporary scene of bowing, bending and stooping and the ancient obeisance paid to the Earth Mother, the source of all fertility. In a further endeavour to develop this notion of the connectedness of past and present, Heaney somewhat anachronistically, describes the potatoes are 'flint-white' at the beginning of Part Two. Several more rapid and bewildering metamorphoses see the potatoes transformed successively into 'inflated pebbles', plump white rabbits living in 'the black hutch of clay', oriental 'slit-eyed tubers', and 'petrified hearts', which when split open 'show white as cream'. Part Two's second verse similarly suffers from 'an overplus of image-making.'[35] Their sudden 'volcanic' arrival, from out of the crusty humus, is likened to a birth, which promises a 'taste of ground and root'. These positive metaphors are displaced in line twelve when historical memory breaks through. The fate of the potatoes is to be 'piled in pits', like 'live skulls, blind-eyed', phrases suggestive of the concentration camps and their victims, and the stark prints of Ireland's famine dead.

The catastrophic events, sights and smells of 'forty-five' are re-created in Part Three by means of a succession of bitter, dehumanising verbs – 'scoured', 'wolfed', 'putrefied', 'rotted', 'tightened', 'chilled', 'hungering', 'grubbing', 'rotted' again, and 'fouled' – and some memorable, terrible lines which recall the horrors described in Woodham Smith:

> The bones of the frame were covered with something which was skin but had a peculiar appearance, rough and dry like parchment; eyes had sunk back into the head, the shoulder bones were so high that the neck seemed to have sunk into the chest; face and neck were so wasted as to look like a skull.[36]

Distinctions between human, vegetable, and animal life have become blurred and meaningless in Heaney's poem, and significantly, the kindly 'black mother' of the opening is now cursed as 'the bitch earth'. For Heaney, as for Wordsworth, each human being is a 'Child of Earth',[37] but, as we have seen in 'Follower', his feelings about parents are not without a certain ambivalence. He laments the utter dependence on the 'faithless ground' of generations of his forebears, and shares something of the scepticism of Kavanagh's hero, "not so sure now if his mother was right/ When she praised the man who made his field his bride".[38]

Part Four restores us to the relatively easeful present. However, each complacent image from contemporary life is affected by an ironic undertow from the previous section. The famine-bird has been replaced by greedy gulls; 'luxuries' such as brown bread and tea are now familiar parts of the diet; the ditch is a place for temporary, rather than eternal rest. In this time of plenty, perhaps unconsciously, perhaps in a conscious act of propitiation, the workers still leave offerings for the Earth Goddess. Estyn Evans records in his book from 1957 how, "when taking a drink out of doors, the old countryman will casually spill a portion of the draught on the earth as a complimentary libation to the good people", the *dei terreni*.[39]

Despite its flaws, 'At a Potato Digging' is an important early achievement. With its less accomplished companion piece, 'For the Commander of the Eliza', it represents an extended sortie into 'the matter of Ireland'. There is some validity in Edna Longley's view that the haunting images and figures in both hint at 'something rotten in the state of Northern Ireland'.[40] In the second famine poem, in which a boatload of starving people are refused food by the English commander of a revenue cutter, several lines seem to reflect the pre-'68 Whitehall and Westminster response to Catholic cries of injustice.

> Let natives prosper by their own exertions
> Who could not swim might go ahead and sink.

The one poem in *Death of a Naturalist* which does address itself to the sectarian present is 'Docker', a satirical piece dating from 1963. One of the biggest employers in Belfast is the shipbuilding company, Harland and Wolff, a company whose labour force then and now was/is predominantly Protestant.[41] Appropriately the poem opens with dockland metaphors – 'gantry', 'cowling', 'sledgehead', 'vice'

– and moves on to depict a man who personifies menace and prejudice, and whose only language is violence. The docker, a Unionist cousin of the miner in Ted Hughes's 'Her Husband',[42] would happily 'drop a hammer on a Catholic', and expects silence from his 'inferiors' to continue. Hindsight and subsequent events make the rueful line, "Oh yes, that kind of thing could start again", even more rueful, and its wry successors less a subject for mirth. It is tempting to see 'Docker' as prophetic. However, one must remember that a six-year-long I.R.A. campaign had only recently concluded, and that during the year it was written, the Reverend Ian Paisley first came to prominence; he had 'certain definite views' about the lowering of the Union Jack at Belfast City Hall as a mark of respect for the death of Pope John XXIII, and communicated them.

A major factor in Heaney's development as a poet, as the previous chapter suggested, was his wife, Marie. *Death of a Naturalist* is dedicated to her, and the volume contains a number of lyrics celebrating their relationship. John Wilson Foster in his 1974 article 'The Poetry of Seamus Heaney' expresses his disappointment with these poems, which, he believes, are "removed in a metaphysical style from immediacy of feeling."[43] Indeed, on occasion, clever conceits do master the emotion. However, despite a certain reticence and obliqueness some early love poems – in part the product of his youth and Catholic upbringing, in part perhaps the result of the influence of Ted Hughes – the emotional current and its force can be clearly identified underneath the surface glints and lightnesses. After the early promise of 'Her scarf à la Bardot', 'Twice Shy' reverts to 'borrowed clothes', hawk and hunting metaphors straight out of 'The Dove Breeder' and 'A Modest Proposal' in Hughes's *The Hawk in the Rain;*[44] it is all too, too 'tremulous', nebulous. In 'Gravities', 'Valediction' and 'Lovers on Aran', the instress of their love communicates itself through sea images, and by references to art and landscape. Reunited after a stormy quarrel, and enduring a 'hopeless day' apart, the lovers 'Re-enter the native port of their embrace'. The poet undergoes a kind of exile without her, like Joyce in Paris grieving for Dublin, or Columcille in Iona wearing 'Irish mould next to his feet' ('Gravities'). With her, he feels secure and 'anchored'; separated, he is left 'unmoored' and 'at sea' ('Valediction').

In the two most successful poems, 'Lovers on Aran' and 'Honeymoon Flight', each of the four elements are invoked to celebrate the unity and exhilaration of love and marriage. 'Honeymoon

Flight' rides on the excitement of two new experiences, both of which involve risk and the overcoming of fear through trust. The landscape itself is enfolded metaphorically into the 'country of the mind'[45] the couple are creating. It is given feminine features, and even the prosaic roads remind the poet of the recent ceremony.

> the *patchwork* earth, dark *hems* of hedge,
> The long grey tapes of road that *bind and loose*
> Villages and fields *in casual marriage*

'The long grey tapes' perhaps suggest the priest's stole, which is used in some Catholic countries to bind symbolically the hands of the bridal pair. For Heaney this new relationship possesses 'a religious force', sustaining him, confirming him with faith. In his essay, 'The Sense of Place', he talks of the 'equable marriage between the geographical country' and the landscapes of the imagination, and comments on the origin of the word 'religious'; from *'religare*, to bind fast'.[46]

Whereas Hopkins chose images of sand ('I am soft sift/ In an hourglass') and water ('I steady as a water in a well') to define himself and his relationship with God, Heaney in 'Lovers on Aran' realises his new secular/ sacred state of grace picturing the eternal embrace of land and sea. Metaphors of light ('bright', 'dazzling', 'glinting') mingle with sexual images ('Came', 'possess', 'yielded') in a joyous swirl and swell of sound and rhythm. Aran's ancient Celtic shoreline, like that of Hardy's Castle Boterel, becomes renewed and illumined under the influences of love and imagination, like the lovers themselves.

> Did sea define the land or land the sea?
> Each drew new meaning from the waves' collision.
> Sea broke on land to full identity.

Throughout his poetic career, Heaney has associated water with the feminine, the Gaelic, the Catholic, the creative elements in his nature. Although from its outset, *Death of a Naturalist* acknowledges his debt to his father and to 'masculine' English mentors such as Hopkins and Hughes, it concludes 'bowing down to the mother'[47] of life in 'Personal Helicon'. Earlier in the collection, in 'The Diviner', he had connected the poetic gift and quest for 'what lies hidden'[48] with the dowser's mysterious craft. Renewal

and identity for both poet and diviner come through 'hunting
the pluck/ Of water', through attuning themselves to the 'secret
stations' and frequencies of our common nature and common
world. 'Personal Helicon' is a poem also 'stirred' by 'the heart of
the mystery',[49] and glances back at earlier experiences and poems
of childhood, yet forward to a future of poetic maturity. At its core
is the potent symbol of the well, in which his pagan and Catholic,
past and present selves are reconciled.

Three mythologies pour into the poem. At St Columb's, one
recalls, Heaney was an excellent Latin scholar, As every classical
scholar or reader of the *Concise Oxford Dictionary of English Literature*
knows, Helicon was a mountain in Boeotia, sacred to the Muses.
From it two fountains flowed, the Hippocrene and Aganippe, and
those who drank from their waters were inspired with the gift
of poetry. In Irish mythology, hagiography and geography, wells
feature significantly. Heaney informs us in *Preoccupations* how his
'first literary *frisson*' came 'on home ground' during his Irish history
lessons, which were 'in reality a reading of myths and legends.'[50]
The story of 'Sinend and the Well of Knowledge', for example,
"expresses the Celtic veneration for poetry and science, combined
with the warning that they may not be approached without danger."
Sinend, a goddess,

> went to a certain well named Connla's Well, which is under the
> sea – i.e. in the Land of Youth in Fairyland. "That is a well,"
> says the bardic narrative, "at which are the hazels of wisdom
> and inspiration, that is, the hazels of the science of poetry.[51]

After the conversion of Ireland to Christianity, wells continued to
draw the Irish soul. Estyn Evans notes that there are three thousand
holy wells listed in Ireland, nearly all of which 'have close associations with the saints'.[52] Patrick Kavanagh in his autobiography
describes one such, Lady Well, fifteen miles from his birthplace,
Mucker, recalling that "the priests didn't like the Well and tried to
discourage pilgrimages. They said it was a pagan well from which
the Fianians drank in the savage heroic days. The peasant folk didn't
mind the priests. They believed St Bridget washed her feet in it."[53]
As a symbol the well, of course, is of immense importance to that
other key Catholic influence on the early Heaney, Gerard Manley
Hopkins. For him, St Winefride's Well in Clwyd became a Christian
equivalent to the fountains of Helicon. "The strong unfailing flow of

the water", he writes, "and the chain of cures from year to year all these centuries took hold of my mind with wonder at the bounty of God in one of his saints."[54]

Though conscious of this spiritual freight, characteristically, Heaney does not allow himself to be borne down by it. Within 'Personal Helicon' one can detect subtle shifts in Heaney's style, in that alliteration is used more sparingly, and more weight is transferred to the music of the vowels and to the images themselves. The poem opens with the kind of matter-of-fact tone he frequently employs, the 'adult' voice, but, by the third line, the child's sensual delight has been re-animated in a quick succession of nouns and simple adjectives. Poet and reader relish together the melodramatic diction – 'the dark drop', 'the rich crash' of the bucket which 'Plummeted down' – the sudden spurts of rhythm, and those pleasuring verbs, 'loved' and 'savoured'. Just as in 'Death of a Naturalist', 'The Barn' and 'Blackberry Picking', he makes use of the child's 'over-personal' grammar – 'So deep *you* saw no reflection in it', 'When *you* dragged out long roots', 'Others had echoes, gave back *your* own call' – and a child's word 'scaresome'. The rat's presence reminds him that the pursuit of knowledge is not 'without danger'.[55] The poem's final stanza, however, speaks of transition, triumph, the growth of a poet's mind. Typically for Heaney, the assertive note is framed and qualified, here by self-deflating references to fingering slime and 'adult dignity'. In fact Heaney has never stopped prying 'into roots', exploring. Having now 'outgrown' his earlier, purely sensuous apprehension of Nature, with its 'sensations sweet' of fear and beauty, he cherishes it for itself binding it together with wife, family, community, literary traditions, native and 'foreign', to form

> The anchor of my purest thoughts, the nurse
> The guide, the guardian of my heart, and soul
> Of all my moral being.[56]

While some earlier poems were somewhat marred by too rapid a succession of evocative images, 'Personal Helicon' takes one image, that of the well, and develops it to the full. Though the concluding metaphor may contain traces of some of Heaney's distinguished forebears

> My own voice cheer'd me, and far more, the mind's

Internal echo of the imperfect sound.

(Wordsworth)

As tumbled over rim in roundy wells
Stones ring; like each tucked string tells, each hung bell's
Bows swung finds tongue to fling out broad its name
Each mortal thing does one thing and the same:
Deals out that being indoors each one dwells;
Selves – goes itself: *myself* it speaks and spells.

(Hopkins)

He thought he kept the universe alone;
For all the voice in answer he could wake
Was but the mocking echo of his own

(Frost)[57]

the voice is recognisably the young poet's own, which 'speaks and spells' with a remarkable maturity.

DOOR INTO THE DARK

The year 1966 was *annus mirabilis* for the Heaneys. Hard on the heels of the publication of *Death of a Naturalist*, amid critical acclaim,[58] another creative triumph took place in July, the birth of their first child, Michael. October saw Heaney's appointment as Lecturer in English at Queen's University, continuing the 'poetic succession' of Lerner and Hobsbaum. One of his students I spoke to wrote essays for Heaney on Elizabethan poetry, and recalls discussions on Sir Walter Raleigh and Sir John Davies, both of whom 'appear' in later volumes. Heaney also took him for tutorials on Gerard Manley Hopkins. My informant went on to describe how subsequently when he faced the ordeal of a *viva* to determine the final class of degree he would obtain, after some 'disastrous confusion' in which 'Richard III' underwent an identity crisis and became 'Richard II', Heaney generously tried to help him salvage the situation by drawing him out on Hopkins.

During the winter of 1967 Heaney, Derek Mahon and Michael Longley attended the funeral of Patrick Kavanagh. Late December saw the first of a series of reviews and articles Heaney produced

for *The Listener*, 'Irish Eyes'. That same year saw the founding of
the Northern Ireland Civil Rights Association.

The following year was very eventful. In February the Heaney's
second son, Christopher, was born. In May, along with Michael
Longley and David Hammond, Heaney embarked on an Arts Council tour, entitled *Room to Rhyme*, visiting small Protestant and
Catholic communities. According to David Hammond, the three
"set out not really knowing what we were doing, going into these
places with our songs and poems. I suppose it was some kind of
opening at a time when everything was closing."[59] On August 24,
the first Civil Rights march took place at Dungannon, to protest
about discrimination in housing. Amongst the four hundred marchers were Gerry Fitt and Bernadette Devlin, and hopes were high
that non-sectarian, non-violent action could bring about reform.
Ominously the march 'provoked' the appearance of a thousand
counter-demonstrators.

Though the majority of citizens of Derry/Londonderry were
Catholics, some curious logic enabled a Protestant administration
to rule the Guildhall. On October 5, part of the route for a Civil
Rights march to articulate "the grievances of the Catholic majority: unemployment, lack of housing, discrimination in jobs and
gerrymandering in electoral affairs"[60] was banned by the Stormont
Minister of Home Affairs, William Craig. Defying this ban, the
marchers, who included Fitt and three British Labour MPs, went
ahead with their original route. The R.U.C. were deployed to stop
the demonstration, and, as a consequence, seventy-two civilians,
and eleven police, were injured. In his article for *The Listener* of
October 24, 'Old Derry Walls', Heaney conveyed his outrage at
what had happened. The Minister, Heaney writes,

considered that a demonstration on behalf of the rights of the
majority was a danger to public law and order . . . He placed
the police. He alerted a reserve force. The rest was violence.
Television revealed the zeal of the police. But eyewitnesses have
attested to the irony of the occasion: the eventual victims of the
law were anxious to keep the police calm, urging them as they
confronted the cordon to stay calm and in control of themselves.
Urgings from elsewhere drove the police into brutal control of
the crowd. The events in Derry shocked moderate opinion on
all sides and are likely to become a watershed in the political
life of Northern Ireland . . . But it seems now that the Catholic

minority, if it is to retain any self-respect, will have to risk the charge of wrecking the new moderation (*of Captain O'Neill*) and seek justice more vociferously.[61]

The Derry beatings provoked a protest march in Belfast on October 9 by two thousand students from Queen's University. Heaney's article celebrates the fact that "Catholic and Protestant, Unionist and Republican have aligned themselves behind the civil rights platform to examine the conscience of the community." He concludes optimistically that "The new 'Londonderry Air' sounds very like 'We shall overcome'."[62]

In a brief article, probably for the Queen's magazine, *Gown*, later that winter, Heaney sounded a more cautious note, warning that the student organisation, People's Democracy, "must remember the real hinterland of prejudice which people on both sides are fighting and not lose sight of this reality in a fury of rhetoric." All too quickly the 'heady and boisterous' early days of 1968, were followed by an 'ashy aftermath'.[63]

November brought some reforms from Prime Minister, O'Neill, but, though welcomed by N.I.C.R.A., they were regarded as inadequate by People's Democracy. In response they organised a march from Belfast to Derry on 4 January 1969 which ended in an ambush at Burntollet Bridge. Paisleyite loyalists, led by one Major Bunting, and assisted by some police reservists, the notorious B Specials, attacked the marchers with 'cudgels, bottles, chains, bricks, and petrol bombs'.[64] The Cameron Commission, which investigated the affair noted that there had been 'an unfortunate and temporary breakdown of discipline'. April 19 saw further 'acts of grave misconduct', when police during rioting in the Bogside burst into a terrace house, and batoned those inside unconscious. Amongst the victims was an 'innocent and well-loved'[65] bystander, a Catholic, Samuel Devenney. After two heart attacks, he died in July 1969. By then the doors leading to peaceful reform had been closed.

Although there is clearly a continuity within Heaney's first two volumes, re-reading *Door into the Dark*, one does register an enlarging of the poetic focus and scope. Published in Spring of 1969, amid this heightening political tension, it embraces Mossbawn, but also townlands beyond, often with an elegiac intensity. In his review of *An Orkney Tapestry*, 'Celtic Fringe, Viking Fringe', Heaney compares George Mackay Brown and Edwin Muir with William

Barnes and Thomas Hardy, and describes how each of these writers "create a country of the mind that is related to a real but passing way of life."[66] The same might be said of Heaney himself. As he gathered the poems for *Door into the Dark* together, all was being changed utterly. In this collection, words themselves become doors into "the dark centre, the blurred and irrational storehouse of insight and instinct, the hidden core of the self."[67] Crossing the threshold of the self, the poet descends into a subterranean world, like Aeneas or Dante, in order to explore the mysteries of creating and Creation, in order to retrieve moments of illumination.

Heaney's feelings of affinity with the dispossessed Gaelic poets of eighteenth century has already been noted.[68] In *The Hidden Ireland*, Daniel Corkery quotes a source from 1722 which describes the methods employed in the ancient Gaelic 'poetical seminaries', the Bardic Schools. The novitiate would be given a subject to contemplate, and then

> they work'd it apart each by himself upon his own Bed, the whole next day in the Dark, till a certain Hour of the Night, Lights being brought in, they committed it to writing . . . The reason of laying the Study aforesaid in the dark was doubtless to avoid the Distraction which Light and the variety of Objects represented commonly occasions. This being prevented, the Faculties of the Soul occupied themselves solely upon the Subject in hand, and the Theme given.[69]

Within the 'fecund fog of unconsciousness',[70] the poet strives to pursue a way, to find enabling images. Echoing his mentor, Patrick Kavanagh, Heaney wrote in early 1970, "We have to shut our eyes . . . to see our way to heaven. What is faith, indeed but a trust in the fog: who is God but the King of the Dark? Somehow the dark presides in the Irish Christian consciousness."[71]

Like *Death of a Naturalist*, *Door into the Dark* registers the pull of "your home water's gravity'.[72] The concept of *home*, however, now embraces a wife, two children, and an ever-strengthening sense of his Celtic identity. While his first volume was largely preoccupied with childhood and the giant figure of his father, 'the heart'[73] of the new book centres on adult relationships, on 'poems on love and marriage' in which the positions of wife and mother are sympathetically re-assessed. "Women have never got full credit for their bravery. They sacrifice everything to life", asserted the author of *Tarry Flynn*. In the dramatic monologue, 'Mother', Heaney portrays the exhaustions and frustrations of a farmer's wife, as she works the pump, and bears the heaviness of her latest pregnancy. She feels like the pump, drained of energy. In attempting to satisfy the various physical needs of others

> I am tired of walking about with this plunger
> Inside me. God, he plays like a young calf
> Gone wild on a rope

her own emotional needs are neglected, and she likens herself to the abandoned bedhead, "on its last legs/ It does not jingle for joy any more."[74] The poem ends in a prayer, with the mother longing for a door leading to a distinct identity. "The liberating, humanizing effect"[75] of marriage, one suspects, had perhaps sensitised Heaney to the fate of his own mother and to that of millions of women. 'The Wife's Tale' similarly addresses itself to "the balance between man and woman",[76] and again the poet uses the form of a dramatic monologue in order to articulate the woman's perspective and to distance himself from the male complacency he depicts, and perhaps had shared. One of sources of the poem is the unpublished 'Homage to Pieter Breughel'.[77] In the *Poetry Book Society Bulletin*, Heaney explained that the poem began "as an irrational desire to write about a woman bringing tea to a harvest field. Earlier I might have set down the picture and trusted that it was redolent of the emotion it evoked for me."[78] No longer satisfied with the pictorial, Heaney wanted, like Frost, to get inside the frame, to bring the figures to the foreground and fill them with breath.

After her initial action of spreading a linen cloth for the harvesters' tea, the wife-narrator becomes a passive, silent observer. On approaching her, her husband shows no sign of affection, but instead, nonchalantly, issues her with an order, "Give these fellows theirs./ I'm in no hurry". After initially showing some approval of her labour, he quickly qualifies it by suggesting her feminine sense of decorum is misplaced, wasted on 'boys like us'. Like most boys/men he expects instant applause for his efforts, however. ("'It's good clean seed. Away over there and look.'") Finally he turns back to his male companions, as boyishly "proud as if he were the land itself", while she, unacknowledged, collects the tea things and rises to go, as if her care and service were as natural and free as sunshine and shade. In its form, in its natural rhythms and unrhymed decasyllabics, and with its pairing of a sensitive wife and unsympathetic husband/'master', 'The Wife's Tale' reminds one of Frost's 'Death of a Hired Man','Home Burial' and 'A Servant to Servants'. The narrator in the latter poem is similarly a resigned woman, treated with little consideration by her husband whose life revolves his work.[79]

Elation and grief in motherhood form the basis of another pair of poems. 'Cana Revisited' and 'Elegy for a Still-born Child'. The two joyous quatrains of the former, which rejoices in the contemporary miracle occurring in the 'bone-hooped womb', contrast with the sombre couplets of the latter. Planetary images and painful half-rhymes are used at first to express the poet's empathy for the bereaved couple. Ultimately, however, the large metaphors of spheres, globes and shooting stars shrink in the face of the tragic actuality of "A wreath of small clothes, a memorial pram/ And parents reaching for a phantom limb." Fittingly the elegy ends with pathos and irony, a 'drizzling sky', 'full to the brim with cloud', a sorrow quickened by Heaney's own fortunate experiences of parenthood.

Much of the light and energy within the volume radiate from the poet's sense of confirmation as husband, father and poet. In an important batch of poems, 'The Forge', 'Rite of Spring', 'Undine', 'Outlaw' and 'Lough Neagh Sequence', Heaney celebrates the fertility of the human and animal world. 'The Forge' provides the title for *Door into the Dark* and a further analogue for the poet's making. While it has much in common with the commemorations of craftsmen from his first book, like many other poems in his second, it defines the act of creation in sexual terms. A short distance from his first home, on the road to Castledawson, a forge was situated, Devlin's forge at Hillhead. It was from here, one summer vacation, that Heaney borrowed an anvil for a Bellaghy Dramatic Society production about the 1798 rising, for his performance as a blacksmith.[80] Dramatised, mythologised, the forge becomes for the poet simultaneously womb and temple, with its 'horned' and sacred anvil 'somewhere in the centre'. A. L. Lloyd in *Folk Song in England* (1967) shows the legitimacy of such symbolism:

> Sexual taboos and rites still surround the miner's calling and the blacksmith's trade in many parts of the world, and their tools – picks, hammmers, anvils and such – are rendered 'living' by being sexualized, their functions considered parallel to the human generative act.[81]

Literary sources for the imagery of the forge probably include Hopkins, Joyce and Corkery.[82] Sketched in with his leather apron and 'hairs in his nose', but not realised, Heaney's surly smith is a relic from a passing world, albeit a magnificent one of 'real iron'.

In contrast to this assertive masculine presence, the female narrator of 'Undine' is a water-spirit, who, like Anderson's Little Mermaid, can only acquire human status and a soul through 'sexual encounter'.[83] Like 'Lovers on Aran', the poem delights in the partnership of male and female, and indicates their potentiality for mutual fulfilment. The vigorous verbs and phrases – 'slashed', 'shovelled up', 'ran quick', 'cleaned out', 'Running clear', 'rippled' and 'churned', 'dug . . . deep', 'took me' – stress that physical and artistic creativity depends on energy and responsiveness. Though guilty of clumsiness, ignorance, and, at times brutality, the male is blessed and sensitised with 'subtle increase and reflection' thanks to the forgiving, female deity. In a review for the *Observer*, the usually astute critic, A. Alvarez, wrote somewhat scornfully of Heaney's 'prim-lipped sexual metaphors' and of his failure 'to commit himself',[84] perhaps unwilling to accept and credit the young poet's conscious decision to work within his own traditions. Within those folk traditions, which can hardly be described as 'prim-lipped', the agricultural and the sexual have always co-habited.[85]

The connection between identity and sexual expression can also be seen in the animal poems in *Door into the Dark*. In its original version, 'The Outlaw', entitled 'Oh Brave New Bull', concluded with Kelly's prosecution, and the white heat of the new technology; a 'white-coated, rubber-gloved' man wandered into the byre, and "as I scratched the Ayrshire's rump/ He chose the labelled seed for his glass pump."[86] No doubt Heaney decided to revise the poem because of the flatness of this ending, and, because he admired the bull's creative power, he did not want to leave the laurels with the 'artsem' man. Kelly's bull is a master of self-possession, like 'The Bull Moses' in *Lupercal*, but his no-nonsense style and macho lack of reticence as 'He slammed life home' does not quite square with Heaney's more sensitive treatment of male/female sexuality elsewhere in the book. Though more effective than its predecessor, 'The Outlaw' is flawed by the excessive demands on the imagination its metaphors make and a somewhat 'slack' conclusion.

The most ambitious and intricate piece in the collection is 'A

Lough Neagh Sequence'. This was published first by Harry Chambers in the Phoenix Pamphlet Poets series in January 1969, in a limited edition of one thousand copies. Drawing out and on the sacred and secular energies within Irish landscape, with its sister poems, 'At Ardboe Point' and 'Relic of Memory', the sequence must be seen as a precursor for the bog poems of *North*, the Glanmore sonnets of *Field Work*, and *Station Island*.

> I envisaged this sequence as a kind of Celtic pattern; the basic structural image is the circle – the circle of the eel's journey, the fishermen's year, the boats' wakes, the coiled lines, the coiled catch and much else.[87]

Its first part opens with a Frost-like directness, 'The lough will claim a victim every year'. Repeated personifications, scaling Man down to size, make the lough a watery equivalent of Hardy's Egdon, a place where contemporary and ancient worlds collide. Paradoxically, humanity both controls and succumbs to natural forces. While at Toomebridge, 'new gates and tanks' have been constructed so that the fishing co-operative can 'lift five hundred stone in one go', further 'up the shore in Antrim and Tyrone' resigned, fatalistic fishermen refuse to learn to swim ('We'll be the quicker going down'), and catch their fellow victims 'one by one'.

In the second poem, 'Beyond Sargasso', cosmic and sexual imagery combine. Within its rhythms the rapid movement of the male eels from mid-Atlantic to the Bann estuary is enacted. Benedict Kiely is surely correct in seeing an analogy between the eel with its instinctual longing for adventure, and 'hungering' for home, and the poet feeling the 'insinuating pull' of his own contradictory, Celtic nature.[88] After the huge distances and timelessness of 'Beyond Sargasso', 'Bait' sees the scale and focus shrink to take in three midnight fishermen. In one of Heaney's most fanciful images, he compares these men to rustlers, though there seems little connection between the 'night raids' on cattle convoys and their groping amid the 'mud coronas'. Like Esau, the worms are 'cheated' of their birthright by the predatory humans, who too easily forget that they too come 'out of the clay'. Religious allusion continues in Part Four, where the fishers are described as merciless, 'Not sensible of any *kyrie*', their 'bouquets' of hooks soon transformed into deadly lines. Just like their prey, they are programmed to 'Pursue the work in hand as destiny',as purposeful as Hughes's 'Snowdrop', who 'pursues her ends/ Brutal as the stars of this month'.[89]

Part Five, 'Lifting', illustrates Heaney's capacity to match Hopkins or Hughes in capturing the *haecceitas* of a creature and an event. He is able to realise in words, sounds and rhythms, the summary fate and frantic flailing of each eel, as it 'knits itself, four-ply' into an oily tangle of strands. The ironic parallel between victims and killers is maintained as the poet pictures the departing boats' wakes winding into each other, indistinguishable, without a separate identity. After the massacre, in the penultimate section, 'The Return', Heaney celebrates the resilience of the female eel, who ensures the survival of the species despite her ordeal in 'the weltering dark'. She 'exhilarates' in her 'mid-water' element, and, again like the maturing poet, delights in the deep, the familiar unknown. Fittingly, 'The Vision' completes the sequence with two nightmarish scenes from childhood. In the first, he recollects a threat and *his* own susceptibility to superstition; in the second, it is as if fears have been made flesh, as he witnesses during adolescence the eels' massed exodus from land to water. In ironic contrast to the 'bright girdle' of faith which once encircled the world of which Matthew Arnold spoke,[90] Heaney presents a 'live girdle', a 'horrid cable' surrounding us. All too soon the poet's ugly vision would be realised. From the malign depths within human nature, fresh violence would hatch, a spawning which would quickly overrun the whole province. Instead of metaphorical frogs or eels, camouflaged men would soon occupy the ditches and hedges, and street corners, having 'gathered there for vengeance'.[91]

The final group of poems from *Door into the Dark* which merit consideration are 'meditative landscape poems', encompassing 'notions about history and nationality'.[92] 'In Gallarus Oratory' commemorates a visit to the famous beehive church on the Dingle peninsula in August 1966. After identifying the feelings of constriction and diminution engendered by this 'core of old dark', the poem moves to renewal and resurrection. Having undergone a symbolic death, buried 'like heroes in a barrow', the original monastic inhabitants/ spiritual pioneers thrilled to a heightened sense of the divine, made manifest in pentecostal Nature.

> They sought themselves in the eye of their King
> Under the black weight of their own breathing.
> And how he smiled on them as out they came

The sea a censer, and the grass a flame.

The primeval, and sometimes pre-Celtic landscapes of 'The Peninsula', 'Whinlands', 'The Plantation', 'Shoreline' and 'Bogland' all illustrate Heaney's increasing concern with Irish geography, history and archaeology, and how 'home' now means something greater than the Mossbawn microcosm. 'Seeking the place of . . . resurrection',[93] his imagination lights upon natural forms and shapes from both childhood and adult experience, ones which articulate the identity of the whole of Ireland, and not merely his own. Recognising the poetic necessity of *peregrinatio* in 'The Peninsula', he seems to echo Eliot in asserting "You will not arrive/ But pass through", and in stressing the virtues of 'the backward look'.[94] His growth and survival as a poet will depend on his ability to 'uncode all landscapes', to remain fluid and responsive like the spirit of 'Undine', to accept new personas, other personalities. These ideas are expressed succinctly in the final quatrain of 'The Plantation':

> You had to come back
> To learn how to lose yourself,
> To be pilot and stray – witch,
> Hansel and Gretel in one.

After the sensual richness of *Death of a Naturalist*, Heaney developed a taste for the austere sublime, influenced in part perhaps by his painter friends, such as T. P. Flanagan, and perhaps partly in response to the Hughes of *Wodwo*. Like Hughes's 'Thistles', the humble gorse blossom in 'Whinlands', is ablaze with identity, spikily determined to hold its ground. Through nature's alchemy, the hills are covered with oxidised gold. The 'small yolk stain'[95] of each bush, which is multiplied many times over, emphasises the fertility, resilience and lyric beauty of this particular feature of the Irish countryside, which "Persists on hills, near stone ditches,/ Over flintbed and battlefield", a feature transcending national 'failures', such as that recalled in 'Requiem for the Croppies'.

Written in 1966 at a time "when most poets in Ireland were straining to celebrate the anniversary of the 1916 Rising",[96] this sonnet rejoices in the seeds of liberty sown during the 1798 rebellion, when a largely Protestant leadership led the dispossessed Catholic masses in an abortive attempt to free Ireland from English domination. Stepping back fifty years before the famine, using the first person plural for greater immediacy, Heaney creates an evocative picture of Irish solidarity, of the rebels' improvised tactics, and of their fate on Vinegar Hill, at Enniscorthy, Co. Wexford. Ten thousand government troops, with twenty pieces of artillery, encircled the twenty thousand 'wretched rebels herded together around the green standards on the summit', and bombarded them with 'grape-shot and the new explosive shells'. According to a local Protestant clergyman, more than half the estimated 50,000 dead in the rebellion had been killed in cold blood.[97]

> Terraced thousands died, shaking scythes at cannon.
> The hillsides blushed, soaked in our broken wave.
> They buried us without shroud or coffin
> And in August the barley grew up out of the grave.

'Requiem for the Croppies' reiterates the grim truth of Irish history that 'There is no bloodless myth will hold'.[98] The religious associations of the scene are close to the surface; the hill and its environs became both a Calvary and a Field of Blood; the legalistic murder was followed by a startling resurrection, as "the graves began to sprout with young barley, growing up from barley corn which the 'croppies' had carried in their pockets to eat while on the march."[99]

The year 1798, like 1968, was a turning point in Irish history. In his marvellous book, *The Year of Liberty*, published in 1969, and reviewed by Heaney in late November, Thomas Pakenham quotes the prophetic words of Lord Cornwallis, the British Commander-in-Chief in Ireland responsible for defeating the 'rebellion', writing to his brother, James, in November 1798.

> You will hear much of a Union: God knows how it will turn out. Ireland cannot change for the worse, but unless religious animosities and the violence of the Parties can be in some measure allayed, I do not think she can receive much benefit from any plan of Government.[100]

At the conclusion of his book, Pakenham sums up the history of Ulster since 1921 in one lucid paragraph, which emphasises the ineptitude and Pilate-mentality of 'successive British governments'.

By a final twist, the second Irish war of independence of 1919–21 not only failed to win a united Ireland, but resulted in a form of self-government in Ulster that had already proved disastrous in '98. Forty years later the stench of history is overpowering. Catholics have remained poor, politically powerless, and alienated from government. Stormont has maintained Protestant ascendancy as stoutly as the Dublin Parliament. Successive British Governments have decided to let well alone, dodging the attacks of the Left with the same tactics Pitt used against Fox – Ireland is an Irish responsibility.[101]

The optimism about Civil Rights Heaney had expressed in October 1968 in 'Old Derry Walls' was to be shattered by the events of the next twelve months. In his review of *The Year of Liberty* for *The Listener*, he was to lament how 'each element of nightmare . . . succeeded the dream of hope'.[102]

In the autumn of 1968, the painter T. P. Flanagan and his wife, Sheelagh, invited the Heaneys to spend some time with them at McFadden's Hotel in Gortahork, Co. Donegal. While their wives looked after the children, poet and painter 'escaped' for trips to look at the Donegal landscape. These were casual 'jaunts', but Flanagan would stop the car at times to sketch. Between them there was 'an unvoiced decision not to discuss the landscape', the recognition that each must 'preserve his isolation'[103] as he examined the bogland scenery. Flanagan informed me that he was unwilling to show Heaney even the outline of a sketch, since any definition might endanger the success of the 'individual imagination's wrestle with its subject.' On Falcara Beach that Hallowe'en, they let off fireworks into the air, and watched the rockets 'snaking up through the dark' towards Tory Island, which 'looked like a seal'.[104] Listening to Flanagan describing his own attitudes to the bogland, one can easily recognise the affinity of spirit linking him and his fellow Ulster artist. The painter described his attraction to 'the fundamentals of Irish landscape', and his love of the moistness, the softness of the bog, its fecundity, its femininity, its connectedness with a pre-Christian, primeval past. Bored with the holiday brochure stereotype of the green Ireland, he delighted in the 'visual surprise' of the bogland, like Hardy's Egdon Heath, with its changing patterns of purple, yellow and ochre in different seasons. His awe at the bogland did not spring so much from its size or colour, but from his 'sense of its ancient life'.[105]

Not surprisingly, Heaney dedicated his poem 'Bogland' to this painter friend, whose familiar, he writes, must be 'Oisin or Wandering Aengus.'[106] In a letter to the author, Heaney contrasted the two men's responses to the 'benign and solitary landscape'.[107]

> I think I did the 'Bogland' poem independently, but the whole feeling of shared pleasure in the landscape, the bleakness and the bareness was a shared one. Terry, however, was very much a visual, painterly reactor: I don't think he had much politico-historico interest in it as an image.[108]

'Bogland' begins defining itself by negation and by establishing a sense of scale, contrasting American prairies which 'slice a big sun at evening' with a distinctive, humble Irish feature, 'the cyclops eye/ Of a tarn'. By the third and fourth stanzas, however, the bog ceases to be merely a physical or geographical phenomenon; it has come to embody a huge span of time, since, as Kavanagh wrote, 'A turf bog is a history of the world from the time of Noah'.[109] It is both grave and reliquary, hoarding the treasures of its past, then, like an arbitrary, but beneficent goddess – or poet? – yielding up its mysteries and miracles, like the elk and the butter.[110] The poem's climax comes with the epigraph quoted at the beginning of this chapter, celebrating the primacy of water, and the endless potential, the bottomless well of the imagination. Writing at a time when prejudice was hardening in each community and 'neighbourly murders' were at hand, he proffered the assuaging, purifying gift of water and of Art, a spiritualised landscape and language, the common inheritance of all the Irish people. Having found in the bog, a door into 'the dark rich places of the human psyche',[111] Heaney crossed the threshold in *Wintering Out* and *North* with conspicuous success. On the other side, along with those 'dark rich places', lay brutality and violence beyond words.

4

Exposure, 1969–75

What excites me about these student protest movements in so many countries is the energy and courage, the determination to act on ideas, to learn from foreign examples; but I dread the violence, the willingness to be moved by slogans no better than those they are opposing, the solidarity based on hate.

James Simmons, *The Honest Ulsterman*, June 1968[1]

His first stroll along the street littered with glass from bomb-shattered windows shakes his faith in the naturalness of his world.

Czeslaw Milosz[2]

WINTERING OUT

The seven years from 1961–68 were years of plenty for Seamus Heaney in both his personal and his literary life. The next seven would prove to be years of pain and adjustment to pain, years in which the 'larger drama of our politics'[3] would preoccupy the private imagination. Though at times geographically distant from the bombs and bullets, for Heaney they were always close at hand. Hearing the reports of guns and of each new 'neighbourly murder', the poet endeavoured to find perspectives which might enable him to face the horror. Although 'the politics of polarisation',[4] and the 'agony and injustice' of events, increasingly compelled him towards adopting a Catholic stance, he struggled for a long time to restrain his feelings of 'race and resentment'.[5] Rather than focussing directly on incidents from the present, he concentrated primarily on the origins and hinterland of the conflict in *Wintering Out*, through elegiac poems celebrating the identity, history, territory and tongue of his people, the Northern Catholic Irish.

In Ulster, the verb 'to winter out' means to see through and survive a crisis, and is derived from a farming custom which involved taking cattle to a sheltered area, feeding them on a minimum diet throughout the winter, before fattening them in the spring and summer. In his article 'Mother Ireland', Heaney suggests the phrase may have been a subconscious 'borrowing' from lines by the poet W. F. Marshall, in which a servant boy who has suffered throughout the winter under a bad master 'looks forward to better times', telling himself, "I wintered at Wee Robert's/ I can summer anywhere." However, in his article 'Mother Ireland', Heaney connects the title of his third collection with *Richard III's* famous opening, "Now is the winter of our discontent", and goes on to describe the book as "a gesture towards the distresses that we are all undergoing in this country at the moment."[6] His enthusiastic response in 'Old Derry Walls' to the political quickening of the North had quickly turned to disillusion and apprehension as events unfolded.

During one week in May 1969, he recalls writing in rapid succession 'about forty poems',[7] perhaps partly as a result of the acceleration in the political pulse at this time, out of a sense of living through a 'once-in-a-lifetime' moment.[8] April had seen ugly fighting in Derry and bombings in Belfast – the latter the work of Protestant paramilitaries – but also the dramatic resignation of Captain O'Neill as Prime Minister. Even on holiday in Spain in the summer, for Heaney there was no respite from home thoughts. Television there brought him news of 'death counts' and domestic 'bullfight reports', while he suffered only 'the bullying sun of Madrid'. Feelings of guilt and helplessness pursued him even when he attempted to 'retreat' into Art and 'the cool of the Prado'.[9] Viewing Goya's famous picture, *The Shootings of the Third of May*, with its central defiant figure in white, its arms outstretched like Christ's, was inevitably to be reminded of the Catholic 'partisans' in Belfast and the Bogside. The cumulative effect on the poet of riots, bombs, sectarian killings, and the deployment in August 1969 of British troops in Derry and Belfast can be seen in his review of Thomas Pakenham's *The Year of Liberty*. Heaney is again struck by historical analogies, on this occasion between 1798 and the situation in 1969:

> The fight was between a ruling class used to power and the exercise of power, who spoke a language of control and assumed their right to govern, and a submerged population activated by a sense of injustice and led by its more politically sophisticated representatives. At this confrontation the moderate retreats from politics, affirming the need for co-operation between all men of

good will and rejecting the destructiveness of civil war as a means to however desirable an end.[10]

His rejection of 'partisan politics' – almost two years later he still clung to the idealistic hope that 'common ground' could be established between Catholic and Protestant – can be contrasted with the attitude of other members of the minority community. Exploiting instead of assuaging 'anachronistic passions',[11] the Provisional Army Council of the I.R.A., which was formed in December 1969, established a powerful position amongst the frightened Catholics of the North during the next twelve months, presenting themselves as champions who would defend them from Protestant mobs and the British army.

Where Heaney did discover 'common ground' in 1969 was in an archaeological study of Iron Age Jutland, P. V. Glob's *The Bog People*. 'The minute I saw the photograph (of the Tollund Man) and the reviews I sent for it', he writes.[12] The book embraced the majority of his deepest concerns – landscape, religion, sexuality, violence, history, myth – a 'knot of obsessions'[13] which would preoccupy him in his next two volumes. It provided an historical perspective enabling him to 'cope with' and confront the contemporary 'Troubles', and created a sense of continuity, kinship, affirmation at a time of social and political disintegration. "The Tollund Man seemed to me like an ancestor almost, one of my old uncles, one of those moustached archaic faces you used to meet all over the Irish countryside.[14] Childhood memories of turf-smoke and wakes, and recent experiences of the Donegal bogland with his painter friend, T. P. Flanagan, were reactivated by Glob's awesome descriptions and evocative photographs. Heaney's empathy for these ancient victims of tribal superstition and ignorance quickly acquired a religious intensity. In describing how he came to create the first of his 'bog' poems, instinctively he resorts to metaphors consonant with marriage and vocation.

> When I wrote that poem I had a sense of crossing a line really, that my whole being was involved in the sense of – the root sense – of religion, being bonded to something. I felt it a vow; I felt my whole being caught in this. And that was a moment of commitment not in the political sense but in the deeper sense of your life, committing yourself to something. I think that brought me to a new possibility of seriousness in the poetic enterprise.[15]

From the autumn of 1970 till September 1971, Heaney worked in
the United States, having been granted a sabbatical from Queen's,
Belfast, so that he could take up the post of Guest Lecturer at
the University of California. Berkeley. Modestly, apologetically, he
has commented, "I got in there through the back alley of poetry,
rather than through the front door with a doctorate. California was
an exotic place after Belfast."[16] At the time, no doubt, Heaney
welcomed the move not merely as a confirmation of his literary
success, but also as an opportunity to give himself and his young
family a 'breather'. The situation in the North had deteriorated
during 1970. The Westminster election in June had brought to
power a Conservative administration which showed itself far less
sensitive to Catholic sensibilities than its Labour predecessor. As
a result of the decision by the British Home Secretary, Reginald
Maudling, allowing the Army to search the Catholic ghettoes,
a large quanity of weapons and ammunition were found. Their
'success', however, and the manner with which they sometimes
conducted themselves, intensified antagonism towards the troops
in the Nationalist community, thereby increasing support for the
Provisional I.R.A.

Heaney's experiences in America accelerated the 'politicisation' of
his poetry. It was there that he began the *Stations* sequence, inspired
by the 'innocence' the New World encapsulated for him.

> It had sunlight and money, which was a change. But I discovered
> there that in this highly technological society the whole move-
> ment was back to a kind of reality that I had known in my
> childhood. There was a terrific nostalgia and a compulsion to
> reverence the primitive kind of life. I mean every undergraduate
> in Berkeley, in some ways, wanted to be a Red Indian.[17]

Appalled by the actions of successive governments in Vietnam and
Cambodia, students and staff identified with contemporary and
historic victims of white American cultural supremacy. Underneath
the primitivist urge lay a fervent desire to make reparations for
the crimes their forefathers had committed against the indigenous
people of two continents. Increasingly Blacks, Hispanics and Indians
'were demanding their say' in American affairs, and Heaney was
inevitably reminded of 'the political and cultural assertions being
made at that time by the minority'[18] back home. The major legacy of
his Berkeley experience was his conviction that poetry could become

'a force, almost a mode of power, certainly a mode of resistance'.[19] Political developments at home had forced him to re-evaluate and reinterpret his formative years in the poems that were to form *Wintering Out*, and his encounters with American poets, such as Gary Snyder and Robert Bly, must have strengthened his belief that words could – in some beneficial way – affect events. He felt a sense of affinity with these writers, both of whom were in the vanguard of the movement against the Vietnam war. In order to achieve their poetic ends, they had turned away from the 'intellectual, ironical, sociological idiom of poetry' in order to focus on 'the mythological'.[20] His reading of the work of these poets – and that of William Carlos Williams, in particular – resulted in a stylistic shift towards 'a more relaxed movement' in his verse, and his adoption of the 'little quatrain shapes'[21] which figure so prominently in *Wintering Out* and *North*.

During his year in America he also had the good fortune to meet two eminent figures from the world of Irish letters.[22] The first was Tom Flanagan, author of *The Irish Novelists 1800–1850*, whose deep concern for Irish history and literature strengthened Heaney's resolve to embrace the national theme. Flanagan subsequently introduced the young poet to Conor Cruise O'Brien, who was lecturing in the United States. Rather than providing him with a period of 'escape', therefore, his time in California enabled him to connect the circuits between the Old World and the New.

Heaney returned to Belfast in September 1971, the month after the introduction of internment without trial in Northern Ireland. The first seven months of that year had been bloody enough – seventeen civilians, eleven soldiers and two R.U.C. men had already been killed[23] – but no-one was prepared for the slaughter which followed internment, except perhaps the Provisional I.R.A. which benefitted tremendously from yet another largely anti-Catholic measure. As a result of the Special Powers Act, by the end of 1971, 1,576 people had been interned, and an additional one hundred and forty-four lay dead.

The manuscript of *Wintering Out* arrived at Faber and Faber on 30 September 1971. The collection opens with a dedication to David Hammond and Michael Longley, and a lyric introducing the themes (disorientation, place, history, and the collective fate), routes (the drive from present to past, past to present, future to past), and moods (resignation/resolution/identification/separation) which will dominate the volume. 'This morning from a dewy motorway' succinctly and successfully depicts the state of siege in post-internment Ireland, with its physical, psychological and spiritual ramifications. The oppression of the present – invoked by such 'concrete' images as the 'camp', the bomb crater, 'machine-gun posts', and the fresh wounds in the clay – is acknowledged, but not diminished when viewed within the wider context of Gaelic and Catholic history, which sees suffering as continuous. Marrying the scene from the windscreen to childhood memories of war newsreels or feature films intensifies the poet's and the readers' horror that this can be happening now and here. The stockade around 'the new camp for internees' is all too 'real', like the cynical wit and despair it has helped to generate.

> Is there a life before death? That's chalked up
> On a wall downtown.

Heaney concludes the poem, no longer a solitary, detached observer, preoccupied with his own journeying. Enduring the same nightmare has heightened his awareness of the intimate relationship between personal and communal destinies, and properly the final line begins with the first person pronoun, plural. Prisoners of history, and yet defined by it, the Catholic minority embraces its familiar humble fate, hugging 'our little destiny again." The subsequent poems in *Wintering Out* explore that 'little destiny', and constitute a subtle act of resistance, an emotional, yet articulate response to centuries of military, political, linguistic and cultural domination.

The collection proper begins with 'Fodder', the first of many hymns to sacred places, objects and words which continue to quicken and nourish the poet's imagination, at a time when human life seems no longer sacred. As a child he 'loved to lie deep in the warm fodder', while a farmhand milked the cows and sang.[24] After proffering the standard English word 'fodder' as his title, he immediately disclaims it, "Or, as we said,/ *fother*", determined, like Stephen Daedalus, to speak in his own tongue. Recalling that single, simple word from his first home releases a spill of images, suggesting the natural and spiritual riches of Mossbawn, 'multiple as loaves/ and fishes'. Aware that the age of miracles and innocence has passed, Heaney summons its memory to sustain him during the cold, bleak present.

Many of the finest poems in *Wintering Out* are similarly concerned with 'bedding the locale',[25] establishing Mossbawn as a frame of reference from which he can map the Catholic past and present. For the poet in his early thirties – married, with two children, and with a voice increasingly listened to in Ireland, Britain and America – the concept of 'home' now required a wider definition, and involved more than the close family characters depicted in his first volumes. It is now a place and a people stretching back into time, into various periods of Irish history, an underworld which can be visited in relative safety, from which the poet-hero can return bearing relics and trove. In 'Bog Oak', he shoulders metaphorically a beam of timber, cut down during the clearances of the sixteenth and seventeenth centuries, and 'long-seasoned' in the bog.[26] It is both a 'trophy' and a 'rib' supporting the body of his first home, a symbol of strength and endurance that has outlasted generations of the 'moustached/ dead' whom once it served. Eulogy becomes elegy, as Heaney lingers among these Celtic ancestors, whose lives are conditioned by 'their hopeless wisdom', their resignation to defeat and dispossession. Even the smoke from their fires 'struggles' to escape, and beyond their hearths only the 'mizzling rain' and the occupying power await. Theirs is no idyllic Twilight world of 'oak groves' and mistletoe, for neither 'is native to Ireland's wilder, more bitter experience'.[27] His pursuit of the past finally brings him face to face not with a druid priest or Gaelic bard, but rather with an English poet and colonial civil servant, Edmund Spenser.[28] The advent of the Troubles had heightened Heaney's ambivalent feelings towards the rich traditions of *English* literature, and while he is conscious of its role in 'founding' him as a poet, he is acutely aware that its cultural triumph has been at the expense of other cultures. Though he initially depicts the author of *The Faerie Queene* 'dreaming sunlight' – composing at Kilcolman Castle in Co Cork, one of many lucrative estates he had 'acquired' in Ireland for services to the Crown – the concluding lines of 'Bog Oak' remind us that while Spenser created, the people he had helped to subjugate starved. The Elizabethan poet's *A Veue of the Present State of Ireland*, a political work from 1596, endorses Lord Deputy Grey's belief that civilization could not be built in Ireland until 'force have planed the ground for foundation'.[29] Aptly, ironically, Heaney quotes from Spenser's description of the famine in Munster which followed the crushing of the rebellion. Its victims exhibited

> such wretchedness, as that any stony heart would have rued the same. Out of every corner of the woods and glens they came

creeping forth upon their hands, for their legs could not bear them. They looked anatomies of death, they spake like ghosts crying out of their graves[30]

but Spenser adds, lest he be accused of pity for the 'rebels', that the extremity of the famine was something 'they themselves wrought'.[31] For Heaney, however, there is no ambiguity of response towards them. They too are 'geniuses', and it is their land and their liberty which is again being 'encroached upon'. 'Servant Boy' looks back to another key period of Catholic 'disaffection', returning to the eighteenth century world of the Big Houses. By 1703, according to Froude, 'nine-tenths of the land' was occupied 'by Protestants of English or Scottish extraction'.[32] These are 'the little/ barons' of Heaney's poem, waited upon by the 'resentful/ and impenitent' Irish. While Corkery describes the continuous bustle of the House's various menial labourers, such as turf-boys, pump-boys, and cow-boys – "Before the dawn had risen, the farmyard was loud with activity; and when darkness had fallen, lanterns went swinging across it, over and thither, from byre to shed, and from shed to barn[33] – Heaney chooses to portray a solitary servant, one with whom he clearly identifies,

> wintering out
> the back-end of a bad year,
> swinging a hurricane lamp
> through some outhouse

Like the poet himself, he is 'a jobber among shadows'. In the second verse Heaney employs an ironic, stylistic strategy which will recur frequently in *Wintering Out* and *North*. He uses Anglo-Saxon kennings – 'work-whore, slave-/ blood' – against the English, who regarded (and, some would argue, still regard) the Irish as barbarous savages incapable of self-imposed 'discipline' and 'control'.[34] In fact the predominant Irish response to colonisation was to work hard, and to keep 'patience' and 'counsel', attitudes which Heaney's parents fostered in him. By verse three, the servant boy's spirit has been so successfully invoked by the poet's words, that Heaney feels confident enough to address him directly – "how/ you draw me into your trail". Having panned in like a camera onto his subject, Heaney then re-establishes the illusion of distance in the next verse, focussing on the 'broken' line trail of fodder left by the servant on his journey 'from haggard to stable', and on 'the warm eggs' he bears. These final images, the fodder and the eggs, stress the nourishing power of Gaelic culture, its resilience and fertility, positive qualities, which Heaney and the Catholic community will require to see through the latest winter.

Another major legacy of colonialism, broached first in 'The Last Mummer', and then explored in a succession of poems – 'Traditions', 'Anahorish', 'Broagh', 'Toome', 'A New Song' and 'Gifts of Rain' – is the linguistic dispossession of the Irish people. Though on one level these poems mourn the 'Vanished music' ('A New Song') of Gaelic, on another they deny silence and loss. Acknowledging the debt contemporary Irish writers owe to Joyce, Heaney has commented that thanks to him, "English is by now not so much an imperial humiliation as a native weapon."[35] In 'The Last Mummer', the more complex companion piece to 'Servant Boy', Heaney again employs a persona to examine and renew his vocation as a poet. 'Shrouded' in mist and mystery, the mummer arrives at a modern equivalent of the Big House, bearing both an ash-plant – the stick a cattle-dealer, like his father, would carry – and a stone, a contemporary 'native weapon'. Unable to lure the occupants away from 'the luminous screen in the corner' which has them 'in thrall', he beats against their iron gates and hurls the stone onto their slate roof in a gesture of frustration. To survive he has been obliged to adopt the language of his English Masters – or as the poem has it, to go 'whoring/ among the civil tongues'[36] – and to maintain a suitably servile pose. Underneath the 'fabulous' mask,[37] however, this teller of tales retains his integrity. Like Heaney, he is 'trammelled/ in the taboos of the country', simultaneously central and tangential to the community he serves, and he too is forced to 'pick a nice way' through the ritual dramas of 'blood/ and feuding' which make up the national repertoire. Although the mummer/poet may seem an obsolete relic, and hardly more substantial than the fog from which he appears, nevertheless, he fulfils an essential priestly function. At a time when 'the centre cannot hold', he attempts to restore ceremony, communion, communication. Through him, with him, in him, reconciliation and order are possible, as the mingling of Celtic ('holly trees') and Catholic symbols ('host', 'monstrance') indicates. Like the 'dark tracks' on the dewy grass which point towards 'summer grazing', his words promise renewal. The mummer strives to make straight the way, to 'untousle' some of the 'knots'.[38]

Prefiguring the more pessimistic 'Act of Union' in *North*, 'Traditions' opens depicting the 'rape' of the Irish language, "bulled
long ago/ by the alliterative tradition." 'Bulled' certainly suggests
a 'forced mating'[39] but, according to *The Shorter Oxford English
Dictionary*, can also mean 'deceived' or 'cheated out of' something.
As a result of acts of violence and deceit over the centuries, the
Irish lost their language and identity, along with their territory.
The Gaelic tongue languished like 'a Brigid's Cross/ yellowing
in some outhouse', and until this century survived principally
in the West, and in fragments such as family names and place-
names. Ulster dialect retains 'strikingly Elizabethan'[40] words and
turns-of-phrase, but Heaney again shows his ambivalent attitude
towards these 'cherished archaisms', his English inheritance. 'Correct Shakespearean' they may be, but they remind him of defeat,
like the name of his birthplace, which brings together *Moss* from
the Scots of the Planters, and *bawn*, an English colonist's fortified
farmstead.[41] Characteristically, in the poem's third section, Heaney
moves towards a positive resolution. Here he denounces the comic
whinging Irish stereotype from Shakespeare's *Henry V*, contrasting
his lisped question from the late sixteenth century – 'What ish my
nation?' – with a confident answer from the twentieth. The final
quatrain pays tribute to James Joyce, who played such a vital role
in establishing the moderm Irish literary tradition, and in giving its
writers 'a mounting confidence in the validity and importance'[42] of
their ground, their culture, *their* English.

For Heaney, the poet remains a diviner, a kind of Magus
'summoning and meshing . . . the subconscious and semantic
energies of words',[43] and by drawing upon the Gaelic place-names
which encircled his Mossbawn home, he attempts to re-connect the
'energies of generation'[44] coursing through Man, land and language,
to restore continuity while acknowledging change. 'Anahorish',
'Broagh', and 'Toome' renew an ancient genre of Irish poetry called
dinnseanchas, which are 'poems and tales which relate the original
meanings of place names and constitute a form of mythological
etymology'.[45] The very act of naming the names conjures 'a kind
of magic reality'.[46] Within the 'soft Gaelic syllables'[47] of Anahorish
– derived from *Anach fhior uisce*, the 'place of clear water' – Heaney
rediscovers a sense of harmony, and founds himself by means of
myth. The whole poem moves with a joyous energy, embodied in
its rhythms by means of *en jambement*, expressing a delight in the
creativity of water and memory. Reconciling dark and light, solid

and fluid, concrete and symbolic detail, it evokes the Eden of his childhood, 'the first hill in the world'. Soon, however, this personal vision is expanded to include Ireland before the colonial Fall. Like the 'lamps swung through the yards/ on winter evenings', names cast shadows, and before long the poet is wading back into a remote Celtic past, its humble images of fertility, 'wells and dunghills', set against the violence of the present.[48]

Voicing the word 'Broagh' stimulates a spill of images from his earliest years, and brings together in its opening lines the three traditions he encountered then – the Gaelic (*Bruach,* a riverbank), the Scots (*rigs,* a Planter word for a riverside field), and the Anglo-Saxon (*docken,* an Old English plural for the dock plant). Heaney attempts to construct a ford between past and present, and, somewhat optimistically, between Nationalist and Unionist. If left to themselves, he implies, perhaps the Ulster Catholics and Protestants might one day learn to accept each other's traditions and acknowledge the rich diversity of their linguistic heritage. There is a wry humour in the poem's final line, for the poem ends with a guttural sound common to both communities, but 'unavailable to an English person';[49] a reminder that it is not only the pronunciation of the *gh* which the 'strangers found/ difficult to manage'.

'Gifts of Rain' is one of Heaney's most successful reflections in time of civil war. Like 'Bogland', it reveals the poet struggling for self-definition, making tentative 'soundings' into the deeper tracts of consciousness, as he strives to reconnect himself to the watery land which bore him. At the same time, it looks forward to 'The Tollund Man' and the poems of *North* since it is motivated by 'the shared calling of blood' – family and racial. The dramatis personae of his first two books – father, mother, wife and the poet himself – have been joined by a larger cast from the present, past and future, which includes his children and all the perished innocents of Mother Ireland. Increasingly the poet is drawn to *still*ness, longing for a Wordsworthian tranquillity and an assurance of continuities.[50] Through his attentiveness to the 'Soft voices of the dead', and through their intercession, he hopes to reconcile what he sees as his dual responsibilities, to himself as an artist and to his community. A dominant presence in the poem – as in 'Anahorish' and 'Broagh' – is water, the healer, the assuager, the shape-changer. In contrast to the first quatrain of 'Anahorish' which hinted at the Garden, the dour opening of 'Gifts of Rain' anticipates a second Flood. Into this bleak setting Heaney introduces a human figure, one who attempts to adjust to the oppressive climate of the present, like some latter-day Gabriel Oak, or Hughesian outcast.[51] To survive he must acknowledge his kinship with and dependence on the rest of the natural world, for he is part of the pattern not its centre. Heaney contrasts the figure's hesitant progress with the assured movement of the water, which seems to possess a sense of purpose, like a hedgehog, a badger, or like a fox 'concentratedly/ Coming about its own business'[52]

> A nimble snout of flood
> licks over stepping stones
> and goes uprooting.

In Part Two, the solitary figure becomes clearly identifiable. It is the poet himself, a déraciné, returning to the 'lost fields' of his childhood, and the lost field of Ulster.[53] Literal and symbolic levels of meaning are maintained in subsequent images, as Heaney 'breaks the pane' and the pain immersing the land by his imaginative fording and wording. In the disturbed mirror – the water, memory, Ireland – a metaphor of beauty surfaces, only to be immediately displaced. The simile of the cut, 'swaying/ its red spoors through a basin', helps the reader to visualise the troubled water, but also reminds one how in Irish history and myth, words like 'land' and 'blood' are kin.[54] The bond between man and earth is re-established in the lines that follow, which depict the clumsiness and intimacy of the relationship. The man's fingers seem like worms as they 'grub' and 'grope' the soil. Life and living depend on the 'sunken drills' of potatoes, which, like the tragic past, Digger – Croppy? – Heaney 'uncastles'. The concluding images of this section suggest that places can generate currents of energy, connecting the human, natural and elemental worlds to each other and to their past. The circuitry and circularity are created aurally by the alliteration of 'h', 'p', 'd', 'n' and 'gr' sounds, and by the image of the hoop.

In Part Three the poem's movement from separation to integration is carried a stage further. Here and in Part Four Heaney celebrates the River Moyola, the source of his initiation into music, his baptism in sound. Though returning to its initial image of continuous rainfall, the focus now has shifted to childhood and the past tense, and away from the tense present. Once more the adult poet captures the child's exhilaration with noise and sights and danger, referring to the water's 'roaring' at night, its bathetic 'slabbering' by day, and the 'long tresses' which pour in abundance from the overflowing rain-barrel. (The immediacy is heightened through the use of enjambed lines, and the repeated '-ing' forms – 'gathering', 'roaring', 'slabbering' and 'harping'). Heaney distinguishes, like Wordsworth, between childhood's sensual revelling in Nature, "when all knowledge is delight,/ and sorrow is not there",[55] and the more sober, 'sublimer joy' that comes with poetic maturation. Now "When time is broke and no proportion kept",[56] he longs to question the river-oracle, "about crops rotted, river mud/ glazing the baked clay floor", in an endeavour to found an Irish future ('for my children's sake') through communion with the Gaelic past ('Soft voices of the dead'), and to place present failures ('crops rotted') into perspective. There are positive associations in the image of the river bed as a kiln, as if hope might harden into definition one day.

In Part Four harmony is restored. Heaney pays a final homage to the Moyola, transformed by his myth-making into a river goddess, an accessible deity to whom he can appeal for imaginative guidance and strength. Like the dancer in Yeats's 'Among School Children', she symbolises creative unity, the inseparability of composer and 'score', nature and art, history and contemporaneity, physical and spiritual being. She is articulate, melodic, self-possessed and self-assured, a familiar spirit whom he can addresses affectionately as 'an old chanter'. While Wordsworth speaks of the Derwent as 'a Playmate whom we dearly lov'd', Heaney emphasises the 'adult' relationship connecting him to his river by means of suggestive imagery. Words such as 'consort', 'bedding' and 'mating' prepare the way for the final climactic image of Moyola, which 'rises to pleasure me', as sensuous as the 'tawny' Cleopatra. She may be 'swollen' and 'wrinkled deep in time',[57] but nevertheless Heaney acknowledges the gifts and the grace she has bestowed upon him, transforming him into a rich young man, a second Dives.[58] The poem ends with the pious wish that his cherishing of home territory, the interlocking Catholic and Protestant farmsteads of South Derry, might in turn encourage others to find common ground in a landscape jointly inherited.

The possibility of *rapprochement* is the subject of 'The Other Side', a poem which does not duck the difficulties of improving cross-community links, but rather faces them squarely with wry good humour. It begins and ends with encounters between Heaney and a Protestant neighbour, and illustrates how centuries of conflict and distrust cannot be easily brushed aside. Much of the poem's

strength stems from Heaney's successful characterisation of the
Protestant farmer, who is treated throughout with a warm and
not unsympathetic irony. From the outset ironic contrasts are in
operation, as the poet mischievously locates the *'white*-haired',
*black*thorn-carrying ascetic *'Thigh-deep* in sedge and marigolds', and
undercuts the neighbour's ominous presence ('his shadow/ on the
stream') and pronouncements ('It's poor as Lazarus, that ground')
by stressing his own relaxed, unflustered response.

> I *lay* where his lea sloped
> to meet our *fallow,*
> *nested* on moss and rushes.

Urban Protestantism in the shape of the docker from *Death of a
Naturalist* clearly posed a physical threat to Catholics; its rural
representative, however, comes across as a fascinating phenomenon, enduring and, in a way, endearing. Admittedly the neighbour
affects a certain arrogance and self-righteousness. He is dismissive
about his neighbours' land, and regards them perhaps as akin to
Lazarus. The possessor of 'promised furrows' rather than 'scraggy
acres', he assumes that he is one of God's 'chosen people', and
can speak with their 'tongue', and with the authority of the Book.
Not only his words take root. As he strides away, he creates 'a
wake of pollen', which in due course will become 'next season's
tares' on his neighbours' property. Despite this unintentional act of
agricultural 'vandalism', and despite his abrupt manner, his 'fabulous' archaic turns-of-phrase make him an object of wonder for the
young of the family, rather than a potential source of menace. The
frequency of his allusions to biblical characters becomes a source of
amusement to them, "For days we would rehearse/ each patriarchal
dictum". Yet beneath the mirth perhaps one glimpses their embarrassment about someone they *perceive to be* socially, economically,
and culturally their superior. From his lips heavyweight biblical
names tumble naturally, before the poet undercuts the grandeur
by means of the bathos of the haycart image, plummeting diction,
and a string of monosyllables ("like loads of hay/ too big for our
small lanes") in the wake of those sonorous polysyllables. What
seemed incongruous and absurd to the child can be respected by
the adult poet who is not averse to employing biblical and classical
allusions himself, sparingly, of course. So open and so *honest* is
the neighbour in acknowledging his prejudices, and so sparse is

his intellectual furnishing that it is difficult for poet or reader to take offence.[59] In fact, one's affection increases observing the man's tact in not disturbing the evening rosary, and one suspects that his decision to visit was a studied, not a present thought. Beautifully, poignantly, Heaney captures the embarrassment felt by both sides when the sectarian divide seems about to be breached. While the adult Protestant "taps a little tune with the blackthorn/ shyly" as he waits for the contact he fears and desires, the young Catholic weighs up the possible consequences of an 'escape' from the 'moan of prayers'. Should he risk his parents' disapproval by deserting the family rite in the interests of good neighbourliness, and once outside, will he have anything to say to this stranger? 'The Other Side' aptly concludes with a question, a dilemma unresolved. The image of the 'grass-seed' has been read as indicating Heaney's hope for a more fertile relationship in the future. However, one must question the value of a conversation only able to embrace superficial topics such as 'the weather' and 'the price of grass-seed'.[60] Then again, talks about talks have to begin somewhere.

Inevitably, inexorably, the collection inches its way back to the present crisis, where it began. At the centre of *Wintering Out*, the nightmare is confronted in the sequence, 'A Northern Hoard', and in the justly acclaimed poem, 'The Tollund Man'. 'A Northern Hoard' derives its epigraph from 'The Rime of the Ancient Mariner', a poem first published in *Lyrical Ballads* in 1798, the year which saw the shattering of Coleridge's hopes for the French Revolution. Paralysed, powerless and full of remorse, like the Mariner, Heaney's speaker occupies a world inhabited by ghostly beings, endures a life made ghastly by acts of violence. Whereas the repetition of his crime ultimately becomes a redemptive act for the Ancient Mariner, in Heaney's poem there seems no prospect of redemption. Crimes multiply, and the 'new history' promises merely a revival of ancient tribal savagery.

One of the weaknesses of the poem is Heaney's inability to maintain his gaze and our focus on the horror of the present. The diversity of biblical, historical and literary allusions which he employs as filters results in a blurring, rather than a sharpening of perspective. 'All shifts dreamily', he writes, except for the imagery. Readers are put through their paces, dodging the 'clucking gas' in 'old Gomorrah', avoiding the opening of an Audenesque 'fault' only to encounter Yeatsian 'tidal blood', glimpsing victims of the plague huddled in a 'pow-wow'. In addition, there seems an undue emphasis on the poet's personal burden of guilt and inadequacy, his 'smeared doorstep',

> I've soaked by moonlight in tidal blood
>
> ('Roots')
>
> I deserted / . . . . Must I crawl back now
>
> ('No Man's Land')
>
> Why do I unceasingly arrive late to condone?
>
> ('No Man's Land')
>
> I am riding to plague again
>
> ('Stump')
>
> What do I say if they wheel out their dead?
> I'm cauterized, a black stump of home
>
> ('Stump')

and too little space given to the victims of atrocities. The comparison of their 'wounds' to Christ's 'palms' and the insensitive reference to the 'lumpy dead' deny those victims their individuality. Fortunately in 'No Sanctuary' and 'Tinder', the last two sections, attention turns from the self-condemning 'I' to the collective 'we' and its culpability.[61] It is in 'Tinder' that Heaney achieves most success and coherence, for here he confines himself to a relatively simple analogy between pre-history and the present. Rooted by another memory from childhood, the poem begins with what seems an innocuous pastime, some boys collecting tiny pieces of flint, trying to make fire. Within a few lines these flints are transformed into 'Cold beads of history and home', a rosary consisting of the martyrs and disasters in Nationalist mythology recited in Catholic households along with the Our Fathers and Hail Marys. Obsessively fingering the shards of the past has been spiritually disabling, and in trying to raise a spark, the boys inflict wounds upon themselves, "our knuckle joints/ Striking as often as the flints." Heaney recognises how on his and on the other side, centuries of indoctrination have bequeathed a legacy of intolerance and fear, and fostered the tribal mentality which now expresses itself in bombings, shootings and arson. These 'adult' activities are the source of the 'unhallowed light' that hangs over both Protestant and Catholic alike; a spurious equality has been established at last. Within each Christian community there are those who seem more at home with the Old Testament philosophy of "a life for a life, an eye for an eye, burning for burning, wound for wound".[62] The fertile island, like that of *Lord of the Flies*, has been desecrated, reduced to patches of 'cinder' and 'ash', but worse is to come. On the heels of this holocaust comes a nuclear winter, a new Age of Ice. The survivors squat like animals, eyes red from sleeplessness, guilt or blood-lust. They prepare to defend this 'cankered ground' ('Veteran's Dream'), with anything that comes to hand, such as the debris from the 'civilisation' that has just fallen – bricks, bottles, petrol, nail-bombs or even bare nails if necessary. Seemingly "fighting had become its own justification, and they could not stop."[63]

The most accomplished poem resulting from Heaney's search during the early 1970s "for images and symbols adequate to our predicament"[64] is without doubt 'The Tollund Man'. A potent combination of historical analogy and myth and intense emotion, it exhibits the depth of Heaney's religious nature. He speaks of it as 'an offering'. In it he articulates a "perception not only of the pastness of the past, but of its presence", "a sense of the timeless as well as of the temporal and of the timeless and of the temporal together".[65] Composing from a sense of reverence for a victim from the distant past came more easily to him than responding to the all-too-immediate horror of the present.

My emotions, my feelings, whatever those instinctive energies are that have to be engaged for a poem, those energies quickened more when contemplating a victim, strangely, from 2,000 years ago than they did from contemplating a man at the end of a road being swept up into a plastic bag – I mean the barman at the end of our road tried to carry out a bomb and it blew up. Now there is of course something terrible about that, but somehow language, words didn't live in the way I think they have to live in a poem when they were hovering over that kind of horror and pity.[66]

The 'entrancement' he experienced looking for the first time at photographs of the Tollund Man matched that of Professor Glob, the distinguished Danish archaeologist, summoned one May evening in 1950 to Bjaeldskov Dal in central Jutland to inspect a body discovered a few hours earlier by two men digging peat for their winter fires. In his book, *The Bog People*, the professor describes the shock of finding himself "face to face with an Iron Age man, who twenty millenia before, had been deposited in the bog as a sacrifice to the

powers that rule men's destinies."[67] Chief amongst these powers
was the fertility goddess, Nerthus, a North European equivalent
of the Mediterranean earth goddesses Ishtar and Aphrodite. It was
for her sake that the Tollund Man endured his death by hanging, so
that the "great ritual drama" of the seasons might continue. Heaney
was quick to recognise the poetic potential of Glob's book, and to
utilise its anthropological insights in interpreting the present state
of Ireland. The fatal attraction of Nerthus lives on in such figures
from the Nationalist pantheon as Kathleen ni Houlihan, the Shan
Van Vocht, and Mother Ireland. Promising a rich harvest in return
for the sacrifice of their lives, she still stirs the Irish young to words
and murder. Through the intercession of one of her ancient victims,
the poet prays that the contemporary blood-letting in Ireland might
in some miraculous way result in "the renewal and fertility of the
territory".[68]

Though the visual images from *The Bog People* may have begun
the process of germination in Heaney's imagination, it was certainly
accelerated by Glob's evocative and poetic prose.[69] Heaney's poem
opens quietly, like Glob's initial description. The language is simple.
Monosyllables predominate. In the first line where the poet resolves
to visit the shrine, no vowel or consonant is repeated, as if music
should be retained solely for the young victim. Subsequently in
the quatrain a simple pattern of sounds ('s', 'p', 'd', 'i' and ' ɑɪ ')
emerges, and a spare and subtle imagery appears. The reference to
the '*mild pods* of his eye-lids' establishes the gentleness of the face,
and connects an adjective frequently associated with Christ and a
noun introducing the fertility motif. The image of the 'winter seeds'
in verse two consolidates this idea, but by this time a starker, bleaker
note has been sounded, partly by means of the diction ('flat', 'dug',
'gruel', 'Caked'), partly through the use of alliteration (the harsh
stops 'c', 'k', 'g', and the fricative 's'). Empathy increases with the
disclosure that he is, to all intents and purposes, naked, a fact which
stresses his defencelessness and prepares us for his ambiguous role
as groom/victim. (The cap and girdle can hardly be said to
constitute clothing. Though they might form part of the nuptial
attire, the intrusive noose cannot be regarded as such.) The unequal
marriage between the mortal 'bridegroom' and 'the goddess' proves
to be a durable one, despite the contradictions and contrariness of
Nerthus. She constricts and releases ('tightened', 'opened'), is verb
and power, but has a soft spot for her man and for the creative
process, ('working/ Him to a saint's kept body'). Swift and deadly

in her embrace, as the alliterated 't's suggest, she is generous in her choice of wedding gift, constant with her sexual favours. Her torc, the plaited noose, turns out to be "the pass which carries him over the threshold of death",[70] and her 'dark juices' confer immortality.

Part One of the poem ends, as it began, *pianissimo*. This effect is achieved by the succession of 'z' and 's' sounds, the strategic placing of 'Reposes' at the heart of the final 'couplet', and its near-rhyming with 'Aarhus'. Heaney's Tollund Man seems at this stage a modest, unassuming saint, in comparison to the magnetic, transcendent figure Glob depicts.[71] For the archaeologist, the Tollund Man embodies the triumph of nature over art. For the poet, however, he is potentially an active spiritual entity, capable of restoring sanctity, forgiveness and reconciliation to the now unholy ground of Ireland. Consequently, in the dramatic opening to Part Two, Heaney contemplates an appeal to the Tollund Man to intercede for Ireland. He hesitates over the propriety of such an action, which would set him at odds with his own faith, and in effect elevate the anonymous pagan to the communion of saints. Perhaps the risk is worth taking, however, if the destructive passions in the 'cauldron bog' can be purged away, and a fertile unity might be re-established.[72] In contrast to the almost 'civilised' ritual killings of ancient Jutland, which at least could claim the dignity of a religious purpose, he cites an incident from the 1920s as an illustration of the barbarity to which the some of the 'Christian' inhabitants of the island have sunk in the service of Kathleen and Carson. "Part of the folk-lore of where I grew up", concerns four Catholic brothers "massacred by Protestant paramilitaries". Their bodies "had been trailed along the railway lines, over the sleepers as a kind of mutilation."[73] An entire generation from one family – or at best a major part of it – had been wiped out. Whereas the Tollund Man was forewarned of his death, perhaps accepted its justification, and was left physically intact by his 'executors', the young brothers were 'ambushed', slaughtered for no conceivable 'common good',[74] their bodies broken and shredded. It is as if only fragments of what were human beings remain to disclose their fate and indict their murderers. Pathos tinges the horror when Heaney draws attention to the '*Stockinged* corpses', an image which makes them appear even younger. Following the almost serene, painless demise of the Iron Age man, the sadism and brutality surrounding contemporary killing is all the more appalling.

In the course of recreating the scene at Aarhus and at the edge of the fen, the poet has increasingly become bonded to his subject, moved by the 'stillness' of history. His imagination eagerly seizes affinities and ironies, and though conscious that a huge distance of time and vast difference in destiny separate him from the Tollund Man, Heaney nevertheless perseveres with the bold comparison.[75]

> Something of his sad freedom
> As he rode the tumbril
> Should come to me, driving

Sombre rhythms and sounds anticipate the meeting of the dispirited son with his adopted father. Each of the first three lines is weighted with a trochee – '*free*dom', '*tum*bril', '*dri*ving' – and the alliteration ('s', 'd' and 'm'), assonance ('freedom'/'he'/'me'), internal rhyme ('tumbril'/'come') and near-rhyme ('sad', 'rode') create their own burden. The Tollund Man may well have travelled on his last journey in a highly ornate waggon sacred to the goddess Nerthus, but Heaney chooses the word 'tumbril' for this vehicle, a choice which has the effect of bridging Time. One pictures the Danish sacrificial victim as a lonely French aristocrat *en route* to the guillotine during the revolution. Motoring through a foreign country hardly seems a comparable experience, an adequate 'objective correlative', yet Heaney successfully reflects *something of* their feelings of isolation, vulnerability, exposure, by reciting the place-names with their alien vowels, sensing an implied threat in 'the pointing hands', and voicing his fear that he will be unable to communicate with anyone. Rather than freeing him from disorientation and his present desolation, ironically the pilgrimage would end confirming them. After living in Belfast under the shadow of immanent death, 'the old man-killing parishes' of Jutland would seem familiar territory, where he will feel "lost/ Unhappy and at home." In structure these final lines echo those of Part One. At the core of this divided decasyllabic, instead of 'Reposes', we find 'Unhappy', pointing the contrast between achieved and continuing suffering, the Tollund Man and the poet.

The writing of 'The Tollund Man' constituted a major epiphany for the poet, a 'coming up into the light'.[76] The climax to Part One of *Wintering Out*, it illustrates Heaney's increasing confidence with a larger canvas, his ability to handle the national theme maturely and responsibly. Places, crises, personalities, and sometimes seemingly minor phenomena from the outer world he 'interiorises', absorbing them into the depths of the inner world. There they are 'preserved' through the action of memory, understanding, and imaginative will, attaining contiguity with his personal myths, prior to the act of retrieval.

At the outset of the second part of *Wintering Out*, the private world asserts itself, but here too the 'backward look' engenders sorrow and memories of conflict, familial, rather than tribal. 'Wedding Day' and 'Mother of the Groom' hark back to his marriage in August 1965, but neither poem dwells upon romance or nostalgia. Instead they focus on the underside and undercurrents of the 'happy event'. To the outsider, the emphasis on tears and fears might well appear excessive. Indeed, without the benefit of Polly Devlin's illuminating comments in *All of us There*, one might be at a loss to explain why such a funereal atmosphere should prevail at a wedding. There exists "a thin membrane . . . between grief and joy in Irish celebrations", she explains.[77] To illustrate her point, she specifically cites her sister's wedding day. At the reception, the poet's wife gave a poignant rendering of the ballad, *Slieve Gallion Brae*. "My sister's husband noted how his bride's song shivered that day, noted too that grief which so often marks my father's face."[78] In fact, the strain seems insupportable for each participant in 'Wedding Day'. Re-winding the film, playing back the soundtrack, the narrator initially recalls his own tense state, and his bewilderment that his and his bride's happiness should breed so much distress. The melancholy is contagious, irrational, manic, and even the young bride succumbs to it. Eclipsed by the 'tall cake', wilting under the intense emotional heat, momentarily she loses herself. The picture Heaney evokes of her inevitably reminds one of Miss Havisham in *Great Expectations*, and in the subsequent image of the 'skewered heart' there is perhaps an ironic echo of her melodramatic words to Pip.[79] Instead of finding relief in the gents, he is confronted with this ironic emblem, and believes he will only regain his composure when he and his wife have put a distance between themselves and their past ties. In his final plea, "Let me/ Sleep on your breast to the airport", lies an acknowledgement of his immaturity, his need to be consoled since his new partner is cast in the role of mother. In the companion piece to 'Wedding Day', 'Mother of the Groom' – and in many of the poems which follow it – Heaney articulates his enhanced awareness of women's lot and losses. The lonely, unappreciated wife and mother-figures found at the heart of *Door into the Dark* reappear in the latter half of *Wintering Out* in a variety of guises. From his portrayal of the displaced mother in 'Mother of the Groom' one senses a son's guilty unease. Its first scene – bathing baby – comes perilously close to sentimentality, yet when Heaney records a more recent *domestic* event he captures vividly the mother's feelings of emptiness, redundancy. The separation which began at birth is completed, and though others greet the new member of the family she at first finds it hard to face the intruder. Her lap now is 'voided', and it is as if "he kicked when lifted / And slipped her soapy hold". Despite her grief at 'losing' her firstborn, her companion and champion, the older woman is generous to her 'rival'. She rallies and applauds. Though lacking the possessiveness of a Mrs Morel or a Mrs Yeobright,[80] she suffers an equal hurt. Observing the ring 'bedded forever now' on her 'clapping hand', the poet is painfully reminded of her length of service as wife and mother. Within that 'forever now' a finality resides, an awesome permanence, pangs of loss. For the son too, a door has closed on the 'honeyed' past, and in 'Goodnight' he identifies the familiar shapes of home – 'latch', 'yard', 'puddle, cobble-stones, jamb and doorstep' – which once provided the boy with 'den' and definition. Now, however, he is part of a parting 'they'. The unnamed female figure watching his – or is it the couple's? – departure is probably his mother, striding in "again beyond her shadows", cancelling "everything behind her."

Although "the private core' in Heaney's domestic lyrics 'will always remain hermetic",[81] within them he reflects the crises, joys and agonies in his personal life with an astonishing openness and bravery, reminiscent at times of Lowell or Plath. In a poem such as 'Summer Home' he exhibits his growing mastery of *technique*, his ability to 'control and manipulate experience'[82] and to transmute "that first stirring of the mind round a word or an image or a memory"[83] into Art. Like the best of what has been labelled 'confessional' poetry, 'Summer Home' simultaneously embodies and transcends the private experience which gave it birth. Originating in the poet's feelings of remorse and desire to make reparation, it becomes, like Shakespeare's *A Winter's Tale*, a journey in five acts from sin to a chastened redemption, a poetic exploration of male guilt and Man's need for 'feminine intercession'.[84] The poem opens dramatically, marrying intimacy and artistry, addressing itself both to wife and readers. We are made immediately conscious that something, as yet unnamed, is afflicting the marital state. The homely recognisable stench of the 'flax-dam' has given place to something less near and more disturbing.[85] Rhythm, sound and imagery combine to evoke an oppressive atmosphere. The regularity established in the first line by the two anapestic feet is immediately disrupted in the second by that 'something', and thereafter strong stresses stalk the verse at will. There is dense use of alliteration ('w's, 'd's, 'm's, 'n's, 'g's, 'ŋ's and 's's) and assonance ('o', 'ɪ', 'ʌ', 'aʊ'). Vowel rhymes and images wit unpleasant associations snake from one line to the next ('dumps'/'something', 'in heat/ dogging us', 'sour'/'fouled'). The question generates a brief moment of self-questioning. Whether self-possessed – in contrast to the alarmed 'inquisitor' – or infected with madness, or both, the 'possessed air' offers no answers. It is only when he stares downwards – and inwards? – that he discovers with horror the progeny of evil, but cannot as yet acknowledge his responsibility as its source. Frenetically he attempts to purge away his 'larval' enemies, his 'scald, scald, scald' a domestic equivalent of Lear's 'kill, kill, kill, kill, kill, kill'.[86] After the dramatic expenditure of energy with which Part One concludes, Part Two begins with a framed portrait. By gathering an abundance of 'wild cherry and rhododendron', the speaker hopes to restore harmony and cross the threshold that leads to reconciliation. In ironic contrast to this vision of plenty is the sound of his wife's distress. Though reduced by grief, her voice, amplified by the hallway, challenges his largeness and 'loudness'. Immediately he recognises that the appositeness of the rhyme connecting his name with 'blame'. Like Cordelia's tears, his wife's 'weeping' sets in motion the process of restoration. Characteristically, Heaney enlists the aid of Catholic imagery[87] and ritual to renew and re-'compose' their sacred and secular union. 'The loosened flowers', like her 'frank and falling' tears, might 'taint' if they fail to 'Attend. Anoint the wound.' The poet's determination to will a settlement is undermined by the presence of three words, 'falling', 'taint' and 'wound'. That the 'original sin' which caused the conflict cannot be so easily forgotten becomes evident in Part Three. Their attempts at making love leave them bruised and 'winded', and another purification rite is necessary. Disconsolate, torn by desire and guilt, he finds temporary relief observing what seems an almost symbiotic relationship between woman and water, for both are 'full of grace'.

Even when in Part Four a sexual climax is achieved, it brings neither gratitude nor gratification, and at the outset of the final section the pair appear to be as far away as ever from resolving their differences. The atmosphere of unhappiness and estrangement claims fresh victims, but at least now the poet can identify the source of the 'foulness'. Honesty prevents him from imposing a cosy resolution on the poem, yet in its last lines Heaney strains towards a positive conclusion, invoking metaphors of music and light. Like the native 'maize, and vine', who serve as their exemplars, the couple must shoulder their 'burden' of growth, and be at home and at one with 'the light'. In its final images, however, 'Summer Home' returns to the dark 'that wombed me',[88] turns back to a moment of music and communion in order to manage the present tense. The cave functions both as an actual physical location – it is a place where the couple share a common wonder at the sublime – and as a symbol of sexual unity.[89] It enables them to regain a sense of perspective, of their place in the scale of creation. The beautiful, delicate image of the 'tuning fork' acts as a reminder of the harmony they can achieve together, its tiny fragile sound a counterpoint to the 'small lost weeping' of Part Two. Certainly 'Summer Home' has travelled a long way from the perturbed free verse of its opening to the nearly regular rhythms and half-rhymes of its ending. Perhaps the slightly jarring effect of that concluding 'dark'/ 'fork' rhyme indicates that the healing is not yet complete. In the meantime, the poem exists to assuage, to 'Anoint the wound'.

Although at first sight 'Limbo' and 'Bye-Child' would appear to be concerned with private cruelties and guilt, these chilling tales can also be read as parables for the present state of Ireland and its moral paralysis. Tribal taboos and laws can so easily outweigh 'civilised' humane values, these poems tell us. Rather than risk ostracisation by the 'Christian' community in which she lives, the unmarried mother of 'Limbo' drowns her new-born baby. Similarly, the mother in 'Bye-Child' attempts to hide her sin from the world's eyes, confining her son to a hen-house, feeding him on scraps, like a dog. Each poem reveals Heaney's remarkable skill at manipulating the reader's emotions. The calculated callousness of the opening lines of 'Limbo'[90] provokes both an immediate and complex response. The juxtaposition of 'infant' – a word which suggests helplessness, and which has strong associations with Christ – and 'salmon', the wry verb 'Netted', the ugly noun 'spawning', and the sardonic reference to the dead child as 'A small one thrown back/ To the waters', emphasise that for the poem's first narrator the baby's death did not constitute 'an important failure'.[91] In line six, however, this detached, journalistic account of events is interrupted by a second voice which probes the tragic sub-text of the story. By means of his quietly assertive, 'But I'm sure', and through his use of the adverb, 'tenderly', Heaney makes it clear that the woman is no heartless monster, but rather a frightened and confused human being. Having endured the fear and loneliness of her secret pregnancy and the harrowing ordeal of childbirth ('Tearing her open'), she agonises over a deed which will bring not the temporary 'relief' she imagines, but rather an eternity of guilt. Though the killing was in part motivated by her desire to protect herself, it can also be seen as a perverse act of love, for if the child had survived, he would have suffered the stigma of bastardy. One must assume that the forgiveness that Christ showed to the woman taken in adultery has no place in Ballyshannon. As a result of her frailty and the community's intolerance, fresh salt is rubbed into the wounds of the Saviour they claim to worship, "Even Christ's palms, unhealed,/ Smart and cannot fish there." Together they have created a new 'limbo' to which the unbaptised child will be consigned forever, a 'briny zone' beyond reach and redemption. The relatively 'recent' incursion of Christianity into the Celtic psyche, the poem implies, has not displaced the ancient religion which prizes tribal loyalties and considers human life cheap.

Despite the cruelty it contains, 'Bye-Child' seems optimistic in comparison with the poem it faces across the page. Although his short life-time has consisted of continuous physical and emotional deprivation, the child has been able to transcend his kennel prison and achieved a hard and bright lucidity of spirit. Like Hardy's Tess,[92] he has developed the ability to separate soul from body. He has journeyed 'beyond patience' and beyond the limitations of human 'love', and identified in the still and changing moon the constancy and grace, the love and loveliness his earthly mother lacked.

The moon serves as the presiding symbol in the final poem of *Wintering Out*, 'Westering', which garners together some of the key images of the volume. In his search for common ground, Heaney has explored place, name, history, myth, home, but struggled to find a sense of shelter anywhere on earth. Homesick in California, sitting under a paper moon – a map, the handiwork of Rand McNally, surely a fellow Irish exile – his mind flees from the proximity of 'frogskin' and 'Pitiscus' to the distant familiar music of 'cobbles' and 'Donegal'. Recalling his last night in the West of Ireland initially provides him with reassuring memories. The home moon gave him a sense of definition, and illuminated for him 'The cobbles of the yard' making them as 'pale as eggs'. His exhilaration at the thought of going to America he likens to 'a free fall'. This is one of those inspired, ambivalent images of which Heaney is so fond. For the parachutist the thrill of exposure to the air gains something of its piquancy from the danger and unpredictability involved. Part of the pleasure must derive from meeting that moment when the security of the aeroplane becomes a thing of the past. One cannot imagine that the theological associations of the word 'fall' were absent from Heaney's mind, since he next refers to the fact that they were travelling on a Good Friday. Although he experiences a truant pleasure and excitement in leaving behind the 'still churches' with their 'congregations bent/ To the studded crucifix', performing the Easter devotions, one detects also a sense of separation, of exclusion, as if part of him resents being merely 'A dwindling interruption'. His attitude here seems not dissimilar to that of John Donne, in his 'Good Friday, 1613. Riding Westward', surely a literary forbear of Heaney's poem. Though 'carryed towards the West', Donne's soul 'bends toward the East'. He too would like to avoid viewing the harrowing spectacle of Christ on the Cross, "Yet dare I almost be glad, I do not see/ That spectacle of too much weight for mee."[93] Attempting to find relief from the pain of exile, he searches for an appropriate symbol to bridge the distance between Berkeley and Belfast. Looking to the serene, timeless, transcendent moon, however, brings little comfort, for its surface too seems marked with 'stigmata', emblems of universal grief and sin. Much as he would like to imagine the existence of an Ireland where there was 'untroubled dust' and a loosening and lessening in the 'gravity' of the situation, reason tells him that this is just another American dream. Nowhere is there 'a place/ still innocent of us'.[94] Even when 'freed' from the cross, Heaney, like his free-falling Christ, still feels the weight of guilt on his hands.

In order to understand Heaney's work at this stage in his career and since, it is essential to try to define his complex and ambivalent attitudes towards Catholicism and Christianity, especially since some critics determinedly seek definitive proof for his absolute rejection of both. In a guide to the *Selected Poems 1965–75*, for example, Nicholas McGuinn rashly asserts, "It is because Heaney feels that Christianity is at best irrelevant and at worst a force for harm in Ulster that he rarely refers to it in *Wintering Out*."[95] Yet if Christianity and Christian allusion did indeed possess neither relevance nor moral force, why would it feature in such major poems as 'The Last Mummer', 'Gifts of Rain', 'The Other Side', 'A Northern Hoard', 'The Tollund Man', 'Summer Home', 'Limbo', 'Bye Child' and 'Westering'? Derek Mahon, writing in 1970, suggested that Heaney was a Catholic who was a poet, rather than a *Catholic* poet, yet this is to imply a dissociation between artistic and religious impulses, a dissociation which in Heaney's case it is almost impossible to make. Clearly Catholicism permeates both his poetic consciousness, with its weighty emphasis on ritual supplication, on awe, grace, guilt, humility, responsibility, discipline, and its burdened and burdening vocabulary. His fondness for the pieties of his Mossbawn childhood has survived both the impact of his secular 'British' education and the psychological-spiritual trauma of the Troubles, and has not been diminished.[96] The highly-charged language in which the Church's teachings were couched permeate the poet's idiolect. His religious metaphors and allusions are not to be dismissed simply as the products of nostalgia, the detritus of a belief long since abandoned; rather they incarnate a potency of feeling remembered and renewed.

County Derry Catholicism shaped his identity in a double sense, however. It founded him, but at the same time made him and his people founder. 'The blueprint for the spirit' frequently turned into an intellectual, emotional and spiritual 'straitjacket'.[97] In addition the Church as an institution in the North had failed to provide the social and political leadership the Catholic community needed and deserved, and in a sense had 'collaborated' with the Unionists' repression. After having endured decades of defeatism and submissiveness, many Catholics in the late 1960s and early 1970s turned first to the Civil Rights Movement, and then later, regrettably, to the Provisional I.R.A. to assert *their* sense of racial identity. As an 'aggravated young Catholic male',[98] he too resented having to turn the other cheek, and while he would not condone the violence, he understood the legitimacy of the rage which gave rise to it. Increasingly during this period of aroused tribal consciousness, the poet defined himself as a Catholic writer, though he tended to stress 'the cultural, rather than the religious load implicit in that term'.[99] Internment, sectarian killings and deteriorating relations between the British Army and the Catholic community inevitably made him "side with his own side".[100] On one occasion around this time when Heaney was travelling to a Civil Rights March with Michael Longley, his companion asked him what they should do and say if they were stopped by a sectarian murder squad. He replied simply, "I think we should sink or swim by what we are." [101] Drawn in one direction by the pull of collective outrage which demanded unequivocal support for the Tricolour and St Patrick, another part of him determined to fly his own flag, and recognised Oisin as his patron saint.

> As a member of the minority, solidarity was expected; and yet you were not just behaving in accordance with expectations, you were behaving naturally along ingrained emotional grain lines . . . But there is a second command besides the command to solidarity – and that is to individuate yourself, to become self-conscious, to liberate the consciousness from the collective pieties. [102]

In the pursuit of his poetic vocation he felt compelled to examine other modes of feeling and perception – *in addition to* Catholic and Christian ones – and to employ pre-Christian mythic material to enable him to confront and interpret the slaughter of innocence.

One source of confirmation for such an approach was to be found in the writings of Carl Gustav Jung. (That unusual reflexive verb 'to individuate oneself' derives from his work.) Clearly Heaney felt a strong sense of affinity with the eminent psychologist, whose crucial phase of self-analysis was triggered by a break with friends and collaborators, and largely coincided with the years of the Great War. Heaney's poetry of the Troubles exhibits a Jungian longing for the wholeness and integration he associates with childhood, and a search for myths which would restore 'purpose and value' to life, which would incorporate Christian values and yet be free of 'conventional Christianity', which would bring about a rapprochement 'between the conflicting sides of his own nature.' [103] Unfortunately, Christian values, such as forgiveness and reconciliation, which he himself still espoused, appeared no match for regressive tribal instinct. Indeed, just as he became accustomed to the scale, severity and savagery of the sectarian hatred, the actions of the British Army in Derry added a new dimension to the conflict. It was no longer simply a clash of two seemingly irreconcilable religious and political ideologies each with a legitimate claim over the possession of the territory. It had become translated into a colonial struggle between the natives and the invader.

1. (*above*) Barn, Mossbawn

2. (*left*) The Pump from
'Changes', an *Omphalos*

3. (*below*) The Eel Fisheries,
Toome

4. St. Columb's College, Derry

5. (*left*) Queen's University, Belfast

6. (*below*) Michael Longley, Derek Mahon, John Hewitt, Seamus Heaney, Cushendall, 1969

7. David
   Hammond

8. (*left*) T. P. Flanagan

9. (*below*) Seamus Heaney and
   Philip Hobsbaum, Glasgow, 1989

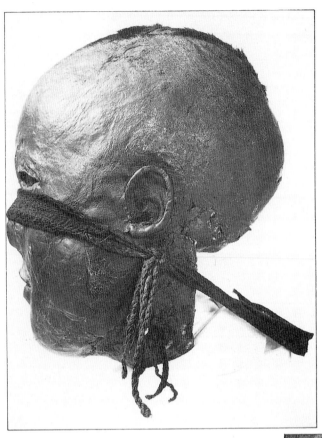

10 a and 10 b (*insert*)
  The Windeby girl, the subject of Heaney's
  'Punishment'. He encountered this image in
  P. V. Glob's *The Bog People*

NORTH

The period between September 1971, when he despatched his third collection to his publisher, and June 1975 when his fourth volume, *North*, appeared, witnessed dramatic changes in the poet's life. His year-long 'exile' had unsettled him. In an interview from November 1971, Heaney described coming back to Northern Ireland as being 'like putting on an old dirty glove again'. America, he went on to say, "gave me the idea that I would have to come back and say that this place is a kind of disease preventing personality from flowering gracefully. It is a very graceless community, a very scared and stunted community."[104] His account of Belfast's Christmas, 1971, is full of fear and menacing references to soldiers, police, vigilantes, cocked guns, roadblocks, flash-lights, night-sights, but few fairy lights. Although he includes one brief moment of sardonic humour – such as when a bomb-disposal squad 'defused a bundle of books' while their owner was supping up in the Queen's University Staff Common room – the proximity of violence and the threat of violence oppresses him. Immediately after citing this 'far from risible' incident, he recalls the horrific explosion of December 4 at Patrick McGurk's bar in Belfast, where fifteen people were blown up by the Protestant Ulster Volunteer Force. The more personal anecdotes begin with his irritation at being marched to a police barracks, along with his three-year-old son, "because my car tax was out of date", and end with his wife's terror, as "an office block in University Road exploded just as she was out of range."[105]

The New Year took up where the old year had left off. On January 22, an anti-internment march on Magilligan strand, near Derry, was broken up by British troops. Suspecting that the protesters intended storming the nearby transit camp, the soldiers first charged at the crowd with batons, and then used rubber bullets and C.S. gas to disperse them. This incident, however, served as a prelude to an event whose repercussions are still being felt. On Sunday, January 30, during an illegal parade in Derry organised by the Civil Rights Association, British paratroopers opened fire, killing thirteen unarmed civilians, and wounding twelve others. Seven of the victims were under nineteen years of age. The subsequent inquiry into 'Bloody Sunday', set up by the Prime Minister, Edward Heath, exonerated the soldiers, who claimed that they had been returning fire. However, according to one highly-respected Irish journalist, "no one else in Derry that day . . . heard any shots until the army began firing . . . . On the evidence it would appear that either the army simply wanted to teach the natives a lesson or that they were given a heightened and misleading impression of what was likely to happen."[106] Grief and anger swept over Catholic Ireland. In Dublin, three days later, the British Embassy was burnt to the ground. Within the Nationalist community of the North, alienation was now total, and Mid-Ulster M.P., Bernadette Devlin, prophetically proclaimed, "The Government may well have lit a fire in Ireland, the flames of which may not die out until the last vestige of British rule has gone from that country."[107] In defiance of Stormont, one week later, on Sunday, February 6, another march was organised, this time in Newry. One of the leaders was a local man, Kevin Boyle, a lecturer in law at Queen's, an early Civil Rights activist. Among the demonstrators were Heaney and Michael Longley. Both have vivid recollections of the helicopters hovering over them menacingly. Despite the loudhailers' warning, "If you go a step further, you are breaking the law," the 'scared, irrevocable steps' had to be taken to show solidarity with those who had died.[108]

By the time Heaney celebrated his thirty-third birthday, the crisis had taken another dramatic turn, leaving "the political future of the province in doubt".[109] The last Prime Minister of Northern Ireland, Brian Faulkner, had resigned, as anticipated, when his government was relieved of its responsibilities for law and order, and the fifty year-old constitution had been suspended. The upsurge in violence provoked by the introduction of internment and the outcry that followed Bloody Sunday had convinced the British Government that Stormont's 'tough' policies were merely exacerbating the situation. Direct Rule from Westminster, however, neither halted the killings, nor eased the tension. It had the unfortunate effect of raising unrealistic expectations among Catholics, and confirming deep suspicions among Protestants about British intentions.

It was natural that the government of the Republic and public opinion both there and among Catholics in the north should see this as a step towards the incorporation of the six-county area in an all Ireland state. It was equally natural that the northern Protestants should feel that their position was now under threat and that they might find themselves placed, without their consent, under what they regarded as alien rule.[110]

At this uncertain moment in the history of the North, the Easter of 1972, Heaney decided to resign from his post as a lecturer at Queen's University, to pursue a career as a freelance writer. He was determined to leave Belfast, and though initially he had hoped to find a place in County Derry, the offer of a cottage in an idyllic, secluded part of County Wicklow resulted in his leaving Northern Ireland for the Republic. By August he and his family were installed at Glanmore.

The motives for this move have been variously explained by Heaney, and, not surprisingly, he has chosen to emphasise its emblematic significance in later interviews. Heaney certainly felt that he had reached a crucial age, and critical stage in his development. His instincts told him it was time 'to go it alone',[111] to devote himself totally to his poetic vocation without the burdens and distractions of teaching.[112] Another major reason for going South, according to his family, was an economic one, a desire to escape the high tax rates in the North. His resignation from Queen's meant forfeiting a healthy and regular salary, and so the chance to keep all of his income from freelance work was not to be spurned. He refers to the 'freedom from tax enjoyed by writers here' as a factor in an article from 1972, and states that his intention is to write full-time 'for a year'.[113] If he had difficulty making ends meet, he could always return to teaching, he believed. It made sense to embark on a new way of life in a new location. His choice of rural Wicklow reveals a longing for a simpler, less frenetic, perhaps more *Irish* way of life. In the words of Daniel Corkery, "The Gaels never made of their own the cities and the towns."[114] According to one friend, Belfast was 'never his city'[115] anyway, and, after his year in the United States, it must have seemed too constricted and constricting. He had had difficulty settling back into his old life-style there, and believed his young family deserved somewhere better; it was "not a good place to bring up children."[116] Heaney also disliked what he has termed the 'committee atmosphere'[117] in Belfast, and no longer needed the instant approbation or censure of any group, however well-intentioned.

Though political considerations undoubtedly affected his decision to take up residence in the Republic,[118] they were by no means pre-eminent. In retrospective accounts of this period, however, he has laid great stress on his determination to distance himself ideologically from 'the corrupt set-up' in the North. He had no intention of allowing his presence and poetry to be used to bolster a state whose legitimacy he denied.

> For the Protestant sensibility, the Troubles were an interruption and disruption of 'the status quo' . . . For the Catholic writer, I think the Troubles were a critical moment, a turning point, possibly a vision of some kind of fulfilment. The blueprint in the Catholic writer's head predicted that a history would fulfil itself in a United Ireland or in something . . . In the late '60s and early '70s the world was changing for the Catholic imagination. I felt I was compromising some part of myself by staying in a situation where socially and, indeed, imaginatively there were pressures 'against' regarding the moment as critical.[119]

Heaney certainly now sees his crossing of the border as a conscious political act. Perhaps it was. While the Paisleyite *Protestant Telegraph* welcomed the departure of 'the well-known papist propagandist' at last heading for 'his spiritual home in the popish republic,' and in Dublin the *Irish Times* rejoiced at his arrival with the headline 'Ulster Poet Moves South', their many friends in Belfast were saddened to see the Heaneys leave. Their sorrow grieved him, and though he claims to have had 'no doubt about the rightness of the move', he was clearly uneasy about 'seeming to break ranks'[120] with them. Some felt rejected. Though Heaney insists that 'it wasn't a matter of me rejecting anyone',[121] he was rejecting something which had sustained him and sustained them – the myth of a happily integrated state called Northern Ireland.

Once ensconced in Glanmore, Heaney began anew the search for myths which might enable him to make sense of 'the swirl' of his own 'private feelings'[122] and fulfil more effectively his social role as a poet. Heaney's first task in his new home was to embark on his translation of *Buile Suibhne*, a major work from the canon of medieval Irish literature. Its subject matter had an obvious appeal for Heaney, since it was the story of a King of Ulster, Sweeney, who was cursed, turned into a bird, and forced into exile. Though Sweeney 'is always whinging' about the secure and happy days of the past, another more Joycean part of him delights in celebrating his 'free creative imagination'.[123] In undertaking this act of retrieval, he may well have been following the example set by Thomas Kinsella, one of the Republic's foremost poets. In March 1970, Heaney had written an enthusiastic review of Kinsella's fine translation of *The*

Tain, an eighth-century Gaelic epic, praising the poet for his 'large ambition', his adoption of 'a more public stance', his 'conscious and explicit relating of the self to the community', and his effort "to bring a literate Irish public into meaningful contact with its earliest literature".[124] The first version of what was to become *Sweeney Astray* was completed by Heaney in April 1973. Soon afterwards, however, he shelved the project. It had lost some of its momentum when the actor whom he had hoped to cast as Sweeney died. He may also have felt that he had taken too many liberties with the original in endeavouring to draw parallels between the Ulster of 637 and 1973, and refers to the translation as being 'too infected by the idiom of the moment'.[125] Freed from that burden, he would be able to concentrate exclusively on his own original creative work, which offered a far more flexible and effective vehicle for commenting on contemporary issues.

During the same month, his wife presented him with a third child, a daughter, Catherine Ann, an event later celebrated in 'A Pillowed Head' in *Seeing Things*. Late April saw the appearance of Heaney's review of *The Rough Field* by John Montague, an ambitious lyric sequence in ten parts, in which the poet skilfully, but sometimes too artfully, wove the strands and strains of family history and regional history into the larger 'matter of Ireland'. The scale and scope of Montague's book excited many of its first readers and Heaney himself cherished it as "an important poem, an utterance from the underworld of love and bitterness, a sign made in the name of tradition".[126] Over the years Heaney and Montague have clearly derived considerable imaginative impetus from each other's work, and one suspects that the breadth of vision and the architectonic power of *The Rough Field* may well have encouraged Heaney in his use of the wide-angle lens and confirmed him in his decision to shape his next collection, *North*, to a conscious design. Though the two poets at this time are similarly engaged in "a search for metaphor and material", "a retrieval of ancestry, an attempt to shore up more than fragments against the ruin",[127] and share a common historical, cultural, linguistic and emotional terrain, Heaney's repossession of his 'home ground' is achieved with a greater immediacy of feeling, a deeper metaphorical energy, a richer sensuous and aural texture than his mentor can muster.

In July Heaney travelled to London to perform in an adaptation of *The Rough Field* at the Round House, and in August he read at the Yeats Summer School in Sligo. Only in recent years had he explored Yeats's work in any depth. His intensive study had left him with a profound respect for Yeats as a poet, as a promoter of Celtic literature, as a propagandist for others, as a man whose 'purity of motive' and 'enormous creative energy'[128] had inspired the Irish Literary Revival.

Another monumental figure revered by Heaney from late 1973 onwards for his integrity both as a man and artist was the Russian poet, Osip Mandelstam, 'the Lazarus of modern Russian poetry.'[129] His short life was punctuated by social and political turmoil. When he was twenty-three, the Great War broke out; at twenty-six, the Revolution; for the next four years, Civil War; and then in his final years, from 1934–38, he experienced first-hand the obscene brutality of the Stalin era. Banned, interrogated, tortured, exiled and finally condemned to certain death in a labour camps on Stalin's orders, Mandelstam kept faith with words and his words kept faith with him. Deleted from official Soviet literary history, his name and fame were secured as a result of the prodigious efforts of his widow, Nadezhda. Despite war and persecution, she managed to preserve in three school exercise books the work of his last ten years, and in 1971 she herself produced an outstanding memoir of Mandelstam's life, *Hope against Hope*. Together this book and the *Selected Poems* sanctioned Heaney's own attempts to wrest beauty from extremity and to use his art as an expression of his resistance to the 'security forces' and 'fat-necked speculators' who would like to control the world.[130]

July 1973 saw Heaney covering for Radio Eireann the publication of three volumes of verse – *History, For Lizzie and Harriet* and *The Dolphin* – by the great American poet, Robert Lowell. This was for a programme called *Imprint* which Heaney hosted between 1973 and 1977. Lowell was grateful for the younger poet's generous comments, and from the mid-seventies onwards a friendship developed between the two writers which Heaney has described as fortifying. In a relatively recent interview Heaney has said of Lowell, "I loved the ignorance, I loved the destruction he had practised upon the lyric . . . the bull-headedness, the rage and the uncharmingness of the writing attracted me enormously."[131] Though it is generally accepted that the influence of Lowell is most evident in *Field Work*, the attitudes he speaks of admiringly would seem to apply to many of the poems in *North*. Speaking to Harriet Cooke in December 1973, Heaney proclaims:

In Ireland at the moment I would see the necessity, since I'm involved in the tradition of the English lyric, to take the English lyric and make it eat stuff that it has never eaten before . . . like all the messy, and it would seem incomprehensible obsessions in the North.[132]

During October 1973 he made the first of two trips to Denmark, after receiving an invitation from the Danish Association of English Teachers. The experience had "an enhancing effect on me. I saw the Tollund Man in Silkeborg and the Grauballe Man at Aarhus."[133] He had been encouraged to write more 'bog' poems by Ted Hughes, and one result of his second visit to Jutland was the poem, 'The Grauballe Man'.

Reading Glob had given him a taste for archaeology, and this interest was quickened during the early seventies as a result of excavations being carried out by Brendan O'Riordan and Tom Delaney into Dublin's Viking past. The role of the Vikings in history was undergoing a radical reassessment at this time, and the National Museum in Dublin mounted an exhibition which challenged the raping and pillaging stereotype of school history books. Heaney remembers being 'terrifically awakened' by this exhibition, and describes with child-like glee his delight in 'the combs, the little scale- pans and so on . . . all that Bronze Age stuff', and, above all, 'the gold.'[134] In November and December Heaney collaborated with David Hammond on a school series for Northern Ireland's Radio 4, entitled *Explorations*. His texts glisten with images which would find their way into the poems of *North*. In 'Words working', he speaks with relish of the rich and secret treasure within words, drawing the students' attention to the Anglo-Saxon phrase, "opening the word-hoard".[135] During this and subsequent broadcasts in the series, Heaney, in his Yeatsian role as literary propagandist, recommends to his listeners exemplars in the main from within the Irish literary tradition.[136] In a programme entitled 'The Long Garden', he retells the story of St Colmcille who 'exiled himself' from the North of Ireland.

Although he was far from the land he loved, he kept in touch with it, he kept the feel of it, by putting soil from his home place inside his shoes, and literally walking on his home ground, even though he was living miles away from it.[137]

Figuratively, Heaney has continued to walk in Colmcille's footsteps; the rich earth of Mossbawn, along with the dirt and dust of the North has remained and remains firmly lodged in his footwear. Although some people interpreted his move to Glanmore as 'an abdication from Ulster, a running away', and he himself feared that it would marginalise him, such suspicions proved to be unfounded as he himself recognised. History in Ireland has always been reluctant to let people alone, and from 1972 up until the publication of *North* – and since – Heaney admits that he was "up to my neck in it."[138]

Before embarking on an analysis of that collection, it is perhaps appropriate to establish the pattern of events which helped to shape the poet's consciousness during this critical period.

In the months following Heaney's resignation from Queen's, there had been a brief spell of optimism, as a result of a ceasefire between the I.R.A. and the Army. William Whitelaw, the British Home Secretary, held secret talks in London with the leaders of the Provisionals on July 7, but the truce broke down two days later, following clashes in West Belfast. The I.R.A had urged the Army to protect some Catholic families who had been allocated houses on the Lenadoon estate. These people were the victims of sectarian intimidation, and had been forced to leave their homes in Rathcoole. When the U.D.A. threatened that they would burn down any houses at Lenadoon occupied by displaced Catholics, the Army backed away from a confrontation with the Protestant paramilitaries, and turned away a van carrying the Catholics' furniture. Before long a Catholic crowd of some three thousand gathered and began to stone the troops which replied with rubber bullets and C.S. gas. Each side accused the other of breaking the truce.

Two weeks later nine people died in Belfast on 'Bloody Friday' as a result of twenty-two explosions, designed to show that that there was no 'slackening of will' on the part of the Provisionals. Ten days later the Army responded by launching Operation Motorman, occupying 'no-go' areas in West Belfast and the Bogside. In the six months following the ceasefire, from July 9 till the end of 1972, fifty-eight soldiers lost their lives – in comparison with forty-three for the whole of 1971 – and civilian deaths totalled one hundred and eighty-six.

The year 1973 witnessed an almost fifty per cent drop in killings in Ulster, but it also saw the I.R.A. carrying its fight to the British mainland. In London on March 8 two bombs were detonated killing one man and injuring one hundred and eighty. This attack had been timed to coincide with voting in Northern Ireland on whether the border should remain. Catholics boycotted the poll, in which 97.8 per cent of the voters expressed their desire that the North should maintain its links with the United Kingdom. The search for some kind of political solution began in earnest close to the end of that year. In late June polling took place for a new Assembly for Northern Ireland, and in December a conference involving the British and Irish Governments, some of the Unionists under Brian Faulkner, the Nationalist S.D.L.P., and the non-sectarian Alliance Party was convened at Sunningdale in Berkshire, with the aim of setting up an Executive for Northern Ireland in which power could be shared by both Catholics and Protestants. The Sunningdale Agreement also proposed the setting up of a Council of Ireland, with representatives drawn from both parts of the island. In effect this was an admission by London of the legitimacy of the Republic's interest in northern affairs, an admission which ignited fears among the Protestant population that before long the perfidious English would hand them over to the Republic.

On the first day of January 1974 the Northern Ireland Executive took office with the former Stormont premier, Brian Faulkner, as its Chief Executive and Gerry Fitt of the overwhelmingly Catholic S.D.L.P. as his deputy. In the Assembly elections of summer 1973, Unionist supporters of Faulkner held a commanding lead over their opponents, yet after Sunningdale his popularity with rank-and-file Unionists rapidly dwindled. Within four days of the Executive's coming into existence, its authority was challenged by the United Ulster Unionist Council, which voted by 427 to 374 to reject power-sharing and the Council of Ireland. Faulkner's Unionist opponents, led by Harry West and the Reverend Ian Paisley, undermined his position still further when in the Westminster General Election of February 28 they gained eleven out of the twelve available seats. Although Heaney's poem 'Act of Union' belongs to the previous year, its reference to 'an obstinate fifth column/ Whose stance is growing unilateral' seems prophetic in the light of the events of May 1974. The struggle between the power-sharing Executive and its true-blue adversaries reached its climax on the fourteenth of that month. Immediately after winning an Assembly vote by 44 to 28 on the Sunningdale Agreement, the Executive was faced by a devastating strike organised by the Ulster Workers Council, an *ad hoc* body consisting of opposition politicians, trade unionists and paramilitaries. For two weeks from May 15 until May 28, the economic life of the country was paralysed. Power cuts blacked out homes and factories, and petrol supplies dried up. On May 16, the new Labour Secretary of State for Northern Ireland, Merlyn Rees, denounced the strike, accusing its leaders of employing intimidation. He considered – briefly – using the Army to man the power stations, but since this would have involved British troops confronting large numbers of angry Protestant workers, he bowed to senior army advice and held back. Four days into the strike, Loyalist paramilitaries struck out at the Republic. In Dublin and Monaghan town thirty-one people were killed and over a hundred were injured by three car bombs. Two of the three cars used in the attack had been hijacked in Protestant areas of Belfast. With the electricity service's public relations officer predicting "terminal damage to the power plants" and the threat that sewage would shortly be "bubbling through the manhole covers",[139] the power-sharing Executive – along with the British Government which had backed it – was forced to admit defeat. On May 28 Brian Faulkner resigned, the Executive collapsed, and direct rule from Westminster was duly resumed. The following day, the strike was called off, sectarian fears having duly claimed another victory.

Although deeply affected by events such as these, Heaney in *North* avoids the temptation of the instant response to the latest atrocity. Instead by drawing upon two and a half thousand years of European myth and history, he presents in Part One a universalised image of the suffering that attended/ attends the struggle for territory, while in Part Two he maps out the contours of a personal mythology, identifying formative moments from his Catholic past. The *North* poems certainly embody a legitimate anger, but they also display the poet's determination to seek out images, rich in energy, which might serve as a 'binding force' for his community, and provide him with the solace of a shape. *North*'s bi-partite structure itself is an attempt to impose order on the tensions and paradoxes that beset his imagination, to 'marry' external obligation and internal need.

In contrast to the eerie unreality of the violent present which served as the point of departure in *Wintering Out*, the dedicatory poems of *North* respond to the security situation by placing us in a past perfected, a tangible world of warmth, solidarity and almost mellow fruitfulness. 'Sunlight' and 'The Seed Cutters' beautifully invoke the spirit of Mossbawn, transmuting the passionate, transitory world of childhood through the redemptive power of Art. 'Sunlight' opens with a mystery, with the illumination of an 'absence'. The vacancy, however, is quickly filled by one and then two substantial family 'personalities' to which images of light, heat and sweetness accrue. The pump, like its human counterpart, Heaney's Aunt Mary, is realised in the poem as a physical and mythic entity. The adjective, 'helmeted', which initially describes it, suggests not only its shape and its human attributes, but also establishes its role as guardian of the territory. It embodies cast-iron reality, occupies, literally, a concrete place within the Mossbawn scheme of things, yet also serves as a symbol or ikon for the subterranean energies of the place and its people. Through the intercession of the sun, it participates in a miracle, as water collected in the casually 'slung bucket' undergoes a transubstantiation. To a child's eye, even the immensity of the sun can be contained and domesticised, and Time itself can seem to stretch. The sun's huge heat is made comparable to 'a griddle', the word, like 'pump', 'stove', 'goose's wing', 'tinsmith's scoop', 'meal-bin, calling to mind an earlier age. It also serves to smoothe the move from outside to inside the house, from a wall of warmth to a 'plaque of heat', and towards the principal figure of the poem, Mary Heaney, busy at her baking. Her presence is made immediate to us by the poet switching into the present tense on line 17, and dramatically conjured for us by means of the accumulation of visual, sensual detail, ('floury apron', 'whitened nails', 'measling shins'), and verbs emphasising her alternating bursts of activity and passivity ('scuffled', 'stood', 'dusts', 'sits'). Heaney's pleasure in recollection energises the short, enjambed lines, whose momentum is virtually unchecked until a second 'space' appears in line 22. As with the original 'sunlit absence', the poet experiences a sense of fullness, not of loss. Aunt and nephew, baker and writer, pause to allow the 'yeast' to rise in the scones and the poem. Each in their act of making affirm kinship and the depth of family feeling. Despite the tarnishing of time, their love, like the 'tinsmith's scoop', is tangibly 'here' in the present tense, and retains its gleam. In his endeavour to find emotional sustenance in a cold, starved time, to wrest moments, values, rituals from the hard, pervading darkness, Heaney resembles John Montague, who begins section two of his major collection with a short poem dedicated to his Aunt Brigid.[140] She too is depicted, engaged in a quotidian domestic task which has acquired symbolic meaning. Heaney, by means of simple unglamorous 'ingredients' – sunlight, water, honey, scones and meal – and Montague, by means of humble and equally sacred images – hearth, ashes, fire, brands, turf – both endeavour to renew the covenant between past and present, in the hope that hope might have a future.

Aptly Heaney employs the sonnet form in the second 'Mossbawn' poem, 'The Seed Cutters', for, like its companion piece, it is concerned with continuities, reaching back to a pre-colonial, seemingly pre-lapsarian age, 'hundreds of years away', when there was only time to kill, and no thought of killing.[141] Its origins lie in 'images drawn from art', and though it started life as an entry in a prose journal, "the more exactly I described what I remembered, the further and further away it became and it went so far away it turned itself into a sonnet".[142] On the surface, the poem is no more than an affectionate portrayal of a seasonal custom which could be located anywhere in Northern Europe during the last four centuries. His rustics are grouped in a half-circle, kneeling behind an ineffective windbreak which the 'wind is breaking through'. The only 'tuck and frill' in their lives is to be found on the sprouting potato leaves, the only stain 'the dark watermark' inside the milky root. Theirs is a world of innocence and indolence, yet their activity perpetuates the creative cycle, connects them to the earth, and in their deaths they are blessed by the 'broom/ Yellowing over them'. The world which the poet inhabits, however, is the tainted world of experience. Though he delights in using the collective 'us' and 'our', and longs to merge into 'the frieze/ With all of us there, our anonymities', the adult in him *knows* that anonymity and collective security are presently things of the past. Not surprisingly in his reading of the poem for the radio programme, *In their element*, the words 'O calendar customs!' and 'anonymities' are intoned with a heavy cadence. What may have begun to feel like celebration, ends in elegy. "The shelter was once there but is there no longer."[143] In order to ensure the authenticity of his rural scene, Heaney invokes the aid of Pieter Breughel the Elder (c. 1525–69), the Flemish painter, whose work had provided part of the stimulus for 'The Wife's Tale' in *Door into the Dark*. As Ciaran Carson has pointed out, the poet's apostrophe "works perfectly; we realise how Breughel's realism, his faithfulness to minutiae, are akin to Heaney's, and what could have been portentousness takes on a kind of humility."[144] Breughel's art, like Heaney's, is not that of "a retiring escapist. His art shows that he had been the witness of the brutal aspects of contemporary life. The misery of the prisoner, the barbarity of judicial punishment . . . the havoc wrought by soldiers sent to search and destroy."[145] He too belonged to a time when 'religious questions' were 'a matter of life or torture and death'.[146]

After the light, assured touch of the dedicatory poems, *North* proper sets off somewhat lugubriously with 'Antaeus'.[147] The poem dates from 1966, and, like some of his earliest work, it suffers from a profusion of confusing images. His Antaeus, 'flushed as a rose in the morning', is a cave-dwelling wrestler, for whom rubbed sand, taken externally, operates as an 'elixir'. He must be one of the few prize fighter in history who 'cannot be weaned', but considering the 'earth's long contour' is the unlikely breast from which he feeds one can appreciate the scale of his problem. Happily, myth and history are utilised to greater effect in the subsequent cluster of poems, 'Belderg', 'Funeral Rites', 'North', 'Viking Dublin' and 'Bone Dreams', which centre upon the Viking presence in Ireland and Northern Europe as a whole. Their imprint persists in language and landscape – place names such as Mossbawn and Wicklow both have Norse elements – and, despite the passing of a thousand years, a congruence exists between their lives of tribal violence and ours. The occasion behind the initial poem in this sequence, 'Belderg', was a visit the poet made to an archaeological site in Co. Mayo. It covers much of the terrain to be explored in Part One of *North* – bogland, Norse history, etymology, culture and agriculture – and contains many of the collection's characteristic features of style, such as the dense usage of words and images of Anglo-Saxon or Viking origin (*eye, house, quern, stone, wheat, plough*); the occasional use of compound nouns and adjectives (*turf-coomb, stone-wall, world-tree*), the kennings beloved by Norse and Saxon *scops*; Gaelic words (*glib*); archaic and dialect words (*coomb*); vivid linguistic relics from 'the soft-piled centuries', set into two- or three-stressed lines. Almost a sequel to 'Tinder' in 'A Northern Hoard', 'Belderg' examines persistence, change and recurrence. The circle is its dominant shape and symbol, occurring in the images of eyes and the 'growth-rings' of trees, but most obviously in the quernstones, used for grinding of corn. At first these objects merit only a flat, matter-of-fact tone. They are common, and though personified, seem to pose no threat. Gradually, however, the 'charge of primal energy'[148] housed within them comes to affect and afflict the poet. The 'innocence' of wonder in verse two, where he imagines discovering one for himself, soon becomes buried beneath a succession of neolithic sights, 'the first plough-marks', 'stone-age fields', 'stone-wall patternings' which repeated themselves 'In the stone-walls of Mayo'.[149] The more his eyes and ears take in, the more oppressive the massy weight of history becomes. Even changing tack and discussing the music of his old home's name brings him back to invasion, division, separation; its 'foundation' proved as 'mutable as sound'. Even supposedly academic questions – 'moss' from Norse or Planter Scots? Gaelic 'bán' or English 'bawn'? Fort or sanctuary? – conspire with the stones to draw him into a vortex, towards the fatalism of the Norse and perhaps now the Northern psyche. He pictures Yggdrasil, the World-Tree[150] – a Viking equivalent of Jacob's ladder – reduced to an ossified ruin, a skeletal winding stair that leads nowhere. The humble wheels which turn in Heaney's mill are not so different from Yeatsian gyres.

In 'Funeral Rites', one of the highpoints of the collection, Heaney journeys from the natural deaths/unnatural savagery of the past and present towards "a dream of forgiveness, the dream of the possibility of forgiveness."[151] Its descriptive detail, in Part One especially, and depth of feeling anchor the myths the poem floats. As the worksheets for 'Funeral Rites' were published in *Quarto*, a Queen's University literary magazine, in November 1975, it is poss-ible to comment on some of the transitions the poem went through in the making.[152] It takes as its starting point Heaney's detailed recollection of family funerals. In his youth, he had "shouldered *a* kind of manhood" and "the coffins/ of dead relations",[153] though, as we learn later, nothing prepared him for the slaughter on the streets he would witness in his thirties. Like the boy narrator in Joyce's 'The Sisters', he notes dispassionately the face and hands of the dead. In contrast to the scuffling hands and whitened nails of his animated aunt in 'Sunlight', he observes the leaden 'dough-white hands' and darkened nails of the deceased, how curiously in death 'Their puffed knuckles/ had unwrinkled', and how they had been fixed by the living in the same pose of pious submission. With his eye for gentle irony, he compares the rough shroud which covers the body with the finer material which lines its coffin-bed, the 'quilted satin cribs', and contrasts the lively erratic movement of the candles and women with the stasis of the corpse. The only ominous presences are the coffin-lid – but even that is redeemed by its gleaming symbols of Christian consolation – and the likening of the funeral cortège to a 'black glacier', an image which looks back to 'igloo brows' and paves the way for the Viking allusions.[154] That a breach has opened up separating the recent past from the present becomes immediately apparent from the outset of Part Two. The stark adverb, 'Now', ushers in a mournful succession of resonants ('*news*', '*comes*', '*in*', '*neighbourly murder*', '*pine*', '*ceremony*', '*customary rhythms*') and the awful truth that murder occurs with such numbing regularity that the telling of it seems almost to have eclipsed the crime itself. Atrocities have become such frequent and familiar events, whether next door or in the next street, that they merit the epithet, 'neighbourly', a bitterly ironic word, since Christ, the founder of 'the Catholic faith' and 'the Protestant religion', commanded his followers to 'love thy neighbour', not to blast them to Kingdom come.[155] His use of 'we' and 'our' and his later reference to 'the whole country' indicate that Heaney's dream of restoration embraces both communities. Initially it is couched in diction which is highly reminiscent of Yeats, an acknowledgement perhaps of the cultural contribution of the Anglo-Irish tradition. Words such as 'ceremony', 'customary', 'temperate', 'cortège' seem to lead back to Yeats's idealised vision of Urbino and Renaissance Italy, and to the *ordered* world of Coole Park. Heaney, however, seeks his 'place of resurrection' not in ancestral houses, but rather in pre-colonial, pre-sectarian, pre-Christian Ireland. He imagines a mass funeral procession snaking its way out of the North, away from its 'blinded' homes, blinded by grief, blinded by prejudice, blinds drawn in mourning.[156] The mourners' destination would be the ancient tumuli of Newgrange, in the valley of the sacred river, Bo-an or Boyne, 'the fountain of all knowledge'.[157] According to Celtic legends this mound contained the palace of Aengus, the god of love. Perhaps at this place, the bereaved of both communities could perform a joint act of contrition at a new 'sepulchre', and find relief and renewal. Skillfully, the poet shifts scene from the 'great chambers of Boyne' to the 'emptied kitchens' of Belfast, conveys us to the 'cupmarked stones' in 'family cars', mingles the symbolic and the naturalistic. What began as a pilgrimage of woe ends in a consummation devoutly to be wished, as the megalithic womb receives the serpent's head. Perhaps through some such fertility rite, the island could be freed from the spiritual paralysis gripping it. After all, in times past, at these tombs, the barren hoped to find a cure.[158]

The third part of 'Funeral Rites' begins with the sealing of the sepulchre and concludes with an image of resurrection, a further reminder of how the poet retains a love of Christian myths and respect for Christ's values, despite the lamentable behaviour of

'Christians' in Ireland. Driving 'north again/ past Strang and Car-
ling fjords', Heaney recalls in those names the Viking legacy, and
an episode from the thirteenth century Icelandic epic, *Njal's Saga*,
in which the tribal appetite for feuding and revenge is 'allayed for
once'. While the word 'imagining' two lines later may imply that
what follows is just wishful thinking, the scale and clarity of the
vision suggests it may be true. The poet's earnest prayer is that
those in the North who have died in the Troubles may achieve
in death the serenity of Gunnar Hamundarson, "beautiful/ inside
his burial mound." Like the poet, he has earned a respite from the
feuding. His chanting of verses effects a miracle, and, as the chamber
of death opens, he turns to that assuaging, eternal, feminine symbol,
the moon, to achieve release through the rituals of Art.

The following two poems, 'North' and 'Viking Dublin', develop
further contrasts and analogies between contemporary Ireland's and
Europe's Dark Ages. 'North' plunges us immediately back into
cold, salty reality, after the beatific affirmation of 'Funeral Rites'.
Re-visiting the Donegal shoreline to take breath, to take stock, to
find or will some kind of confirmation, Heaney hears at first "only
the secular/ powers of the Atlantic thundering", rather than the
voice of God or Thor. From out of this noise emerges a sound,
warning him against the temptations of 'violence and epiphany',
raiding atrocity to make art. Heaney's admiration for what Magnus
Magnusson has called the 'pent-up dynamism'[159] of the Vikings,
borne in that swashbuckling adjective 'fabulous', is qualified by his
knowledge of the more prosaic facts. Beneath the veneer of religion,
their world too was preoccupied with 'geography and trade', political treachery and violence, 'lies and women'.[160] Heaney's longship
source appears to be 'buoyant' with foresight as well as 'hindsight',
and his scathing attitude towards many members of the 'althing'
(the ancient Icelandic parliament) anticipates the poet's contempt
for the scurvy and cynical politickers in Stormont and Westminster.
The earliest drafts of 'North's seventh stanza speak of 'poets', rather
than 'memory', 'incubating the spilled blood', but both these and
the final version indicate how Heaney is all too aware of the morally
hazardous relationship between art/myth and killing; though the
artist has a responsibility to his community to commemorate the
deaths of 'martyrs in the national struggle', there exists an all
too real danger that the very act of commemoration will breed
further slaughter. Anticipating the advice of Michael McLaverty
in 'Fosterage' ("Go your own way./ Do your own work") and of

develops the features of landscape – Heaney speaks of her 'breasts'/ soft moraines' – and changes after the intimate attentions of the Ice Age, 'the nuzzle of fjords/ at my thighs'. She is rudely awakened from her long hibernation by 'a turfcutter's spade'. Though the injury results in a temporary re-burial, her triumphant re-birth soon follows

> and I rose from the dark,
> hacked bone, skull-ware,
> frayed stitches, tufts,
> small gleams on the bank.

In its images 'Bog Queen' connects itself not merely to earlier poems in *this* collection. 'Turf', 'spade', 'jar of spawn', 'fermenting' and 'bruised berries' hark back to *Death of a Naturalist*. Reversing the process of disintegration with which the poem started, Heaney, as so often before, achieves renewal through marrying elements of national and personal history, through myth and image.

Such moral/ spiritual victories become increasingly uncommon in the remaining 'bog' poems. Whereas 'The Tollund Man' began in a reverential tone, gentle consonants, fertile images and a future tense, 'The Grauballe Man' is tarred by the present, 'and seems to weep/ the black river of himself'. A succession of similes and metaphors drawn from nature – 'the grain of his wrists/ is like bog oak', 'the ball of his heel/ like a basalt egg', 'His instep has shrunk/ cold as a swan's foot' – confine him to his peat-bed. His integration in the animal and vegetative world is perhaps at the expense of his humanity, and all possibility of transcendance seems 'arrested' when 'The head lifts' to expose 'the vent/ of his slashed throat'. Subsequent images struggle against that stark fact, and though Heaney applies healing adjectives ('cured', 'vivid') and positive nouns ('repose', 'elderberry', 'foetus') to the wound, ultimately 'the pain and terror', which Glob saw in the face, assert themselves.[171] In the final three stanzas, Heaney weighs art and actuality, along with 'beauty' and 'atrocity'. However much instinct and imagination urge him to elevate this casualty of religion to the communion of saints, the savage fate suffered by the Grauballe Man compels him towards a heavier conclusion. No-one in the North can or should escape the burden "of each hooded victim/ slashed and dumped", and the evidence of his eyes.[172]

Conflicting loyalties, and pity and guilt, private and collective,

James Joyce in 'Station Island', XII, to resist external pressures,[161] his Viking mentor counsels him to put his trust in the 'nubbed treasure' of the word-hoard' and the 'gleam' of his own private experience. Maintaining the analogy between the North's 'fabulous raiders' of then and now, he compares the artistic enterprise with a 'long foray',[162] its difficulty intensified by the prevailing moral blackness. Like the Norse scops and Celtic bards before him, he will become acclimatised to the task of 'composing in the dark'.[163]

Heaney's preoccupation with lines – of history, poetry and ancestry – continues with 'Viking Dublin: Trial Pieces' and 'Bone Dreams'. In the verse of 'Viking Dublin', he strives to reproduce the buoyancy and speed of the longship, but his craft is impeded by its cumbersome ballast, its diverse and bewildering imagery.[164] In section IV, he self-mockingly compares his predicament, and his ineffectuality, with that of Hamlet, an act of ironic identification which has prompted a charge of 'posturing' from one critic.[165] Rather the extended allusion illustrates his anxiety over the equivocal and equivocating role of the poet, over the parasitical relationship that can exist between art and violence, concerns which will surface again in 'Punishment'. A more justifiable objection to this part of the poem might centre upon the tenuous connections linking the Vikings and *Hamlet*. 'Bone Dreams' is a pivotal poem within the first part of *North* since it concludes one sequence and initiates another. Behind it lies a Joycean longing to wreak vengeance upon England for the cultural and linguistic violence it has done to Ireland, and the political violence it still does. However, after announcing his readiness to employ his 'sling of mind' against the Philistines, this would-be Samson/David quickly succumbs to the seductive pleasures of the invaders' language and landscape. His imagination is aroused by these 'strange fields', which yield to his attention one particularly sacred relic, the compound word, 'bone-house'. He may well have first encountered this Anglo-Saxon kenning for the human body in Hopkins, as it features in the opening lines of 'The Caged Skylark', "As a dare-gale skylark scanted in a dull cage/ Man's mounting spirit in his bone-house, mean house dwells."[166] During his fosterage at St Columb's and at Queen's, he had discovered in language and literature, and the 'tongue's/ old dungeons', a surrogate home. Though *ban-hus* could never eclipse Mossbann, nevertheless its associative potency encourages him to undertake yet another pilgrimage back through time and 'dictions', in order to hear "the scop's/ twang, the iron/ flash of consonants/

cleaving the line", and to re-create that austere first world of English. It generates also the image of the mead-hall, where, like a bird, 'the soul/ fluttered a while/ in the roofspace', which had joined the barn – described in *Death of a Naturalist* – as a permanent construct in his memory. In preparation for the erotic explorations which will follow, the focus shifts at the end of section three from the 'small crock' of the brain, of indeterminate gender, towards an identifiably female 'structure', to the hearth of the *ban-hus*, where the 'cauldron/ of generation/ swung'. The domesticity of that image seems to clash rather with the more emphatic sexuality/animality implicit within 'love-*den*' and 'blood-*holt*', and with the romanticism of 'dream-bower'.

From the womb of words he moves to the origins of conflict, which began with England's occupation of Ireland. In contrast to the rapes to be depicted in 'Ocean's Love to Ireland' and 'Act of Union', his 'invasion' of England is a lyrical affair, a gentle love-act, in which the partners 'end up/ cradling each other'. After touring the pretty erogeneous regions of Wessex and Northumbria, in the course of which he visits Maiden Castle and Hadrian's Wall, and somewhat fancifully portrays himself as the Cerne Abbas giant, his final destination is Devon and death. The dead mole discovered there provides yet another image for England, complete with 'Pennines' and a rich 'pelt of grass and grain/ running south', but serves also as a *memento mori*, like the white bone with which the poem began.[167]

Paradoxically, it is in a series of poems about sacrificial victims of the Iron Age that Heaney attempts to confront the barbarity of the present. Many readers have difficulty coming to terms with these 'bog' poems. Some even 'recognise' in them the poet's 'necrophiliac' tendencies, or his 'neo-sadism',[168] but this is to be unaware of the fact that underneath the sexual topsoil allegorical material lies buried. Their subject is the Republican tradition, and how the cruelties inflicted upon 'dark-bowered queen', Mother Ireland, Kathleen ni Houlihan, Shan van Vocht, have brutalised her sons, engendering a love of territory and ancestry that can carry them to appalling extremes. The title of the very first bog poem comes from a Republican song, 'Will you come to the bower?', which celebrates the wild and terrible beauties of Ireland and its martyrs. By appealing to their love of religion, landscape and history, by invoking the sacred names of St Patrick, Brian Boru who 'drove the Danes', O'Neill, O'Donnell and O'Connell, the song calls on Ireland's exiles and sons to rally to the mother country, "Where

the soil is sanctified by the blood of each true man. analogies between ancient cults and contemporary cult endeavours to explain the persistence in Northern Ir fiercely defensive, and, at times, pitilessly destructive i that of its twin – Loyalism. On a simpler level, these his continuing relishing of the bogland landscapes, and at the fragments and treasures they cast up. They bear w determination to retrieve some shards of hope and beau in the scales against 'atrocity'.

The sequence opens with two dramatic monologues nated by this unappeasable goddess of the ground. T queen of 'Come to the Bower' and 'Bog Queen' is anoth tion of Nerthus, the earth goddess, to whom the Tollun sacrificed. Though for centuries pinned to the bog by willow' rods, she is now undergoing a resurrection. She for renewal, and 'spring water/ Starts to rise around tense is not past perfect, but present continuous. The measured account she gives of herself in the second poen with the nervous sexual excitement expressed in the fi eagerness to possess her, her finder disregards 'the burst Of coin-hoards', hungering instead for 'the bullion/ Of bone'. For him, her whole being is compressed into that of bliss, but for the reader the queen has no real identity clearly associated with natural forces, the images of 's and tangled vetch' and the 'fox's brush' suggest that. the physical description with which we are provided, con item one 'The pot of the skull', item two 'The damp tuck curl/ Reddish as a fox's brush', and item three, 'A mark of in the flesh/ Of her throat', seems so cursory that the boc bog remains an abstraction.

In 'Bog Queen', however, she enjoys the advantages of and a history. In the Spring of 1781, in a peat bog on Drun Mountain in County Down, the skeleton of 'very small was discovered on land belonging to Lord and Lady Moi numerous garments on and around the body and the "orn found on the skull . . . belonging to a diadem" indicated t was a lady of high rank, probably a Danish Viking.[170] The of Heaney's poem accepts the indignities of Time with fo and confidence in her ultimate salvation. Like the dispos people of her adopted home, she survived centuries of 'w by becoming at one with the land and its sufferings. Her

supply 'Punishment' with its emotional charge. One of the very major achievements of *North*, it embodies and dramatises Heaney's 'contradictory awarenesses'. Acutely distressed by the humiliations inflicted upon the 'scapegoat' victims of communal intolerance, he nevertheless recognises the legitimacy of the community's feelings of betrayal. "At one minute," he observes "you are drawn towards the old vortex of racial and religious instinct, at another time you seek the mean of humane love and reason."[173] Though ashamed of his passive complicity in the brutal 'justice' meted out on young women who had gone out with British soldiers or who were suspected of acting as informers – they were shaved, tarred and feathered, and tied or chained to railings – he concludes that simply to condemn such acts would constitute 'connivance' with the historical enemy. After all, as the events of August 1971 – January 1972 had recently shown, they could not always be relied on to show 'humane love' or civil reason.[174]

The material for 'Punishment' is again drawn from *The Bog People*.[175] In it perspectives shift constantly as Heaney struggles to establish a tenable position. The poem begins assertively with a dramatic statement in which the author identifies himself with the Windeby girl and her tragic fate. The regularity of 'the tug/ of the halter' is conveyed in the rhythm of alternating anapests ($\cup\cup$/) and iambs ($\cup$/), and reinforced by stressed consonants ('k', 'f', 't', 'h', 'n') and vowels (' Λ ', ' eɪ ', ' ɜ '). Though he feels for her in her defencelessness – alone with her executioners and the kinder 'wind/ on her naked front' – the repeated third person possessive adjective, 'her', effects a separation between his imagined and her actual exposure. The 'divorce' is evident in the long shots from verse three onwards, as touch gives way to sight. Distanced in Time, dehumanised by a succession of images in which she is compared to 'a barked sapling', transformed into 'oak bone', her blond hair reduced to 'a stubble of black corn', she undergoes a restoration in verses five to seven, regaining human attributes, albeit those of a condemned prisoner. Brighter references from earlier versions to 'her red/ and yellow headband', her 'soiled halo',[176] Heaney suppresses, in order to concentrate on the starkness of 'blindfold' and 'noose'. By means of this ironic 'ring', in which her brief 'memories of love' will be stored forever, she is led to her drowning, a scene that Heaney can picture so vividly that he is moved to address her directly. Artfully he excites our sympathy for the girl with a series of adjectives – Little', 'flaxen-haired', 'undernourished', 'beautiful'

– which have the effect of diminishing her guilt. He goes further, for in calling her a 'scapegoat', he invites a comparison between her fate and that of Christ, sacrificed to atone for the sins of the community. "I almost love you", he declares, but that qualifying adverb proves crucial, and the 'acquittal' one might have expected never materialises. Instead Heaney shifts our attention from the accused to the accusers, and the equally culpable onlookers, like himself. He admits that he lacks the moral courage shown by Christ when he confronted the Pharisees, who were determined to stone the woman taken in adultery.[177] Like so many within the frightened enclaves of the North, he would not have intervened to save the girl, but rather,

> would have cast, I know,
> the stones of silence.

Stirred to self-reproach, he condemns himself as merely an 'artful voyeur', conscious that he has been in a sense exploiting the girl's body in order to satisfy an *artistic* need for resolution. Although his liberal education and conscience make him incline towards 'civilized outrage', witnessing the degrading punishment inflicted on her 'betraying sisters' of today, 'imaginatively'[178] he can understand the reasoning behind the brutally 'exact' laws of the tribe. To understand is not to condone, nor to be freed from conflicting allegiances which threaten to make him a traitor.

The next poem in the collection derives its title of a mournful Billie Holliday song, depicting white 'justice' in the southern United States. Innocent blacks, lynched by racist mobs and left to hang on trees, are referred to as 'strange fruit'. Heaney's sonnet stares unremittingly at the decapitated head of a girl exhumed from the Roum Fen in northern Denmark in June 1942. The familiar pattern of associations – which sees her compared to a baby ('unswaddled') and to fruit and other flora ('gourd', 'prune-skinned', 'prune-stones', 'fern'), and views her head as a mirror of her landscape ('Her broken nose . . . a turf clod', 'Her eyeholes blank as pools in the old workings') – Heaney breaks in the last four lines, realising that the metaphor game – or his 'artful voyeurism' – is leading him towards 'beatification', 'reverence', consolation. Just in time he redeems himself with a grim catalogue of adjectives that stick with the cruel facts, and allowing the victim to retain its desolate integrity.

In 'Kinship', the last of the bog poem sequence, Heaney returns to his home territory, to turn over his 'memories of wilderness/ on the kitchen mat' after his long journeyings, literal and imagined, to Denmark and Iceland. Ireland, his Ireland is also the land of 'the strangled victim', but as he paces among the fields of peat, delighting again their springy feel and watery sounds, their 'cheeps and lisps', he tastes again the innocent *frisson* of childhood awe in images since stained with adult experience – 'black', 'incisions', 'ritual', 'a gallows drop'.[179] Terribly familiar, accessible, impenetrable, this ambiguous landscape is both lyrical, 'a moon-drinker' and, at the outset of part two, loathsome. The flax-dam, where innocent frogs once 'gathered for vengeance', has been annexed into the killing fields, 'domains of the cold-blooded'. In an attempt to halt himself from sinking totally into synonymity,[180] Heaney grasps hold of the Gaelic roots of the word, 'bog', 'meaning soft'. Delicate, visual metaphors are succeeded by a series of kennings, accentuating the scale of the bog in time and space, depicting it as a massive living organism. It manifests itself first as a huge stomach and a womb ('Ruminant ground', 'deep pollen bin'); a store-house ('Earth-pantry', 'sun-bank'); a necropolis ('bone-vault'), preserving with equal care both human gifts ('votive goods') and victims ('sabred fugitives'). Personified, it becomes an 'enbalmer', a comic circus-performer ('Sword-swallower'), and most menacingly, an 'Insatiable bride', like the man-consuming goddess, Nerthus, in Part Three. Finally, landscape transforms itself into mindscape through which the 'floe of history' passes, creating fertile areas of 'nesting ground' for the imagination, but also a less inviting region, the 'outback' of uncertainty.

After his long engagement to – and with – his enigmatic mistress, a symbolic consummation occurs in the third section of 'Kinship'. Certainly the insistent sexual allusions to the 'soft lips of growth', the 'tawny rut', the 'bearded cairn', the 'love-nest', 'the cloven oak-limb', and to the 'wettish' and 'upright' shaft of the phallic spade, stress the intensity of the bond – physical, psychological, emotional, and spiritual – between the poet and his ground. Their deeper function, in this poem and in *North* as a whole, however, lies in Heaney's desire to bring about the *political* and *cultural* repossession of Ireland after centuries of English occupation. What may have begun as a private love-act with words has developed into a conscious endeavour to articulate the Irish Catholic identity. At what he perceived to be a turning point in the history of the island, not surprisingly he wished to emphasise the contribution which could be made by *Northern* Catholics in the process of cultural renewal and reclamation. The turf-spade, which has lain hidden, 'overgrown' with a mossy 'green fog' – the ;fecund fog of unconsciousness'?[181] – he retrieves and sets up as an 'obelisk', regarding it as another piece of 'treasure trove', "a symbol of what and who we take ourselves to be as a nation."[182] It could, and has been argued, however, that while the bog and the spade have excellent Celtic credentials, images such as the 'cloven oak-limb', and indeed the whole Nerthus myth, exclude rather embrace, mystify rather than illuminate, unless one has read Glob, that is.[183] Stepping back from the myth for a moment, in Part Four Heaney records 'the wheel of the year' which 'turned on the hub of the bog'. In contrast to his prose account in which human responses take centre stage,[184] the poem emphasises the natural cycle, when each season slipped into the next as lyrically as his enjambed verses. The opening lines ('This centre holds/ and spreads') refute those of Yeats in 'The Second Coming', delivering us seemingly into a world of harmonies and integration, where even death is easeful, a gentle cadence, 'a melting grave'. Having composed himself and lulled the reader into this maudlin mood, he breaks the spell in the final stanzas, firstly through the shock of the word 'rots' and the hanging preposition 'into', and secondly by means of wry self-mockery.

> I grew out of all this
> like a weeping willow
> inclined to
> the appetites of gravity.

The melancholy sight of a turf-cart at the beginning of Part Five recalls the hidden spade of Part Three, but, like the spade, it is retrieved from Time to be 'perfected' in the poet's memory. Seeing again the hand-carved felloes and the 'cupid's bow' rekindles his reverential love for his great-uncle, Hughie Scullion, the mythic being who drove the cart and disseminated warmth. In contrast to Dylan Thomas's *self*-centred paeans to childhood, "honoured among waggons I was prince of the apple towns",[185] Heaney's celebrations laud adult heroes, who irradiate power and glory, and depict his own role as secondary. The circle the 'god' and the 'squire' describe, like kinship, includes, confirms, enfolds. Re-experiencing this delight, he converts 'I' to 'we', past tense to present, statement to command. A simple journey acquires the status of a royal 'progress', and the 'squire' the pride and status of a man.

Having been addressed by one voice of his education, he turns to address another in the concluding part of 'Kinship'. Heaney appeals to the Roman historian, Tacitus, to verify the accuracy of his account of contemporary Ireland. Written in the first century A.D., his book, *Germania*, had given an account of the rituals of the ancient Celts, and their sacrifices in honour of the goddess, Nerthus. Her festivities commenced with 'journeyings through the countryside' in her sacred waggon, and were completed with 'the drowning of the goddess's attendants' in lakes or bogs.[186] Heaney recognises that although the goddess of territory has stimulated and sustained his poetic energies, during these self-same period she has excited others to channel their frustrated energies – political, spiritual, sexual even – into horrific acts of slaughter. As Seamus Deane has succinctly put it, "the roots of poetry and violence grow in the same soil."[187] Where once 'Our mother ground' was strewn with 'sour' autumnal leaves (Part IV), now it is 'sour with the blood/ of her faithful'. Adherents of the 'sacred heart' of Nerthus in both 'Christian' communities vie with each other in supplying her with daily transfusions, while the bemused 'legions', the British troops sent in by Westminster in August 1969, look on from their fortified barracks.[188] This poem has no time for the pious tentative hope expressed in 'The Tollund Man' that the killings might serve as a fertility rite. In answer to the question Yeats posed in 'Easter 1916' after the bloody aftermath of the Rising, 'O when may it suffice?', Heaney replies that for the inhabitants of this 'island of the ocean', like their Iron Age ancestors, 'nothing will suffice'. With bitter irony, he concludes that perhaps the best Ireland can hope for is a balanced analysis from a historian of the calibre of Tacitus, who will take into account the 'noble' principles behind the butchery. This kind of stark 'self-lacerating recognition'[189] reminds one of another poet 'unhappy, and at home' in the North of Ireland, who wrote in the year of Heaney's birth,

> I envy the intransigence of my own
> Countrymen who shoot to kill and never
> See the victim's face become their own
> Or find his motive sabotage their motives.[190]

In the next section of *North*, Heaney pinpoints two crucial moments in the historical conflict between Ireland and England, in order to account for the re-emergence of archetypal patterns of human behaviour in contemporary Ireland. Both 'Ocean's Love to Ireland' and 'Act of Union' offer allegorical versions of history, depicting 'the rape of the territories of Ireland.'[191] One of the precedents for Heaney's portrayal of Ireland as a 'ruined' maid and England as her conscienceless, hypocritical attacker can be found in the work of the seventeenth century Munster poet, Aodhagán ó Rathaille (Egan O'Rahilly), to whom a chapter of *The Hidden Ireland* is devoted. In 'The Wounds of the Land of Fodla', he anticipates Ireland's future under colonial rule,

> Beir feasta aca it mhéirdrigh fé
>   ga críonchóisir,
> 'S gach ladrann caethach d'éis
>   do chlí-dheólta.

> Henceforth shalt thou be an unwilling
>   handmaid to every withered band,
> While every foreign churl shall have
>   sucked thy breasts.[192]

'Ocean's Love to Ireland' debunks the myth of English 'civility' in its treatment of what is euphemistically termed Anglo-Irish 'relations' between the late sixteenth and early eighteenth centuries, the period of the 'wars of extermination' (Yeats). Borrowing a scene from John Aubrey's *Brief Lives*, Heaney presents Sir Walter Ralegh, so gallant a courtier and so lyrical a poet for his Queen, raping one of her 'Mayds of Honour'.[193] As Ralegh 'drives inland' and extends the Pale southwards, linguistic violence follows in the trail of military conquest. Heaney implicates him not merely in the massacre of six hundred Spanish 'papists' at Smerwick, Co. Kerry, in 1580 – they had been sent to help in the Munster rebellion against Elizabeth – but also in the destruction of Gaelic culture. Thanks to Ralegh and his fellow colonist, Edmund Spenser, the woods that inspired the Gaelic bards now resound to the incessant beat of the 'Iambic drums/ Of English'. The sexual-political analogy is employed with greater immediacy in 'Act of Union'. A 'pregnancy poem',[194] its composition coincided with his wife's third pregnancy which lasted from the summer of 1972 until the spring of 1973. In its earliest draft, it looks like becoming another uncertain love poem. What began as a celebration of her human geography, and an admission of his clumsiness as a male,[195] veers away from sexual politics towards the unholy coupling of Ireland with her next door neighbour in its first published form in *The Listener* (22 February 1973). Entitled 'A New Life', this version consists of four sonnets, and introduces specific references to Ireland's colonial history, exposing the rawness of the wounds in the Irish mind, memory, tongue, body, landscape.[196] The transformation of these four sonnets into the two sonnets of 'Act of Union' occurred following a 'mini-Group discussion' in Wicklow. Philip Hobsbaum writes:

> I was staying with Heaney in Glanmore Cottage when he showed me 'A New Life'. Another guest at the house at the time was Anne Stevenson. We had a mini-group discussion over the drafts. Both Anne and I thought the poem was too long and I think I am right in saying that I suggested how it might be cut; I also supplied the title. (But I don't want to minimise Anne's role in this – it was a discussion, not a tutorial!) But of course behind any group discussion is the fact that no poet of any talent will take what seems to him a bad suggestion.[197]

'Act of Union' is a tighter, leaner poem than its predecessor. It is set in dramatic motion with three brief phrases, heralding a flood, or rather a 'gash' of energy. The aloofness of the narratorial voice is immediately conveyed by the 'aerial' view he gives of his beloved. After a brief proprietorial caress, the speaker makes it plain to his listener that the only feasible response to his enforced suit is submission, "I am the tall kingdom over your shoulder/ That you would neither cajole nor ignore." In contrast to the colonial power in 'A New Life' which admits to the 'dark deeds' it has committed against Ireland – "And as my secret papers come on show/ You rightly drag my name into the mud" – this England reveals no trace of guilt over the 'legacy' he has bequeathed to Ireland, the 'heaving province' of Ulster, which has come to a hideous maturity. His choice of the word 'inexorably' to describe this process implies that the 'rending' in the colony has a certain inevitability about it; it is all a matter of fate, rather than human – i.e. his – responsibility.

The dispassionate tone continues into the second sonnet, which notes how the union has spawned 'an obstinate fifth column', even now 'Mustering force'. Although the monstrous, 'ignorant', 'parasitical' child sired by England is generally taken to be a reference to Protestant paramilitaries, as some commentators have pointed out, the I.R.A. can equally be viewed as the offspring of the rape; both have a passing family resemblance to Yeats's 'rough beast', and threaten not just the health and security of the mother, but also that of the father. Narrator and author join together in the poem's conclusion, which sees no end in sight to Ireland's anguish. For Heaney, the wounds created by the Act of Union will always remain 'raw' in the Irish consciousness. Treaties and truces might provide temporary relief, but they can never heal the 'running sore',[198] After all it was an Anglo-Irish treaty in 1921 partitioning Ireland which bred the present Troubles.

The poems which make up Part Two of *North* spring from "a need to be explicit about the pressures and prejudices watermarked into the psyche of anyone born and bred in Northern Ireland."[199] Perspectives narrow as the focus settles on recent history, private myth and anecdote. Appropriately the language becomes more conversational, less poetically charged, as Heaney settles into a form and a style which will both complement and contrast with those of the first half. Both 'The Unacknowledged Legislator's Dream' and 'Whatever you say, say nothing' see Heaney wedged into a corner, expected to make some kind of statement, to take up some kind of political stance. In the former, the poet finds himself trapped in a Kafkaesque nightmare, a prisoner in a land of cages. The commandant is another 'Hercules', an eminently rational being, who reassures his honoured guest that the security provided by the bars is infinitely preferable to the chaos on the other side. Rejecting this 'civil' advice, Heaney tests his weight on the cell floor, to assess his chances of digging his way out. In 'Whatever you say, say nothing', Heaney has been cornered by an English journalist, demanding his 'views/ on the Irish thing', soon after his return to Belfast. Impatient at the latest invasion of Ireland, by analysts and hacks whose paraphernalia 'Litter the hotels', whose experience of

> the long campaign from gas
> And protest to gelignite and sten

has convinced them of their rights to the territory – and impatient too with his own tight-lipped 'servility'[200] in speaking to them – he asserts defensively, 'Yet I live here, I live here too'. His annoyance at their intrusiveness and their clichés is nothing compared to the scorn he heaps on himself and his fellow countrymen. For too long he and they have connived in a conspiracy of 'evasion and compliance',[201] which has made co-existence possible, but has left bigotry intact. Now that 'gelignite's a common sound effect', the 'voice of sanity' and civility – and stasis – can scarcely be heard; and the 'liberal papist note' cannot compete with the cacophonies, 'That shake all hearts and windows day and night'. Just as he had to in 'Strange Fruit' and 'Act of Union', he checks his natural tendency towards optimism. Ironically, one of the problems with the second section of the poem is that the author ends up saying too much about himself and his problems. At a time when 'Men die at hand' (Yeats, 'Meditations in Time of Civil War'), his personal anxieties over his 'pestering/ Drouth for words' and his longing 'To lure the tribal shoals to epigram/ And order' seem somewhat minor matters.[202] In Part Three, he castigates the offensive nature of society in the North. Sectarianism permeated not only government, institutions, education, employment and housing. Even the simplest social exchange required shifty "Manoeuvrings to find out name and school". At the root of 'The famous/ Northern reticence', he suggests, is paranoia, bred by a siege mentality. Comparing Ulster's Catholics with the 'wily Greeks' trapped inside the Wooden Horse could hardly reassure Protestant readers. When the siege of Troy was lifted, the Trojans were not given the option of peaceful integration within Achaean society; they were enslaved or massacred. Now the protest movement had exposed the rottenness in the state, his fervent wish was that "the great dykes the Dutchman made"[203] would collapse. His decision to end 'Whatever you say, say nothing' with the dedicatory verses from *Wintering Out* indicates his fear that the dykes, ramparts, stockades and camps are likely to remain in place for a while yet.

That the Catholic Church had collaborated in and contributed to the political and spiritual repressiveness of the North is the charge levelled by Heaney in 'Freedman' and the opening section of 'Singing School', 'The Ministry of Fear'. In the former he equates the success of children from the Catholic working class and small-farmer class in the wake of the 1947 Education Act with the achievements of former slaves who reached major positions of authority in imperial Rome, as well as referring to his own intellectual liberation during the Group years. In the latter he hints at the psychological scarring that accompanied the process of academic enfranchisement, thanks to kindly ministers from Church and State. 'Freedman' begins with an epigraph from *The Romans* by

R. H. Barrow, which states that "*A man from a 'backward' race might be brought within the pale of civilization, educated and trained in a craft or a profession, and turned into a useful member of society.*" Appropriately the poem's first word is of Latin origin. 'Subjugated' sets both theme and mood, and receives prompt support from 'Manumitted', meaning 'released from slavery', and 'murex', a shellfish which yielded a purple dye, a colour associated with Lent. Whereas at home, in South Derry, the liturgical cycle was locked into the rhythms of the countryside – rushes for St Brigid's Eve, buttercups and ladysmock for May Eve[204] – at school too often it seemed 'all fast and abstinence' and ashy submission. Each Ash Wednesday, when the priest recited the words, '*Memento homo, quia pulvis es*', 'Remember, Man, you are dust', as he badged their foreheads with 'the mortal dust',[205] the Northern faithful were reminded of their lowly status in the scheme of things. Already suffering political and economic discrimination, their feelings of inferiority were intensified by the clergy, who exuded authority like the 'groomed optimi', the senatorial class in Ancient Rome.[206] Heaney confesses to having been 'under that thumb', until poetry 'arrived' in that city – thanks principally to Philip Hobsbaum – wiped his brow, and secured for him a new source of the sacred. Ironically, the final line, 'Now they will say I bite the hand that fed me' betrays something suspiciously like guilt. The print of the ash is indelible.

'Singing School', *North*'s final sequence, develops the trial motif, proffering snatches of autobiography in which the poet is 'arraigned', but not 'freed' ('From the Frontier of Writing'). Interrogations by police and priests experienced or witnessed in childhood and in early manhood give way in the later sections to stern self-questionings from and about the present. Accused and self-accused, he attempts to defend himself from the charge of evasion by asserting his identity as a creative artist, and invokes the aid of major figures from native, English and European tradition to justify and verify his stance. His title, derived from Yeats's 'Sailing to Byzantium', refers to the Platonic idea of the soul enriching itself through the contemplation of great works of art,

> Nor is there singing-school but studying
> Monuments of its own magnificence.

The six poems embrace allusions to Kavanagh, Joyce, Wordsworth, Hopkins, Katherine Mansfield, Graham Greene, Lorca, Goya and

Osip Mandelstam, a litany of names almost as potent to his memory as Mossbawn, Moyola and Anahorish. In 'The Ministry of Fear' he celebrates having come through four ordeals in his teenage years; his experience of exile and brutality while 'billeted' at St Columb's; his first flirtation with poetry; the beginnings of sexual initiation, when "I came to life/ In the kissing seat of an Austin Sixteen"; and finally a cross examination by a crass R.U.C. patrol. What must have been moments of extreme stress and distress are re-examined through a filter of irony, bathos, self-deprecation. Homesick and abandoned at boarding school, he throws away the biscuits 'left to sweeten my exile'. Unflatteringly, Heaney compares this act of pique with the 'act of stealth' carried out by the young Wordsworth, when he 'borrowed' a skiff for the night and slipped out onto Patterdale water. Several lines later his supposedly clumsy attempts on the Muse are contrasted with the proficient efforts of his companion from school and university, Seamus Deane. In Deane's graceful, 'svelte' verses, 'Vowels and ideas bandied free', yet when he comes to describe his own endeavours to find a voice, he portrays himself as a country oaf, his 'hobnailed boots' stomping all over 'the fine/ Lawns of elocution." This image connects language with property, sound with race and class, and was probably influenced by the opening line of 'Ancestral Houses', in Yeats's 'Meditations in Time of Civil War', which speaks of 'a rich man's flowering lawns' and of his *'planted* hills'. Certainly the whole accent of the poem shifts towards the psychological violence of racial conditioning – "'Catholics, in general, don't speak/ As well as students from the Protestant schools.'" – and the physical abuse committed in the name of Mother Church or Father State, both of whom aimed to keep heads 'bowed'. Dissonances feature prominently in subsequent episodes. The sadism of the Big Study is conveyed partly through the onomatopoeic qualities of the words 'strap' and 'epileptic', and also by means of the reference to the 'echoes plashing', sound effects designed no doubt *pour encourager les autres*. The sexual fumbling and murmuring inside the Austin is accompanied unromantically by the reverberations of the engine, left running for warmth and a quick getaway. The light and buoyant mood and rhythm in this scene – 'the air/ All moonlight and a scent of hay' – capturing the exhilaration of 'summer's/ Freedom', are undercut by the sudden appearance of the policemen, who at first seem to present only a bovine threat, "crowding round/ The car like cattle, snuffing". This cosy, rural image is rapidly modified when he mentions the 'muzzle' of the sten-gun being pointed at his eye. Their repetition of his name – *'Seamus?'* – indicates their pleasure at having stopped a Taig and/or their disbelief that one of the peasants should be driving a car. Though they seize Heaney's private letters as an assertion of their authority – or in the hope of discovering something incriminating – Deane's florid 'hieroglyphics' prove indecipherable. Members of the Protestant majority might still control the roads and most of the territory of Ulster, but Heaney and Deane had begun to stake their claim to the English lyric. By making 'full chimes' in their own tongue, they could defeat 'the ministry of fear'.

After employing traditional decasyllabic blank verse for this first poem, he returns to the book's dominant verse form, the taut short-lined quatrain, in the second, third and sixth sections, 'A Constable Calls', 'Orange Drums, Tyrone 1966' and 'Exposure'. In 'A Constable Calls' Heaney recollects the anxiety and 'Small guilts' he experienced as a child during the visit of a policeman, sent to check details of his father's crops. Our attention is initially focussed on the bicycle leaning against the window-sill, an intrusion in the Mossbawn yard. The images with which it is described – 'rubber *cowl*', *'fat black* handlegrips', 'the 'spud'/ Of the dynamo gleaming and *cocked back*', the pedals 'hanging *relieved* / Of the *boot* of the law' – alienate the reader even before we meet the unperson to whom it belongs. The policeman is portrayed as a 'shadow' being, rather than as an individual. His uniform makes him the embodiment of the Protestant State, and, like his bike, he seems composed of distinctly separate features – a cap, sweating hair, a polished holster, braid cord, a baton-case, a voice without a face. Heaney's introduction of his child self in the fifth stanza is prompted by the reference to 'acres, roods, and perches', measurements which conjure memories of primary school Arithmetic lessons. The secure, familiar worlds of home and classroom, however, are jeopardised by the presence of this armed stranger. Like the peasant boy, Luis, in Graham Greene's *The Power and the Glory*,[207] the young Heaney cannot at first take his eyes from this object of fear and fascination. Entrancement turns to alarm when he hears the constable's inquiry as to whether his father is growing any root crops being met with a denial. It is a lie. An accessory to his father's crime, he pictures the place of retribution.

> I assumed
> Small guilts and sat

Imagining the black hole in the barracks.

Any relief he may have felt as the policeman rises to go is immediately qualified by the sight of the 'baton-case' and the ominous description of the ledger as 'the domesday book'. Having lived through Ulster's Armageddon as an adult, with its bombs, bullets (metal and plastic), C.S. gas, killings and maimings, the solitary R.U.C. man on his ticking bike seems almost a figure from an age of innocence.

In the third and fourth parts of 'Singing School' – 'Orange Drums, Tyrone 1966' and 'Summer 1969' – Heaney records the approach and arrival of the dark cyclonic violence, yet in the fifth he retreats temporarily into 'pre-lapsarian' Belfast and affirmative experience, a meeting with the writer, Michael McLaverty. Both the title, which refers to an ancient Gaelic custom,[208] and the dedication to the poem, indicates Heaney's gratitude to McLaverty, one of his most important literary 'benefactors'. A past and present master – his major novel, *Call my Brother Back*, was published in the year of Heaney's birth – he stressed to the young poet the virtues of originality ('Go your own way'), of economy ('Don't have the veins bulging in your biro'), the value of intimate detail, and the emotive power within 'that note of exile'.[209] He comes across in Heaney's poem as an earnest, assertive, but sensitive man for whom art has 'become a life', a lyric and moral force which grips. His position as a headmaster is reflected in the fact that five of the six sentences he utters are commands, yet the sixth shows his empathy for Hopkins and his suffering. Certainly he confirmed in Heaney his sense of the high seriousness of the poet's vocation, for "he sent me out, with words/ Imposing on my tongue like obols."

The transition from 'Fosterage' to 'Exposure' is a journey from certitude to uncertainty. The very title suggests a feeling of vulnerability, and indeed the poem as a whole is an act of self-exposure, a confession of his fear that he has missed a 'once-in-a-lifetime portent' by going into exile at Glanmore, and of his unease at being exposed to the criticism of friends and foes. Equally unsettling was the exposure he was receiving from the media, which confusingly expected more pronouncements on political developments in the North once he was settled in the South. The poem begins simply, evocatively, with a spareness of which McLaverty would have approved. Trochaic cadences dominate the first verse ('Wick*low*', 'Al*ders*', 'drip*ping*', 'bir*ches*'), whose chill, dank images mirror the state of Heaney's spirit, which longs for summer and an abundance of light. He tries to escape from the drag of physical realities, 'damp leaves' and wintry discontent, by indulging in visions of *Should* and *If*. He imagines glimpsing the 'comet that was lost', and coming upon fragments of 'meteorite' – hard, bright words which might open up possibilities of definition, illumination, renewal – but the chances of either happening seem as remote to him now as the season of 'haws and rose-hips'. Even though he is in a dejected mood, he refuses to discount the notion of resistance. The hero he sets down 'On some muddy compound' seems a composite portrait, the sling suggesting David and Cuchulain, the 'compound' an Irish political prisoner or perhaps the Russian poet, Osip Mandelstam, who paid for his gift and his words of defiance in exile, pain and death. The thought of such men of action, of such exemplary moral integrity intensifies Heaney's feelings of inadequacy, his doubts about the value of his own 'artistic enterprise'.[210] 'How did I end up like this?', he asks himself, and moves on to dismiss his work as just so much 'weighing and weighing', just so much ponderous 'responsible *tristia*'.[211] In verecund mood, Heaney questions who he is writing for, but the only answers he receives are oblique and uncomforting. The voices of the rain in the alders complain of 'let-downs and erosions', mourn the irretrievable certainties of the past. Heaney's relief at being at liberty and free from the stigma of betrayal, 'neither internee nor informer', is qualified by his recognition that though he has 'Escaped from the massacre', he has not escaped responsibility for its victims, nor the guilt that accompanies survival. Adapting a phrase applied to Mandelstam and Akhmatova by the Soviet authorities who branded them as 'internal *émigrés*',[212] Heaney sentences himself to becoming 'An inner emigré'. One line later, he employs a further historical analogy when he compares himself to 'a wood-kerne', an outlaw, forced to take cover in the woods of Glanmore, but exposed even there to 'Every wind that blows' from the North. In contrast to the 'meagre heat' generated by the sparks of his imagination, he invokes one final image for the epiphany he feels has eluded him; the almost Yeatsian perfection of 'The comet's pulsing rose'.

Although *North* provoked a positive critical response from the likes of Anthony Thwaite in *The Times Literary Supplement*, Conor Cruise O'Brien in *The Listener*, and Richard Murphy in *New York Review of Books*, it was received with less than enthusiasm by two important Ulster commentators. Ciaran Carson condemned what he saw as a tendency towards sentimentality and mystification in many poems, attacking Heaney for creating a "world of megalithic doorways and charming, noble barbarity."[213] Another major critic, Edna Longley, lamented what she saw as a narrowing of Heaney's poetic vision since *Wintering Out*, which invalidated his claim to be a seeker of 'common ground'. It was regrettable that the rites of *North*, whether "ancient, modern or imagined" should be so "profoundly 'Catholic' in character",[214] and that his work had become so 'artful', so stylised, as a result of his move to the distant South. In the course of this chapter, I hope to have shown how 'barbarities' are confronted in the bog poems, and treated as neither 'charming' nor 'noble'. In answer to Edna Longley's charge, it should be pointed out that Heaney's attitude towards his Catholic inheritance is not by any means uncritical or unquestioning. He had not simply slipped into a reactionary, nationalist, Catholic position. Though some friends might have wanted him to adopt the fully 'liberated' stance of a Mercutio – "A plague on both your houses!" – this was not possible. His "upbringing and experience" of events from late '71 to late '74 gave "him cogent reasons to feel that one side is worse than the other," and, as Conor Cruise O'Brien recognised in his review, "his poems have to reflect this."[215]

North represents the culmination of a poetic process begun with *Death of a Naturalist*; it is 'the book all books were leading to'.[216] At the same time, however, it anticipates his later development. It reveals his growing receptivity to other cultures and their experiences, a movement outwards which will lead him towards those exemplary, obdurate, ironic north and mid-European voices of Mandelstam, Herbert, Milosz, Holub and Brodsky. Like them, he will endeavour to create an art which is both particular and universal, immediate and oblique.

5

Quickenings, 1975–84

She, in the midst of all, preserv'd me still
A Poet, made me seek beneath that name
My office upon earth, and nowhere else,
And lastly, Nature's Self, by human love
Assisted, through the weary labyrinth
Conducted me again to open day,
Revived the feelings of my earlier life,
Gave me that strength and knowledge full of peace.

Wordsworth, The Prelude[1]

FIELD WORK

At the core of Heaney's fifth collection, *Field Work*, is a sequence of sonnets and lyrics celebrating his wife, Marie, and their home, the cottage at Glanmore. The experience of living together there – as husband, father, poet – was the 'makings of my adult self', he has said, an experience which left him renewed and fortified physically, spiritually, imaginatively.[2] His aim had been to change the rhythms of his life and verse, to 'displace' himself in order to develop as a man and writer, and in this he succeeded as the longer, assured, melodious lines of the poems of *Field Work* testify. By the time the book was published, however, the Heaneys had been living for three years in a handsome Edwardian house in the Sandymount area of Dublin. He had taken up a permanent teaching post in October 1975 at Carysfort Teacher Training College, and in the following year was appointed Head of the English Department, a post he retained until 1981.[3] They had decided to leave Glanmore partly because the initial attractiveness of its remoteness had worn off to some extent. The circumstances of domestic life were difficult as the house was a long way from the main road; it was sparsely furnished, and extremely cold in winter; it was too small for a growing family of five, and though they had made it a home, the property belonged to Anne Saddlemeyer. In addition, their eldest son, Michael, was fast approaching secondary school age, and

> I foresaw that if we stayed in Wicklow, in Glanmore, about twenty five or thirty miles south of Dublin, I foresaw the teenage years of the children as being slightly disconsolate, running into Dublin and all that . . . I suppose that for the first time in my life, I thought of the future, and in order to set the domestic machinery quietly and effectively to work, I thought we'd move into Dublin.[4]

Essentially it had served its purpose. It had enabled the couple to achieve a deeper intimacy and understanding as husband and wife, and had given the young Heaneys something of the 'simple animal joyousness' and sensuous innocence which had characterised their father's 'hedge-school' experience at Mossbawn.

> I wanted the kids to have that sort of wild animal life that I had. They were like little rodents through the hedges . . . I wanted that eye-level life with the backs of ditches, the ferns and the smell of cow-dung, and I suppose I didn't want to lose that in myself.[5]

The tang of their delight helped the poet to savour again his 'original place',[6] and lent both piquancy and poignancy to many of the lyrics in his fifth and sixth collections.

A recurring concern within *Field Work* and *Station Island* is the tension between song and suffering. In counterpoint to the spiritual harmony and artistic growth enjoyed by the poet, the 'implacable, disconsolate wailing'[7] of sirens continued in the North. During their last two years in Glanmore, 1975 and 1976, killings in the province totalled 247 and 297 respectively – amongst the victims, his second cousin, Colum McCartney, killed in a random sectarian attack – and over 5,000 people received major injuries. Just over a week before Heaney's thirty-sixth birthday, seven died and seventy-five were injured in two pub bombings in Belfast. Exactly one week after the British Government announced in July 1975 that all internees would be released by Christmas, news came of the shooting by the U.V.F. of three members of a pop group, the Miami Showband. The same

Protestant paramilitary organisation was responsible for the killing of twelve people, including four women, and the wounding of forty-six, in a series of attacks in October. Early in the New Year, the murder of five Catholics near Whitecross, South Armagh, prompted a group called the Republican Action Force to kill ten local Protestant linen workers in revenge.[8] Only in 1977 and 1978 did the level of violence begin to abate, in part due the efforts of the Peace People. The movement was established in August '76 following the tragic deaths of three children in Andersonstown, killed while out walking with their mother, Anne Maguire, when a car slewed into them. Its driver, an I.R.A. man called Danny Lennon – a friend of Bobby Sands[9] – had been shot dead at the wheel by an army patrol. Four days later, in what Bernadette Devlin described as 'an explosion of female rage',[10] ten thousand people marched through the streets in Belfast to demand an end to the slaughter. A week later, peace rallies held in Belfast and in Dublin attracted twenty thousand each. Yet, by the time its founders, Betty Williams and Mairead Corrigan, were awarded the Nobel Prize in October 1977, much of its momentum had been lost. Some of their pronouncements alienated Republican sympathisers in the Catholic ghettoes, and internal squabbles split the leadership. Little wonder that the motto of the 'Harvest Bow', *The end of art is peace*, is described as a 'frail device'.

With this all-pervasive context of violence in mind, Heaney dramatises his anxieties over the morality, justification and efficacy of poetic utterance in contemporary Ireland. As one of the meanings of the title implies, *Field Work* is exploratory, preparatory, sometimes a tentative projection of what might be. The first poem, 'Oysters', sets the agenda, and asks whether it is appropriate for the poet to exercise the gift of his lyric art, his free-ness, in the midst of the unfree, the oppressed, the dying. While innocent children, men and women are being crushed, shot or blown to bits, might not song constitute 'a betrayal of suffering'?[11] By reflecting upon the exemplary conduct of other poets who lived through and responded to the viciousness of their times – such as Wilfred Owen, W. B. Yeats, Osip Mandelstam, Zbigniew Herbert, Miroslav Holub – and by celebrating the sacral in his day-to-day experience, Heaney began to answer such questions and to learn to trust 'in the clear light'.

The opening lines of the new collection make a break with the austere mood of *North*'s ending. The solitary, meditative, regretful, leaf-shuffling narrator of 'Exposure' has come indoors, rediscovered the first person plural and shares in a feeling of collective pleasure. The sound of the shells creates an atmosphere of cheery domesticity, securing the poet, allowing him to indulge in a spot of fanciful excess. After his failure to sight the lost comet, one can forgive him his starry 'conceits', his taste for 'Orion' and 'the salty Pleiades'. Immediately his eyes open in stanza two, however, Heaney's *gravitas* re-asserts itself, challenges his social self, attacks his conscience. The oysters are hauled from the heavens, their fall from grace effected in a succession of related images humanising, or, rather, feminising them. He emphasises their genital shape, and portrays them as victims of the ocean's rape; they are 'Alive', but now 'violated'. The shock waves extend to the rhythms, for in the tenth line the two strong stresses within 'Millions' and the three final trochees – 'ripped and shucked and scattered' – break the pattern of iambs. Recognising the 'regressive' tendencies of these images – leading him back to 'Act of Union', to the 'spent flukes' of 'Exposure', perhaps to the diaspora which followed the Famine – he governs his tongue, changes tack. The intention of the meal, after all, had been to celebrate 'friendship', amid the 'cool of thatch of crockery', and yet here he was succumbing again to black melancholy, imperial history, stings of guilt. When his lyric evocation of the Romans journeying over the Alps with their 'damp panniers' of oysters is halted by the tart, dismissive phrase, 'Glut of privilege', he becomes "angry that my trust could not repose/ In the clear light, like poetry or freedom/ Leaning in from the sea." To enjoy the oysters is no more reprehensible than to relish poetry or freedom or one's own individuality. Like Chekhov, drinking down a whole bottle of cognac on the first night of his visit to the penal colony on Sakhalin, Heaney's deliberate act demonstrates his belief that he has earned his 'right to the luxury of practising his art'.[12] He refuses to be bound forever to sentences from the past, to 'slave blood', slave attitudes.

In 'Triptych', Heaney acknowledges the grip history retains on his island 'of comfortless noises' and upon his way of viewing events. The opening image of 'After a Killing' – a poem written after the murder in Dublin of Christopher Ewart-Biggs, the British Ambassador on 21 July 1976 by the Provisional I.R.A. – picks out the shapes of two gun-men on a hillside. Although they seem at first *like* the ghosts of 'the unquiet founders' of the Irish Free State, the I.R.A. of 1919–1921, their robust appearance, their rifles and their deeds have made them all too real. To describe these figures as 'Profane and *bracing*' (my italics) seems to acknowledge the persistence of a boyish awe for these deadly men of action – one which the Provisional I.R.A. is at pains to promote – a legacy of the culture of the G.A.A. Hall.

A note of deep sadness brims in the second verse, which begins with a standard expression of condolence in Ulster framed as a question, 'Who's sorry for our trouble?'. The answer, of course, is the people of Ireland themselves, who face the brunt of the Troubles, but also England which now shares in the suffering because it would not suffer the Irish to "dwell among ourselves/ In rain and scoured light and wind-dried stones?" In a Lowell-like catalogue of nouns, Heaney identifies key features in the Irish landscape, 'Basalt, blood, water, headstones, leeches.' That last image illustrates Heaney's doubt about the future. Will the blood-letting prove purgative, or will the patient die from so much loss?

Turning away from blood, Heaney reaches towards innocence. The backward look can only offer him the 'neuter original loneliness' of pre-lapsarian Ireland, which once stretched from Brandon on the west coast to Dunseverick in the north. Even then before native borders were supplemented by imported varieties, only 'small-eyed survivor flowers' flourished, and the delicate 'unmolested orchid' – an emblem of integrity – was a rarity.[13] Turning away from the myopia afflicting the Garden's past and current stock, the poem's vision expands to take in the solidity of 'a stone house by a pier', to consider the spaciousness such a desirable property can provide for a large family, 'Elbow room', or an artist, 'Broad window light'. In the final stanza, one perceives that Heaney's strategy for overcoming the 'insoluble conflict' inherited from history will be to outgrow it, and to develop "in the process 'a new level of consciousness'".[14] This will come from relishing the 'unlooked-for joy' in the lyric present, its beauty as accessible as fresh mackerel, *new* potatoes.

> today a girl walks in home to us
> Carrying a basket full of new potatoes,
> Three tight green cabbages, and carrots
> With the tops and mould still fresh on them.

The girl is like an Irish Ceres, and her basket contains and embraces both green and orange.[15]

The feminine presence of the second panel of the Triptych, 'Sibyl', proffers little in the way of affirmation. When questioned about the collective future, the Oracle is soon reduced to phrases of dwindling length and hope. She predicts that physical repercussions will accompany humanity's social, moral and spiritual decline. Evolution is in reverse, and the 'paragon of animals' will soon be no better than a stinking ant,

> Unless forgiveness find its nerve and voice,
> Unless the helmeted and bleeding tree
> Can green and open bud like infants' fists.

Christian values *might be* restored if the people – and the poets – are given the grace and have the courage to speak out in favour of tolerance and the helmeted tree, the symbol of political liberty. The high ideals which inspired the French Revolution of 1789, the Irish Rebellion of 1798, and the Civil Rights Movement *might* 'bud' again if the blood can be staunched, and the Terror ended.[16] The mood is subjunctive, and the dream seems doomed finally by the implausible image of 'Bright nymphs' emerging from the 'fouled' volcanic 'magma', and because of the virulent materialism abroad in Ireland. 'My people think money', trawl silence, bank on 'acquisitive stems', not 'green buds'. The island is possessed by Antonio, Trinculo, the ghost of Sycorax; Prospero and Miranda are adrift again. The third poem of 'Triptych','At the Water's Edge', transports the reader to three sacred islands on Lough Erne – centres of faith, fertility, certainty in ancient Celtic Ireland – and from thence to a fearful border town in the present, Newry, the scene of a protest against brutal secular authority. It is another poem of shifts and oppositions, which sees Heaney, in the aftermath of Bloody Sunday, poised between old pieties requiring submission to God's will – wanting "to bow down, to offer up,/ To go barefoot, foetal, penitential" – and the dictates of his adult, poetic, political self which demand that certain steps be taken. At each holy place, he seeks stillness, prays for guidance, longs for a voice which will confer absolution, or at least reassurance. On Devenish, once occupied by a monastic community founded by St Molaisse in the sixth century, the only human representative he meets is a solitary keeper, a fellow reciter of elegies. The chant of a snipe has replaced plainsong. Order is melting before his eyes, communion dissolving.

> Carved monastic heads
> Were crumbling like bread on water.

Depotentiation and decay are similarly in evidence on the other islands. On Boa, divine silence greets his silence. The Godhead has been 'trepanned', sawn into by time and the elements. Although it is described as 'sex-mouthed', the stone contains no promise of regeneration or resurrection. Graves besiege it, and its groove has become merely a 'stoup for rain water'. On Horse Island, 'a cold hearthstone' affords him little comfort, brief sanctuary. The house-hold gods – Lares and Penates – are long gone, and the sky and air are filled with shadow and noise, the inauspicious, 'thick rotations/ Of an army helicopter patrolling.' Turning away and inwards, back to a domestic frame of reference, he discovers 'A hammer and a cracked jug full of cobwebs', the former perhaps a symbol of the 'armed struggle', the latter emblematic of the present arid state of Ireland, lacking the renewing, healing, assuaging power of water. Once more his earliest instincts for veneration, for water-worship, are aroused, only to be checked in the final quatrain, which seems to dismiss such a response as primitive, servile, immature, associating it with the political and moral defeatism and passiveness which impeded the Catholics' spiritual growth. 'How we crept before we walked', he exclaims, finding in those first person plurals – 'we' and 'our' – a solidarity, easing his feeling of exposure.

As violence advances on every front, Heaney attempts to secure some lines of defence in the two poems immediately following 'Triptych'. In each he manoeuvres with the sonnet form to assert tra-ditional rights, to shore up traditional values. Once more the poet is fortified by the memory of Mossbawn, and returns to one of its most potent presences, the family pump.[17] In 'A Drink of Water' it retains the role it acquired in 'Mossbawn Sunlight', serving as a symbol of loving-kindness, as an enduring source of physical and spiritual refreshment; in 'The Toome Road', however, it acquires a political dimension, embodying defiance.[18] The poem depicts a depressingly recurrent scene from Irish history, a foreign army moving at will, violating the integrity of the territory. The traditional, agricultural world of the ballads invoked in the poem's first three words – 'One morning early' – has been invaded by the contemporaneity of 'armoured cars' – unlyrically 'warbling along on powerful tyres' – and 'headphoned soldiers'. In what seems a ludicrous effort to integrate these vehicles into the countryside, at least from a ground's eye view, alder branches have hacked off and used for camouflage – early casualties of the army presence. With the fifth line, the poem's focus returns to the narrator, one of the displaced.

His first question invites us to place this particular incursion within the context of at least three centuries of dispossession. ("How long were they approaching down my roads/ As if they owned them?") In the course of his second, he seems to recognise the unlikelihood of anyone being energised into action. All those back doors left 'on the latch' in expectation of 'bad news' suggest a people conditioned to defeat, for whom military occupation, like natural disaster, must seem an entirely predictable feature of the cycle between 'seed' and 'headstones', just another fact of life. Rather than end the sonnet on this note of resignation, Heaney adds a further three lines, as if determined to snatch victory from the colonial power. Although the power and glory belongs to the 'charioteers', the professionals concerned with extending or defending Empires, ultimately it is the 'Sowers of seed', like his forbears, who will inherit the Kingdom. Their champion is the *omphalos*, a transcendant, ever-present, unseen being which 'stands' and will remain standing long after all these warriors, with their anachronistic chariots and 'dormant guns' will have passed away.

The elegies to his three murdered friends, Colum McCartney ('The Strand at Lough Beg'), Sean Armstrong ('A Postcard from North Antrim') and Louis O'Neill ('Casualty'), similarly demonstrate Heaney's refusal to allow bullet and the bomb to have the final word. The appalling, unnatural circumstances in which these deaths occurred are powerfully recorded – 'the blood and roadside muck', the 'pointblank teatime bullet', the fact of being 'blown to bits' – yet, through the intercession of memory, Art and Nature, Heaney manages to assuage his sense of loss, and to strike sharp, clear notes in celebration.

A key confirmatory presence behind these elegies is that of Dante. In both 'The Strand at Lough Beg' and 'A Postcard from North Antrim', Heaney tries to converse with and question the dead, admittedly with less success than the author of *The Divine Comedy*. The first Canto of *Purgatorio* provides the epigraph to 'The Strand at Lough Beg' and one of its most delicate, memorable images, which sees Heaney kneeling in the 'brimming grass' to 'gather up cold handfuls of the dew' to wash his cousin's face, a purification ritual prescribed by Cato in order to prepare the Florentine for Purgatory:

> Go, take this man, and see thou gird his waist
> With a smooth reed, and from his brow likewise

Cleanse all this filth with which it is defaced[19]

In the poem's opening movement, Heaney pictures his cousin, Colum, driving steadily uphill towards Newtonhamilton, towards his encounter with his killers. It is an ascent into darkness, far from the secure, almost sacral, 'white glow of filling *stations*'. On this same road – ironically referred to as 'a high, bare *pilgrim*'s track' – where Sweeney, King of Dal-rie, was pursued by 'a demon pack/ Blazing out of the ground',[20] his guiltless modern counterpart, a humble carpenter from Armagh, confronted the more prosaic, but deadlier menace of a 'red lamp swung' – or was it 'tailing headlights'? – followed by hooded heads, and a sectarian killer's 'cold-nosed gun'. Against that brutal, temporal 'authority', Heaney sets the sacred spire of Church Island, towering above the mortal 'clays and waters of Lough Beg', and 'its soft treeline' of 'unmolested yew'.[21] The second section relocates the young victim in the landscape of his boyhood, but only to recognise chill portents to his future. Even though as a child he became accustomed to hearing the gunfire of the duck hunters, violating the tranquillity of his home, 'long before rising', the evidence of their spent power, 'Acrid, brassy, genital, ejected', appalled him. As he crossed 'the strand to fetch the cows', he could never have imagined that one day he would be regarded as 'fair game'. At this point Heaney turns individual cameo into a collective portrait. Significantly he makes no reference to McCartney as a carpenter, but rather stresses his earlier role as innocent, pastoral herdsman, as a typical representative of his community and class.

> For you and yours and yours and mine fought shy,
> Spoke an old language of conspirators
> And could not crack the whip or seize the day.

Despite their long and deep resentment against Unionist rule, few among the rural Nationalist population – '*Big-voiced* scullions', '*talkers* in byres'[22] – would ever have dreamt of shaping their grievances into political action. Their agenda was headed by 'Haycocks and hindquarters', rather than the vexed question of how to achieve a United Ireland. For McCartney's killers, however, the belief that he shared that common Catholic aspiration was sufficient to justify his murder.

The immediacy achieved in the poem's third and final movement owes much to Heaney's effective use of the present tense and of visually 'concrete' detail, such as the description of the cattle 'Up to their bellies in the mist', Lough Beg 'Like a dull blade with its edge/ Honed bright', and the imagined funeral rites. Unable to leave the 'bleeding, pale-faced boy'[23] on his knees, Heaney elevates the victim, before setting him down once more. Poem becomes *pietà*. With rushes which miraculously, and ironically, '*shoot* green again', he plaits 'Green scapulars', decking the body in these sacred vestments which symbolise humility and his hope in the resurrection. Although his next volume voices the suspicion that he had 'saccharined' his cousin's death in 'The Strand at Lough Beg', confusing 'evasion and artistic tact', whitewashing the ugly facts, I am not convinced that the poem merits denunciation, or that lyric tenderness is inevitably a weakness. To enable him to come to terms with the cruelty of 'what happens' -- the gun, the blood, the muck, the shroud – Heaney needed Dante at this time, just as he had needed the Tollund Man earlier. Faced with a similar tragedy, Heaney's painter friend, T. P. Flanagan, also turned to an old master for inspiration. When his close friend, Martin McBurney, a civil rights lawyer, was killed by the P.I.R.A., Flanagan's tribute to him, 'Victim', employed a figure from Poussin's 'Echo and Narcissus' to convey the moral beauty of the murdered man.

At first sight it would appear that the central figures celebrated in 'A Postcard from North Antrim' and 'Casualty' could not be more different. Sean Armstrong was a friend from Queen's, and for a while 'part of the commune-pot smoking generation' in Sausalito. Returning to Belfast in the early seventies 'to get involved in social work', he was shot 'by some unknown youth'.[24] Louis O'Neill, however, belonged to a much older generation. A regular at the public house in Ardboe owned by Heaney's father-in-law, he often invited the young poet to accompany him on fishing expeditions on Lough Neagh. Three days after Bloody Sunday, he was blown to bits in a bar 'miles away', having broken the curfew the Provisionals had imposed out of respect for the thirteen dead. Whereas O'Neill comes across as a laconic, solitary figure – he rarely raised his voice, and could order a drink merely by 'a lifting of the eyes/ And a discreet dumb-show'[25] – Armstrong seems loud, brash, and ebullient; 'Postcard' ends with Heaney's affectionate, and probably embarrassed memory of Armstrong as *mein host*. What the modest fisherman and the generous, genial clown share, however, apart from their status as victims, is uniqueness, individuality, irreplaceability. Both men

were part of Ulster's 'old decency', and were as representative of
that *comparatively* innocent, integrated, world as Old Bushmills, soda
farls, stout and eels.

Each elegy is a delicate act of restoration, in which the poet
re-places a lost friend in his proper element. Whereas in 'Casualty' the movement takes us from a lonely interior to a scene of
companionship 'Somewhere, well-out, beyond . . . ', the panels of
'A Postcard from North Antrim' start with a stark exterior view,
and finish in a congenial interior. Our first sight of Sean Armstrong
is in long shot, his life hanging on the precarious thread of the
Carrick-a-Rede rope bridge, the first of several thin lines encountered in the poem.[26] The eye passes next to the 'warm-planked,
democratic wharves/ Of Sausalito', a soft-focus, easeful world of
'twilights and guitars' shattered in the poem's third quarter, by
the chill facts of a typical Belfast killing. As if to escape from the
devastating consequences of the 'pointblank teatime bullet', and
the hopelessness of his own injunction to "Get up from your blood
on the floor", Heaney tries to recapture the pleasure of watching
and listening to Armstrong holding the floor with his songs and
recitations. One of his favourites recalled Henry Joy McCracken
kissing 'his Mary Ann' just before his execution. Another was
The Ballad of William Bloat, by Raymond Calvert, a grisly tale of
attempted murder and suicide. After cutting his wife's throat, the
'hero' is unmanned hearing 'the steady drip . . . / Of her lifeblood',
seeing 'the pool of gore on the bedroom floor'.[27] Re-examining the
final image of 'A Postcard from North Antrim' in the light of these
allusions, what seemed at first to be purely affirmative becomes
tinged with irony too. The wine reflects a memory of blood, as
well as a moment of celebration. Underneath the expansiveness
of Armstrong's personality, the 'raw' emotion and 'brute force' of
his material and delivery, Heaney recognises a strain of anxiety, a
vulnerability, made even more poignant in retrospect.

Tentativeness is more a characteristic of the narrator in 'Casualty', than of his subject. For the most part Louis O'Neill appears
self-assured, self-possessed, content 'to swim/ out on your own', to
follow instinct and his 'own frequency',[28] and the only situation in
which he displays a trace of unease comes when he raises the subject
of poetry during his conversations with Heaney. Endeavouring to
be diplomatic, and wishing to avoid the risk of condescension, the
educated, younger man would present a 'turned back' to that topic,
and would steer their talk towards more 'neutral' territory, "to

eels/ Or lore of the horse and cart/ Or the Provisionals." The sad irony is that now, as a result of his friend's tragic, horrific death, a poem exists, bridging what had seemed to be distinctly separate worlds, distinctly separate personalities. Within 'Casualty' Heaney is compelled once more to engage himself in complex issues of personal and collective morality. Whereas in 'Punishment' he had seemed to endorse the legitimacy of feeling behind the tribal revenge, in this poem he appears to challenge the justice of O'Neill's fate. By breaking the curfew, the fisherman had in a sense broken faith both with his own people and the dead, but what was the extent of his guilt, Heaney asks. Was he fully responsible for his actions, or was he merely responding to the impulses of his nature? And could his crime have merited such a terrible punishment? Even the victim seems to admit there is no 'right answer'. In their lucid analyses of 'Casualty',[29] Blake Morrison and Neil Corcoran agree that an acquittal is called for, and that Heaney's sympathies are essentially with O'Neill. Although I would concur with their general conclusion, I would suggest that the issue and Heaney's loyalties are much more finely balanced than they suggest. Their desire to extricate the poet from those 'old currents' and constraints of tribal feeling leads them to diminish and distort the emotional impact on Heaney of the Bloody Sunday funerals. Morrison speaks of 'a sense of constriction and suffocation' in the following images

> The common funeral
> Unrolled its *swaddling band*,
> *Lapping, tightening*
> Till we were *braced* and *bound*
> Like *brothers* in a *ring*

while Corcoran – perhaps with Blake's 'Infant Sorrow' in mind – detects 'constriction and the infantile'. For both critics 'swaddling', 'band', and 'bound' – together with 'tightening' – possess exclusively negative associations.[30] Neither registers the fact the phrase, 'swaddling bands', features in one of the most famous of all Christmas carols, 'While Shepherds Watched Their Flocks', and is used to describe how the infant Christ is dressed as he lies in the manger.[31] Heaney employs the allusion to stress that the thirteen victims of Bloody Sunday were innocent of any crime, and to remind us how collective horror at their murder had the effect of strengthening bonds within the Catholic community ('braced', 'brothers'), marrying a people in grief and anger ('in a ring'). The bitter humour of 'PARAS THIRTEEN . . . BOGSIDE NIL' and the evocative image of the coffins afloat, 'Like blossoms on slow water', imply a complicity in these communal emotions, rather than detachment from them. Even though some members of his community used the atrocity to justify their own vicious acts, it is hard to believe that Heaney's intention was to indict the entire Catholic 'lumpen-proletariat' (Morrison) on a charge of psychological/emotional/spiritual retardation simply for mourning their dead as a community. Unable to file in line with 'Those quiet walkers/ And sideways talkers/ Shoaling out of his lane', Heaney ends his tribute in O'Neill's 'proper haunt', cherishing one particular morning of shared freedom. The analogies he draws between the fisherman's way of working and the poet's way of making bind them together, enabling him to view his creative enterprise as an extension of O'Neill's life. The final couplet contains an almost filial plea that this 'old father',[32] this 'Dawn-sniffing revenant', will return as a spirit to question him, to quicken his sense of poetic purpose, to guide him on 'the land/ Banked under fog' and through misty waters.

One other fortifying presence in the elegy needs acknowledging before passing on. There is an affinity in form and content between 'Casualty' and Yeats's dawn-set celebration of 'isolation, self-containment, natural life',[33] 'The Fisherman'. Both are written in trimeters, employ iambic rhythms, and rhyme on alternate lines (*ababcdcdefef*). For each poet, the fisherman is 'The most unlike', a kind of 'anti-self',[34] who embodies independence, wisdom, integrity – a refusal to submit to the will of the crowd.[35]

Images of the sea, of fish and fishing surface in the poems immediately following 'Casualty', and serve not merely to recapture brief moments of restoration and pleasure in the company of artistic friends and equals. More importantly, in poems such as 'The Singer's House', 'The Guttural Muse', 'In Memoriam Sean O'Riada' and 'Elegy', their function is to celebrate a renewed belief in the redemptive power of art. Contagious violence and guilt had left him feeling 'like some old pike all badged with sores', needing the healing touch of 'doctor fish',[36] exemplary presences, living and dead. The rites of purification begin in 'The Singer's House', its eight stanzas permeated by the invigorating 'tang' of music, words and salty places. Heaney's central premise, and image, may well be derived from St Mark's contention that "Salt is good; but if the salt has lost its saltness, how will you season it? Have salt in yourselves and be at peace with one another."[37] The justifiable suspicion that the North is slipping rapidly into irreversible decline, "So much comes and is gone/ that should be crystal and kept", is checked in new acts of naming, placing, savouring. For Heaney, the very names, *Carrickfergus* and *Gweebarra*, possess a piquant, 'brine-stung' energy ('Oysters') consonant with song.[38] Saying them enables him to 'conjure' the 'old decencies' of Ulster, the values of industry, creativity, modesty, frugality, courtesy, grace and good husbandry, values he associates with his close friend, David Hammond, the singer of the title. In Hammond's company, whether in Belfast or in Hammond's Donegal home, 'a whitewashed turf-shed' overlooking the Atlantic and Gweebarra Bay, the poet could experience again 'amicable weathers', the delight of a 'glittering sound' – a voice and a view sustaining faith in the 'efficacy of song'.[39] Such is the magic of the voice that seals – kin to Yeats's immortal dolphins – swim to the strand to pay their homage, a sight which tempts Heaney into the subjunctive, and hope, tentative as 'a rowboat far out in evening'. Perhaps the inimical, 'blood-dimmed'[40] tide *might* turn. Once people imagined "that drowned souls lived in the seals" and that "At spring tides they might change shape." In folk-myth, the miraculous was always possible; but how feasible is belief today? Later in *Field Work*, in 'September Song', he will speak of toeing the line between the tree in leaf and the bare tree', of being caught 'in the middle of the way' between hope in the resurrection, and fear in the finality of death. Listening to Hammond on this occasion, however, he is convinced of the potency of the note, the Word, the 'sound-waves' – "Raise it again, man. We still believe what we hear" – and that there is more in heaven and earth than just the 'secular powers . . . thundering'.[41]

The elegy for Sean O'Riada (1931–1971), one of Ireland's most acclaimed composers, delights in his mastery of pen, baton and rod, and recalls one afternoon spent together when, like the disciples in St Luke, Chapter V, they watched as 'mackerel shoaled from under/ like a conjured retinue'. The depth of his feeling for the man and artist can be measured by the comparison he makes between O'Riada and that first 'expert'[42] in his life, his own father – "He conducted the Ulster Orchestra/ like a drover with an ashplant" – and in the allusions to Yeats. References to 'a quickened, whitened head', to *sprezzatura*, to 'falconer and fisherman', to 'a sceptic eye' connect O'Riada's absorption of – and with – the rich Irish folk tradition to Yeats's. Despite the brevity of his life, his contribution to the national culture was a considerable one, and fittingly Heaney concludes his praise-poem mingling allusions to the historical struggle[43] – "he was our jacobite/ he was our young pretender" – with images from nature and each of the arts.

> O gannet smacking through scales!
> Minnow of light.
> Wader of assonance.

Robert Lowell in 'Elegy' is presented to us in almost as many bewildering guises as Proteus, the *Odyssey*'s Old Man of the Sea. He appears first as master mariner, as 'helmsman', riding 'on the swaying tiller of yourself', generally commanding, but sometimes succumbing to the turbulence in his life. The immense force of his intellect and imagination is likened to a 'night ferry/ thudding in a big sea', its subtlety with a 'water-breaking dolphin'. In the potentially constricting arenas of poetry of politics, Lowell exhibits the craft of a gladiator, a 'netsman, *retiarius*', who can turn thought into word into deed. Awed through much of the poem by the epic, heroic stature of his subject – 'you found the child in me' – Heaney completes the eulogy on a quieter, intimate note, recalling Cal's last farewell, and a flash of timorous affection. After this point of departure, which takes place under the 'opulent and restorative', 'full bay tree/ by the gate at Glanmore', the reader arrives at the core of the collection, the 'Glanmore Sonnets', ten epiphanies celebrating 'opened ground', personal and poetic quickening. A central factor in this process of renewal was the place itself. The austerity of the accommodation – Glanmore is small and possessed of 'very frugal appointments'[44] – is more than compensated for by the beauty of the setting. Like Dove Cottage,[45] the Heaneys' cottage 'looks straight into bushes and into a hillside', and is surrounded by luxuriant vegetation and animal life. Abandoning the regularity of nine-to-five enabled him to establish his own rhythms, and heightened that acute responsiveness to seasonal change, to 'planetary, biological reality',[46] which had been with him from infancy. At Glanmore Heaney seems to have experienced a deeper assuredness than any he had known since his days at Mossbawn. The poet himself sees the two places as analogous. Both Glanmore and 'the original place' were presided over by generous, benevolent, female deities, and bustled with children and their enthusiasms.

Sharing the 'strange loneliness' of the Wicklow countryside together strengthened the marriage, enriched the Heaneys' family life. As the sequence develops, the poet's wife, Marie, becomes an increasingly important presence – she appears in Sonnets III, VIII, IX and X – as a stabilising and energising force.

> We had been married six years, and, you know, I think it takes a while to get to know how to be married. What happened to us personally as a couple, as a family, was that we got married again in a different way. We started life again together.[47]

Nine months after their move to Wicklow, their third child was born, a daughter, Catherine Ann.

Heaney's choice of the sonnet form indicates a desire to re-establish the 'old values' of order, harmony, and lyric ceremony in his work, after the highly-politicised, thrusting quatrains of *North*. Appropriately the sequence begins with a dedication to his 'patron' at Glanmore, Ann Saddlemyer, the academic who had leased the cottage to the couple. She is addressed as 'our heartiest welcomer', a phrase borrowed from Yeats's 'In Memory of Major Robert Gregory'. 'Settled', like Yeats in his new home, Heaney prepares himself to receive some of the ghosts of his past, the 'dream grain' of memory. In the opening line of the first sonnet, Heaney sets in the soil preparatory vowel sounds – 'αʊ, 'αʊ ', ' ɪ '/ 'u ', 'ʌ '/ 'ə ', 'əʊ '/ 'ə ', 'αʊ ' – graphic and aural circles in which he will plant fecund images. The field he is about to plough is 'deeply tilled', and places the poet in a pastoral tradition reaching back through Kavanagh to Horace and Vergil. The 'opened ground' he speaks of harks back to the furrows turned in 'Follower', rather than to the historical faults and wounds examined in 'At a Potato Digging' or 'Act of Union'. Sloughing off the burdens of history, politics, and the grandness of myth, he reconnects himself to the 'cropping land'.[48] He listens as the acres 'breathe' into his spirit, and from the breath attempts 'to raise/ A voice'. Inspired, fortified by the arrival of his own 'Midwinter Spring',[49] he senses again the scent, promise and possibilities of Art, 'the fundamental dark unblown rose'. In comparing 'the good life' to a simple act like crossing a field, he alludes to the final line of Boris Pasternak's 'Hamlet' – "Everything drowns in Pharisaism./ Living life is not crossing a field"[50] – but only to reject its note of despondency, the note he had himself sounded in 'Exposure'. The first Glanmore sonnet, by way of contrast, ends with sacral images conveying fertility, energy and continuity, a succession of long vowels, and a buoyant iambic confidence.

> *Breasting* the mist, in *sowers'* aprons,
> My ghosts come *striding* into their *spring stations.*
> The dream *grain whirls* like freakish *Easter* snows.

In II, Heaney restates his essentially religious, Jungian view of the act of creation, a view first articulated in 'The Diviner'. The poet experiences initially stirrings somewhere in the 'dark hutch' of the subconscious, 'sensings' which seek a shape, a form, achieve an incarnation in words.[51] An impenetrable mystery, or conspiracy almost, lies behind the creation of any work of art, he suggests. The stone connives with the chisel, the wood-grain instructs the mallet. Finding himself now 'in the hedge-school of Glanmore', Heaney prays that his humble surroundings will tutor him in song, provide him with a poetic instrument that might 'continue, hold, dispel, appease' his epiphanies and fears.

Sonnet III records one such epiphany, a marriage of sound and sight. The sensual music, the lyric images are almost too intense, too exquisite. Crisp, plosive 'k's consort with each other

> This evening the cuc*k*oo and the cornc*r*a*k*e
> (So much, too much) *c*onsorted at twilight.
> It was all *c*repus*c*ular and iambi*c*.

and climax in that delicious polysyllable, 'crepuscular', which can mean 'indistinct', 'glimmering', or simply 'pertaining to twilight'. Uneasy, guilty even, about where all this 'melodious grace'[52] is leading him, Heaney places 'checks' in the poem, such as the phrase in parentheses and the deflating comment of his wife at the mention of 'Dorothy and William.' It is a shaft against *hubris* typical of Heaney. Having recognised and voiced his feeling of affinity with a poetic giant such as Wordsworth, he fears his own presumptuousness. To allude, for Heaney, is to pay tribute, to claim kin, but not equality. And so in the final couplet he retreats to tenable ground, to nature, to a spare 'rustling and twig-combing breeze', to modest 'cadences'.

These lyric experiences at Glanmore induce memories of Mossbawn, and prompt the shift of time and place in IV, V and VI. Each sonnet records moments in the making of his poetic sensibility, aural, visual, tactile stimuli. IV makes analogies between the childhood longing to hear the engine's 'iron tune' and the adult poet's striving after verbal strength and resonance; both involve keeping 'an ear to the line'[53] for something that might never materialize. Instead of tasting the potent, promised sound of 'flange and piston *pitched* along the ground', the music of that alluring, frightening, populous, mechanised world beyond his borders, the child's faith, patience and persistence earn only a meagre reward – the dull thump of 'Struck couplings and shuntings', and the sight of a few ephemeral ripples shaking 'Silently across our drinking water'. The failure is only relative; refreshment can be drawn even from the well of loss.[54]

In V he reoccupies imaginatively the 'boortree' bower of his first home, to play a new variation on an old game, 'touching tongues'. From this vantage point 'in the throat'[55] of the tree, he examines the distinctive textures of the two languages and traditions that shaped his upbringing, the intimate native tongue of Mossbawn and the more formal, extended register of language acquired at St Columb's and Queen's. Saying the dialect word, naming the *boortree*, can still evoke its 'soft corrugations', its 'green young shoots' and 'greenish, dank' security, yet the sharpness of these images suffers under the influence of time and the 'alien' tongue. Like the disappearing Gaelic culture mourned in the place-name poems of *Wintering Out*, it is reduced to being only a 'snapping memory', displaced by its English 'equivalent'.[56] An appropriate note of stiffness enters in the fifth line, when Heaney recalls how Standard English forms were imposed upon him, 'elderberry I have learned to call it'. In the next line, however, he turns quickly away from past lessons 'learned' to present 'love', and celebrates the original's blooms and berries with a succession of resonants ('l's, 'm's), stops ('b's, 'p's), continuant 'r's and fricative 's's, and a variety of long vowels. 'Elderberry', by contrast, is merely "shires dreaming wine", an image suggestive perhaps of English opulence and pretentiousness, a world away from the homeliness and fecundity of 'saucers brimmed with meal'. Despite his clear preference for the 'bruised' language of home, Heaney is not insensible to the benefits that derived from that other culture. The poem is itself an act of grafting, setting into sensual 'Irish' stock linguistic slivers from his 'English' education, 'cultivated' words such as 'corrugations', 'swart', 'caviar', 'etymologist'. Exile, after all, provided him with the words and forms with which to articulate his *desiderium nostrorum*.[57]

Guilt – perhaps over his present lyric 'truancy', and past reticence on political matters – surfaces again in the somewhat oblique sixth sonnet. Having ended the previous poem retreating into a foetal position in 'the tree-house' of Mossbawn/Glanmore, Heaney reproaches himself for his 'timid cicumspect involvement',[58] determining in a future tense to 'break through . . . what I glazed over', to take more risks. He is quickened by the memory of an anonymous, local act of heroism from the winter of 1947, when a man 'dared the ice/ And raced his bike across the Moyola river'. This tale of bravery, retold 'after dark', generates another childhood recollection in the next sonnet. Just before 'Midnight and closedown', he would listen to the litany of names from the BBC weather forecast – 'Dogger, Rockall, Malin, Shetland, Faroes, Finisterre'[59] – and picture awesome, mysterious regions, inhabited solely by keening winds. In contrast to these exposed spaces, possessed for long periods by 'Green, swift upsurges' of natural violence,[60] are 'the lee' and leas 'of Wicklow', which Heaney had made his 'haven'. Solace and sanctuary prove to be temporary. In VIII and IX, threatening elements converge on Glanmore, bringing with them black presences, bloody reflections, which serve as a reminder of, an objective correlative for, 'scaresome' experiences from his Mossbawn childhood,[61] explosions and carnage from his recent past.

> *Thunderlight* on the *split* logs: big raindrops
> At body heat and lush with *omen*
> *Spattering dark* on the *hatchet iron*

His fearful, fertile imagination breeds evil familiars – the magpie, the toad, the rat – and leads him to interpret their natural activities as sinister manouevrings. Behind the magpie's curiosity, the poet detects a cynical opportunism worthy of 'The Twa Corbies'.[62] Its appearance, like that of the toad, presages some unknown horror, and he dreads 'What', not who, he might meet 'blood-boltered, on the road?'[63] In order to break the spell his terror has induced, and purge away his increasingly alarming sense of exposure, Heaney introduces the figure of his wife into the poem, and a shared memory. The old woman from Les Landes embodies maternal love and protectiveness, and reminds him of the enduring, assuaging power of song. Instead of calming him, this image of appeased suffering intensifies the urgency of his needs, his hunger for a sexual catharsis which will free him from the pangs of conscience and consciousness.

IX sees the roles reversed, and it is now the turn of the poet's wife to feel distraught. *She* isn't merely 'Imagining things'. Having come to the 'hedge-school' of Glanmore to contemplate and compose, Heaney resents being forced into action and away from imagining, into abandoning the idealised 'burnished bay tree' of poetry for the 'tart-leafed' reek of reality and responsibility. The thought of having to kill the rat generates repugnant images from childhood, "Blood on a pitch-fork, blood on chaff and hay/ Rats speared in the sweat and dust of threshing". Though he is spared the the role of executioner by the empty briar's 'swishing', he cannot escape the pain that still 'Haunts' his wife's face, and his own guilt at having failed her. And so in the final sonnet, he proffers his act of atonement, in the form of a dream embracing the most intimate of memories. Marriage again supplies the poem with its 'central trope',[64] the couple passing from a chaste, sepulchral separation ('laid out/ Like breathing effigies'), through ritual purification ('Darkly asperged and censed') towards consummation ('the lovely and painful/ Covenants of flesh'. Throughout, the surreal is firmly bedded in the physical, the literary within personal experience. The actuality of the 'moss', 'Donegal', 'turf-banks', 'wetting drizzle' and 'dripping sapling birches' prevents the allusions to famous runaway lovers – Lorenzo and Jessica from *The Merchant of Venice* and Diarmuid and Grainne from Celtic myth – from seeming cloyingly romantic. After the ninth line where biblical resonances ('And in that dream I dreamt') dally with the tender conversational tones of an Elizabethan love lyric – Sir Thomas Wyatt's 'They flee from me' is the source for 'how like you this?'[65] – the sonnet moves from the 'public' domain of literature into the private past. Significantly it is the decisive act of his wife, her 'deliberate' kiss, that breaks the spell, that frees them from stasis and catalepsis, that raises their relationship onto a new, exquisitely sensuous and sacred plane. Through this and subsequent acts of love, a space has been created which is uniquely theirs, a 'separateness', a place for dewy dreams. The sequence closes with the poet asserting the primacy of domestic love over political/social responsibilities, yet at the same time acknowledging the fact that sexual communion, like the poetic act, seems to offer only a temporary 'respite' from the 'cold climate'

of external realities. Though adverse political conditions will continue to threaten the lyric impulse, Heaney remains determined to
sow the 'dream grain', to let the 'dream grain' whirl.

In the poems immediately succeeding 'Glanmore Sonnets',
Heaney again dwells on the critical role played by his wife in
his personal and artistic maturation. Whether plunging into a pool
in Tuscany ('The Otter'), or rooting around 'in a bottom-drawer / For
the plunge-line nightdress' ('The Skunk'), her vigour and glamour
awe and enthrall him, leaving him 'tense as a voyeur'. Like John
Fowles's heroine, Sarah Woodruff,[66] she is part 'ordinary', part
'mysterious', simultaneously 'palpable' and inaccessible,[67] and
achieves her subtlest and most erotic definitions in natural
contexts and images. She becomes a nest in 'Homecomings'
('damp clay pouting'), a reclaimed waterland in 'Polder', and a
'wounded dryad' in 'Field Work', her veins 'crossed / criss-cross
with leaf-veins'. 'The Otter' praises her almost divine ability to
displace light, its verbs – 'wavered', 'swung', 'Surfacing', 'Turning',
'Re-tilting', 'Heaving', 'Printing' ('The Otter') – thrilling at the
impact she makes, the energy she articulates, the adjectives –
'wet', 'smashing', 'fine', 'lithe', 'thigh-shaking', 'intent', 'frisky'
and 'freshened' – relishing her beauty, sense of purpose, and sexual
allure. Her role in 'An Afterwards', however, is as a corrective
influence on the poet, voicing her legitimate anger at her husband's
neglectfulness. The opening stanzas picture a woman in vengeful
mood, consigning Heaney's fellow-scribblers to hell because of their
eternal 'backbiting', 'Jockeying for position', and treachery.[68] When,
in the fourth verse, his 'sweet' is allowed direct speech and gives
vent to her pent-up frustration, the effect is dramatic; the satirical,
self-mocking note disappears. Her words are rooted in the real
world, and speak of responsibilities unevenly shared, of missed
opportunities, of loneliness within marriage, a concrete world of
rooms, children, elder and rose blossoms. Love, and the tender
lyrical images, soften her reproach. His inability to unwind, and
the rarity of his laughter concern and move her, to the extent that
she offers him a partial absolution in the final quatrain. At least in
his poetry he had striven to be even-handed in his approach to the
Troubles and, though he had been unfair to his family, something of
value – 'those books', *Wintering Out* and *North*? – did emerge out of
his 'responsible *tristia*'.[69]

Field Work maintains to its very end the interpenetration of domestic and political experience. In the last three poems, 'The Harvest

Bow', 'In Memoriam Francis Ledwidge' and 'Ugolino', Heaney turns once more to his earliest ties, to his father and to his father's sister, and reveals his feelings of affinity with a young Catholic poet, killed in the First World War, and with five figures from Dante, locked into appalling suffering. An assertion of familial and cultural continuities, 'The Harvest Bow' fulfils an identical function to that performed by 'Mossbawn: Two Poems in Dedication' in *North*. On this occasion, however, the poet draws inspiration for his act of making from an *accomplished* artefact, the handiwork of his father, one whose form and material have proven their capacity to endure and to illuminate. Created from 'wheat that does not rust/ But brightens as it tightens', the bow embodies an art 'which shares . . . / With great creating nature'.[70] It implicates within its intricacies 'the mellowed silence' of a father and his generation, the 'burnished' tongue of a son and his, and plaits together the craft of one, the technique of the other, the lives and languages of each, into a beautiful 'love-knot'. Of all the portraits of Patrick Heaney, the one provided in 'The Harvest Bow' is perhaps the most affectionate.[71] The attributes depicted in earlier poems again appear – his physical vigour and dexterity, his strong sense of purpose, his difficulty in communicating his feelings – but here the images and diction seem to kindle a tenderer response. The first verb encountered, 'plaited', suggests a feminine skill. The act and object are expressive of the gentle wisdom of the 'mellowed', 'aged' maker. To the poet the bow is a work of art both accessible and elevating ('a knowable corona'), and demonstrates its creator's 'gift' and 'fine intent'. To its maker, however, it is merely another seasonal 'throwaway', easily, almost effortlessly produced by fingers grown 'somnambulant'. Focusing on the old man's hands – rather than his 'straining rump' ('Digging') or 'globed' shoulders ('Follower') – Heaney can contrast delicate manipulation in the present with power wielded in the past; now Patrick deals with pliable straw, rather than obstreperous cattle and game-cocks at battle-pitch.

Once in the poet's possession, the bow is restored to its original function as a fetish.[72] When touched, it validates him as an interpreter for his 'tongue-tied' father. When looked through, it enables him to scan their shared past to retrieve memories and make them as 'palpable' as 'old beds and ploughs in hedges'[73] or Mossbawn's 'outhouse wall'. When listened to, it plays back 'Beats' and heartbeats 'out of time'. The particular scene he settles on conveys both closeness and distance within the father-and-son relationship. Silence divides and joins them. They are separated by the break between stanza three and four, "You with a harvest bow in your lapel/ Me with the fishing rod", and yet connected by *en jambement*, and by the boy's delight in 'the big lift of these evenings'. The knowledge that such evenings in his *Daddy*'s company are passing away sharpens his pleasure, and dulls it. Each seeks/sought to capture something, fish or flesh, but 'flushes' nothing. Even the harvest bow, for all its beauty and cunning, seems like a 'drawn snare', since ultimately everything is given the slip by Time.

> Even the roses split on youth's red mouth
> Will soon blow down the road all roses go.[74]

And yet, despite its frailty and the minor failures associated with it, retained within 'its golden loops' are a luminosity, a warmth that will endure. From the twists in the bow the reader gleans not only details from a private history, however, for within the 'throwaway love-knot of straw' resides the spirit of a lost communal past. The relic belongs, like the ashplant, to an age of innocence, before sectarian tribalism and the strangers' intervention[75] destroyed the shape of the year. Heaney's celebration of a late summer rural ritual needs to be seen in the context of contemporary urban history. Each year since 1968 summer in the North has not merely signified the marching season, but a time when the violence in Belfast and Derry can be expected to reap its ugliest harvest.

Images of lost innocence feature prominently in the next poem, 'In Memoriam Francis Ledwidge', an elegy which intercuts, for ironic effect, moments from Heaney's childhood and from his aunt's girlhood with sketches from Ledwidge's brief life. Francis Ledwidge (1887–1917) was 'a remarkable ploughboy poet'.[76] Following his patron, Lord Dunsany's example, but much to his annoyance, Ledwidge enlisted in the Royal Inniskilling Fusiliers in October 1914 because he felt that the British army "stood between Ireland and an enemy common to our civilization".[77] His attitude modified somewhat after the suppression of Easter Rising, when he returned to Ireland. Along with Padraic Colum, Æ, Gogarty and Stephens, he contributed to a book of verse for the dependants of the prisoners of the Rising. His last poems, according to Jeffares, show him increasingly 'turning to religious meditations' and reveal a growing interest in 'Irish literary and historical material'.[78] Having survived the Gallipoli campaign, when he had to suck stones to make his 'dry mouth water', he met his end 'rent/ By shrapnel' in the third battle of Ypres.

Clearly in many respects Ledwidge's 'cultural and political colourings'[79] are not dissimilar to Heaney's own. At first sight it seems curious that it is not until the sixth stanza of the thirteen that we actually 'meet' the subject of the elegy. Heaney's poem opens instead contemplating an existing work of art, an archetypal figure, a bronze statue such as one might find in any village or town throughout Britain, complete with its roll-call of 'loyal, fallen names'. Its stiff cape, helmet, bayonet and haversack, make it an icon belonging to a remote, dead past, so familiar as to be taken for granted, and, not surprisingly, it barely registers on the consciousness of a seven or eight year-old child. By means of this persona – ignorant, nervous, spoilt, like our adult selves – the poet tugs at his own and the readers' sense of guilt at having paid so little heed to the victims of war, and so begins the act of atonement and re-evaluation. The sculptor's 'imagined wind', the soldier's arrested pose, contrast with the movement of 'real winds' that buffet the living, the boy and his aunt, the pilot, the courting couples, and the farmer. What connects them, tenuously, to the dead soldier are the references to 'the barbed wire' (that 'had torn a friesian's elder') and the seaside location. Ledwidge had himself gone courting at the seaside, near Drogheda,[80] a journey presaging other fateful journeys, taking him away from roots and origins, 'the dolorous/ And lovely'. Heaney's imagery emphasises Ledwidge's distinctly Celtic, Catholic *mythos*, the mingled elements of *pagus* and Christian *disciplina*[81] while internal rhyme (altar/flowers/water/Easter) and those alliterated images of strength (rocks/raths/raftered) stress the seasonal, cultural, liturgical and historical pattern that shaped and sustained him. Once clothed in a 'Tommy's uniform', however, serving in the army of Ireland's traditional enemy, Ledwidge's identity seems drained of its life-blood. He acquires 'a *haunted* Catholic face, *pallid* and brave/ *Ghosting* the trenches', and, though he wears his sprig of hawthorn to remind himself of home, like his silence, 'cored from a Boyne passage-grave', the white blossom points forward as well as back.[82] His commitment to a foreign cause left him parched physically and spiritually, and, in the aftermath of Easter 1916, rent by the contradictoriness of his position, 'To be called a British soldier while my country/ Has no place among nations'. When, six weeks before his death, he expressed his sorrow that 'party politics should divide our tents', he could not have imagined how soon those same racial, cultural, and ideological differences would lead to the division of his land. Ironically the very place which gave his soul its confirmation, the ancient hills and sacred valley surrounding the Boyne, remains the seat and site of those divisions between the green and the 'true-blue'.

The last two stanzas pull together the various 'strains' of the poem. Through a succession of musical images and references – 'enigma', 'tunes', 'strains', 'drum', 'note', 'flute', 'keyed', 'pitched', 'consort' – Heaney expresses his view that, like every artist, Ledwidge should have attended to the tenor of his own spirit, instead of succumbing to 'the sure confusing drum', 'the cracked metre of a marching tune';[83] his instrument was the flute, not the gun. His note was pastoral, melancholic, Gaelic, not percussive or Anglo-Saxon. Sadly Ledwidge did not live long enough to resolve and exploit the 'Criss-cross' of conflicting influences in his background. His elegist has, and to a remarkable extent.

Following perhaps the precedent set by Yeats in his middle and late volumes, Heaney has shaped the end of his fifth collection with a piece invoking memories of and comparisons with its earliest poems. The macabre fate endured by Anselm, Gaddo, Hugh and Brigata, the 'young/ And innocent' of 'Ugolino', has been anticipated by that of other *Field Work* victims, 'the murdered dead' of 'Triptych', 'A Postcard from North Antrim', 'The Strand at Lough Beg', 'Badgers', and 'Casualty', where the betrayal motif has surfaced already.[84] The book closes as it opened focussing on the dramatic impact of political realities on private living, the contrasting meals of 'Oysters' and 'Ugolino' emphasising the poet's acute consciousness of the gulf between his experience of suffering and that of others, and his determination to give others a voice, to 'report the truth'. The poet's guilty anxiety, enjoying the 'tang' of words and the 'brine-stung/ Glut of privilege' in congenial, convivial company seems a far remove from Ugolino's terrible silence and grief and ghastly revenge, feasting on 'the sweet fruit' of his enemy's brain. 'Ugolino' takes us far from *Field Work*'s lyric centre, a world away from the Owenesque 'underground' of 'In Memoriam: Francis Ledwidge', where reconciliation is almost thinkable. Despite its remote setting in one of the iciest recesses of Dante's Hell, one quickly adjusts to the surreal violence, the familiar, intractable territory. The two figures of the second and third line, locked into an all-consuming hatred, might easily be a Republican and a Loyalist paramilitary, an I.R.A. man and a Brit.

If we pursue the analogy, as Heaney intends, Ulster becomes the 'nightmare tower', its innocent and guilty inhabitants plagued by moral famine, spiritual dearth. There, the 'future's veil' is 'rent', and children and young men can still be regarded as 'legitimate targets', despite the fact that the sins of fathers "Should never have been visited on his sons."

STATION ISLAND

The five years following the publication of *Field Work* saw further major changes and developments in the poet's career and in the political situation. In October 1980, Heaney's *Selected Poems 1965–1975* and *Preoccupations: Selected Prose 1968–1978* appeared. The year of the hunger strike crisis, 1981, saw him joining forces with the founders of Field Day, Brian Friel and Stephen Rea, in their endeavour to raise the level of the debate over critical issues of culture and identity, politics and art throughout Ireland. During the same year he resigned from his post at Carysfort College, having secured a five-year contract to teach at Harvard University for one term a year, beginning in January 1982. In 1982 he co-edited with Ted Hughes, *The Rattle Bag*, a poetry anthology which received considerable critical acclaim, and was awarded an honorary doctorate by his old university, Queen's, Belfast. The following year, 1983, the Field Day Press in Derry brought out *Sweeney Astray*, his translation of *Buile Suibhne*, and published *An Open Letter*, a good-natured, satirical, 'lyrical sideswipe at Penguin Books'[85] for including his work in an anthology of Contemporary *British* Poetry. Breaking 'Old inclinations not to speak',[86] he reminds the editors, Blake Morrison and Andrew Motion, and his many English and American readers, that Hibernia is his *patria*, not *Britannia*.

> be advised
> My passport's green.
> No glass of ours was ever raised
> To toast *The Queen*.

The year 1984 brought triumph, and loss. At Harvard he was elected to the Boylston Chair of Rhetoric and Oratory, but in the late autumn, while he was on tour promoting the joint publication by Faber & Faber of *Station Island and Sweeney Astray*, his mother died. His love for her and grief at her loss found shape and sound in the beautiful sonnet sequence at the heart of *The Haw Lantern*, 'Clearances'. Her absence would create a space 'Utterly empty', but 'utterly a source'.

The composition of the poems of *Station Island* coincided with a period of extreme political tension in the province. In late August 1979, shortly before the arrival of Pope John Paul II in Ireland, Earl Mountbatten of Burma, his fourteen year-old grandson and a fourteen year-old friend, were blown up at Mullaghmore, Co. Sligo. A few hours after this attack, eighteen soldiers were killed by two Provisional I.R.A. bombs at Warrenpoint in Co. Down. These killings, and the outrage they stirred, forced the Church authorities to abandon the idea of a papal visit to the archdiocese of Armagh. The nearest he came to the North was Drogheda, where at a vast open-air Mass on September 29, a month later, he appealed to the I.R.A. and to the other warring parties to end their campaigns of violence. "On my knees I beg you to turn away from the paths of violence and return to the paths of peace. You may claim to seek justice. I too believe in justice and seek justice. But violence only delays the day of justice." [87] Though this may have caused a dint in support for the Provisionals within the nationalist community, their popularity revived and increased over the next eighteen months as a result of the hunger strikes of 1980 and 1981. Relations between Republican prisoners and the British Government had been rapidly deteriorating since 1 March 1976, when 'special category' status had been withdrawn for offences committed after that date.[88] The Government's aim was to 'criminalise' the violence – and thus to deny it *mystique* – and to accommodate newly-admitted prisoners they built eight new cell blocks at Long Kesh (the Maze Prison), near Lisburn, the H-blocks. The initial Republican response to this denial of their political status was the 'blanket protest' which began in September 1976, when nineteen year-old, Ciaran Nugent, the first prisoner to be moved into the H-blocks, refused to change into prison clothing. After spending his first night and the next day naked, he was given a blanket to wear during exercise; it would become for him and for others a badge of defiance, and as more Republicans were moved into the H-blocks, the number 'on the blanket' multiplied. 'By the end of the decade there were more than two hundred blanket men and women in the Province's jails'.[89] Inside and outside Long Kesh, the temperature continued to rise. At the request of the leadership inside, the I.R.A. outside started to target prison officers for assassination.[90] While some warders reacted to this threat by showing kindness to the men in their charge, others responded with beatings. In March 1978 a number of prisoners refused to leave their cells, for fear of being beaten on their way to the showers and the lavatory, they said. In late April, immediately after a fight between an inmate and a warder allegedly resulted in the prisoner being 'dragged off to solitary confinement' and 'badly beaten',[91] Republican prisoners began smashing up the furniture in their cells. In response, the authorities removed everything from the cells except blankets and mattresses, and refused to use warders to 'slop out' for the prisoners while they maintained their sit-in. The prisoners replied by smearing their walls with excrement, in order 'to make a clean space where they could sleep and to dissipate the stench'.[92] Though for a good while this tactic earned them considerable media attention, particularly in America, and led to Archbishop Tomas O Fiaich's denunciation of the authorities,[93] it brought the restoration of political status no nearer. Consequently, in the autumn of 1980, the Republican leadership inside the prison embarked on the third phase of their 'endurance' campaign, the hunger strikes.[94] The first of these involved seven men and lasted fifty-three days, from October 27 to December 18, and ended when the Northern Ireland Office offered some concessions in a thirty-four page document and the lure of negotiations. 'Part of the deal was that the prisoners would be allowed to wear their own clothes in recreation time, and prison issue during working time',[95] but when this compromise arrangement broke down in late January 1981, a second strike was decided upon.

For the second H-block hunger strike, a dramatic new strategy was devised. Both the blanket and dirty protests were halted in order to encourage the media to focus exclusively on the fasting men. Instead of beginning their fast simultaneously on March 1 – the date when special status had been phased out five years earlier – each man joined at fortnightly intervals in order to extend and max- imise the emotional impact of the strike. Shortly before the start of his ordeal, their leader, Bobby Sands, declared, "This is between me and the British government and that is it. Between the two of us."[96] In the battle of wills that ensued, ten Republican prisoners perished, but support for their cause on the island soared to its highest pitch since Bloody Sunday.[97] Forty days into the strike, on April 9, Sands was elected Westminster MP for Fermanagh and South Tyrone in a by-election, securing 30,492 votes. Less than a month later, sixty six days into his fast, he died. An estimated seventy thousand attended his funeral.[98] Although Sands had requested that the strike should end with his death, it continued for a further five months. In the course of that time, nine more hunger strikers died – the second 'victim' was twenty-five year-old Francis Hughes, a Bellaghy man whose family the Heaneys knew well[99] – along with thirty members of the security forces and thirty civilians. Successive administrations in the South, Church leaders and various intermediaries pleaded with Mrs Thatcher and her Government to modify her 'inflexible approach'[100] and to come to some kind of accommodation with the strikers, but all to no avail. Had they succeeded, perhaps Northern Ireland might have been spared 'from one of the most bitter and polarising crises of the present troubles.'[101] Two days after the strike ended on October 3, James Prior, the new Secretary of State for Northern Ireland, granted the prisoners' original demand, to be allowed to wear their own clothes in prison.

Although *Station Island* contains only one overt reference to the hunger strike – section IX of the title sequence begins with a fourteen-line 'speech' by a hunger-striker who could easily be based on Francis Hughes – there are a significant number of allusions throughout the collection to prisons, cells, compounds, policemen, punishment, informers, betrayals, victims of violence in such poems as 'Chekhov on Sakhalin', 'Sandstone Keepsake', 'Granite Chip', 'An Ulster Twilight', 'The Loaning', 'Station Island' II, IV, VII, VIII, 'The First Flight' and 'The Old Icons'. The anguish and anger of his fellow Catholics in the North in the wake of the strikes must have had no little influence on Heaney's 'decision' in *Station Island* to embark upon a rigorous reappraisal of his conduct and role as an artist. Exile in Dublin, 'migrant solitude' in Harvard had brought him fame and financial security, but also sharpened an already acute moral consciousness and "made his own anxieties seem both insignificant by contrast and yet also more intense."[102] Though one part of him sensed that his poetic growth was being impeded by the continuing burden of political and religious obligation – the need 'to be faithful to the collective historical experience'[103] – another part felt compelled to meet the claims of his community, to pay his 'debt'.[104] By taking 'the strain',[105] by 'pulling his weight',[106] by proffering the 'service' of his verse, the poet hoped to earn the right to lyric freedom, buoyancy, flight.[107]

What characterises *Station Island* is this 'double note', this setting

down and sounding out of conflicting perspectives. Like its companion publication, *Sweeney Astray*, it tenses within itself the conflicting
elements at play in the Irish psyche and in so much of Irish
literature, the collision between Oisin and Patrick, the *pagus* and
disciplina, 'relish and penitence',[108] the carnal and the sacral. In both
volumes, Heaney lays bare the 'ingrained emotional grain lines'[109]
within the individual and collective Catholic subconscious, bringing
together narratives, characters, rites, images and locations belonging
to a shared and private past, from ancient Ireland to the present
unfree state. Part of that unfreedom is due to the all-pervasive
influence of the Catholic Church, which all too frequently denies
the individual choice and authority.[110] In a far more oblique way
than Joyce – or the apostate Sweeney – Heaney in *Station Island*
attempts to slip free of the Church's grip, to establish the legitimacy
of his own line and lines. Despite the presence of many coded
declarations of independence within the volume, however, one
senses that, like Joyce's Stephen in *Ulysses*, "he has not yet won the
battle behind his forehead to free . . . the mind from the mind."[111]
Naturally he feels some disquiet making the necessary move from
his first affiliations, leaving the security of 'cover'.[112] "Writers need
images and situations which release in them whatever is latent and
submerged and allow them to appease their perhaps unconscious
yearnings and tensions."[113] In order to allow such feelings to surface
and to further the process of individuation, he sets at the core of
his sixth volume a pilgrimage, returning imaginatively to a place
of retreat and renewal that he had visited three times during his
teenage years. He could not have chosen a site with richer spiritual,
historical, cultural, political, and literary associations.

　　Station Island, the island of the title, is situated on Lough Derg,
the lake of the cave, in County Donegal. There, according to tradition,
in a cave, during a fast that lasted forty days, St Patrick had a vision
of the Otherworld and actually experienced the pains of purgatory.
Subsequently, one of his disciples, St Davog, established a penitential retreat on the island, which from medieval times onwards was
referred to as 'St Patrick's Purgatory'. In the mid-twelfth century,
a knight called Owein visited the site, and 'had visions of souls
being tormented by devils'.[114] Accounts of his experience quickly
spread throughout Europe, and may have influenced Dante in his
conception of the first book of *The Divine Comedy*. Lough Derg is
the only place in Ireland considered worthy of inclusion on a 1492
map of the world, and its depiction in a recently discovered fresco

from Todi in Italy indicates that it was well-known there in the mid-fourteenth century.

The history of the pilgrimage over the last three hundred years suggests a definite correlation between its popularity and the state of politics in Ireland.[115] Interestingly the largest number of pilgrims this century visited Station Island in 1952, during a phase in which clerical influence on the government of the newly-formed Republic was at its height.[116] In that year 34,645 performed the pilgrimage and the thirteen year-old Heaney may well have been one of them. Interviewed in a film for R.T.E. in 1986, Lough Derg's current Prior, Monsignor McSorley, spoke of a significant increase in pilgrims over the previous four or five years, attributing it in part to the political situation in the North.[117]

The pilgrimage itself involves three days of rigorous spiritual exercises, during which time, through prayer and fasting, penitents 'die to the world', like Christ at Easter, in order to rise again. Barefoot and hungry, they must complete nine circuits of the island's holy places, kneeling before crosses dedicated to St Patrick and St Brigid and within six rings of stone, or 'beds'.[118] The paths around the beds contain jagged stones which serve as a reminder of the suffering endured by Christ on his 'stations', and how physical pain and difficulty can help purify the soul. At the centre of the pilgrimage is a 'long restless vigil',[119] lasting twenty-four hours, in which the penitents enter 'a twilight zone', a period in which their energy and awareness is 'gradually reduced', in which they are reminded how 'life is inescapably linked with death.'[120] By subjecting themselves to these rites, the pilgrims consciously connect themselves and their suffering with those of earlier generations of Irish Christians, a 'communion of saints' who may intercede on their behalf when after death they arrive in the real Purgatory.

With its stress on the bond between the living and the dead, its emphasis on the path of renunciation and sacrifice, its reliance on dramatic metaphor and symbol, its use of repetitive, mantra-like prayer, along with the – pious? masochistic? – practice of inflicting punishment on the body in order to cleanse the soul, the Lough Derg experience seems to enshrine quintessential features of Irish Catholicism. Many of these modes of thought and feeling have, of course, been taken up into Republican ideology, and surface in the language and actions of such men as Padraic Pearse, Terence McSwiney, and Bobby Sands.[121] Heaney makes no explicit connection between the ancient, ascetic spiritual rituals of Lough Derg and the twentieth-century use of the hunger strike as a political weapon, yet they do both spring from what he refers to in his brief introduction to *Station Island* for the *Poetry Book Society Bulletin* of Winter 1984, as *'self-afflicting compulsions* (my italics) . . . that once lived at the very centre of the Irish Catholic psyche.'

Within this same piece, Heaney attempts to differentiate between the particular, personal 'use' he has made of Lough Derg in the *Station Island* collection and earlier literary responses, those of William Carleton (1794–1869), Sean O Faolain (1900–91), Patrick Kavanagh (1904–1967) and Denis Devlin (1908–59). Two of these writers, both of Northern Catholic stock, actually materialise in Heaney's title sequence, in sections II and V respectively, and, together with Joyce, function as 'subversive' shades, challenging 'the claims of orthodoxy',[122] the poet's old allegiances. William Carleton and Patrick Kavanagh had very different motives for their visits to the island. Carleton's book, *The Lough Derg Pilgrim* (1828), arose from a need to find grace with his new Protestant masters, and was intended to serve as a piece of anti-Papist propaganda. However, what comes across most forcibly in his writing is how attuned he is to the poetry he intends to condemn, the 'pale, spectral visages' of the officiating priests, 'the sepulchral light of the slender tapers', 'the deep, drowsy, hollow, hoarse, guttural, ceaseless and monotonous hum' of the pilgrims at prayer.[123] In his *Lough Derg*, written in 1942 during one of the worst periods in his life, Kavanagh appears as an ironic and compassionate commentator, dwelling on the mismatch between the sacred and the secular – "'I renounce the World,' a young woman cried/ Her breasts stood high in the pagan sun" – diagnosing the malady from which he and most of his pilgrims suffer, a carnal and spiritual hunger, 'love's terrible need'.[124] It is significant that immediately after his encounter with Kavanagh – at the close of section V – Heaney becomes 'sunstruck', and recalls his translation from frustrated sexual fantasist, mocked by 'bags of grain/ And the sloped shafts of forks and hoes', to fulfilled activist, revelling in 'honey-skinned shoulder blades amd the wheatlands of her back', inhaling the sweet scents of 'the land of kindness'.[125]

From its inception, *Station Island* owed much to Heaney's involvement with translation. His substantial work on *Buile Suibhne* fed into the 'lyric events'[126] which make up the third section of the book, and supplied him with a rich store of image and allusion. His delight in Dante after reading the *Commedia* in translation resulted first in his rendering of the 'Ugolino' episode in *Field Work*, but subsequently influenced the shape, content and procedures at the core of his next volume. In his essay, 'Envies and Identifications: Dante and the Modern Poet', he explains how Dante gave him the confidence to tackle Lough Derg and create his own *purgatorio*, and identifies key elements in the poet's work on which he endeavoured to draw.

> What I first loved in the *Commedia* was the local intensity, the vehemence and fondness attaching to individual shades, the way personalities and values were emotionally soldered together . . . The way in which Dante could place himself in an historical world yet submit that world to scrutiny from a perspective beyond history, the way he could accommodate the political and the transcendent, this too encouraged my attempt." [127]

In order to achieve verification in his poetic vocation, to find his own equivalent of *la diritta via*, 'the right road', [128] Heaney determined to engage the spirit voices of his past and through them 'explore the strains' [129] of a riven consciousness.

From the outset of the collection dissonant notes trouble the harmony. At first reading the deft pace and fanciful conceits of 'The Underground' place it at a far remove from the hell of 'Ugolino' (the final poem of his previous book) and the purgatorial 'stations' ahead. It commemorates an event from the Heaneys' honeymoon in 1965, a frenetic dash through subterranean London to make it 'for the Proms'. The excitement of the chase is captured beautifully, dramatic participles ('running', 'speeding', 'gaining') and emphatic verbs ('japped', 'flapped', 'Sprang', 'fell') flying off like the buttons on his wife's coat. He establishes a warm, intimate tone through his direct address to his wife, with his use of features from spoken English ('There we were', 'And me, me then', 'damned if I look back'), and by the playful, erotic allusion to Pan's pursuit of Syrinx, [130] but distance and time make and mar the pleasure. Shared past tenses and first person plurals fade like 'echoes in that corridor', as Heaney retraces the path of memory in a separate present. The unromantic 'draughty *lamplit* station' where he ends up is a world away from the fairy tale innocence of a 'new white flower', '*moonlit* stones', Hansel and Gretel, the experience of the years intervening having left his soul 'japped with crimson', 'Bared and tensed'. Like Orpheus, he knows he is 'damned' if he risks looking back, yet love compels him to do so. *Station Island* will be about risking 'the backward look', enduring exposure. 'To remember everything is a form of madness', says Hugh in *Translations*. Madness, as Sweeney learnt, is the bitter price to be paid for flight.[131] For a little while, in the two poems which follow, the customary *gravitas* keeps its distance, and Heaney is free to relish sensuous experience – a seductive glimpse of a sacred body , delicious mouth-music in the words 'slub silk' ('La Toilette'); a tart smell, and a 'bitter and dependable' taste ('Sloe gin'). With 'Away from it all', 'Chekhov on Sakhalin' and 'Sandstone Keepsake', however, the old anxieties about 'doing the decent thing' – and not doing it – reemerge. In the first of these, 'Away from it all', a sequel to 'Oysters', Heaney seems to be suffering from what could be termed post-alimentary depression. A convivial occasion, a late night supper, develops into a heated debate during which the poet is forced to scrutinise his conduct as an artist. Lamely he proffers his friend 'rehearsed alibis', such as the quotation from Czeslaw Milosz's *Native Realm*, and in so doing creates an opportunity for an engagement with major questions about the relationship between art and action – Should poets and/or poetry engage in politics? Can poetry constitute an active participation in history? Does the writing of poetry make any difference to the state of Ireland? – an engagement which never materialises. As if to avoid further interrogation – or perhaps to answer it – Heaney turns away to the 'light at the rim of the sea', swims out to a lyric limbo. There, 'somewhere', washed by salutary currents of uncertainty and scruple, the poet treads water.

One of the main weaknesses of the poem is the meal he makes of his original image. After having 'pried' the lobster from its element, 'plunged and reddened' it – and unjustly implicated it in human violence through the reference to 'sunk munitions' – the poet adds insult to injury by changing into it. Assuming the final two lines are *meant to* suggest Heaney's predicament is analogous to the lobster's – 'hampered',[132] 'bewildered' when out of his element – one struggles to see how the poor lobster can be said to be 'fortified' before or after being taken apart.

'Chekhov on Sakhalin' and 'Sandstone Keepsake' would seem to support Seamus Deane's contention that for Heaney 'writing has itself become a form of guilt and a form of expiation from it.'[133] In both he appears to be moving towards the view that the poet may discharge his responsibility to give witness through *lyric* action. Chekhov's dedication to the healing arts – he was a doctor as well as a writer – make him another exemplary figure for Heaney, his life and work embodying right words and right actions, artistic and moral integrity. Heaney pans in on one particular incident in Chekhov's life, which occurred during his visit to the penal colony of Sakhalin. On his first night before embarking on his investigation into the conditions on the island, he opened a bottle of cognac – a parting gift from friends in Moscow – drank down the entire contents, and hurled the glass against the rocks in true aristocratic fashion. Chekhov's temperament was such that he was not given to making flamboyant gestures, but this one signalled an attempt to shatter the distance between himself and the stark deprivation and injustice he was about to meet. The whole enterprise was in fact a deeply symbolic act, a step back through origins far humbler than Heaney's, for Chekhov's grandfather had been a serf. By reporting on the state of Sakhalin, the artist was not only fulfilling a social role; he was also serving himself, performing 'stations' on the island to exorcise his past, and in so doing taking a step towards 'psychic and artistic freedom'.[134] He was to discover, however, like his Irish shadower, that it was one thing to aim 'to squeeze/ His slave's blood out', another to achieve it.

Within the poem Heaney clearly endeavours to square up to 'the burden of his freedom', to face his Sakhalin. Though, as I have suggested, Chekhov's island bears some resemblance to Station Island as a place of purgatory, its closest equivalent in Heaney's world is the prison camp ten miles south of Belfast, Long Kesh, the scene of the hunger strikes.[135] He would pass it each time he used the M1 motorway on his way north. It is a puzzle as to why Heaney should talk about the Russian 'travelling north', or describe Sakhalin as so 'far north, Siberia was south', when in fact it is situated in the far *east*, and beside the Pacific, not the Arctic Ocean. The only explanations for this 'error' or piece of poetic licence, apart from the obvious one that Heaney has no sense of geography, are that the poet is thinking specifically of Long Kesh as Ulster's Sakhalin, and/or that the word 'north' has now come to be loosely synonymous in his mind with a state of confinement, with wilderness, with inanition. A key reason for his obliqueness in referring to recent events may well lie in his view that poets should be "wary of stirring feelings which could be destructive and also wary of massaging collective feelings which could make for too much complacency."[136]

'Sandstone Keepsake' is similarly set in a place resonant with political associations. The beach at Inishowen where Heaney discovered the stone is on the 'Free State' side of the Foyle estuary; across the water, across the border, lies Magilligan Point, the site of an internment camp set up by the British in 1971. An emblem of the poet's division, the stone is first pictured being thrown 'from hand to hand', weighed up. Like its keeper, it belongs to history, and is marked with the colour of blood and guilt. It is a 'chalky *russet*', '*ruddier*' when out of the water, and has been bruised and '*bloodied*'. Physical reality is its domain. It is palpable, substantial, 'dense and bricky', utterly itself like Zbigniew Herbert's 'Pebble', "a perfect creature/ equal to itself/ mindful of its limits/ filled exactly/ with a pebbly meaning."[137] 'Lifted', arrested by the hands of the poet, it becomes 'permeated by false warmth',[138] turned into a symbol of transcendent Nature, translated by fanciful metaphor from the Foyle to the Phlegethon. In the middle of his myth-making, alluding to 'damned Guy de Montfort' and the *Inferno*, he checks himself ('but not really'), as if a humbler, inner, County Derry voice were telling him, 'Catch yerself on!', 'Just listen to yourself!', but even after this literary memory is allowed to finish its say. The final movement of the poem begins with the colloquial 'Anyhow' snapping the spell created by the 'casket, long venerated', and apparently concludes with a *Domine non sum dignus*,[139] an admission of his inadequacy. The sandstone brightens, wet and red, but Heaney, by contrast, appears relegated to shadow-status, slave-status, 'subjugated'[140] once more, ineffectually looking up at those who look down on him. It is interesting that he should offer in the last five lines the perspective of the British authorities, and present himself as a cowed, almost comic figure 'in scarf and waders'; Heaney seems almost to be conniving in their dismissal of him. The lines perhaps reflect his uncertainty whether his verses can indeed set wrongs right. Perhaps all the poem, the man and the stone can do is quietly look back 'with a calm and very clear eye'.[141]

'Shelf Life' brings together further objects for inspection, but not for veneration, as Heaney maps out his private space.[142] The sequence consists of six terse lyrics. In each an object is felt, weighed, repossessed. 'Granite Chip' definitely belongs to the Other Side. 'Acquired' from the Martello Tower at Sandymount, built by the British in 1804 to defend themselves against French invasion, it is unredeemed by its connection with Joyce. Petrified within it are most of the negative features of the Protestant imperialists who occupied the coast and the country; it suggests a culture that is primitive ('stone age'), cruel, repressed and repressive ('circumcising', 'Calvin edge', 'jaggy, salty, punitive/ and exacting'). By way of contrast, the 'Old Smoothing Iron' is a relic from a private world, an inside, female world of 'Soft thumps', 'intent' labour, 'resentment' and responsibility. Instead of sharp, articulate, male granite we have the 'dimpled angled elbow' and 'dumb lunge' of the woman ironing. The lesson she gives looks forward to the lesson Heaney will give his sons in 'A Kite for Michael and Christopher'; these simple – almost Christ-like? – lines point the way forward for Heaney in his endeavour to reconcile the conflicting pressures upon him as a poet. By accepting his duty to others he will merit release:

> pull your weight and feel
> exact and equal to it.
> Feel dragged upon. And buoyant.

The opening stanzas of 'Old Pewter' continue the celebration of Mossbawn persistence and virtue; the plate is 'dented', but 'temperate'; 'sullied', but 'soft'; 'doleful' and 'placid'. In the third, however, Heaney makes a break, recalling his first disobedience when under cover of mist he 'hid deliberately', knowing his parents were terrified that he had drowned in a nearby pool. In the final stanza, which Edna Longley sees as epitomising the whole book,[143] the pewter becomes an emblem of the soul and its imperfections. In the mysterious 'Stone from Delphi', Heaney prays for a renewed sense of piety and purpose, that 'some dawn' he may 'make a morning offering again'. He is compelled to define his religious longings using Catholic images, yet another part of him, as we know, cherishes the possibility of 'untrammelled' speech, like Joyce's.[144]

In the rather bleak, opaque, final poem of 'Shelf Life', 'A Snowshoe', 'an amorous blizzard' generates the only spark of warmth, and even the glow of love-making and word-making, which had left him 'eager and absorbed and capable', soon dims. A cold, empty, divisive wind 'lifts away' the snowshoe-kite, leaving Heaney 'blank' as "morning brightens/ Its distancing, inviolate expanse."

Gradually the pull of conscience eases, memories of family and home permitting a temporary respite from the 'suck of puddled, wintry ground' ('Remembering Malibu'), the 'miasma of spilled blood' ('Stone from Delphi'). After observing others' on the move southwards in 'A Migration', like Brigid, he "gets up and says, 'Come on'", and begins a series of poems of transit and transitions. Westering again in 'Remembering Malibu', walking a Pacific shore, his mind, his 'instep' is 'welted solid' to home strands and cells, the 'monk-fished, snowed-into Atlantic' and Skellig Michael, where anchorites settled in the sixth century. However much he longs to be rid of the encumbrance of *disciplina*, 'to rear and kick and cast that shoe', he can see how quickly footsteps fill 'with blowing sand' in the anonymity of exile. With 'Making Strange' the poet is back at base, and finding an American connection salutary. The occasion for the poem was a guided tour of the home-ground for the Jamaican-born poet, Louis Simpson. Visiting a local pub at opening time, Heaney ran into 'someone from childhood',[145] and was suddenly placed in the role of mediator between the two men, one the embodiment of 'travelled intelligence', smart and self-assured, the other a shy countryman, 'unshorn' and embarrassed 'in the tubs of his wellingtons'. Adeptly, Heaney alludes in the title itself to the different languages and worlds in which he and they have their being. In his first dialect, Hiberno-English, 'to make strange' means 'to be unfriendly', 'to draw back in fear', 'to react defensively', as his fellow-countryman does, as he himself used to. To the world of academe, however, 'making strange' conjures up the name of Victor Shklovsky, the Russian formalist critical theorist, who asserted that art sharpens and intensifies our perceptions of the world by making objects 'unfamiliar', a process he terms *ostranenie*. The task of modulating between two tongues reminds Heaney as to where his poetic roots and future lie, in preserving native speech, private and parochial experience, yet in being prepared to extend his range and pitch, to 'Go beyond what's reliable'. As a result of the stranger's presence, and because of the increased sophistication of his technique, he is able to re-cover his country, rediscover its familiar features and figures by means of metaphor and allusion that 'make strange'. The sudden 'flick' of a chaffinch is enough to set him in motion again, 'reciting . . . all that I knew'.

The scene switches next from Heaney to Hardy country. Re-siting himself at 'The Birthplace', Heaney evokes an intellectual and physical environment, which is Wessex, but could equally be Wicklow. Hardy's cottage is as frugal, 'small and plain' as the one at Glanmore, and, like it, inhabited by 'ghost life'. Beyond the dry confines of 'the deal table', 'the single bed', *dreams* 'of discipline' are

open tracts, a 'deep lane . . . sexual/ with ferns and butterflies' and
a 'damp-floored wood', where, *un*like Hardy's 'troubled pairs', the
poet and his wife disport themselves without serious consequences.
Meditating on these experiences in another dense image cluster,
Heaney stresses the dangers in the nestling instinct. The flight back
to sources, to roots and roosts – literary, spiritual, sensual, emotional
– must not result in a permanent grounding.

In the lyrics which follow, 'Changes', 'A Hazel Stick for Catherine
Ann', 'A Kite for Michael and Christopher' and 'The Railway
Children', the poet renews the 'covenant'[146] within his family,
linking a childhood long past with ones that are passing. Like
Yeats, he nourishes dreams for his young, yet fears perhaps a
descent to 'common greenness'.[147] In 'Changes' he conducts one
of his children through 'the long grass' to the old pump, an act,
a station performed in reverential silence. Still vividly present in
Heaney's inner ear are the sounds which accompanied the original
sinking of the shaft, the rasp, 'the slithering and grumble'. Though
rusted now, the pump retains its function as a point of energy,
renewal, tenderness, persistence. In place of the 'ruffled' women
who used to come to it 'with white buckets/ like flashes on
their . . . wings', there is now a young mother bird, nesting under
the 'citadel', guarding a single egg. Watching and watched by this
tutelary spirit, the poet finds 'a comfort in the strength of love',[148]
a determination to resist the pain in change. 'A Hazel Stick for
Catherine Ann' and 'A Kite for Michael and Christopher' similarly
'enshrine'[149] moments of illumination, fortifying experiences, the
passing-on of the baton and the line from one generation to another.
The 'salmon-silver' hazel stick is a humble offshoot of ancient stock;
it not only 'points back to cattle' and to Patrick Heaney, but also to
Celtic mythology, where salmon and hazels were associated with
'the wisdom of the ages' and 'the accomplishments of poetry and
science'.[150] Like so many other objects in Part One of *Station Island*,
the kite undergoes a startling metamorphosis, transmuted from its
'grey and slippy' origins into a 'small black lark', a heavy 'shoal',
an emblem of the soul struggling to fly 'above Sunday', a symbol
of Heaney's poetry.[151] The line lifts, like fortune or reputation, but
might well plunge.

Reflecting on the political and poetical strains his sons have
inherited, 'the strumming, rooted, long-tailed pull of grief', prompts
Heaney to consider once more the legacy of childhood. 'The Railway
Children' recreates beautifully a child's-eye view of the world,

through the repeated use of first person plural pronouns (six 'we's, one 'us', one 'ourselves' in thirteen lines), the choice of child-like images and diction ('white cups', 'sizzling wires', 'lovely freehand', 'shiny pouches'), the delightful apprehensions and misapprehensions.

> We were small and thought we knew nothing
> Worth knowing. We thought words travelled the wires
> In the shiny pouches of raindrops,
>
> Each one seeded full with the light.

At this point the young Heaneys' deductions about the material world become coloured by their experience of sacred metaphor – words, water, seeds, light – and the poem culminates with their belief that, with God's grace, they 'could stream through the eye of a needle'[152] and enter the Kingdom of Heaven.

· For the adult narrator of 'The Loaning', however, there are no longer such certainties as grace or transcendence, only shadows. At the opening of poem, he finds himself stranded 'in the limbo of lost words', latching onto the only discernible voice, the wind 'shifting in the hedge'. The comparison of this rustling sound to 'an old one's whistling speech' initiates a number of binary oppositions – human silence/stasis/mortality versus natural 'speech'/motion/mutability. Spell-bound, he watches the bird-like spirits of his 'old first place' in their articulate flight, as they pour from 'birch-white throats', or settle 'in the uvulae of stones/ and the soft lungs of the hawthorn'. Their 'streaming', 'fluttering' motion contrasts with the fixity of the human world, the rooted narrator, the 'turned-up carts' in *rigor mortis*, the 'iron bedsteads'[153] now serving as fencing. Instead of the breath of God, he now senses the breath and breadth of loss. His rosary is 'a shiver of beaded gossamers', and in place of the sacred chalice his eye drinks in 'the spit blood of a last few haws and rose-hips'. This latter image would be not be out of place in a poem of Wilfred Owen's, and suggests the extent to which the poet's apprehension of contemporary brutality has stained his perception of the natural world. Putting space and time between himself and this disturbing miniature, Heaney seeks security in sound and dimness, in the 'Big voices' of his father and his friends half-heard during an un-Troubled summer evening long ago. In describing how they 'took the twilight as it came/ like solemn trees', he emphasises *their* integration in the natural order, but, at the same time, their limiting passivity. 'There boy', a voice commands the dog, but the boy's imagination is about to slip the leash. Rejecting the confined, resigned, 'womanless' interior, he translates his 'small dreamself'[154] into the more feminine branches, like some latter-day Sweeney. There, he hears a still, sad counterpoint to the 'ayes' of the men, the wind hinting at the displacement ahead, like the Chorus in a Greek tragedy with their 'αι αι's. Like the 'Spit blood' at the end of Part One, this mournful note anticipates the violence of Part Three, with its dramatic, acoustic shift from exterior, everyday noise ('High-tension cables/ singing', 'barking dogs', 'juggernauts changing gear', the crack as 'a twig snapped') to inner, everyday horror, the sound of a torture victim undergoing his stations. Preceded by nightmarish allusions to Dante's 'bleeding wood', the grim final frames from 'The Loaning' act as a further reminder of the distance separating Heaney from the age of innocence and airiness, as a result of his intellectual, literary, political and spiritual 'enlightenment'. In creating the concluding scene once more he employs references to the language and rites of Catholicism with ironic effect, depicting the new universal 'liturgy' and its vicious, 'murdering ministers', operating in a state near you.[155]

It is within the poetic rites and penitential encounters of the title sequence of *Station Island* that one discovers Heaney's most sustained attempt at achieving absolution and permission as a writer. In order to resolve the competing claims of orthodoxy and individuality, and to inquire into his own conduct, Heaney engages in dialogue with 'figures from the unconscious'.[156] These include shades from his private past – Simon Sweeney, in I; his Aunt Agnes in III; a young priest, Terry Keenan, in IV; his old primary teacher at Anahorish, Barney Murphy, in V; an old footballing friend, William Strathearn, in VII; the archaeologist, Tom Delaney, and his cousin, Colum McCartney in VIII; a neighbour, a hunger striker from Bellaghy, in IX – along with exemplary, confirmatory presences from the literary domain, such as William Carleton (II), Patrick Kavanagh (V), St John of the Cross (XI) and James Joyce (XII), and the spirits of Sweeney, Dante, Mandelstam. Each has either a narrative or an admonition to impart, or a direction to offer, and, as a consequence, the text contains frequent allusions to roads, trails, tracks and paths which might or might not lead to betrayal, might or might not forward the process of individuation.

'Station Island' begins, like *Buile Suibhne*, with conflicting sounds in the air, with the power of the Church pitched against 'the older, recalcitrant Celtic temperament'.[157] There is a breathless urgency in the opening phrase with its four strong stresses – 'A húrry of béll nótes' – a pressure which will be maintained by the rapid-movement of the six-syllable, enjambed lines. Once the 'morning hush' has been violated by the sound of *Sunday*, it 'could not settle back' and soon a second presence materialises on the scene. Symbolically defined by his bow-saw, 'held/ stiffly up like a lyre', and by his association with hazels, Simon Sweeney, like his royal namesake, belongs to an Ossianic, pre-Christian Ireland, embodies pagan energy and lyricism, a trail of thought and feeling Heaney had been taught to fear. The rather provocative way with which he is addressed, as "an old Sabbath-breaker/ who has been dead for years", irritates Sweeney, who already disliked the pious, holier-than-thou attitude he detected in the young Heaney. Although initially he is bluntly dismissive of the poet and his learning – "Damn all you know" – and teases him over his 'First Communion face' and boyish superstition, Sweeney's final words demonstrate a concern for Heaney's welfare. His advice to 'Stay clear of all processions' prefigures Joyce's in XII, but, at this early stage in the psychomachia, the pull of conventional piety is still too strong. When the 'quick bell-notes' sound again, Heaney falls into mournful line with the 'shawled women' whose somnolent movement 'saddened morning'. In response to their litany – or perhaps as a result of his fasting – a host of 'half-remembered faces' appears, a communion of the dead. His submission to their collective will, and rejection of Sweeney, is clearly signalled; the poet 'drew behind them', followed 'their drugged path' as a fellow pilgrim, 'trailed' their foot-steps, despite the damaging effect this course had on 'the tender, bladed growth' of his imagination.

The ease of commerce between past and present is cleverly established in II, which, following biblical precedents, is set on a road, in a high place.[158] Heaney drives effortlessly from the twentieth century world into a past which seems contemporaneous. Despite the distancing created by historical references and macabre, Gothic effects,[159] essentially the Ulster childhood that Carleton describes, "nights spent listening for/ gun butts to come cracking on the door," mirrors that of recent generations, particularly of those brought up in Belfast and Derry in the early 1920s, the late 1960s and early 1970s. Although Carleton's "O holy Jesus Christ, does nothing change?" is spoken in response to the fervour Heaney expresses both for Lough Derg and *Lough Derg Pilgrim*, it sums up the poem's consistent perspective on the politics of the North. The situation may have appeared comparatively tranquil in the poet's younger days, when Catholic taste had turned from the harsh 'unforgiving' chords of the Fenian 'harp' to more submissive notes, thanks to the combined efforts of Church and Stout, "By then the brotherhood was a frail procession/ staggering home drunk on Patrick's day", but sectarian tensions remained. Along with bright, celebratory, relaxed memories of a 'normal', rural childhood and adolescence ('flax-pullings, dances, summer crossroads chat'), Heaney recalls more sinister ones in stanza eighteen. The wording, listing and tone all suggest the impassioned voice of a younger self breaking through.

> All that. And always, Orange drums
> And neighbours on the roads at night with guns.

Though small beer in comparison to the acute suffering detailed in IV, VII, VIII and IX, these personal, painful recollections clearly affect his listener. The repetition and reassurances sound positively paternal.

> 'I know, I know, I know, I know,' he said,
> 'but you have to make sense of what comes.
> Remember everything and keep your head.'

In the course of their exchanges, Carleton's attitude to Heaney has altered dramatically. It had taken 'a shower of rain' to transform the anger and the disbelief into calm disapproval, but here he displays sensitivity and sympathy, acknowledging an affinity of spirit and experience. Another aspect of his complex character has come alive. Underneath the tough, irascible, self-assured exterior of the 'old fork-tongued turncoat' – 'If times were hard, I could be hard too' – Heaney detects a divided sensibility like his own. By means of this second 'mask', the poet articulates his own determination to travel alone, to examine the 'signatures of all things I am here to read',[160] to demonstrate his Joycean conviction that art must address itself both to lyrical and unlyrical matter, the 'trout . . . in a spring' and 'maggots sown in wounds'.[161] In the choice of his parting image, as in the rest of his language, Carleton reveals the common ancestry he shares with Patrick Kavanagh (see V) and the poet from Co. Derry;

it is rural, unromantic, and typically Ulster Catholic in its *humilitas*. Intellectually a dissenter, like Heaney, he retains a potent, more than residual loyalty to 'the first kingdom',[162] his earliest physical, emotional, spiritual, linguistic terrain.

In the interconnected poems III and IV, Heaney returns to private spaces, to focus on death, faith and innocence. In order to reach back and quicken memory at the beginning of III, he resorts to traditional ritual practice, dubbing it wryly as 'Habit's afterlife'. It works, however, and soon he is back at source, 'among bead clicks and the murmurs/ from inside confessionals', meditating on another secular/sacred object from home, a tiny, shell-covered, seaside memento. This had belonged to his father's sister, Agnes, who had died in the 1920s, a child victim of tuberculosis. Like the delicate harvest bow in *Field Work*, it acquires the status of a holy relic. Shrouded by tissue, silence and mystery, invested with the Lamb-like innocence, the virginal spotlessness of its possessor, the simple trinket becomes a 'grotto' in the imagination of the impressionable, intensely religious boy, and subsequently a fetish, a taboo object, forbidden fruit that he would 'forage' for. The epithets used to describe it in stanza four, 'shimmering ark, my house of gold', closely echo phrases from the *Litany of the Blessed Virgin*, where Mary is addressed in successive lines as 'Tower of Ivory', 'House of Gold', 'Ark of the Covenant', and, three lines later, as 'Health of the Sick'.[162] The prayer, recited each night as part of the family Rosary, also includes the *Agnus Dei*,[163] which may explain why the name of this long-dead child haunted Heaney so much, and why he felt her spirit had been transferred to him. Suddenly a 'cold draught' breaks the spell memory has conjured, and prompts Heaney to consider other absences, such as that of the young missionary father, the subject of IV, who had died as a result of his stationing in 'swamp-fed', sweltering air of a rain forest. Imagining the physical and spiritual decay of that dank mission compound, he recalls a grim intimation of mortality from his own past, the discovery of the decomposing body of the family dog. The 'bad carcass' serves as an ironic contrast to the hallowed, bodiless vision he has of snowdrop-white Agnes, and may consciously or unconsciously echo an early scene from Joyce's *Ulysses*.[164]

Poem IV – or perhaps one should say canto IV – is recognisably set on Station Island itself, between the crosses of St Patrick and St Brigid. In narrating the story and recording the effects of one young man of living out his priestly vocation, it generates a subtext in which Heaney voices his need to 'outstrip obedience' ('Alerted') if he is to fulfil his poetic vocation. Here the formal influence of Dante is seen again, with the Irish poet employing his own version of *terza rima*, which he had already used in II and would subsequently use in key poems, VII, XI, XII. Within the opening stanza, binary opposites come into play, the 'Blurred swimmings' of poetic sight contrasting with the seemingly fixed certainties of the Catholic faith enshrined in the stone pillar and iron cross. Twice in the poem Heaney is about to embark on his first station; in line three, he is 'ready to say the dream words', while in lines 16–17, his arms are outstretched in the required gesture of renunciation, 'but I could not say the words'. What prevents him is a hazy image to which he gives definition, and his conviction that the World, the Flesh and the Devil should not be renounced, but rather accepted, relished and confronted. The clash with orthodox Catholic 'truths' begins with the 'Blurred oval prints of newly ordained faces', the first adjective and final noun implying that the individuals had already relinquished much of their individuality. In accepting what they interpreted as a calling from God, many of these idealistic, inexperienced young men were in fact responding to the call of parental piety or ambition, and had allowed themselves, body, mind and spirit, to be taken in by 'dream words', illusions about the nature of the world. Encoded in the physical description of the fledgling priest, Terry Keenan, are omens of the struggle between Faith, Flesh and the World which will be fought out inside him. 'I met a young priest', Heaney writes, 'glossy as a blackbird'. The blackbird image, as has been noted, has pagan, pre-Christian associations. The simile and the perky rhythm imply a bright, chirpy, vigorous personality, at variance with the ancient role that has subsumed it, the sober *disciplina* possessed by stole and cincture. (There is similarly something incongruous about the 'polished shoes' – smart, practical, contemporary? masculine? – beneath the effeminate frippery of the 'pleated, lace-hemmed alb'.) The young man's tragic fall from this pristine state comes quickly, and is anticipated in the unflattering analogy of the fifth stanza. The old, forgotten bicycle wheel, buried in a ditch, becomes a metonym for Keenan himself, trapped under 'jungling briars/ wet and perished'. Fever rips him out, and all that is left behind is abandoned space. The ghost's account of the futile waste of his life is vividly dramatised, by making him short of breath, like a tubercular victim, capable only of speaking in curt sentences or noun phrases, and by means of striking images. ('I rotted like a pear. I sweated masses.') A clue to his failure – and the Church's failure – may be seen in his extremely limited perception of those he has been sent to redeem. His attitude to the indigenous population is a typically European, colonial one – in his eyes they consist solely of 'Bare-breasted / women', 'rat-ribbed men' and 'head-dresses' – and ill becomes an Irishman.

Whereas with Carleton in II, Heaney placed himself in the role of Naïf, in IV he reveals a greater maturity than that of his subject. Heaney's empathy for a fellow Catholic 'victim', and the terrible price he paid, is mixed with anger at the Church and the priest's connivance with it. To be 'doomed to do the decent thing',[165] the poet now believes, means to submit to the authority of a fallible Church and blindly ignore one's own individual moral instincts. He accuses Keenan with complicity in an act of betrayal, of offering cheap chat and easy consolations to the local community, instead of helping them resist the forces oppressing them, and their own spiritual, cultural, political and economic subjugation. The legitimacy of the charge makes the priest falter, but then provokes a counter-charge, 'And you . . . what are you doing here?'. It is the question with which Heaney has endeavoured to grapple throughout *Station Island*. The defendant presses home his attack, challenging Heaney to explain why he had allowed himself to become confined once more in the narrow compound of Catholic pieties and loyalties, 'Unless you are here taking the last look'. Whether Heaney's silence indicates that he has broken completely with the Catholic faith, as many critics conjecture, is itself a matter of conjecture. Only the poet can give the definitive reply. Certainly within this poem he is striving to 'disentangle the soul'[166] from what he sees as the pernicious elements in his own and the collective Catholic past, in order to clear the ground for future growth.

In poems V and VI Heaney reverts to the role of disciple, and celebrates the contribution to his creative development by a number of masters. The first of these is Bernard Murphy, his primary teacher, a foster-figure whom the poet delights to shake by the hand and jokes with. The images describing him are firmly rooted in the old culture of Co. Derry, and are generally connected with fertility, energy and rural labour. He is compared to a bear and a bull; his feet resemble 'a dried broad bean' which later bursts into life; his territory is full of hay and bird's nests, birches and dairy herds; he is like a mower, and his breath whooshes like a scythe; his disciplined teaching converted young mouths into 'busy whetstones' and sharpened their minds. It

was Master Murphy who had quickened the young Heaney's intellectual and linguistic appetites, and provided him and others with a
practical means to improve their life-chances – education. Although,
like Keenan's mission, the scene of his earthly 'station' has now
been reclaimed by nature, the difference is that at Anahorish school
something was achieved, endured, and grew. After this refreshing
encounter, however, Heaney finds himself again out of synch with
his fellow pilgrims – as he will be throughout VI – facing the 'wrong
way' as they stream towards him. His mind is on another literary
mentor and his catechetics.

> *For what is the great*
> *moving power and spring of verse? Feeling, and*
> *in particular, love.*

The tone switches once more at the close of the poem with the
appearance of Patrick Kavanagh, for whom Lough Derg was also
a source of 'contradictory awarenesses'.[167] Colloquial, comic, full
of easy intimacy, his 'parting shot' prepares the way for VI's focus
on secular secrets, sexual growth. Shutting out the bell, the basilica
and the 'somnolent hymn to Mary', Heaney word-plays with an
early sweetheart, relishes a wisp of Horace, a longer waft of Dante,
and a redemptive moment with his own Beatrice, and so revives
his *'wilting powers/ . . . like somebody set free'*. After holidaying in
sunlight, lyric sex and lyric poetry, however, a three-part reckoning
comes.[168]

Four dead young men seize centre stage once more in poems VII,
VIII and IX, leaving Heaney at his most exposed. Each forces him
to live their final moments, to scrutinise his conduct in the face of
their deaths. That he regards his responses to have been inadequate
can be seen in the short shrift he gives to his own lame excuses.
Accusations are succeeded by self-accusations, and ultimately, in
IX, by admissions of self-disgust. It might be argued that in this
phase of 'Station Island' the poet fulfils a critical requirement of
the pilgrimage, which is 'to chastise one's own soul'.[169] VII is
a particularly well-crafted piece. Within the terza rima, Heaney
reproduces the authentic rhythms and language of Ulster speech,
and blends in deft touches of narrative, dramatic and poetic detail.
(The horrific event recounted in the poem was clearly suggested
by the murder of a shopkeeper in Co. Antrim. William Strathearn,
a footballing companion of Heaney's youth, was the victim of a

sectarian killing carried out by two off-duty policemen.) Much of the
poignancy of the poem comes through delicate ironies and musical
effects. The languorous ripples of stanza one – particularly in line
two with its long vowels ('u ', ' ɑɪ ', 'ʊ ', ' ɑɪ ', ' əʊ ')
and alliterated 's', 'l', and 'ng' sounds – are cleverly disturbed in
lines 4 and 5 first by a reflection that does *not* appear, then by 'a
presence' which does. Such a vague, insubstantial word in no way
prepares us for the shock that is coming. When at last he faces –
and makes us face – the ravaged face of his friend, the semantic
impact is sustained by the keening music in the lines. The regular
pumping of the four 'b's sound like a gun, and even the vowels
appear stricken:

> His br*ow*
> was bl*ow*n *o*pen ab*o*ve the *eye* and bl*oo*d
> had dr*ie*d on his neck and ch*ee*k.

Ironically it is the murdered man who offers consolation, with
his 'Easy now' and his comforting, but inappropriate footballing
analogy, reminiscent of Owen's 'Disabled'.[170] In counterpoint to
the shopkeeper's almost dispassionate, matter-of-fact manner is his
wife's more perceptive, impassioned responses. He talks of having
the 'sense not to put on the light', is shaken by the persistent
Macbeth-like knocking, and yet ignores his fears and naively goes
downstairs to open the door, so used is he to doing 'the decent
thing'.[171] He dismisses her fears as hysteria, 'Is your head/ astray,
or what's come over you?', and maintains the grim irony as he talks
of her 'lying dead still'. Before leaving her for the last time, instinct,
which might have saved his life, makes him reach across the bed
and squeeze her hand. A commonplace intimacy, its poignancy is
enhanced by the ordinariness of the language which follows it.
Even Heaney's 'plainest style'[172] is charged with double meanings,
and *'cooked meat'* and *'open up'* are soon followed by other ironic
phrases, references to 'the be-all and *end-all*' and to Stratheam's
'open-faced' nature. Moved by the dead man's playful humour –
his light dig at Heaney's weight – appalled that such physical grace
and style should be butchered by 'shites', the poet embarks on a
ponderous apology, its first line mannered, its second stuffed with
polysyllables. The reply he receives is again a plain one, "'Forgive/
my eye', he said, 'all that's above my head'", and perhaps contains
an ironic echo of Kavanagh's *Lough Derg*. In that place of restoration,

'a poor soul' could be "freed/ To a marvellous beauty above its head".[173]

Set between one 'neighbourly murder' and another lies a tribute to another stylist, Tom Delaney, who had opened up the world of archaeology to Heaney in the 1970s. An assistant keeper in the Antiquities Department of the Ulster Museum, he had died in 1979 at the age of thirty-two.[174] Again the poet is overwhelmed by feelings of inadequacy in the face of death, regretting that he had left so much unspoken when he visited his friend for the last time in hospital. Gifted and gift-giving, Delaney had lovingly pursued his calling, looking into the 'still' face of history, lined, like the present, with 'muck', 'force', and, more rarely, 'grace', until illness had cruelly intervened to deny him 'what seemed deserved and promised'. Acutely conscious of the injustice of Delaney's fate, and how his own path through life had been 'irradiated'[175] with good fortune, Heaney lapses into silence once more, a guilty silence which breeds three visions. The first is a befitting emblem for the history of the North, a hoard of neolithic axe heads, each charged with 'force' and 'menace'.[176] Displacing these 'eggs of danger', a more peacable image from Catholic Ireland comes to mind, a cast of a medieval abbess, 'mild-mouthed and cowled, a character of grace', which the 'woodkerne' Delaney had presented to the Heaneys. At the very moment Heaney feels strong enough to look his friend in the eyes, a third figure confronts him, a 'bleeding, pale-faced boy'. When at first Heaney fails to register who it is, his cousin quietly, but scathingly, reminds him. While sectarian gunmen were blazing into Colum McCartney, the poet was relaxing with literary friends amid 'the most interesting Cistercian remains in Ireland',[177] at Jerpoint Abbey, Co. Kilkenny. Making up for his wordlessness in 'The Strand at Lough Beg', McCartney indicts Heaney on a number of counts, accusing him of a woeful failure to his 'own flesh and blood'. Instead of returning to Bellaghy immediately when he 'got the word', he had remained in the South, and had shown less emotion at the news than the poets who were with him. In his 'defence', Heaney initially deflects attention from himself, suggesting that his friends' responses were in part voyeuristic, and that his own was conditioned by a certain fatalism ('encountering what was destined') and a feeling of utter emptiness ('I felt like the bottom of a dried-up lake'.) The reference to Lough Beg – and yet another self-centred image – sparks off McCartney's second attack. He claims that Heaney was guilty of evasion, and, worse, complicity in the crime against him; he had "whitewashed ugliness, and drew/ the lovely blinds of the *Purgatorio*/ and saccharined my death with morning dew." Accusations that he had sometimes softened cruelty and sentimentalised brutal events were not new.[178] That the poet should apparently denounce previous work for 'aestheticising and trivialising the ethical'[179] is remarkable, as Barry Goldensohn has suggested. However, one should perhaps be on one's guard when rhetoric is wielded to whip the lyric. In the opening essay of *The Government of the Tongue*, Heaney has argued so persuasively on the effectiveness of the lyric riposte to violence that I am extremely doubtful whether he is in fact repudiating the earlier poem; perhaps both 'The Strand at Lough Beg' and 'Station Island' VIII should be accepted simply as 'competing discourses', and equally valid.[180]

The five sonnets of IX complete the vigil and the rigorous self-inquisition which has accompanied it. The poet plummets to his lowest point yet, sucked down in a vortex of self-disgust, until restorative images in the last three sonnets bear him upward. The descent begins with the monologue of a dead hunger striker, almost certainly based on Francis Hughes. It was composed, along with the rest of the poem, in circumstances which parallel to some extent those detailed in VIII; while the poet's family were paying their respects at the dead man's wake in Bellaghy, Heaney was in privileged surroundings, attending a poetry reading in Oxford, staying at All Souls, in rooms belonging to Sir Keith Joseph.[181] Steeped in guilt, anger and frustration, the poem determines neither to endorse nor to condemn overtly the striker's actions. The opening couplet starkly records the physical effects of the fast, the verbs ('dried', 'Shrank', 'tightened' and 'cracked') emphasising the withering, the process of contraction afflicting the vital nouns, 'brain', 'turf', 'stomach'. Each of these three had been a repository for new life in 'Bog Queen', but in this poem Heaney steers clear of fertility myths. Two decades earlier, looking at the serene expression and 'stained face' of the Tollund Man, he had translated himself into a 'Bridegroom to the goddess'. Now, however, he is sidelined, observing the ceremony from a distance, with its 'white-faced groom' perishing for the sake of the same elusive, insatiable bride.[182]

Ambivalence characterises the presentation of the striker; he is tracker and tracked, ambusher and ambushed, 'emptied and deadly', aggressor and victim. In the second sonnet, several phrases recognise the 'common ground' shared by the paramilitary and the poetic activist. Each possesses an 'unquiet soul'; each has been shaped by and trapped by the ancient bog, allured by the 'maimed music' of tribal loyalties; each longs for 'medicinal repose'. Repose, however, belongs to another time.[183]

In the third sonnet he is adrift on a surreal sea, all efforts having 'run to waste'. Like 'The Steadfast Tin Soldier' in Hans Andersen's tale, he is swept along a gutter and down into a sewer on a 'swirl of mucky, glittering flood'.[184] This composite metaphor bears not only the poet's disgust with himself, but also the sickening tide of hatred reactivated by the hunger strikes, and the near-irresistible pressure to conform demanded by Catholic and Republican ideology. Perhaps this is the 'shed breast' which threatens to maintain his subjection to 'connivance and mistrust'. When he cries out, the spell is broken, and first one, then another magical apparition rises up before him. Both represent the redemptive power of Art; the candle, like a ship of light, illuminates 'the course and currents' of his past life, while the old brass trumpet promises access to harmony. Before he can make music, rage must burn itself out. The bitter outburst which begins the fifth sonnet – "I hate how quick I was to know my place/ I hate where I was born, hate everything/ That made me biddable and unforthcoming" – seems one further attempt 'to squeeze/ His slave's blood out',[185] but a calmer note establishes itself at the poem's mid-way point, in which Heaney, through three similes, comes to accept himself for what he is, realising that his place, origins and 'half-composed' condition are his greatest source and resource.

For the final stage of the pilgrimage, Heaney utilises three different routes towards renewal that had already proved so efficacious in his development as an artist, and would continue to do so; he plumbs private memory to achieve a lyric epiphany (X); he uses the act and impact of translation as a means of enlarging his poetic sensibility and 'historical sense',[186] of re-defining himself within a broader cultural context (XI); he keeps faith with parochial literary *genii* (XII). The mug of X and the kaleidoscope of XI he translates into magic vessels through which the restorative rites of Art can be enacted. For the child the mug out of reach, just as the spade of 'Digging' was, but for the adult poet it becomes a richly accessible symbol, standing as a symbol of cultural origins to be treasured and transcended. Mossbawn can be read in its every sprig and crack, and each its 'turbulent atoms'; far humbler than Keats's 'silent form', it is nevertheless possessed by 'truth and beauty'.[187] While its cornflower pattern may imply its own and its owners' integration with the natural cycle, the adjective 'unchallenging' and the verb phrase 'repeating round it' suggest a dull predictability, from which it can only be released through the defamiliarising processes of Art. Physically the mug remained unaltered after its theatrical debut, but the family's perception of it changed dramatically, and it had helped to transform the whole audience's apprehension of reality; they were made conscious, if only for a while, of a world beyond their 'small hearths', awesome, miraculous, capable of change. Principally a celebration of poetic retrieval and transfiguration, X has a political dimension too. Although from very different motives and with very different goals in mind, both the poet and the paramilitary of IX, lured by 'The dazzle of the impossible', are reacting against the passive, inward-looking attitudes that had prevailed within the minority Nationalist community of Northern Ireland through most of its existence.[188] In XI we witness two further acts of retrieval, and a double translation. Whereas in his *John Malone Memorial Lecture*, Heaney's account of the scuttling of his kaleidoscope ends in a terrible sense of failure,[189] in XI its immersion and descent turns to triumph. In a metonym for Heaney's future poems, it becomes 'a marvellous lightship'; 'abased', it rises again. The promise of resurrection pervades the rest of the poem, which consists of a fine rendering of a poem from St John of the Cross, set as a penance to Heaney by a travelled Irish monk. 'The Song of the soul that is glad to know God by faith', according to one commentator, speaks of the need for the individual soul to 'go through a dark night' to find God, to experience 'a kind of death' in which 'the prerogative of our own way of thinking' is sacrificed in order that 'our emptiness will be filled with a new presence . . . the contact of divine love.'[190]

As a counterpoint to the traditional, sacramental images of XI (Christ as the 'eternal fountain' and 'this living bread') and its litany-like refrain ('although it is the night') comes the 'cunning', but equally 'narcotic' voice of James Joyce in XII. A fellow of infinite tongues, he switches quickly out of the sonorous Heaneyspeak of his opening lines, with its talk of obligations and rites, discharged or not discharged, into a far more down-to-earth, immediate style, and concludes with metaphors from his favourite element, the sea. Appearing at the sequence's conclusion, he is Heaney's most important guide, is addressed as 'Old father', and even bears the emblem of paternal authority, an ashplant. The physical, emotional and psychological ordeal on the island has left the poet drained, but on the mend, 'Like a convalescent'. Immediately he steps off the ferry and back onto the too, too solid earth, he receives first Joyce's helping hand, and then the clearest, straightest of directions. Urging Heaney to abandon the earnest, penitential mode, Joyce promotes an antithetical, individualistic view of the poet's role and responsibilities, stressing self-assertion and the dream of lyric fulfilment, instead of the orthodox Catholic 'virtues' of self-abasement, collective solidarity, self-denial. Although they contain 'nothing I had not known/ already', Joyce's images and imperatives, which speak of agricultural labour ('harness', 'Cultivate'), sensual pleasure ('hands at night', 'sun', 'breast'), flight ('Take off from here') and music ('Now strike your note'), impact upon him, like the blows of the rain. Restored from torpor and exhaustion, the poet excitedly informs Joyce of the bond between them, which he describes as 'a revelation/ set among my stars', 'the collect of a new epiphany'. Heaney feels ratified as an Irish writer of English by the fact that his birthday, April 13, coincides with a key diary entry in *A Portrait of the Artist*. It is the moment when Stephen Daedalus sloughs off his 'previous linguistic inferiority complex',[191] on discovering that the English Jesuit, who is his Dean of Studies, is as ignorant as he is arrogant. The Dean had queried Stephen's use of the word 'tundish' for a funnel, implying that it must be an example of quaint olde Irish dialect.[192] Rather than being gratified by his disciple's reverential attitude, Joyce, like Carleton in II, is irritated, and accuses Heaney of 'raking at dead fires' in raising the language issue.[193] 'The English language belongs to us', he affirms; the battle to possess it and to repossess their own Irish identity had been won long ago by Yeats, Wilde, O'Casey, Synge, Kavanagh, and Joyce himself. Instead of trying to swim with the tribe and act as a voice for others,[194] Heaney should strike out alone, he suggests. Strength, vision, confirmation must come from remaining 'at a tangent', 'out on your own', as Mandelstam realised.

> Courage. Keep the eye wide.
> Be the dark speech of silence laboring.[195]

Despite the downpour which closes in on him at the end of XII and punctuates his final speech, the ghost of Joyce refuses to be deflected from 'his straight walk'.

Although Joyce can dismiss the imagined pilgrimage to Station Island as 'infantile', or as 'a backsliding enterprise'[196] as an earlier version has it, for Heaney it was a journey that had to be undertaken.

Whereas in 1972, in the wake of Bloody Sunday, he found it easy to heed the call of 'religious, political and domestic obligation',[197] by the late '70s and early '80s, issues were no longer so clear-cut, and necessarily his stance became more ambivalent. The hunger strikes with their much more complex psychic freight compelled him and others within the Nationalist community to agonise over their position, pressuring them, in the words of one historian, 'to side again with a bankrupt ideology that had become alien to most and irrelevant to many.'[198] According to Padraig O'Malley

> The hunger strikes caught the South in the middle of a social transformation. A new order was emerging as the country changed from a producer to a consumer society . . . The older visions of self that sustained the producer society – hard work, thrift, "sacrifice in the name of a higher law, ideals of duty, honour, integrity," the sublimination of self-needs" – were being pushed aside for the newer vision of personality with its emphasis on "self-fulfilment, self-expression, self-gratification." But the old order did not yield willingly, and the hunger strikes became a powerful symbol of the old values, the hunger strikers silent accusers, adding to the sense of dislocation, compounding the stirrings of latent guilt.[199]

In Part Three of *Station Island* Heaney attempts to transcend the present by flying back into the past to 're-collect', and 're-member' a world once whole. Not surprisingly, given the length of time he had devoted to *Buile Suibhne*, and the acute tensions he had been experiencing, when 'his brain convulsed/ his mind split open',[200] Heaney chose the figure of Sweeney as a vehicle through which to explore his own sense of displacement. 'The First Gloss' begins the search for a 'justified line', which takes him back to the margin, to the eastern edges of Co. Derry, away from 'great historical action' to 'the rhythms of the yard'.[201] In 'Sweeney Redivivus' he stirs the magic sand,[202] and pays out the line leading back to Mossbawn. On his return he discovers everywhere the marks of change, as he did in 'The Loaning'. There is still a bitter smell 'blowing off the river', but the scutch mill has long gone, and his tree retreats are 'nowhere'. Seeing lush, abundant hedgerows reduced now to 'hedges thin as penwork', and spaces he had cherished cut into by 'hard paths and sharp-ridged houses', leaves the poet uncertain as to whether his whole perception of 'the first kingdom', from which he had derived his sense of himself, was merely the product of a wild and flawed imagination.

'In the Beech', by contrast, shows a secure memory at work. A beech served as a secret hideout for the young Heaney, who, like Sweeney, could have lived 'happy/ in any ivy bush/ high in some twisted tree'/ and never come out'.[203] From the very first line, however, a threat is implicit, since a 'lookout' is generally posted to watch for danger. Even 'the concrete road' conspires against him; at the end of the poem it will be occupied by foreign tanks,[204] and, a few years after that, it will carry him away to Derry and St Columb's. What began as a place of sanctuary, stability, and relatively 'innocent' sexual pleasure, all too quickly suffers a fall; the beech becomes a 'tree of knowledge'. When industry, in the form of the chimney stack, inches its way onto the skyline, the boy seems unperturbed, for the steeplejacks are comically small and unmenacing 'up there at their antics/ like flies against the mountain'. When political realities invade his land- and air-space, in the form of tanks and low-flying planes, the encroachment is not so easily forgotten; though excited by their power and proximity, he 'winced at their imperium', which left a permanent dint on the concrete and his consciousness.

Acutely critical perspectives of Mossbawn, and the culture and values with which Heaney was brought up, operate in the two sardonic poems which succeed 'In the Beech'. 'The First Kingdom' plunges immediately into mock heroic. 'The royal roads were cow paths', Heaney begins, and then introduces the queen of the farm – his mother presumably – in a somewhat ungainly pose, 'hunkered' beside a cow. Any uplift created by the literally lyric image of her plucking 'the harpstrings of the milk' sinks under the bathos of the fourth line, 'into a wooden pail'. The other members of the royal stock fare little better, lording it 'over the hindquarters of cattle'. The unheroic, inglorious history of this 'backward' people is a mere rag-bag, in which major tragedies and minor 'mishaps' have become indistinguishable from each other. He once cherished his inheritance ('I blew hot'), but now is no longer 'in step with my own folk'.[205] Praise for their endurance is outweighed by scorn and sorrow that they should be 'two-faced' and 'accommodating', 'demeaned' by their submissiveness to State and Church and circumstance. 'The First Flight', by contrast, tells of mastery and defiance, of climbing out of the mire of 'attachment'.

Heaney draws on images and scenes from *Sweeney Astray* as

analogues for his 'asylum'[206] at Glanmore, and through the poem to defend the poet's right to witness from a point of solitude and separation. According to Heaney's mythic version of events, like his alter ego, Sweeney, he was not allowed to enjoy his 'point of repose' in Wicklow, but instead subjected to deputations armed with sweet words and threats ('a stone in each pocket') and accusations ('old rehearsals/ of debts and betrayals'). Unable to lure him back to Belfast, they pronounced him 'a feeder off battlefields' – a reference presumably to the attacks on *North* – a charge which he nullified simply by ascending higher in his art in *Field Work*. Distance lent perspective, and, from his 'new rungs', he was able to discern and damn the atavisms of both communities, the Protestants with their 'hosting'[207] and 'levies from Scotland', the Catholics with their 'fasting' and 'rhythmical chants'. Like Derek Mahon in his marvellous poem, 'The Last of the Fire Kings', Heaney here refuses the role of bard to the 'fire-loving/ People' of Ulster, refuses to 'perpetuate/ The barbarous cycle'.[208] He too posits 'a place out of time', a perfect, delicate, enduring Art, the vision he will endeavour to realise in *The Haw Lantern* and *Seeing Things*.

As the collection moves to its close, Heaney strives to lay down a base and basis for future work. Many of the qualities he aspires to – fortitude, energy, an unrelenting, uncompromising dedication to Art – he detects in the character and work of the French painter, Paul Cézanne (1839–1906), another Group man who finally chose to go solo.[209] Like Heaney, an admirer of 'wonderful balance and perfection' achieved by the old classic masters, in his work 'everything is in its place, and nothing is casual or vague. Each form stands out clearly and one can visualise it as a firm, solid body.'[210] 'An Artist' is almost Hughesian in its relish of force and rigour, in its celebration of the bond between abstract and concrete. Whether painting a still life or a mountain landscape, Cézanne's art is hewn from 'anger' and 'obstinacy', wrested by 'coercion', braced by a determination to face and outface self, to see and reach beyond limits. In order to inch towards such a state of independence and strength, he makes one further effort to slough off the old images and allegiances. In contrast to the openness of Cézanne's visions, he presents what he sees now as the confining iconography of Republicanism and Catholicism. Appropriated by, and dishonoured by the contemporary warriors for Irish 'freedom', 'The Old Icons' consists of a triptych depicting an imprisoned patriot, a hunted priest from the Penal Times, and a committee of 'sedition-mongers' complete with the 'tout' who betrayed them. This last composition seems to epitomise Ireland's history for Heaney, almost *une farce macabre*,[211] a continuing narrative of aspirations and treacheries. Significantly, what holds the poet's attention most in the picture is the striking invidivuality of the traitor, the pivot of 'an action that was his rack/ and others ruin'. Though Heaney would like to believe he had outgrown these formative images, they clearly retain a grip on him; in them are fused solidarity and the spectre of betrayal, reminding him that how 'dear-bought' is the reward for opting out.

Once awesome, now seemingly redundant symbols of clerical authority tower over the opening stanzas of 'In Illo Tempore'. Dominating the first of these, by means of its size, its rich, exotic material, its bright, regal colours, is the missal.[212] Potent as Ronan's psalter, it stimulates Heaney into a consideration of the grammar and politics of The Mass. Of the twelve words in stanza two, half are verbs, chosen to stress the passive, submissive, secondary role of the laity in the drama of the Word, a position re-emphasised by the cyclical nouns of stanza three.

> Altar stone was dawn and monstrance noon,
> the word rubric itself a bloodshot sunset.

Leaving sunset and huge religious metaphors from that time (*illo tempore*) behind him, Heaney turns to 'the small hours' of the diminished present, in which certainties and convictions have lost their allure. While one can hardly credit the modesty of his supposed claim to fame, "Now I live by a famous strand", one cannot but respond to the pathos of the seabirds, the doubt-full simile, and that 'Dover Beach'-like feeling that night now prevails.[213] A soulless, solely material world will never be sustaining.

Station Island ends, as it began, with a descent below ground, a journey whose goal is wholeness, music. What buoyed 'The Underground' was its light, delightful conceits, its regular decasyllabic, rhymed and half-rhymed lines, its assuredness that Orpheus *would* regain his Eurydice. 'On the Road', however, is an altogether more serious, more solitary affair. The final flight of the displaced Sweeney/Heaney, it darts forward in the clipped, tense quatrains of four to six syllables that appeared frequently in *North*. The opening is deliberately unremarkable, with Heaney remarking on the unremarkability of car travel. Outside, a dripping landscape hints back perhaps to 'Exposure'; inside the steering wheel, translated briefly by a fanciful simile into 'a wrested trophy', reverts to normality, an 'empty round'. Half-rhymes tick past as predictably as road signs. His body and senses are dulled from continuous driving, which renders 'all roads one'. Suddenly, language and rhythm move up a gear as he recalls "the seraph-haunted, Tuscan/ footpath, the green/ oak alleys of Dordogne", before a moral brake is applied to lyric impulse, *'Master, what must I do to be saved?'* What constitutes an exemplary life is a question that continues to concern him, but for Heaney, as we have seen, the role models are far more likely to be artists than religious. Acknowledging the fact that throughout his life he has been 'a rich young man', 'steeped in luck',[214] largely because of the gifts accruing from his Catholic home and education, makes the break with the faith of his fathers even harder. He tries to utilise the memory of a bird with an 'earth-red' back, circling over him as if in benediction, to resist the pull of *disciplina*, to get 'up and way', to achieve one last translation. Like Sweeney – perhaps like every Irish Catholic writer – he can never be utterly free of the Word, which caused and enabled his flight. The very images he employs emphasise his cultural and linguistic indebtedness; in endeavouring to realise his 'escape', 'to lean, without toppling, beyond the plumb of his native language',[215] he employs harmonious figures drawn from medieval monasticism ('black letter latin') and the Bible ('Noah's dove'). The poet who confidently proclaimed, 'I rhyme/ To see myself', at the close of *Death of a Naturalist*, now depicts himself as 'a panicked shadow/ crossing the deerpath' of poetry. From fixed past – fifteen years of violence, alienation, and growth, learning how to stand 'his ground determinedly in the local plight'[216] – he turns to an uncertain future of conditionals. As the earth of home has been stained blood-red, become 'cold', 'hard-breasted', he chooses a 'soft-nubbed', roosting-place abroad. Taking a leaf out of the book of the Polish poet, Zbigniew Herbert, he renews his art by migrating to a rich prehistoric sanctuary, discovering in the cave paintings of Lascaux 'a blinding, obvious unity',[217] an 'Unearthly sweetness'[218] transcending the 'brutal practice' of the world which fed them. In the delicate, fluent picture of the drinking deer he recognises another image of his old self, 'strained', 'expectant', 'long dumbfounded', but also the promise of a fresh identity. *Station Island*, after all, is 'a book of changes', bringing to completion the first stage of Heaney's poetic development. By taking the risk of breaking cover in *The Haw Lantern* and *Seeing*

Things, he hopes to uncover new sources, to 'rise' and 'raise a dust/ in the font of exhaustion'. The seemingly 'arid' images[219] are in fact 'generative',[220] and look forward to a time when

> the lame shall leap like a deer
> and the tongues of the dumb sing for joy;
>
> for water gushes in the desert,
> streams in the wasteland,
> the scorched earth becomes a lake,
> the parched land springs of water.'[221]

6
Space, 1984–91

When you write about the dead, you are expiating your connection with them, you're cleansing it. And that means that
they are also present. Even if they're not there as spirits, your
own mother and your father . . . are actually present inside
you and therefore you must come to terms with them.

John Montague[1]

The emptier it stood, the more compelled
The eye that scanned it.

'Squarings', xlvii

THE HAW LANTERN

Although the period from 1984–91 was an intensely creative one
for Seamus Heaney, resulting in three poetry collections, *The Haw
Lantern* (1987), *New Selected Poems 1966–1987* (1990), *Seeing Things*
(1991), a collection of critical essays, *The Government of the Tongue*
(1988), and a play, *The Cure at Troy* (1990), and saw his elevation
in 1988 to Professor of Poetry at Oxford University, loss shadowed
success. "The most important thing that has happened to me in the
last ten years", Heaney told Blake Morison in a recent interview, "is
being at two death beds."[2] The deaths of his mother in the autumn
of 1984 and of his father in October 1986 left a colossal space, one
which he has struggled to fill through poetry. Many of the finest
lyrics in *The Haw Lantern* and *Seeing Things* – 'Alphabets', 'The Stone
Verdict', the 'Clearances' sonnets, 'Man and Boy', 'Seeing Things',
'Squarings' – spring directly from this well of grief, and are a reflex
action/vatic reaction to it.

Critics have noted, and Heaney himself has commented on, a
greater sense of ease and release within these last two volumes, a
'freeing up'[3] which may not be unconnected with bereavement. No
longer constrained perhaps by his feeling for parental feelings, he

211

appears less tentative, more candid in his observations on Catholic and Nationalist tradition. There are other factors at play, however. The advent of the late forties/early fifties has made him less anxious, and more inclined in his writing to "enjoy the whole truancy and sport of the lyric process."[4] Working in America for four months of the year, crossing and re-crossing the Atlantic, has brought an *'airiness'*[5] to his poetry, he believes, and his perspectives have been enlarged by his contacts with Eastern European writers such as Czeslaw Milosz, Zbigniew Herbert, Miroslav Holub, and by his friendships with the Russian poet, Joseph Brodsky, and the St Lucian poet, Derek Walcott.

From its outset *The Haw Lantern* employs parables to trace stages of growth, phases in the learning process, and is concerned with the recognition and evaluation of shapes and spaces, the balancing of losses and gains. Appropriately, since education begins at home and with play, 'Alphabets'[6] opens with the poet's father, or, rather, his father's shadow, amusing the child, making images 'materialise' on the wall. Immediately afterwards, however, 'shades of the prison-house' close in, signalled by a weighty, repeated polysyllable and a switch into formal register, "He understands/ He will understand more when he goes to school." In stanza two he quickly adjusts to the new environment. From the amorphous smoke pictures of 'the whole first week', he progresses to letters and numbers, learning by building 'cross-ties' between the familiar and unknown, between a world of forked sticks, swans, hoes and rafters, and the hieroglyphs of school. Soon the simple pleasures of seeing things and saying things are impinged upon by a growing awareness of the rules governing adult thinking, early inklings of the absolutism running through the State and the Church

> there is a right
> Way to hold the pen and a wrong way.

Widening horizons are suggested by the concluding images of Part One, 'A globe in the window', but before these can be reached he must master new tongues, and negotiate his way round a new script. Repeating the *pagus* versus *disciplina* motif of *Station Island*, again the poet emphasises his preference for pre-Christian, Gaelic culture; whereas the Latin he learnt at Anahorish and St Columb's is associated with repetition and abstraction ('column after stratified column'), menace ('minatory') and discipline, ('stricter', 'pealing of a bell'), acquiring Irish is viewed as a journey home, as a temporary return to the Garden. There he enjoys his first audience with the Muse, 'All ringleted in assonance and woodnotes', and gains his earliest taste of lyric possibilities, before the door into the light is slammed shut once more. The space where blackbirds and lively verbs were wont to 'dart and dab' becomes reoccupied by dour nouns, 'self-denial', 'fasting', 'cold', 'north'. As so often in the previous book, the Northern Catholic variety of Christianity is depicted as a destructive influence, likened to a sickle slashing through the luxurious, luscious undergrowth of the imagination.

The weight of historical time lifts at the opening of the third movement, as Heaney, at university, first as student, then as lecturer, takes his place 'at the centre' of his time, but feelings of achievement and assuredness are shortlived, checked by a consciousness of all that has been lost from his 'circumference'.[7] The home ground with its familiar icons – stooks like lamdas, potato pits with faces like deltas, horseshoes like omegas – has been 'bulldozed' by the machine/computer age, ("Balers drop bales *like printouts*"), and has taken on a uniform, 'meanly utilitarian air'.[8] Now so much has 'gone', he strives through shapes and sounds to create his own figures of the universe, to make 'his pen catch up with his soul'.[9] Ultimately Heaney sees his condition as comparable to that of an astronaut, shuttling between two worlds,[10] defined by the limitations of his present (his 'small window'), awed by images of distant perfection ('The risen, aqueous, singular, lucent O'). To complete the poem's 'full circle' ('The Stone Grinder'), his station from A to Ω, he returns in his final image to the original place and to 'the marvellous as he had known it'.[11] In a procedure reminiscent of *Death of a Naturalist* and anticipating *Seeing Things*, child and adult are reunited, the one and the other stunned by the miracle of letters. For the poet, the plasterer is a fellow scribe; in the round eyes of the child, however, he was an other-worldly being, another Jacob. For the one the apparition on the gable end was another Knock;[12] for the other the achieved poem is a wonder in itself. For Heaney, as for Wordsworth, it is a source of 'perpetual benediction' that 'nature yet remembers / What was so fugitive', that 'shadowy recollections' – a father, all fingers and thumbs – can provide such 'fountain-light', such 'master-light'.[13]

Adult perspectives prevail in most of the subsequent poems in *The Haw Lantern*, which see Heaney having 'second thoughts' about the values and culture of home. Divisions and dualities empower in 'Terminus', and determine its form and content. In each of the eleven couplets there is a balancing act, natural objects/locations weighed against industrial objects/locations in I, blessed prudence set against the worship of Mammon in II, leading Heaney to the conclusion that 'Two buckets were easier carried than one'. Education and literary success may have set him on the road to exile, into a 'migrant solitude',[14] but they have also ennobled him and enabled him to remain 'in earshot of his peers'. He ends the poem comparing his situation with that of Hugh O'Neill, the subject of Brian Friel's 1988 play, *Making History*, a man caught 'in midstream', a born Celt, an English fosterling. In the title poem the haw serves as a composite emblem for the poet's 'people', their exacting influence on his art (the 'blood-prick'), and the art itself. Despite the fact that it is displaced in time ('burning out of season'), despite its humble pedigree and low-wattage, it fulfils its function and is a source of illumination. Translated and personified, the haw embodies strength, persistence, maturity, integrity, becomes a classical, golden mean against which the poet measures himself.

The notion of being subjected to scrutiny and 'earning the right to proceed'[15] lies at the heart of 'From the Frontier of Writing'. The first of a series of ambitious experiments using other voices, written over a three week period, it owes much to his readings in Eastern European poetry. Though Heaney's frequent need to cross from the Irish Republic into the North and vice versa provided the occasion for the poem, the situation he describes with such detachment and immediacy, the knotted, tense, diminished feelings he evokes so precisely, are universal. Like its 'merry', 'fierce'[16] companion pieces – 'Parable Island', 'From the Republic of Conscience', 'From the Land of the Unspoken', 'From the Canton of Expectation', 'The Mud Vision' – the poem takes place at the intersection of the real and the surreal, the concrete and the abstract, public and private spheres. Moving quickly, quietly, with sinister intent, it actualises a whole field of force and fear which contains both the soldiers and you, the driver, until, half-way through, it daringly shifts ground. Previously Heaney had employed myths and metaphors as a way into examining political realities; here he turns that process on its head, using political realities as metaphors for the troubles faced by the writer.[17] Once the words are set down, the book published, the author has to endure the prospect of 'marksman' critics 'training down' on him, has to await the 'squawk/ of clearance'. What makes the pressure bearable is the lift that comes when 'suddenly you're through', and the interrogators and their illusory, 'armour plated' power seem no more substantial than 'tree shadows', 'flowing and receding' on the 'polished windscreen' of his art.[18]

Occupying the still centre of the volume is a sequence of eight sonnets, 'Clearances', dedicated to the memory of his mother. The introductory poem, written in *terza rima*, stresses her role as teacher/exemplar/muse, as a practical and inspirational force in his life. It was she who taught him the importance of getting the angle 'right'; now, in the verses that follow, he appeals to her once more in his endeavour to hit the mark, 'to face the music' of her loss, to 'strike it rich' telling her cause aright. In Sonnet I Heaney picks up and relishes a 'cobble thrown a hundred years ago', recalling the stones and accusations of betrayal levelled at his maternal great-grandmother. Although he cannot perhaps keep faith with her faith, he is prepared like her to run the gauntlet in following his conscience. II moves forward a generation, with Heaney wittily re-creating the 'polished' interior of his grandparents' house, and the almost military rules – 'The kettle whistled. Sandwich and teascone/ Were present and correct' – governing behaviour there.

> And don't be dropping crumbs. Don't tilt your chair.
> Don't reach. Don't point. Don't make noise when you stir

his mother's voice resounds as the octet ends. Leaving tension behind, the sestet homes in on and transfigures the fact of her death, tenderly imagining the reunion of father and daughter in a celestial 'shining room together'.

Coming close again by holding back' (V) could describe both Heaney's subject and method in the next four sonnets, which articulate beautifully, unsentimentally, the unspoken love of son and mother.[19] Simple, humble, domestic chores, such as peeling potatoes (III) and folding sheets (V), are transmuted into courtship rituals/ acts of communion;[20] 'hampered' (IV) by speech, the pair rely on 'fluent', synchronised movement (III, V, VI), delicate gesture ('her head bent towards my head' in III), brief moments of physical contact ('So we'd stretch and fold and end up hand to hand' in V, 'Elbow to elbow, glad to be kneeling next/ To each other' in VI), the poetry of the liturgy and the poetry of the Bible ('*As the hind longs for the stream*') to 'voice' their feelings for one another. In reining back the emotion, it is intensified, in the poems as in life, and when, at times, the language seems to be becoming too adolescently passionate, as in III – 'I was all hers', 'Her breath in mine' – Heaney checks himself with 'little pleasant splashes' of prosaic reality 'To bring us to our senses'. After luxuriating in sensation and stylised love-play throughout sonnet V – with its cool pull, its thwacks of sound, its minimal, exclusive alphabet 'where I was x and she was o' – in the final phrase he jolts us back to the hard economics/frugal philosophy governing life on the farm, and how vital it was to make ends meet. Rural Ulster in the 1940s was no pastoral or advertisers' idyll; the linen sheets were sewn from 'ripped-out flour sacks', and would never have belonged on a *Persil* washing-line.

Heaney returns in sonnet IV to themes raised in the early poems of the collection and in the first of the sequence, to education and betrayal. One of the cruellest results of being sent away to St Columb's, of being ripped untimely from the womb-like home, is the intellectual, cultural and linguistic rift which now separates mother and son. Each colludes in a game of pretence in order to maintain the semblance of unity. Loyalty to her origins, however 'hampered and inadequate' she perceives them to be, makes her affect ignorance (*Bertold Brek*), and reprove her son ('You/ Know all them things') for the division that has arisen. His response in the sestet constitutes a betrayal 'Of what I knew better', one that he is uneasy about. Though 'redeemed', to some extent, by the fact that it is 'governed' by love and loyalty to her, the final image – itself a sign of separation – suggests that the conflict will inevitably resurface. His *naws* and *ayes* will only earn him a temporary respite; space will always remain.

In VII and VIII, the concluding sonnets, Heaney movingly relives the moment of bereavement, explores the effects of clearance in family and personal terms. VII opens with a shock, a matter-of-fact, third person singular estimate of a tragic, ironic, absurd, poignant state of affairs. Only at his wife's deathbed was the husband released from 'a lifetime's speechlessness' ('The Stone Verdict'). In vain he tries to fend off the impending loss by encouraging her to picture a future tense, bending his head towards hers,

'You'll be in New Row on Monday night
And I'll come up for you and you'll be glad'

but 'She could not hear', and only the circle around the bed derives comfort from his intimacies. The bareness of the language, father's and son's, is intensely affective – "He called her good and girl. Then she was dead"[21] – as is the assertion of collective solidarity in the last four lines. The image of a 'felled' tree, with which VII ends, is carried over into sonnet VIII, which sees Heaney turning space and silence into a resource for sound. Seeking an *objective correlative* for his feelings of loss, he recalls the toppling of another giant fixture from his past, the chestnut tree. Not surprisingly, since it was planted by his aunt in the year of his birth, as he grew up he 'came to identify my own life'[22] with that of the tree, which was eventually cut down by the 'new owners' of Mossbawn when Heaney was in his early teens. Its links with that first place, that first sense of himself, with mother, father, aunt, brother, community, made it a potent symbol. In contemplating 'the space where the tree had been or would have been' some thirty years later, the poet was able to come to terms with his own unrootedness, his feelings of 'luminous emptiness'[23] in the wake of his mother's death. Out of the 'cut, the crack, the sigh/ and collapse', he begins a new phase of self-translation, working other intense moments of 'childhood sensation'/adult experience into wonders.[24]

SEEING THINGS

Seeing Things is another 'book of changes',[25] translations, visions. Between the fine renderings of Virgil and Dante, which open and close the book, there are innumerable magical transformations of 'ordinary' experiences, and celebrations of instances when renewing 'light breaks over me'[26] through door, window, skylight. Gone is the anguished wrestling with authority that characterised key sections of *Field Work* and *Station Island*, where exhaustion seemingly had the last word. In this latest collection Heaney sounds far more at ease with himself, suffused with *claritas*, lightness of being. Confidently bearing the golden bough of metaphor before him, he combs the underworld of memory for 'clear truths and mysteries', and ascends into the 'upper air'.[27]

A recurring presence in this ninth volume is the shade of the poet's father, Patrick Heaney, who had featured so importantly in his first book. With the passing of time, awe of the living Father has given way to an affectionate acceptance of a fellow man, flawed and mortal like himself. He first 'appears' in the guise of Anchises, in the translated extract from the *Aeneid*. A sacred burden, he is borne on his son's shoulders away from the 'flames' and 'enemy spears', the situation reversing the roles in 'Follower', twenty-five years previously, when Heaney recalled how his father 'rode me on his back/ Dipping and rising to his plod'. Similarly the scene in 'Markings' II, which finds him, spade in hand, 'nicking the first straight edge' in the garden, nods back to the seminal poem, 'Digging', re-establishing the tenuous affinity between father and son as lovers of lines, as foundation-makers, ploughmen.

The most perfect expressions of filial affection in *Seeing Things* are recorded in 'Man and Boy', 'The Ash Plant', 'Squarings' XV, and in the title poem. The first of these begins with advice that Heaney has, in a sense, heeded, an old fisherman's joke, 'Catch the old one first'. He then develops the familiar portrait of a 'down-to-earth', 'broad-backed, low-set man', whose distrust of lyric moments 'On slow bright river evenings' led him 'lightly' to check his children's spirits. (A mild reproof, that 'lightly'.) Though generally a man of few words, occasionally he would 'make a splash' with figurative language – like his son – describing a salmon 'As big as a wee pork pig by the sound of it', or asserting '*I could have cut a better man out of the hedge*' ('The Ash Plant'). A more sombre mood sets in, however, with Part Two of the poem, which employs the present tense to show ripples of equivalence linking three generations, and to heighten the immediacy. In this second section stillness and frenetic animation combine. In contrast to the salmon, leaping on its return to the spawning ground, a mower stands stock-still in the middle of a field. Part of time, rather than Time himself, he 'leans forever on his scythe', the centre of a dial on a stopped watch. Now, having known what it is to lose a father, Heaney can identify more fully with the emotions his father experienced, when, as a 'barefoot boy', he raced through the fields 'On the afternoon of his own father's death.' The poet's language in the eighth stanza is simplicity, economy itself. Repeated 'h' sounds create a breathlessness, intensify the immediacy of the present tense, while the black half-door opens on to death and eternal division:

> The open black half of the half-door waits.
> I feel much heat and hurry in the air.
> I feel his legs and quick heels far away

Reversing the positions in 'The Golden Bough', Heaney concludes with one last metamorphosis in which his father becomes Aeneas, and he becomes the 'light-headed', 'thin-boned', 'witless elder'.

The third part of 'Seeing Things' restores another panel from the fresco of his childhood. Riskily starting with 'Once upon a time' and ending 'happily ever after', it craftily avoids sentimentality in between. Heaney invents a scene he never actually saw, when his generally solid, stolid father was pitched off balance into a deep stream. 'Cartwheels, barrel/ And tackle' tumbled into a whirlpool in a fall presaging his final 'fall'. With typical deftness, Heaney completes the picture focusing on the farmer's hat carried 'merrily' along to 'The quieter reaches', the jaunty adverb reminding one, in the words of the song, that 'life is but a dream'. The last lines capture the illumination of a son seeing his father 'face to face' for the first time, without the halo, or, in Mr Heaney's case, the hat of authority.

In 'Squarings', a sequence of forty-eight, twelve-liners which make up the second half of the book, one discovers an even finer miniature, rich in 'Stable straw, Rembrandt-gleam and burnish', a worthy successor to 'Mossbawn Sunlight'. The sight of his father foraging in 'a tea-chest packed with salt', inspecting 'unbleeding, vivid-fleshed bacon' by the light of a hurricane lamp, made him feel heir to a fortune, another Joseph:

> That night I owned the piled grain of Egypt.
> I watched the sentry's torchlight on the hoard.
> I stood in the door, unseen and blazed upon.
>
> (XV)

Equally impressive is the marriage of sense, image and sound found in poem XXIX, where Heaney makes available again 'a music of binding and loosing/ Unheard in this generation', the music of a latch. Something clicks in the inner ear as we listen to its 'Scissor-and-slap abruptness'; for the poet its 'see-saw lift' gives entry to the potent and the ominous in his past.

Unfortunately, not all of *Seeing Things* reaches this pitch. The first part of 'Markings', for example, bumps on unremarkably like a heavy football, despite attempts to loft it upwards with three abstract nouns, three abstract adjectives. Other poems similarly insist on cataloguing rather than creating effects, such as 'The Pitchfork', or fall into 'High-pitched strain and gradual declension', like 'A Royal Prospect' and many of the sonnets in the 'Glanmore Revisited' sequence. In an interview with Clive Wilmer for BBC Radio 3 in 1990, Heaney spoke of his desire to create a poetry which resembled 'window glass' rather than 'stained glass'. At times, unfortunately, the windows look out on limited prospects, and spareness of style matches slightness of content.

Along with the flat notes, there are some marvellous highs, particularly in poems such as 'Wheels within Wheels', 'The Biretta', 'The Settle Bed', and within the eerie cadences of the second half of the book. The music of fishing, its swishing and whispering and sharp ratcheting, is vividly caught in 'Casting and Gathering', another of those Heaney poems in which the twin voices of his education collide and collude.

> One sound is saying, 'You are not worth tuppence,
> But neither is anybody. Watch it! Be severe.'
> The other says, 'Go with it! Give and swerve.
> You are everything you feel beside the river.'

In 'The Pulse' from 'Three Drawings' fishing is again seen as analoguous to the act of, the 'achieve of' poetic creation, that feeling of completeness, of ratification when

> you reeled in and found
> yourself strung, heel-tip
> to rod-tip, into the river's
> steady purchase and thrum.

Repeatedly in *Seeing Things* it is the unpredictability and changeability of water and sky which excite the poet and prompt new and unusual angles of vision. The eye-level distrust at the 'scaresome' shilly-shallying of the boat to Inshbofin, with which Part One of the title poem opens, is finally divinely transcended when the craft moves to its outcome. As it glides across the water

> It was as if I looked down from another boat
> Sailing through the air, far up, and could see
>
> How riskily we fared into the morning,
> And loved in vain our bare, bowed, numbered heads.

Incertus was a long time dying.

In 'Glanmore Revisited' VII, it is his wife's insistence on a skylight in their Wicklow retreat which results in yet another burst of air and illumination, admitting wonder; cutting into the pitch pine' is an act of liberation, rather than violation. Once more the 'lapsed' poet is compelled into biblical allusion, feeling 'for days'

> like an inhabitant
> Of that house where the man sick of the palsy
> . . . .
> Was healed, took up his bed and walked away.

Perhaps the only afterlife is the one created by the Imagination, he suspects, yet, paradoxically, the more space Heaney puts between himself and orthodox belief, the less embarrassed he is speaking of souls and spirits. As many reviewers have pointed out, there is a growing conviction that "there is no next-time round" (I), that *"All gone into a world of light?"* means *"All gone"* (XLIV); any consolation 'perhaps' and 'may' in XLIV and XLV might have possessed comes up against the definite images of transience with which those poems end, the dead leaf swirling, ashes and house-dust.

As the first poem of 'Lightenings' implies, *Seeing Things* is full of 'Unroofed scope', 'Knowledge-freshening wind', 'soul-free cloud-life'. Though the old hearth, and the old certainties, may now be cold, they retain an afterlife in his imagination. One cannot imagine Heaney not returning to them to rekindle memory, to admit 'things beyond measure'(XLVI), to relish 'the dazzle of the impossible' ('Station Island', X). 'I trust contrariness', he says early on in the collection.[28] 'Squarings', like so much of his poetry since *Death of a Naturalist*, exemplifies his determination to keep faith with his 'Plain, big, straight, ordinary' origins (XXXIII), and his preparedness to flash beyond them like light from 'a god's shield' (XXXV) or a 'goldfinch over ploughland' (XXX).

Notes

Abbreviations used throughout the notes to refer to works by Seamus Heaney, published by Faber and Faber.

DN = *Death of a Naturalist*, 1966
DD = *Door into the Dark*, 1969
WO = *Wintering Out*, 1972
N   = *North*, 1975
FW = *Field Work*, 1978
SI   = *Station Island*, 1984
SA = *Sweeney Astray*, 1984
HL = *The Haw Lantern*, 1987
See = *Seeing Things*, 1991

and

P   = *Preoccupations: Selected Prose*, 1980
GT = *Government of The Tongue*, 1988

plus

S   = *Stations*, 1975
       (published by Ulsterman Publications, Belfast)

Interviews conducted by the author are prefixed with the initials MRP, and took place on the following dates.

with Harry Chambers, Cornwall, 9 March 1985
with Michael Longley, Belfast, 11 June and 27 November 1985
with Raymond Gallagher, Derry, 12 June 1985
with Ann and Hugh Heaney, Bellaghy, 13 June 1985
with Seamus Heaney, Dublin, 2 September and 28 November 1985
with J. B. S O'Kelly, Belfast, 27 November 1985
with T. P. Flanagan, Belfast, 27 November 1985
with David Hammond, Belfast. 28 November 1985
with Frank Ormsby, Belfast, 11 June and 27 November 1985
with Seamus Deane, Dublin, 28 November 1985
with Philip Hobsbaum, Glasgow, 1 and 2 February 1986

1: A Good Anchor: Home and Education, 1939–61

1.   Daniel Corkery, *The Hidden Ireland*, Gill and Macmillan 1924, p. 24.
2.   Seamus Heaney, interviewed by John Haffenden, *Viewpoints*, London: Faber, 1981, p. 69.

3.   See Benedict Kiely, 'A Raid into Dark Corners: The Poems of Seamus Heaney', *The Hollins Critic*, Vol. 4, 1970, p. 8.

> The cattle dealer's stick was his lance, his sabre, his staff of office. Civilization, law, has disarmed him, deprived him . . . The open markets, with dung and din of bargaining, and hand slapping, and drink to clinch the bargain have been replaced by roofed-in marts where matters are conducted in an orderly fashion by one auctioneer.

4.   *Phoenix*, No. 1, ed. Harry Chambers, March 1967, p. 35.
5.   E. Estyn Evans, *Irish Folk Ways*, London: Routledge, 1957, p. 260.
6.   Michael Longley, 'The Northerner', *Sunday Independent*, 26 September 1976, p. 2.
7.   *N*, p. 59.
8.   Seamus Heaney, interviewed by John Haffenden, art. cit., p. 63.
9.   *HL*, 'The Stone Verdict', p. 17.
10. *P*, p. 45.
11. Quoted in Polly Devlin, *All of us There*, London: Pan, 1984, p. 22.
12. *HL*, p. 27. In an earlier version of this poem, appearing in *The Honest Ulsterman*, No. 80, Spring 1986, p. 4, Heaney's opening line begins, "When the other woman was away at Mass." This refers, no doubt, to his Aunt Mary, and implies that at times he longed for the exclusive company of his mother.
13. There may be a faint echo of *Othello*, Act Two, scene i, "They met so near with their lips that their breaths embraced together."
14. Seamus Heaney, interviewed by John Haffenden, art. cit., pp. 60–61.
15. *HL*, 'Clearances', VI, p. 30.
16. St Paul's Epistle to the Hebrews, Chapter 6, v. 19.
17. Seamus Heaney, 'A Raindrop on a Thorn', interview for *Dutch Quarterly Review*, 9, No. 1, 1979, p. 30.
18. Seamus Heaney, interviewed by Caroline Walsh, *Irish Times*, 6 December 1975, p. 5.
19. *P*, p. 21.
20. Seamus Heaney, interviewed by James Randall, *Ploughshares*, Vol. 5, part 3, 1979, p. 18.
21. 'A Poet's Childhood', *The Listener*, November 11, 1971, p. 661.
22. In 'Epic', by Patrick Kavanagh, the Monaghan poet asserts the significance of 'parochial' events, arguing that Homer "made the Iliad" from "a local row." *Collected Poems*, London: Martin Brian and O'Keeffe Ltd, 1972, p. 136. Dan Taggart appears in 'The Early Purges', Big Jim Evans in 'Mid-Term Break', Henry MacWilliams in 'Obituary', an unpublished poem from the first Group meeting. MacWilliams' bed became part of the fencing at Mossbawn and is referred to in several later poems, including 'Mother' (*DD*) and 'The Harvest Bow' (*FW*). The precedents for these celebrations of neighbours lie in Kavanagh's and Montague's verse. In *Station Island*, 'An Ulster Twilight', yet another carpenter features, Eric Dawson.

23. Seamus Deane, 'Talk with Seamus Heaney', *New York Times Review*, 84, No. 48, 1979, p. 79.
24. Seamus Heaney, *Stations*, Belfast: Ulsterman Publications, 1975, p. 18.
25. Seamus Heaney, 'William Wordsworth Lived Here', BBC 1974.
26. The pump appears in 'Rite of Spring' and 'Mother' in *Door into the Dark*; in *'Sinking the Shaft'* in *Stations*; in 'A drink of water' and 'The Toome Road' in *Field Work*, and in 'Changes' in *Station Island*.
27. *N*, 'Kinship', p. 43.
28. *P*, p. 17 and *Stations*, p. 4.
29. *P*, p. 19.
30. Ibid., p. 35.
31. Seamus Heaney, interviewed by James Randall, art. cit., p. 17.
32. William Wordsworth, *The Prelude*, 1805, III, l.192.
33. 'A Poet's Childhood', art. cit., p. 660.
34. *S*, 'Hedge School', p. 6.
35. Daniel Corkery, op. cit., p. 67.
36. Seamus Heaney, 'The Poet as a Christian', *The Furrow*, xxix, 10, p. 604. cf. 'The Holy Spirit is in the fields', Patrick Kavanagh, *Tarry Flynn*, p. 30, and see Mark Patrick Hederman, 'Seamus Heaney, the Reluctant Poet', *Crane Bag*, 3, No. 2, 1979.

> 'Landscape' Heaney says, 'is sacramental, a system of signs that call automatically upon systems of thinking and feeling'. He talks of discovering 'a poetic voice' as though that voice were somewhere between his ordinary consciousness and some other consciousness beyond any that is presently available to us' (p. 65).

37. *N*, 'Kinship', p. 45.
38. Seamus Heaney, 'The Poet as a Christian', art. cit., p. 604. "Words for me have always become instinct with a fresh energy when they are hovering over my home ground in County Derry."
39. *P*, p. 20.
40. Ibid., p. 25.
41. Seamus Heaney, 'Le clivage traditionnel', *Les Lettres Nouvelles*, March 1973, p. 87.
42. *Among Schoolchildren, A John Malone Memorial Lecture*, Belfast, 1983, p. 7.
43. See *P*, pp. 22–24.
44. *SI*, p. 73. "You'd have thought that Anahorish School was purgatory enough for any man."
45. *S*, p. 19. Heaney's renewed interest in Anglo-Saxon is evident in the pared down style of *North*. The title of Heaney's poem and a number of images – those of the ring-giver, the burning halls, the deserted benches, the splintered fellowship – are derived, of course, from the marvellously atmospheric Anglo-Saxon poem.
46. William Wordsworth, *The Prelude*, 1805, III, line 141.

47. Theodore Roethke, 'The Favourite', *Collected Poems*, London: Faber, 1985, p. 26. Heaney returns to the image in *Station Island*, p. 58 and p. 119.
48. *P*, pp. 21–22.
49. Barry White, *John Hume: Statesman of the Troubles*, Belfast: Blackstaff Press, 1984, p. 12.
50. Ibid.
51. MRP interview with J. B. S. O'Kelly.
52. Barry White, op. cit., p. 12.
53. MRP Interview with Ann Heaney.
54. *N*, p. 63. The phrase originates in *The Prelude*, I, 398.
55. MRP Interview with Ann Heaney.
56. Details of timetable from MRP interview with Raymond Gallagher. Detail concerning confessions from Heaney's review of *An Duanaire 1600–1900 Poems of the Dispossessed*, ed. Sean O'Tuama and Thomas Kinsella, *Tribune Review of Books*, p. 38.
57. Seamus Heaney, 'Old Derry Walls', *The Listener*, 24 October 1968, p. 521
58. MRP interview with Seamus Deane.
59. Barry White, op. cit., pp. 12–13.
60. MRP Interview with Seamus Deane.
61. Ibid. In *N*, p. 64. 'Freedman', p. 61, also emphasises subjugation, 'I was under that thumb too like all my caste', and the lack of Christ-like compassion in the 'groomed optimi'.
62. MRP Interview with Raymond Gallagher.
63. Barry White, op. cit., p. 13.
64. *Among Schoolchildren*, op. cit., p. 7.
65. T. S. Eliot, 'Little Gidding', *Four Quartets, The Complete Poems and Plays of T. S. Eliot*, London: Faber 1969, p. 194.
66. *S*, p. 22.
67. *HL*, 'Alphabets', p. 2.
68. John Hume quoted in Barry White, op. cit., p. 43.
69. *HL*, pp. 46–47. The first version of 'From the Canton of Expectation' appeared in *The Times Literary Supplement*, 24 January 1986.
70. Tim Pat Coogan, *The I.R.A.*, Glasgow: Fontana, 1980, p. 371.
71. Ibid., p. 375.
72. Seamus Heaney, 'Le clivage traditionnel', art. cit., p. 187.
73. Seamus Heaney quoted in 'The Poet who came back', Brian Bell, *Belfast Telegraph*, 23 November 1971.
74. Seamus Heaney, 'Le clivage traditionnel', art. cit., pp. 187–188.
75. *N*, p. 63.
76. MRP interview with Seamus Deane.
77. MRP interview with J. B. S. O'Kelly.
78. See *P*, p. 44.
79. Detail from an album of documents and articles collected by Seamus Heaney's mother.
80. MRP interview with J. B. S. O'Kelly.
81. *P*, p. 35.
82. William Wordsworth. *The Prelude*, 1805, I, 305–309. In contrast to

Wordsworth's 'beloved vale', Heaney at St Columb's looked down
to the valley of the unbeloved Bogside.

83. William Wordsworth, 'Preface to *Lyrical Ballads*', from *Poetical Works*,
ed. de Selincourt, Oxford University Press, 1967, p. 738.

84. William Wordsworth, *The Prelude*, 1805, VIII, 390–395.

85. *P*, p. 41.

86. Seamus Deane, *Celtic Revivals*, London: Faber 1985, p. 174.

87. Seamus Deane, op. cit., p. 174.

88. William Wordsworth, *The Prelude*, 1805, II, 328.

89. MRP interview with Seamus Deane.

90. T. S. Eliot, *Murder in the Cathedral*, from *The Complete Poems and Plays*,
ed. cit., p. 147.

91. William Wordsworth, *The Prelude*, 1805, X, 437–440.

92. Another phrase from Wordsworth. For the importance of his mother's stress on 'patience' in the shaping of his sensibility, see Seamus
Heaney, interviewed by John Haffenden, art. cit., p. 60. See also *P*,
p. 63.

93. John F. Danby, *Wordsworth: The Prelude and other poems*, Arnold, 1963,
p. 14.

94. Gerard Manley Hopkins, poet and priest, 1844–1889. Like Heaney,
Hopkins was the eldest of nine, in a household strongly affected
by the presence of a maiden aunt. 'A fearless climber of trees'
who 'would go up very high in the lofty elm tree standing in our
garden', according to his brother's account – see Graham Storey's *A
Preface to Hopkins*, Longman, 1981, p. 12 – his childhood was spent
in 'dreaming and reading, and chewing the cud of his gleanings'
of literature. After an unhappy period as a boarder at Highgate
School, where he excelled at Classics, and after glittering success
at university, where he too was 'champion of the examination halls'
(*Stations*, 'Cloistered', p. 20.), and gained a double first, he appalled
his family by his conversion to Catholicism in 1866 and by joining
the Jesuits two years later. Thereafter his life was devoted to the
priesthood and poetry, two paths from which he could reveal
'the sacramental presence of the creator throughout the universe'
(Graham Storey, op. cit., p. viii).

95. "I find myself with my pleasures and pains, my powers and
experiences, my deserts and guilt, my shame and sense of beauty,
my dangers, hopes, fears, and all my fate, more important to myself
than anything I see." ('Comments on the Spiritual Exercises of St
Ignatius Loyola' in *Gerard Manley Hopkins: Poems and Prose*, selected
and edited by W. H. Gardner, Penguin, 1968, p. 145).

96. Graham Storey, op. cit., p. 34.

97. Ibid., p. 35.

98. While training at Stonyhurst College from 1870–1873, he developed a
deep affection for the wild, and bleak Lancashire countryside, which
he described as 'solemn and beautiful' (Storey, op. cit., p. 44), his
'painterly' eye discerning a 'chastened sublimity' such as Hardy
found on Egdon Heath or Heaney met in the Donegal bogland. During his next three years in Clwyd, a rigorous spiritual programme

commingled with opportunities to bathe 'in the beautiful liquid cast of blue' (Storey, op. cit., p. 47) of the Welsh landscape, not dissimilar to that of Co. Wicklow. At St Winifride's Well, the shrine of a seventh century martyr, an epiphany occurred which left him immersed in 'wonder at the bounty of God' – "even now the stress and buoyancy and abundance of the water is before my eyes" – and provided a literal source for the well image of the fourth stanza of *The Wreck of the Deutschland*.

99. Seamus Heaney, 'William Wordsworth Lived Here', BBC 1974.
100. John Carey, 'The Joy of Heaney', *Sunday Times*, 21 October 1984, p. 42.
101. Gerard Manley Hopkins, *The Wreck of the Deutschland*, stanzas 7 and 9, in Gardner's selection, ed. cit., pp. 14–15. The attraction Hopkins felt towards both the ascetic and the sensuous echoed a tension within Heaney's nature. During his schooldays, on one occasion, Hopkins abstained from drinking liquids for a week to fulfil a bet, and yet the description of bluebells in his Journal of 9 May 1871, for example, suggests a richly sensuous apprehension of the world, which looks forward to the Lawrence of *Sons and Lovers* or the Heaney of 'Blackberry Picking'.

> The bluebells in your hand baffle you with their inscape, made to every sense: if you draw your fingers through them they are lodged and struggle with a shock of wet heads . . . then there is the faint honey smell and in the mouth the sweet gum when you bite them. (Gerard Manley Hopkins, Journal, 9 May 1871, in Gardner's selection, ed. cit., p. 123)

102. *P*, p. 44.
103. Ibid., pp. 79–97.
104. Ibid., p. 45.
105. Seamus Deane, 'Talk with Seamus Heaney', *New York Times Review*, 84, No. 48, 1979, p. 79.
106. George McWhirter, letter to MRP, 31 March 1986.
107. It was automatic for Catholic undergraduates.
108. *Among Schoolchildren*, op. cit., p. 7.
109. Ibid., p. 8.
110. *P*, p. 46.
111. Seamus Heaney, interviewed by James Randall, art. cit., p. 14.
112. In *North*.
113. Seamus Heaney, 'Singing School', *Worlds*, ed. Summerfield, Penguin, 1974, p. 95.
114. Seamus Heaney, letter to MRP, 23 January 1986.
115. Seamus Deane, 'Talk with Seamus Heaney', art. cit., p. 79.
116. William Wordsworth, 'Preface to *Lyrical Ballads*', ed. cit., p. 736.
117. Seamus Heaney, interviewed by John Haffenden, art. cit., p. 70.
118. Robert Frost *Selected Poems*, ed. Ian Hamilton, Penguin, 1973, p. 198. Frost's reveries are sudden broken by the appearance of 'a great buck', which

"Pushed the rumpled water up ahead
And landed pouring like a waterfall,
And stumbled through the rocks with horny tread,
And forced the underbrush – and that was all."

119.   Robert Buttel, *Seamus Heaney*, Bucknell University Press, 1975, p. 29.
120.   *N*, p. 64.
121.   George McWhirter, letter to MRP, 31 March 1986. The term
        'Parnassian' derives from Hopkins letter of 10 September 1864, to A.
        W. M. Baillie, where he defines it as a species of sub-poetry, lacking
        in genuine inspiration, but nevertheless possessing something of the
        dialect of the individual writer, but not the full 'watermarks' of
        the self.

        " . . . in Parnassian pieces you feel that if you were the poet you
        could have gone on as he has done . . . If you examine it, the
        words are choice and the description is beautiful, but it does
        not *touch* you." (Gerard Manley Hopkins, Letters, in Gardner's
        selection, ed. cit., p. 156)

122.   The allusion is to *The Wreck of the Deutschland*, stanza 10. Heaney,
        like Hughes before him, 'secularises' Hopkins's intense religious
        imagery.
123.   George McWhirter, letter to MRP, 31 March 1986.
124.   Seamus Heaney, quoted in Neil Corcoran's *Seamus Heaney*, London:
        Faber, 1986, p. 19.

2: Affinities, 1961–66

1.   Seamus Heaney, quoted in *Mid-Ulster Mail*, June 6, 1984. The origin
        may be Patrick Kavanagh, *The Green Fool*, Penguin, p. 236.

        "To myself I repeated the quotation I had heard somewhere, 'The
        Wise Man stays at home'."

2.   Thomas Kinsella, 'The Divided Mind', in *Two Decades of Irish Writing*,
        p. 209.
3.   Seamus Heaney, interviewed by John Haffenden, art. cit., p. 71.
4.   Mark Patrick Hederman, 'Poetry and the Fifth Province', *The Crane
        Bag*, 9, 1, 1985, pp. 112–113.
5.   Seamus Heaney, quoted in an article entitled 'Turkeys made him a
        Poet', *Ulster Tatler*, 1966.
6.   Sean O'Faolain, quoted on the dust cover of *Collected Short Stories of
        Michael McLaverty*, Dublin: Poolbeg Press, 1978.
7.   Kenneth Neill, *An Illustrated History of the Irish People*, Gill and
        Macmillan, 1979, p. 22.
8.   Seamus Heaney, introduction to *Collected Short Stories of Michael
        McLaverty*, p. 7.

9. Ibid., p. 8.
10. 'Turkeys made him a Poet', art. cit.
11. Seamus Heaney, introduction to *Collected Short Stories of Michael McLaverty*, pp. 8–9.
12. In his article, 'The Poetry of Seamus Heaney', in *Critical Quarterly*, 16, 1, Spring 1974, pp. 35–48, John Wilson Foster does not even mention Kavanagh amongst the influences, and Blake Morrison merely quotes Heaney on Kavanagh, in *Seamus Heaney*, op. cit., pp. 28–30.
13. Patrick Kavanagh, *The Green Fool*, p. 227.
14. A phrase used by Heaney in the *Poetry Book Society Bulletin*, 123, Winter, 1984. A deeply religious, almost erotic attachment to the soil that he had inherited warred with Kavanagh's literary ambitions, which lured him towards the city; his devout upbringing and natural humility clashed with his consciousness of the Church's repression of sexuality and identity. His writing manifests at times an exquisite sensual apprehension of the beauty of the world, at others an impotent fury which spends itself unsatisfactorily on satire. His later poems, when he had adjusted himself imaginatively to urban Dublin, display a stoical resignation and a wry acceptance of things, and a determination in his second home to "record love's mystery without claptrap/ Snatch out of time the passionate transitory" ('The Hospital').
15. *P*, p. 122.
16. *P*, p. 125.
17. Patrick Kavanagh, 'The Great Hunger', II, *Collected Poems*, p. 36.
18. Ibid., p. 39.
19. *P*, p. 125.
20. Patrick Kavanagh, 'The Great Hunger', XII, ed. cit., p. 52.
21. Seamus Heaney, *Stations*, p. 20.
22. *GT*, 'The Placeless Heaven: Another Look at Kavanagh', pp. 9–10.
23. Seamus Heaney, quoted in Michael Allen's 'Provincialism and Recent Irish Poetry', in *Two Decades of Irish Writing*, ed. Douglas Dunn, Manchester: Carcanet, 1975.
24. Patrick Kavanagh, introduction to *Collected Poems*, p. xiii.
25. Patrick Kavanagh, *Collected Poems*, pp. 18, 12, 27, 38.
26. The increasing violence from 1969 onwards and the sufferings of his own community, however, made it necessary for Heaney to probe more deeply and critically into his Catholic origins from *Wintering Out* onwards.
27. Patrick Kavanagh, *The Green Fool*, p. 203.
28. *GT*, p. 14.
29. Patrick Kavanagh, quoted in Terence Brown, *Northern Voices: Poets from Ulster*, Dublin, 1975, p. 218.
30. Seamus Heaney, Introduction to *Collected Short Stories of Michael McLaverty*, p. 7.
31. Patrick Kavanagh, 'The Great Hunger', *Collected Poems*, p. 42. Heaney quotes from this poem in his McLaverty Introduction.
32. Patrick Kavanagh, *Collected Poems*, p. 71.

33. Kavanagh's admiration of Hopkins's poetry is mentioned in *The Green Fool*, p. 244.

34. Heaney Groupsheet 1, November 1963. (Groupsheets provided by Philip Hobsbaum) His name may have been derived from a village to the north-west of Bellaghy, McKenna's Town.

35. Patrick Kavanagh, *The Green Fool*, p. 29.

36. *P*, p. 45.

37. Patrick Kavanagh, *The Green Fool*, p. 64.

38. Ibid., pp. 43–44.

39. Thomas Kinsella, in *Myth and Reality in Irish Literature*, ed. Ronsley, Wilfrid Laurier Press, Ontario, 1977, p. 10.

40. Patrick Kavanagh, *Collected Poems*, p. 164.

41. *P*, p. 45.

42. See Robert Buttel, *Seamus Heaney*, op. cit., p. 26.

43. Ibid.

44. Robin Skelton, Introduction to *Six Irish Poets*, Oxford University Press, 1962, p. xiv.

45. John Montague was born in Brooklyn, New York, in 1929, but at the age of four left the United States to live with his father's sisters in Garvaghey, Co. Tyrone. After an education at St Patrick's College, Armagh, and University College, Dublin, and three years as a film critic and a literary correspondent, he returned to America in 1953 on a Fulbright scholarship to Yale, disaffected with the cultural paralysis, the 'almost palpable air of distrust and ineffectuality' (Terence Brown, 'John Montague: Circling to Return', *Northern Voices: Poets from Ulster*, p. 153) that he found in the South. In 1956 after working in Iowa and at Berkeley, he went back to Ireland, however, to act as an editor for Bord Failte in Dublin. From 1961–64 he was a Paris correspondent for *The Irish Times*, and published a fine collection, *Poisoned Lands*, which Heaney bought in August 1963. In the mid-sixties he taught at Berkeley, at University College, Dublin, and at an experimental university at Vinceques in France. In the same year that Heaney made his symbolic move to the Republic – the year of 'Bloody Sunday', 1972, when killings almost tripled – Montague settled back in Ireland, in Cork. In *The Rough Field*, published in November 1972, he attempted to focus his response to the violence of the North with a lyric sequence almost epic in scope and scale, fusing personal, historical and contemporary material, as Heaney would do in *North*. Heaney was one of the readers of the poem at a performance for the British Irish Association on 8 July 1973 at the Round House, London.

46. John Montague, Introduction to *Poisoned Lands*, first edition 1961, new edition, Dolmen Press, Portlaoise, 1977, p. 9.

47. Ibid.

48. John Montague, 'A Welcoming Party', *Poisoned Lands*, new edition, p. 38.

49. Frank Ormsby, in the introduction to his anthology, *Poets from the North of Ireland*, Blackstaff Press, Belfast, 1979, p. 7.

50. The poem appeared in Skelton's anthology, *Six Irish Poets*, Oxford

University Press, 1962. A revised version can be found in John Montague, *The Rough Field*, Dolmen Press, Portlaoise, 1972, pp. 15–16. In the revised version the uncle's tunes have changed to *'The Morning Star'* and the historically emotive *'O'Neill's Lament'*.

51. T. S. Eliot, 'East Coker', *Four Quartets*, Faber, 1944, new edition 1959, p. 24.
52. Both poems use three line stanzas and a final rhyming couplet. Heaney has admitted that 'The Water Carrier' was his model.
53. *HL*, 'Terminus', p. 5.
54. John Montague, 'The Quest', *Poisoned Lands*, ed. cit., p. 39.
55. Polly Devlin, *All of Us There*, Pan Books, 1984, p. 165.
56. Seamus Heaney, 'Unhappy and at Home', interview with Seamus Deane, art. cit., p. 61.
57. Seamus Heaney, Groupsheet 2.
58. Edmund Spenser, *A View of the Present State of Ireland*, 1596, ed. W. L. Renwick, Oxford University Press, 1970, p. 39.
59. Daniel Corkery, *The Hidden Ireland*, Gill and Macmillan, Dublin, 1924, new edition 1967, p. 108.
60. Ibid., p. 85.
61. Ibid., p. 144.
62. Heaney, *Among Schoolchildren*, A John Malone Memorial Lecture 1983, p. 11. See Chapter Five, dealing with 'Station Island, XII.
63. James Joyce, *Portrait of the Artist as a Young Man*, London: Panther Books, 1984, p. 184.
64. Seamus Heaney, *Among Schoolchildren*, Malone Lecture 1983, p. 9.
65. Ted Hughes, 'Fire-Eater', *Selected Poems 1957–81* op. cit., p. 44.
66. Seamus Heaney, 'The Bread of Life', *Trench*, June 1964, p. 6.
67. R. S. Thomas. 'A Peasant', *Sons at the Year's Turning*, Hart Davis, 1955, p. 21.
68. Edna Longley, *Poetry in the Wars*, Bloodaxe Books, Newcastle, 1986, p. 144.
69. Norman McCaig, *Old Maps and New: Selected Poems*, Hogarth Press, 1978, p. 20. The poem 'Climbing Suilven' first appeared in *Riding Lights*, 1955.
70. Ibid., p. 51.
71. *P*, p. 153.
72. William Shakespeare, *King Lear*, Act IV, scene iii, ll. 96–101.
73. *P*, p. 152.
74. Ibid., p. 153.
75. The title of Chapter One of Ted Hughes, *Poetry in the Making*, London: Faber, 1967.
76. Ibid., p. 17.
77. Both poems encapsulate what Camus has called 'the primitive hostility of the world . . . facing us across the millenia' (Albert Camus, *The Myth of Sisyphus*, Penguin, 1955, p. 20). Although Heaney's and Hughes's concern with animals springs from childhood experience of farms and country tracts, literary experience and history have equally shaped and determined their poetic response and philosophy. Within Hughes, one detects the strong influence of

Blake, who equally delighted in energy and 'fearful symmetry' and
raged against the mechanistic thought of Locke and Newton, which
cages mankind by denying faith and inspiration. Perhaps it is not
fanciful to compare Blake's rejection of the worship of Reason with
Heaney's and Hughes's reaction against what Edward Lucie-Smith
has called the 'balanced' banality of some of the so-called Movement
poets, whose 'prissily decorous' verse rarely 'moved' (see *British
Poetry since 1945*, Harmondsworth: Penguin, 1970, p. 136). Reacting
in turn against Dylan Thomas, the *New Lines* tribunes endeavoured
to banish Coriolanus and replace him with poets such as Elizabeth
Jennings

> Now watch this autumn that arrives
> In smells. All looks like summer still.
> Colours are quite unchanged, the air
> On green and white serenely thrives,
> Heavy the trees with growth and full
> The fields. Flowers flourish everywhere.
>
> (*New Lines*, Macmillan, 1956, p. 4)

or John Holloway

> Later round a College 'quad they spoke
> Of subtler things: and understood them well.
> One preferred Aristotle or blunt Locke,
> And one Spinoza's calm, unlikely tale.
>
> (92)

Though education had introduced them to the middle class squares
of the university poets, emotionally both Hughes and Heaney
belonged to the wild rural spaces. (Hughes was brought up in
Hebden Bridge and Heptonstall, in the Calder Valley. and spent
a lot of his spare time in childhood in walking, hunting and fishing.
His father was a carpenter, and later a newsagent. His success
at Mexborough Grammar School gave him access to a university
education. Like Heaney, he was the first in his family to achieve
academic success.) Their poetry rebels against such genteel decorum
and intellectual restraint which permit no epiphanies or revelations,
and goes where A. Alvarez said English poetry should go in his
introduction to *The New Poetry*, the famous Penguin anthology of
1962, 'beyond the gentility principle'.

78.   Ted Hughes, 'An Otter', *Selected Poems 1957–1981*, Faber, 1982,
       p. 54.
79.   MRP Interview with Seamus Heaney.
80.   Neil Corcoran, *Seamus Heaney: A Student Guide*, Faber, 1986, p. 20.
81.   Seamus Heaney, quoted in the above book, p. 20.
82.   MRP Interview with T. P. Flanagan.
83.   Seamus Heaney, Introduction to booklet, *T. P. Flanagan*, Arts Council
       of Northern Ireland 1977.

84. In *Causeway: The Arts in Ulster*, ed. Michael Longley, Arts Council of Northern Ireland, 1971, p. 54.
85. Thomas Hardy, *The Return of the Native*, Macmillan, 1975, p. 44.
86. MRP Interview with T. P. Flanagan.
87. Polly Devlin, *All of us There*, op. cit., p. 11.
88. Ibid., p. 82.
89. Ibid., p. 40.
90. Ibid., p. 157.
91. Seamus Heaney, interview with John Haffenden, art. cit., p. 67.
92. Seamus Heaney, quoted in Neil Corcoran's *Seamus Heaney: A Student Guide*, op. cit., p. 21.
93. MRP interview with Seamus Heaney.
94. *DN*, p. 25. 'Welfare State' appeared in *Interest*, May 1963, Vol. 3, No. 6, p. 16.
95. Neil Corcoran's *Seamus Heaney: A Student Guide*, op. cit., p. 21.
96. Seamus Heaney, 'Poetry from a co-operative society', *Hibernia*, September 1963.
97. MRP interview with Philip Hobsbaum.
98. Ibid.
99. As his comments in 'Poetry from a co-operative society' reveal.
100. Ibid.
101. Seamus Heaney, Groupsheet 4.
102. Seamus Heaney, 'The Belfast Group: A Symposium', *The Honest Ulsterman*, November 1976, p. 63.
103. Ibid., p. 56.
104. Michael Longley, 'The Belfast Group: A Symposium', *The Honest Ulsterman*, November 1976, p. 56.
105. MRP interview with Michael Longley.
106. MRP interview with David Hammond.
107. Ibid.
108. From the age of seven Hammond had been friendly with an unemployed neighbour, Johnny Jamison, who had been disabled in 1921 during the Civil War. His large bookcase contained documentary novels from the early 1900s, like Patrick McGill's *Moleskin Joe*, which dealt with the seasonal migration of Irish workers to Scotland, and Maurice Walsh's patriotic story, *Blackcock's Feather*, which confirmed the young Hammond's sense of his own Irishness within the Protestant-dominated, eastward-looking, south-defying state. At the secondary school stage, he angered his parents by reading late into the night and by embarking on impromptu cycling tours of the countryside, in search of figures like them in rural settings. Like Heaney, therefore, his childhood, youth and early adulthood were permeated by a sense of displacement, a deep-seated unease faced with the clash between 'official' cultural perspectives and those of his Irish homeground.
109. MRP interview with David Hammond.
110. Seamus Heaney, *Among Schoolchildren*, op. cit., p. 3.
111. Seamus Heaney, 'Unhappy and at home', interview with Seamus Deane, art. cit., p. 61.

112. Seamus Heaney, in a letter to the author, 30.10.85.
113. Theodore Roethke, *Collected Poems*, London: Faber, 1968, p. 35.
114. Ibid., p. 38.
115. *P*, p. 191.
116. Seamus Heaney, in a letter to the researcher, 30.10.85.
117. Seamus Heaney, quoted in Neil Corcoran's *Seamus Heaney: A Student Guide*, op. cit., p. 23.
118. MRP interview with Philip Hobsbaum.
119. Seamus Heaney, in a letter to researcher, 23.1.86.
120. Godfrey Fitzsimmons, 'Festival Countdown', November 1965.
121. Neil Corcoran, *Seamus Heaney: A Student Guide*, op. cit., p. 22.
122. Robert Kee, *Ireland: A History*, Abacus, 1982, p. 232.
123. MRP interview with Philip Hobsbaum.
124. Seamus Heaney, 'Out of London: Ulster's Troubles', *New Statesman*, July 1, 1966, p. 23.
125. Ibid.
126. Roy McFadden, 'I won't dance', *New Statesman*, July 1, 1966, p. 24. The full text of the poem appears in the anthology, *The Wearing of the Black*, Blackstaff Press, 1974, p. 84.

3: Pioneer, 1966–69: Notes to poems from *Death of a Naturalist* and *Door into the Dark*

1. 'Bogland', *DD*, p. 56.
2. *The Shorter Oxford English Dictionary*, ed. C. T. Onions, Oxford University Press, 1984, p. 1589.
3. *P*, p. 116.
4. Ibid., p. 47.
5. Ted Hughes, *A Choice of Shakespeare's Verse*, London: Faber, 1971. "The poetic imagination is determined finally by the state of negotiation in a person or people between man and his idea of the Creator" (p. 181).
6. *P*, p. 43.
7. Seamus Heaney, interview with Peter Orr, British Council, 1966.
8. 'A Poet's Childhood', *The Listener*, 1 November 1971, pp. 660–661.
9. Ted Hughes, 'Six Young Men', from *The Hawk in the Rain*, London: Faber, 1957, p. 54.
10. Heaney's carrying of the milk "in a bottle/ Corked sloppily with paper" recalls a moment in *The Green Fool*, when Kavanagh recalls a friend bringing him 'a ten-glass bottle of tea corked with a piece of newspaper' (p. 248).
11. *P*, p. 116. The poem's origins lie in a fusion of personal, folk and literary memory. One finds the antithesis of physical, earthly strength and intellectual power in the earliest Irish invasion myths. In *Myths and Legends of the Celtic Race*, Rolleston informs us that the megalithic peoples of Ireland worshipped *dei terreni*, who controlled 'the fecundity of the earth and water' and dwelt in 'hills, rivers and

lakes'. However, the Danaan deities who displaced them were conceived of in intellectual terms, the God Dana's son bearing the name Ecne, meaning 'Knowledge' or 'Poetry'. The Danaans were noted for their 'magical and healing arts', but gained their ascendancy by means of spears which were 'light and sharp-pointed', while those of the Firbolgs whom they defeated were 'heavy and blunt'. (Rolleston, op. cit., pp. 104–106).

12. The crocks are inappropriately compared to 'large pottery bombs', and only seven lines later have become humanised, each inheriting a 'heavy lip' of cream. Similarly, an excessively dramatic note is introduced with the line, 'our brains turned crystals'.

13. Heaney's interest in the work of the painter is reflected in 'Homage to Pieter Breughel', which appeared in Groupsheet 2. A literary source for the poem may be Hopkins's 'Harry Ploughman'. Harry's 'grey eye's heed steered well', and his back 'bends . . . to the wallowing o' the plough'. In describing the unity of man and team, Hopkins, like Heaney, employs a naval image; they are 'one crew' (Hopkins, ed. cit., p. 64).

14. In *Room To Rhyme*, he comments on his failings as a farmer's son. "In his childhood he learned to milk a cow and mow with a scythe, but never became perfect in either."

15. *P*, p. 65.

16. Seamus Heaney, interview with John Haffenden, art. cit., p. 63.

17. Seamus Heaney, 'After the Synge-Song', *The Listener*, 13 January 1972, p. 55.

18. Edna Longley, *Poetry in the Wars*, op. cit., p. 11.

19. D. H. Lawrence, *The Rainbow*, Harmondsworth: Penguin, 1949, p. 222.

20. Estyn Evans, op. cit., p. 157.

21. Describing a photograph by Robert John Welch in the Ulster Museum, Heaney has written, "The smells of childhood go slightly rank for me when I remember flax and fishing" (*Ulster Museum: A Personal Selection*, item 9).

22. P. R. King, 'I Step through Origins', in *Seamus Heaney*, ed. Harold Bloom, Chelsea House, 1986, p. 76.

23. Albert Camus, *The Myth of Sisyphus*, Harmondsworth: Penguin, 1955, p. 20.

24. P. R. King, art. cit., p. 76.

25. Seamus Heaney, 'A Poet's Childhood', art. cit., p. 661. Heaney's barn, a hellish, nightmarish gulf, can be interestingly contrasted with one described in Hopkins' *Journals*. The Stonyhurst barn left the poet exhilarated by its 'beauty of inscape', reassured with its 'principals' and 'cross-bar high up' (Hopkins, ed. cit., p. 126.).

26. An allusion to 'Punishment', *N*, p. 38.

27. The last stanza seems to endorse Patrick Kavanagh's view in *The Green Fool*, p. 141.

"Townsfolk provide societies for the protection of animals because they are one remove from primitive life. We had no sympathy for the salmon, any more than for the fat pigs which we slaughtered at our front doors."

28. Robert Frost, 'Blueberries', *Selected Poems*, ed. cit., p. 141.
29. Seamus Heaney, interview with Seamus Deane, art. cit., p. 61.
30. Seamus Heaney, in an interview with the author, said that John Montague's poem, 'The Water Carrier', was the source of the form for 'Mid Term Break'.
31. Daniel Corkery, op. cit., p. 29.
32. The man primarily responsible for the British handling of the crisis, the Head of the Treasury, Charles Trevelyan, was eventually knighted for his services, and wrote a history of the Famine, which ended in August 1847 according to his account. However, as Robert Kee (*Ireland: A History*, Abacus, 1982, p. 101) has pointed out, some '*eighteen months later*', the Dublin *Freeman's Journal* posed several pertinent questions about England's Malthusian policy :

> "Is it not possible to contrive some means of saving the people from this painful and lingering process of death from starvation? Do we live under a regular and responsible government? Is there justice or humanity in the world that such things could *be* in the middle of the nineteenth century and within twelve hours' reach of the opulence, grandeur and power of a court and capital the first upon earth?"

33. Estyn Evans, op. cit., p. 259.
34. The sixth line of *The Great Hunger* refers to crows which 'gabble over worms and frogs' (ed. cit., p. 34).
35. John Wilson Foster, 'The Poetry of Seamus Heaney' in *Critical Quarterly*, 16:1, Manchester, Spring 1974, p. 38.
36. Cecil Woodham Smith, *The Great Hunger*, New English Library, Sevenoaks, 1983 edition, p. 190.
37. William Wordsworth. *The Prelude*, V, l. 25, ed. cit., p. 521.
38. Patrick Kavanagh, *The Great Hunger*, I, ed. cit., p. 35.
39. Estyn Evans, op. cit., p. 304.
40. Edna Longley, *Poetry in the Wars*, op. cit., p. 142.
41. According to Tim Pat Coogan, writing in 1980, out of a work-force of ten thousand at Harland and Wolff, probably less than one hundred were Roman Catholics (*The I.R.A.*, op. cit., p. 444).
42. Ted Hughes, *Wodwo*, London: Faber, 1967, p. 19.
43. John Wilson Foster, 'The Poetry of Seamus Heaney', art. cit., p. 42.
44. See Ted Hughes's poems, 'The Dove Breeder' and 'A Modest Proposal', *The Hawk in the Rain*, op. cit., pp. 23 and 25.
45. *P*, p. 48.
46. Ibid.
47. Seamus Heaney, interview with John Haffenden, art. cit., p. 61.
48. *P*, p. 48.
49. Ibid.

50. Ibid., p. 23.
51. T. W. Rolleston, op. cit., p. 129. When Sinend fails to perform due rites at the well, she is drowned by the 'angry waters'. After her body is washed up on the shore, she receives the dubious compensation of donating her name to the river, the Shannon.
52. Estyn Evans, op. cit., p. 298.
53. Patrick Kavanagh, *The Green Fool*, op. cit., p. 55.
54. Hopkins quoted in Graham Storey's *A Preface to Hopkins*, op. cit., p. 47.
55. T. W. Rolleston, op. cit., p. 129.
56. William Wordsworth, 'Lines composed a few miles above Tintern Abbey', ll. 109–111, ed. cit., p. 165.
57. William Wordsworth, *The Prelude*, quoted in *P*, p. 63. Gerard Manley Hopkins, 'As Kingfishers catch fire', ed. cit., p. 51. Robert Frost, 'The Most of It', ed. cit., p. 220.
58. The *TLS* reviewer found it 'substantial and impressive'; Christopher Ricks described it as 'outstanding'; C. B. Cox called it 'the best first book of poems I've read for some time'. It won the Somerset Maugham Award and the Geoffrey Faber Prize.
59. David Hammond, quoted in 'The Other Side of Violence', *Sunday Independent*, 23 November 1982, p. 13.
60. Seamus Heaney, 'Old Derry Walls', *The Listener*, 24 October 1968, p. 522.
61. Ibid.
62. Ibid.
63. Seamus Heaney, in a letter to the author 30 October 1985.
64. Dick Wilcocks, 'Animals, bloody animals', *Union News*, Leeds University, 14 February 1969, p. 4.
65. Barry White, *John Hume*, op. cit., p. 76.
66. Seamus Heaney, *The Listener*, 21 August 1969, p. 254.
67. Seamus Heaney, 'The King of the Dark', *The Listener*, 5 February 1970, p. 181.
68. See Chapter 2.
69. Daniel Corkery, op. cit., p. 74.
70. Patrick Kavanagh, quoted by Seamus Heaney, in 'King of the Dark', art. cit., p. 181.
71. Ibid.
72. 'The Salmon Fisher to the Salmon', *DD*, p. 18.
73. Seamus Heaney, *The Poetry Book Society Bulletin*, No. 61, Spring 1969.
74. The bedhead, 'made into a gate for our back garden', once belonged to a neighbour of the Heaney's, a childless widower, Henry MacWilliams, the subject of one of his earliest poems. See *Groupsheet* 1.
75. *P*, p. 53.
76. Seamus Heaney, *The Poetry Book Society Bulletin*, No. 61, Spring 1969.
77. This poem has never appeared in print probably because it is merely a series of verbalised pictures. It connects with 'Mother'

in its description of 'a bleeding mother' who 'labours still', and contributes its final line to 'The Wife's Tale'.

78. Seamus Heaney, *The Poetry Book Society Bulletin*, No. 61, Spring 1969.

79. Robert Frost, 'A Servant to Servants', from *North of Boston, Selected Poems*, ed. cit., pp. 63–68.

> "It's rest I want – there, I have said it out –
> From cooking meals for hungry hired men
> And washing dishes after them . . .
>
> By good rights I ought not to have so much
> Put on me, but there seems no other way . . .
>
> His work's a man's, of course, from sun to sun . . .
>
> No more put out in what they do or say
> Than if I wasn't in the room at all."

80. Seamus Heaney, *Among Schoolchildren*, art. cit., p. 5.
81. A. L. Lloyd, *Folk Song in England*, St Albans: Panther, 1969, p. 212.
82. In the famous tenth stanza of Hopkins's *The Wreck of the Deutschland*, God is depicted as the 'smith' of the universe. Joyce's *Portrait* ends with Stephen's resolve "to forge in the smithy of my soul the uncreated conscience of my race." Corkery in *The Hidden Ireland* (p. 88), cites an anonymous Gaelic poem, *Aonar Dhamhsa Eidir Dhaoinibh*. This laments the loss of the bardic schools with their 'three forges', where memory was trained, and companionship and criticism dispensed.
83. *P*, p. 53.
84. A. Alvarez, 'Homo Faber', *The Observer*, 22 June 1969.
85. See A. L. Lloyd, op. cit., pp. 199–208. In Ireland even a farm's gate-posts can possess sexual attributes, according to Estyn Evans, op. cit., p. 103.

> In Co. Armagh I have heard the farm gate-piers referred to as the man and wife of the house . . . . we cannot overlook the megalithic practice of selecting alternating pointed and flat-topped monoliths for some of their ritual erections, symbolizing, it is thought, male and female.

One of many 'charms' a girl might employ to gain a young man's affections, cited in Brian Merriman's *The Midnight Court*, was to sleep with a spade (op. cit., p. 286.). Estyn Evans writes also of one type of spade used in Ulster for stripping turf, called a *flachter*, which requires forward 'thrusts of the thighs and groin' (op. cit., p. 188).

86. Seamus Heaney, Groupsheet 1.
87. Seamus Heaney, *The Poetry Book Society Bulletin*, No. 61, Spring 1969.
88. Benedict Kiely, 'A Raid into Dark Corners; The Poems of Seamus Heaney', *The Hollins Critic*, 4 October 1970, pp. 1–12.

89. Ted Hughes, 'Snowdrop', *Selected Poems 1957–81*, ed. cit., p. 58.
90. Matthew Arnold, 'Dover Beach'. See also Notes to *Field Work* and *Station Island* note 213.
91. 'Death of Naturalist', *DN*, p. 16. It is perhaps not wholly inappropriate to tie in Heaney's symbol of the eels with Shakespeare's innumerable serpent references in *Antony and Cleopatra*. One of the two quotations from Francis Day's *The Fishes of Great Britain and Ireland* which preface the Phoenix edition refers to Aristotle's belief 'that eels sprang from mud', an idea picked up the drunken Lepidus's speech,'Your serpent of Egypt is bred now of your mud by the operation of your sun' (Act II, sc.vii, ll. 29–31). For Shakespeare and for Heaney, these creatures symbolise energies with both creative and destructive potential. The 'rigid Augustus' of Ted Hughes's 'Cleopatra to the Asp' (*Selected Poems 1957–81*, p. 58), with his 'virginal' sword, is not a far remove from Heaney's St Patrick. The latter is frequently depicted in statues, Heaney writes,

> banishing the snakes from Ireland. The snakes are the emblems of evil, perhaps, the satanic worms who poisoned Eden, and Patrick is the hero ridding the country. But in another way Patrick's staff could be seen as a spade that's planting a sense of sin in the country . . . Certain life forces have been paralysed. I know several people . . . who will never eat eels because of the profound implications of this statue.' ('King of the Dark', art. cit., p. 182)

The unholy Trinity, the unhappy congruence in Ulster of political, religious and sexual repression was to preoccupy Heaney in each of his subsequent volumes, and stimulate many of his finest poems.
92. Seamus Heaney, *The Poetry Book Society Bulletin*, No. 61, Spring 1969.
93. Nora Chadwick, *The Celts*, Harmondsworth: Penguin, p. 206.
94. Cf. T. S. Eliot, 'East Coker', III, *Four Quartets*, ed. cit., p. 29.
95. Cf. the image of he eggs in 'Servant Boy', *WO*, p. 17.
96. *P*, p. 56.
97. Robert Kee, op. cit., p. 65.
98. Geoffrey Hill, 'Genesis', *Collected Poems*, Harmondsworth: Penguin, 1985, p. 16.
99. *P*, p. 56.
100. Quoted in Thomas Pakenham, *The Year of Liberty*, St Albans: Granada, 1972, p. 389. The first edition was from Hodder and Stoughton, 1969.
101. Ibid., pp. 405–406.
102. Seamus Heaney, 'The Delirium of the Brave', *The Listener*, 27 November 1969, p. 757.
103. T. P. Flanagan, in an interview with the author, 27 November 1985.
104. Ibid.
105. Ibid.

106. Seamus Heaney, introduction to *T.P.Flanagan*, Arts Council of Northern Ireland, 1977.
107. Ibid.
108. Seamus Heaney, in a letter to the author, 30 October 1985.
109. Patrick Kavanagh, *The Green Fool*, op. cit., p. 77.
110. From *Irish Folk Ways*, one learns that magical practice lies behind the custom of preserving butter in bogs, and how 'quantities ranging from a few pounds to as much as a hundredweight' (p. 196) have been discovered by astonished turf-cutters.
111. Edna Longley, in a review of *Door into the Dark*, in *Phoenix*, ed. Harry Chambers.

4: Exposure, 1969–75: Notes to poems from *Wintering Out* and *North*

1. James Simmons, editorial in *The Honest Ulsterman*, No. 2, June 1968, p. 2.
2. Czeslaw Milosz, *The Captive Mind*, Harmondsworth: Penguin, 1980, p. 26.
3. *P*, p. 30.
4. Conor Cruise O'Brien, *States of Ireland*, London: Hutchinson, 1972, p. 173.
5. *P*, p. 30.
6. 'Mother Ireland', *The Listener*, 7 December 1972, p. 790.
7. Interview with Harriet Cooke, *The Irish Times*, 28 December 1973, p. 8.
8. A phrase from the final quatrain of 'Exposure', *N*, p. 73.
9. 'Summer 1969', *N*, p. 69.
10. 'Delirium of the Brave', *The Listener*, 27 November 1969, p. 759.
11. Ibid.
12. Interview with Robert Druce, 'A Raindrop on a Thorn', *Dutch Quarterly Review*, Vol. 9, 1978, p. 30.
13. Ted Hughes, ed. *A Choice of Shakespeare's Verse*, Faber, 1971, p. 181.
14. Interview with James Randall, *Ploughshares*, 5:3, 1979, p. 18.
15. Randall, art. cit., pp. 18–19.
16. Interview with Caroline Walsh, *The Irish Times*, 6 December 1975, p. 5.
17. 'The Saturday Interview', Caroline Walsh, art. cit., p. 5. In Geoffrey Summerfield's anthology, *Worlds*, Penguin, 1974, there is a photograph by Larry Herman of Heaney with a painting of a Red Indian above his head. Two highly successsful feature films from this period which reassessed the history of the Indians and portrayed the atrocities they suffered were *Straw Dogs* and *Little Big Man*.
18. Randall, art. cit, p. 20.
19. Ibid.
20. Ibid.
21. Ibid.
22. Within Tom Flanagan's *The Irish Novelists 1800–1850* (1959), there

is an examination of the work of William Carleton, who figures importantly in Heaney's *Station Island*. Flanagan wrote the excellent novel, *The Year of the French* (1979), which deals with the 1798 rebellion. Conor Cruise O'Brien (b. 1917), a famous Irish statesman and man of letters, author of *States of Ireland* (1972), which contains a valuable account of the origins and development of the recent Troubles.

23. W. D. Flackes, *Northern Ireland: A Political Directory*, Ariel Books, 1983, p. 320.
24. 'A Poet's Childhood', *The Listener*, 1 November 1971, p. 660.
25. 'Gifts of Rain', *WO*, p. 25.
26. See Estyn Evans, op. cit., p. 85 and p. 185. "In the past, too, considerable use was made of buried timber dug from the bogs, of oak for roofing beams and of pine for kindling."
27. Terence Brown, *Northern Voices: Poets from Ulster*, Gill and Macmillan, 1975, p. 180. Brown comments that Heaney is "governed by rational impulses and is disinclined to mythologise the Irish past" (p. 175).
28. Edmund Spenser, English poet (1552–99). Ernest de Selincourt, in his introduction to Spenser's *Poetical Works*, Oxford University Press (1912) writes of the *Veue of the Present State of Ireland*:

> "In its lack of sympathy with the Irish, and its failure to understand the real causes of their disaffection, it is typical of the view held by all Elizabethans and by most English statesmen since." (p. xxxvii)

29. Arthur, Lord Grey of Wilton, quoted in introduction to *Spenser: Poetical Works*, ed. cit., p. xxiv.
30. Edmund Spenser, *A Veue of the Present State of Ireland*, ed. W. L. Renwick, Oxford University Press, 1970, p. 104. Heaney quotes part of this extract in 'The Trade of an Irish Poet', *Guardian*, 25 May 1972, p. 17.
31. Ibid.
32. Daniel Corkery, *The Hidden Ireland*, op. cit., p. 42.
33. Ibid., p. 49.
34. In a mock Advanced Level Literature examination at a sixth form college, where I taught, one eighteen year-old English student mistakenly described this as the message of Brian Friel's *Translations*!
35. 'The Interesting Case of John Alphonsus Mulrennan', *Planet*, January 1978, pp. 34–40, quoted in Neil Corcoran's *Seamus Heaney*, p. 83.
36. Heaney refers to *'civil* tongues' because English became the dominant language in the towns of Ireland, especially in the area known as The Pale.
37. In 'Seamus Heaney praises Lough Erne', *The Listener*, 4 February 1971, p. 143, T. P. Flanagan describes the Mummers thus:

> "They were dressed in old trousers usually gathered under the knee and then on the upper part of the body they wore an old

potato sack or something like that, let down like a shirt. But the interesting thing was this great conical helmet of straw, which was woven and constructed rather like the traditional beehive, and this made them a sort of macabre Humpty-Dumpty. As they walked, because of the considerable weight of straw on their shoulders, their heads within the straw helmets tended to rock gently from side to side . . . " (p. 143)

Estyn Evans, in *Irish Folk Ways*, p. 287, provides illustrations of a mummer's outfit, and Patrick Kavanagh refers to his experience as a mummer in *The Green Fool*, pp. 143–144.

38. The image is from Ted Hughes, see note 13.
39. Aisling Maguire, *Selected Poems: Seamus Heaney*, Longman York Press, 1986, p. 35.
40. Estyn Evans, *Irish Folk Ways*, op. cit., p. 1.
41. 'The Trade of an Irish Poet', art. cit., p. 17.
42. Interview with Seamus Deane, 'Unhappy and at Home', art. cit., p. 64.
43. 'The Trade of an Irish Poet', art. cit., p. 17.
44. Seamus Heaney giving a commentary on a selection of his poems on a Faber Poetry Cassette from 1982.
45. *P*, p. 131. Of the literary custom of emphasising place-names, Thomas Kinsella writes, "It is often enough justification for the inclusion of an incident that it ends in the naming of a physical feature" (Introduction to *The Tain*, Oxford University Press, 1970, p. xiii).
46. Edna Longley, *A language not to be betrayed: Selected Prose of Edward Thomas*, Carcanet 1981, p. 75.
47. Daniel Corkery, *The Hidden Ireland*, op. cit., p. 19.
48. In an earlier draft of 'Anahorish' which appeared in *Phoenix* 13, in Spring 1975, there are references to 'death squeals', 'the big slaughterhouse', and 'the lane streaming/ With blood also'. The draft, has in the left hand corner, an arrowand the date '11th Jan 1972'.
49. Seamus Heaney giving a commentary on a selection of his poems on a Faber Poetry Cassette from 1982.
50. Wordsworth employs the word in this double sense in his famous poem written above Tintern Abbey, speaking of 'The still sad music of humanity.'
51. Gabriel Oak, the hero of Thomas Hardy's *Far from the Madding Crowd*, is attuned to the changes in Nature and the weather. Heaney's figure also reminds me of the central character in Ted Hughes's story, 'The Rain Horse' in *Wodwo*, Faber and Faber, 1967, pp. 45–55.
52. Quotation from 'The Thought Fox' by Ted Hughes, from *The Hawk in the Rain*, Faber and Faber, 1957, p. 14.
53. The old woman in Yeats's *Cathleen ni Hoolihan* laments the loss of her 'four beautiful green fields' – Leinster, Munster, Connacht, and Ulster (*Selected Plays*, London: Macmillan, 1964, p. 250).

54. In *P,* p. 33, Heaney recounts a dream he had while in California. "I was shaving at the mirror of the bathroom when I glimpsed in the mirror a wounded man falling towards me with his bloodied hands lifted to tear at me or to implore." To borrow Yeats's phrase from 'Easter 1916', for Heaney blood is 'in the midst of all'.
55. William Wordsworth, *The Prelude,* 1805 version, II, lines 306–307.
56. Shakespeare, *Richard II,* Act V, v, line 43.
57. Shakespeare, *Antony and Cleopatra,* Act I, v, line 28.
58. *Gospel according to St Luke,* Chapter XVI, v.19 ff. 'Dives' means 'a rich man' in Latin. The story operates in the next poem, 'The Other Side', with its reference to Lazarus.
59. In contrast to this example of unenlightened Protestantism, Heaney presents us in 'Linen Town' with the radical dissenter, Henry Joy McCracken. He founded "the first Sunday school in Belfast which was open to scholars of all religious views" (Thomas Pakenham, op. cit., p. 196) and lead the United Irishmen in the Ulster Rising of 1798.
60. Grass-seed plays an important role literally and metaphorically in an epiphany in his autobiography, *The Green Fool,* p. 194. While queuing to sell grass-seed, he reads some reviews and a poem by Æ in the *Irish Statesman* which have such an impact on him that he decides to become a writer himself.
61. Cf. W. B. Yeats, 'Meditations in Time of Civil War', VI, *Collected Poems,* p. 230.

> "We had fed the heart on fantasies,
> The heart's grown brutal from the fare."

62. *Exodus,* Chapter 21, v.24. Tom Paulin in 'Paisley's Progress', in *Ireland and the English Crisis,* Bloodaxe, 1984, pp. 161–162, comments on the Reverend Ian's fondness for Old Testament analogies.
63. Doris Lessing, *Briefing for a descent into Hell,* Panther 1972, p. 85.
64. *P,* p. 56.
65. T. S. Eliot, *Tradition and the Individual Talent,* in *Twentieth Century Poetry: Critical Essays and Documents,* Martin and Furbank (eds), Open University Press, 1975, p. 80.
66. Seamus Heaney, interviewed by Brian Donnelly, in *Seamus Heaney,* ed. Broadridge, Copenhagen: Danmarks Radio, 1977, p. 60.
67. P. V. Glob, op. cit., p. 20.
68. *P,* p. 57.
69. It is interesting to observe how the poet drew upon and transformed his source material. From the very first chapter of his study, Glob permeates his factual description with a sensitive use of metaphor in establishing the ambivalence of the Tollund Man, as an object of beauty, of piety, as an example of human cruelty and fear.

He lay on his damp bed as though asleep, resting on his side, the head inclined a little forward, arms and legs bent. His face wore a gentle expression – the eyes lightly closed, the lips softly pursed, as if in silent prayer. It was as though the dead man's soul had for a moment returned from another world, through the gate in the western sky.

On his head he wore a pointed skin cap fastened securely under the chin by a hide thong. Round his waist there was a smooth hide belt. Otherwise he was naked . . .

The air of gentle tranquillity about the man was shattered when a small lump of peat was removed from beside his head. This disclosed a rope, made of two leather thongs twisted together, which encircled the neck in a noose drawn tight into the throat and then coiled like a snake over the shoulder and down across the back. After this discovery the wrinkled forehead and set mouth seemed to take on a look of affliction. (Glob, p. 18)

His last supper was 'a gruel' made from 'cultivated and wild grains', which it was hoped would "grow and ripen by the goddess's journey through the spring landscape" (p. 163). In recompense for their sacrifice and suffering, Nerthus – Mother Earth – bestowed a blessing upon the faces of her husbands, "and preserved them through the millenia" (p. 192).

70. Ibid., p. 166.
71. Ibid., p. 36. "The majestic head astonishes the beholder and rivets his attention. Dark in hue, the head is still full of life and more beautiful than the best portraits of the world's greatest artists, since it is the man himself we see."
72. Within the Nationalist community in the early 1970s, it was expected that order could only be restored in the North following the reunification of Ireland.
73. Seamus Heaney giving a commentary on a selection of his poems on a Faber Poetry Cassette from 1982. Kevin Boyle and Tom Hadden, in their *Ireland: A Positive Proposal*, state that "In the period from 1921 to 1924 some 2,000 suspects were interned without trial. Between June 1920 and June 1922 over 400 people were killed, either by security forces or by irregular paramilitaries on either side" (p. 59).
74. 'Kinship', *N*, p. 45.
75. One is perhaps reminded of the dramatic historical analogies employed by Sylvia Plath in poems such as 'Lady Lazarus' and 'Daddy'.
76. Seamus Heaney, commentary from *In Their Element*, BBC Radio Ulster, 1977.
77. Polly Devlin, op. cit. "Perhaps no other nation is more ready to cry, to be borne down with the sadnesses inherent in human existence . . . There is often apparent around us a wild extravagance of grief, as though it is the only possible or permissible show of emotion" (p. 84).
78. The words of the song celebrate the land, yet accept the inevitabilities of loss and exile. It begins brightly with flowers,

As I went a walking one morning in May
To view yon fair valleys and mountains so gay
I was thinking on those flowers, all doomed to decay,
That bloom around ye, bonny, bonny Sliev Gallion braes.

but ends with politico-economic realities

O, it was not the want of employment at home,
That caused us poor exiles in sorrow to roam,
But those tyrannising landlords, they would not let us stay,
So farewell unto ye, bonny, bonny Sliev Gallion braes.

79. Charles Dickens, *Great Expectations*, London: Panther Books, 1964, p. 47.

> "'Do you know what I touch here?" she said, laying her hands, one upon the other, on her left side.
> 'Yes, ma'am.'
> 'What do I touch?'
> 'Your heart.'
> 'Broken!'"

80. The dominant, and, in a sense, deserted mothers of D. H. Lawrence's *Sons and Lovers* and Thomas Hardy's *The Return of the Native*.
81. A quotation from Brian Friel, *Translations*, p. 40.
82. Sylvia Plath, interview with Peter Orr, British Council, 1962.
83. *P*, p. 48.
84. Seamus Heaney, interview with Frank Kinahan, art. cit., p. 409.
85. Allusion to a line in 'The Thought Fox' by Ted Hughes, from *The Hawk in the Rain*, Faber and Faber, 1957, p. 14.
86. Shakespeare, *King Lear*, Act IV, vi, 189.
87. Heaney describes the custom of making a May altar in honour of the Virgin Mary in 'The Poet as a Christian', *The Furrow*, Naas, 29:10, October 1978, p. 605. 'Chrism' is oil mingled with balm and is used in each of the major Catholic sacraments.
88. 'Antaeus', *N*, p. 12. Stalactite and womb images occur in Sylvia Plath's poem, 'Nick and the Candlestick', *Ariel*, pp. 40–41, which also sets off the innocence of children against parental guilt.
89. See Philip Hobsbaum's comments in 'Craft and Technique in *Wintering Out*' in *The Art of Seamus Heaney*, ed. Curtis, Poetry Wales Press, p. 42. Heaney employs the tuning fork image in *P*, p. 70, when he talks of the 'stilled consciousness' of Wordsworth. The poet is 'a living tuning fork planted between wood and hill.'
90. The concept of limbo is itself a cruel one. It was conceived by medieval theologians as a place where the unbaptised and Old Testament prophets and patriarchs could live eternally. Though free from the torments of hell, they were denied the light that emanates from Christ.

91. W. H. Auden, 'La Musée des Beaux Arts', *Selected Poems*, Penguin, 1967, p. 61.
92. Thomas Hardy, *Tess of the d'Urbervilles*, Macmillan, New Wessex Edition, 1977, p. 158. The 1960s was the period of the Apollo moon missions, culminating in the landing of the Eagle space capsule in July 1969.
93. John Donne, *Selected Poems*, Penguin, 1975, p. 174.
94. Lisel Muller, 'The Lonesome Dream', *Contemporary American Poetry*, ed. Mark Strand, New York: Mentor, 1969. The poem explodes the fantasy of the immigrants' view of America, and suggests that human beings regrettably destroy everything beautiful that they touch.
95. Nicholas McGuinn, *Seamus Heaney: A Student's Guide to the Selected Poems 1965–75*, Leeds: Arnold Wheaton, 1986, p. 68.
96. See Seamus Heaney, interview with Frank Kinahan, art. cit., pp. 408–409.

>   "The specifically Irish Catholic blueprint that was laid down when I was growing up has been laid there forever. I think of the distrust of the world, if you like, the distrust of happiness, the deep pleasure there is in mournful litany, the sense that there's some kind of feminine intercession that you turn to for comfort."

97. Seamus Heaney, 'The Poet as a Christian', art. cit., p. 604.
98. Seamus Heaney, 'Unhappy and at Home', art. cit., p. 61.
99. Seamus Heaney, quoted in an article by Martin Dodsworth for *The Guardian*, 1975, reprinted in *Seamus Heaney*, ed. Broadridge, p. 46.
100. MRP interview with Harry Chambers.
101. MRP interview with Michael Longley.
102. Seamus Heaney, interview with Randy Brandes, *Salmagundi*, Skidmore College, Saratoga Springs, No. 80, Fall 1988, p. 8.
103. Anthony Storr, *Jung*, Glasgow: Fontana, 1973, p. 89. The interview in which Heaney describes himself as Jungian is the Frank Kinahan one for *Critical Inquiry*, 8:3, Spring 1982.
104. Seamus Heaney, comments from 'The Poet who came back', an article from the *Belfast Telegraph*, 23 November 1971.
105. *P*, pp. 31–32.
106. Tim Pat Coogan, *The I.R.A.*, Glasgow: Fontana, 1982, p. 437.
107. Bernadette Devlin, quoted in Barry White, *John Hume: Statesman of the Troubles*, op. cit., p. 123.
108. MRP interview with Michael Longley. 'Scared, irrevocable steps' is a quotation from *F*, p. 14.
109. J.C. Beckett, *A Short History of Ireland*, Hutchinson, 1979, p. 174.
110. Ibid.
111. MRP interview with Seamus Heaney.
112. Seamus Heaney, interview with Caroline Walsh. art. cit., p. 5.

>   "Actually I think . . . poets shouldn't work too hard at other jobs, because I think if you commit a lot of your attention and your

tension in another place, you close your receiving stations."
Poetry had not been sufficiently at 'the centre of my life', he
believed. "I didn't know what being a poet was, though I know
now, that it is a dedication to this art and a determination to make
the meanings of your life through the art and then to make the art
in some ways the meaning of your life."

113. Seamus Heaney, in a newspaper article from 1972 which I have been
     unable to trace. I copied the comments from an album of articles
     belonging to his mother.
114. Daniel Corkery, op. cit., p. 23.
115. MRP interview with Michael Longley.
116. Seamus Heaney, the same untraced article from 1972 referred to in
     the above note 113.
117. MRP interview with Seamus Heaney. In the interview with John
     Haffenden he refers to 'committee work' (p. 74).
118. Seamus Heaney, interview with James Randall, art. cit., p. 8.
     "Undoubtedly I was aware of a political dimension to the move
     south of the border . . . ". In the interview with Robert Druce,
     he states, "Of course I realised that there was an emblematic
     significance in moving south of the Border. But what happened
     was that it was mythologised, actually, immediately, because it was
     in the newspapers" (p. 28).
119. Seamus Heaney, interviewed by Seamus Deane in 'Talk with Seamus
     Heaney', *New York Times Book Review*, 2 December 1979, pp. 47–48.
120. Seamus Heaney, interview with James Randall, p. 8.
121. Ibid.
122. Seamus Heaney, 'Unhappy and at Home', art. cit., p. 65.
123. Seamus Heaney, introduction to *Sweeney Astray*, Derry: Field Day,
     1983, p. viii.
124. Seamus Heaney, 'King Conchobor and his Knights', *The Listener*, 26
     March 1970, p. 416.
125. Seamus Heaney, quoted in Neil Corcoran's, *Seamus Heaney*, p. 33.
126. Seamus Heaney, 'Lost Ulstermen', *The Listener*, 26 April 1973, p. 550.
     For Derek Mahon *The Rough Field* was 'a rich and complex work by
     the best Irish poet of his generation'; for James Simmons it was 'a
     very fine book' which 'should be an inspiration to us all'; and for
     Stand magazine 'one of the topmost poetic achievements of Irish
     writing in the last twenty years'.
127. Seamus Heaney, introduction to *Soundings*, Belfast: Blackstaff Press,
     1972.
128. Seamus Heaney, interview with James Randall, p. 10.
129. *P*, p. 217.
130. Ibid.
131. Seamus Heaney, quoted in Neil Corcoran's, *Seamus Heaney*, p. 36.
132. Seamus Heaney, interview with Harriet Cooke, art. cit., p. 8.
133. Seamus Heaney, quoted on covers of *Seamus Heaney*, ed. Broadridge,
     Copenhagen: Danmarks Radio, 1977.
134. Seamus Heaney, quoted in Neil Corcoran's, *Seamus Heaney*, p. 34.

135.   Seamus Heaney, *Explorations I*, produced by David Hammond, BBC
        Northern Ireland Radio 4, recorded 29 November 1973. Broadcast 17
        January 1974.

> Think then of that word 'hoard'. In museums you find coin-
> hoards, hoards of gold, hoards of weapons. Hoard immediately
> brings the idea of hidden riches to our mind . . . Next 'a word-
> hoard'. What are we to make of that? Where are the words
> hoarded? Where is the precious store to be found? Well, obvi-
> ously, the mind, the memory, the imagination of the poet is a
> kind of hoard where words are buried, and in making his poem
> he opens the hidden chests of words in his head; he mines his
> own brain for the words that will gleam with his meaning."

136.   In programme one, he chooses prose extracts from Joyce and Brian
        Friel, and one poem by Kavanagh, 'Shancoduff'; programme two
        begins with Michael McLaverty, then turns to Joyce and Brian Friel
        again; the third programme takes its title from another Kavanagh
        poem, 'The Long Garden', and then extracts from Frank O'Connor,
        Florence Mary McDowell, and Maurice O'Sullivan; programme four
        opens with the 'bitter honey' of knowledge tasted by Wordsworth
        and Maxim Gorky, with Heaney's own 'Blackberry Picking' and
        extracts from *Sons and Lovers* and Gorky's *Childhood* served up as
        the main course; the fifth and sixth broadcasts are emphatically
        Celtic in flavour, and contain poems from *Buile Suibhne*, Dylan
        Thomas, Edwin Muir, Louis Macneice, and prose from Robert
        Louis Stevenson and Flann O'Brien, along with further extracts
        from Florence Mary McDowell and Maurice O'Sullivan.
137.   Seamus Heaney, *Explorations I*, 'The Long Garden', recorded 6
        December 1973. Broadcast 31 January 1974.
138.   Seamus Heaney, quoted in an article by Martin Dodsworth for *The
        Guardian*, 1975, reprinted in *Seamus Heaney* ed. Broadridge, p. 48.
        In his commentary on a selection of his poems on a Faber Poetry
        Cassette from 1982, he states, "Instead of moving away from the
        focus of public events in the North, in some odd kind of way,
        I had moved into it, as somebody expected to to say something
        about it."
139.   Barry White, *John Hume: Statesman of the Troubles*, op. cit., p. 167.
140.   John Montague, *The Rough Field*, Portlaoise: Dolmen Press, 1972,
        p. 19.

> *Each morning, from the corner*
> *of the hearth, I saw a miracle*
> *as you sifted the smoored ashes*
> *to blow*
> *a fire's sleeping remains*
> *back to life, holding the burning brands*
> *of turf, between work hardened hands.*

I draw on that fire . . . ."

Montague chose 'Sunlight' for the anthology, *The Faber Book of Irish Verse* in 1974.

141. The same phrase was used by Marie Heaney's brother, Barry Devlin, as the title for a song on the Horslips L.P., *The Tain*, Oats, 1973. The song in turn provided the title for Jennifer Johnston's novel, *Shadows on our Skin*, 1977, which deals with the Troubles in Derry.

142. Heaney commenting on the poem in the programme, *In their Element*, for BBC Radio Northern Ireland, 1977. The poem may be connected with a photograph of seed cutters which used to hang in the hallway at 'The Wood', a present given to Heaney's father by David Hammond.

143. From the interview, 'Unhappy and at home', art. cit., p. 67. The words quoted are Seamus Deane's, but are ones to which Heaney assents.

144. Ciaran Carson, 'Escaped from the Massacre?', a review of *North*, *The Honest Ulsterman*, 50, Winter 1975, pp. 185–186.

145. Gregory Martin, *Bruegel*, New York: Park South Books, 1978, p. 2.

146. Ibid.

147. In Greek mythology, the giant Antaeus, son of Poseidon and Ge, the earth mother, wrestled with Hercules. Initially he survived because each time he was thrown to the ground he derived fresh strength from his mother; eventually Hercules twigged, and, lifting him aloft, squeezed him to death. Unfortunately, Heaney's giant lacks any 'contact with the soil' of actual experience, and perishes from breathing too much 'literary' air prior to his unnamed rival's arrival. Only in the light of the later poem, 'Hercules and Antaeus', which rounds off Part One, does the mist of the first allegory disperse a little. There Antaeus represents the instinctual Celt, doomed to defeat and dispossession by the rationalist English Hercules. This would enable the first 'Antaeus' speech to be interpreted politically as naive, boastful blather which 'goeth before destruction', the voice of a 'haughty spirit before a fall' (Proverbs, 16, v.18). W. B. Yeats refers to the myth in 'The Municipal Gallery Revisited', *Collected Poems*, p. 368.

148. Seamus Heaney, in the introduction to *A Personal Selection*, Ulster Museum, publication number 248, May 1982.

149. This listing has a deadening effect, which may or may not be intentional. *North*, however, is studded with many such image-cairns, part of Heaney's attempt to achieve a rugged, archaic starkness.

150. Yggdrasil was "the greatest and best of all trees, a mighty ash-tree which was the holy of holies", "which held the fabric of the universe together, a living and sentient being" (Magnus Magnusson, *Viking: Hammer of the North*, London: Orbis, 1976, p. 49). See also H. R. Ellis Davidson, *Gods and Myths of Northern Europe*, Harmondsworth: Penguin, 1964, pp. 190–192.

The idea of a guardian tree standing beside a dwelling place was once a familiar one in Germany and Scandinavia . . . Yggdrasill

was certainly a guardian tree . . . and was visualised as a kind
of ladder stretching up to heaven and down to the underworld.

The seemingly tenuous connection between the Mossbawn conversation and World-Tree myth in the poem is strengthened when one
recalls that the beech trees of the Heaney's old home, beloved by
the poet in his childhood, had been either blown down, or chopped
down by the purchaser. The only tree to survive is a tall ash by
the roadside which had not grown at all since the Heaneys left,
according to the present owner.

151.   Seamus Heaney giving a commentary on a selection of his poems
        on a Faber Poetry Cassette from 1982.
152.   The worksheets are printed in Arthur E. McGuinness's article, 'The
        Craft of Diction: Revision in Seamus Heaney's Poems', which
        appears in *Image and Illusion: Anglo Irish Literature and its Contexts*,
        Portmarnock, Co. Dublin: Wolfhound Press, 1979, pp. 62–91.
153.   Ibid. The first line of Version One states how he was "almost
        immune" to the "Ordinary dead in their own bedrooms", and
        alludes specifically to his grandfather's wake.
154.   Ibid. Version Two (B), entitled 'Growing Pains', ends on a far more
        emotional note, referring to the more recent funeral of 'a cousin
        of my father's'. 'The dead beauty of his face' moves the poet
        to tears, or, as this version ponderously puts it, 'the confirma-
        tion of manhood useless.'. In its final form, Part One conveys a
        sense of decorum, and emphasises the emotional restraint and
        distance he was able to maintain, since as Versions Three and
        Four of the poem have it, "Those dead have left no craters in my
        days."
155.   Ibid. Earlier drafts possess stark, Owenesque references to 'men
        whose blown stomachs were cleaned like dung/ into eight plastic
        bags' (Version 1), 'men whose blown stomachs were cleaned like
        dung/ Off the pavements' (Version 2), and 'shovelled remnants'
        (Version 3), but the poem's final version endeavours to transcend
        the horror and pity of war, and to direct its metaphoric and
        mythic energies towards some future rituals of atonement and
        reconciliation.
156.   Cf. Louis MacNeice in 'Valediction', *Collected Poems*, London: Faber,
        1966, p. 53.

        But no abiding content can grow out of these minds
        Fuddled with blood, always caught by blinds.

157.   Seamus Heaney, commentary in the film *The Boyne Valley*, BBC 1980,
        directed by David Hammond.
158.   Estyn Evans, op. cit., p. 283. See also Seamus Heaney, *The Listener*,
        5 February 1970, p. 182. "Patrick's staff could be seen as a spade
        that's planting the sense of sin in the country. The snakes are

frigid at the foot of his crozier. Certain life forces have been paralysed."
159. Magnus Magnusson, Preface to *Vikings*, London: Orbis, p. 7.
160. Eyebrows have already arched over that phrase, 'lies and women', notably those of Edna Longley. (See her article, 'North: 'Inner Emigre' or 'Artful Voyeur', in *Poetry in the Wars*, Newcastle: Bloodaxe, 1986, p. 159.) It may have been influenced by Heaney's recent reading of *Njal's Saga*, in which many of the tragic events stem directly from the machinations of three female principals, Unn, Hallgerd and Bergthora. The failure of Unn's marriage to Hrut as a result of the witchcraft sets in motion the events which culminate in the death of the hero, Gunnar. The rivalry between Hallgerd, Gunnar's wife, and Bergthora, Njal's wife, prompts a murderous feud in which seven of their servants die. When Gunnar is surrounded by his enemies, Hallgerd refuses to give him one of her hairs as a bow-string, an action that might have saved his life.

The phrase 'exhaustions nominated peace' appears in *Stations*, Belfast: Ulsterman Publications, 1975, p. 21, where it refers to an earlier phase in the Troubles. Heaney may well have had in mind the June–July 1972 ceasefire by the P.I.R.A.
161. *SI*, pp. 93–94.
162. Cf. Eliot's description of poetry in *East Coker* as 'a raid on the inarticulate' (*Collected Poems*, ed. cit., p. 182).
163. Daniel Corkery, op. cit., p. 76.
164. There are too many rapid metamorphoses in too short a space. In section IV, for example, the poet's handwriting can be discovered 'unscarfing/ a *zoomorphic wake*', before turning up 'a *worm* of thought'; someone has fallen asleep in the 'word-hoard'!
165. Nicholas McGuinn, op. cit., p. 97. It is must be hard for Heaney to live with the accusation of *hubris* after depicting himself as a 'dithering' blatherer.
166. Gerard Manley Hopkins, *Selected Poems*, ed. cit., p. 31.
167. The allusion to *The Tempest* ('Those little points/ were the eyes') supports such a reading. Heaney's fascination with this creature may stem from the fact that moles, like snakes, are not found in Ireland. They attained considerable popularity in Jacobite circles, however, when one of their number was responsible for the unsaddling and ultimately the death of King William III, the victor of the Battle of the Boyne.
168. Blake Morrison, *Seamus Heaney*, p. 62, and James Liddy in 'Ulster Poets and the Catholic Muse' in *Eire-Ireland*, 13:4, Winter 1978, p. 135.
169. I am grateful to Sister Mary Clancy of the Daughters of the Cross, Stillorgan, Co. Dublin for supplying me with the words of 'Will you come to the bower?'. The final stanzas run:

You can visit New Ross, gallant Wexford and Gorey,
Where the green was last seen by proud Saxon and Tory,
Where the soil is sanctified by the blood of each true man

> Where they died satisfied, their enemies they would not run
> from.
>
> Will you come and awake our lost land from its slumber,
> And her fetters we will break, links that are long encumbered,
> And the air will resound with Hosanna to greet you,
> On the shore will be found gallant Irishmen to meet you.

170. Glob, op. cit., pp. 103–104. Whereas the Danish archaeologist refers to 'a sort of cape worn on one shoulder and passing under the opposite arm', Heaney employs the more 'Ulsterly' term, 'sash'.
171. Ibid., p. 39. "There could scarcely be any doubt as to the cause of death. A long cut ran round the front of the neck practically from ear to ear, so deep that the gullet was completely severed" (p. 48).
172. A poem similarly initiated by a photograph which may have been at the back of Heaney's mind as he wrote 'The Grauballe Man' is Ted Hughes's 'Six Young Men'. 'Contradictory permanent horrors' stalk in both poems, and Heaney's rhetorical question, 'Who will say 'corpse'/ to his vivid cast?', seems answered by Hughes's assertion in the final stanza. (See *The Hawk in the Rain*, op. cit., p. 55).
173. *P*, p. 34.
174. The word 'civil' is associated by Heaney with English rule, and its hypocrisy. It implies 'controlled', 'disciplined', 'anglicised'. Its opposite, one can deduce from Brian Friel's *Making History*, is 'barbarous' or 'Irish'. It is used, again ironically, in 'Whatever you say, say nothing'.
175. Glob, op. cit., pp. 112–114. The archaeologist describes the discovery of the body of a fourteen-year-old girl on the Windeby estate in Schleswig, North Germany.

> She lay on her back, her head twisted to one side, the left arm outstretched. Between it and her hip was a large block of stone. The right arm was bent in against the chest, as if defensively . . . The head with its delicate face, and the hands were preserved best; the chest had completely disintegrated and the ribs were visible . . . The hair, reddish from the effects of bog acids but originally light blond, was of exceptional fineness but had been shaved off with a razor on the left side of the head . . . The young girl lay naked in the hole in the peat, a bandage over the eyes and a collar round the neck.

In a later chapter, he cites Tacitus's account of 'the special punishment for adultery by women' among the Germani, which was to have their heads shaved in the presence of their relatives, and then to be 'scourged out of the village' (p. 153). Significantly, Tacitus "says nothing about male adultery".

176. See Arthur E. McGuinness, 'The Craft of Diction: Revision in Seamus Heaney's Poems', art. cit., pp. 80–85. Versions 2–6 of the

worksheets refer to the 'birch scourge/ thrown across her settled/ in the posture/ of a palm.'

177. *The Gospel according to St. John*, Chapter 8, v. 1–11. The later reference to her 'numbered' bones contains an allusion to archaeological practice, but also perhaps to St. Matthew (Chapter 10, verses 28–30), where Christ speaks of the preciousness of human life and divine providence.

> And do not fear those who kill the body but cannot kill the soul. Are not two sparrows sold for a penny? And not one of them will fall to the ground without your Father's will. But even the hairs of your head are numbered.

The phrase, 'numbered heads', occurs in the first part of the title poem from *Seeing Things*, p. 16.

178. Seamus Deane, 'Seamus Heaney: The Timorous and the Bold', *Celtic Revivals*, p. 180.

179. In 'The Bog', *Seamus Heaney*, ed. Broadbridge, Copenhagen: Danmarks Radio, p. 39, Heaney writes,

> I must have been no more than three or four years old when I was warned not to go into the little bog at the edge of our farm. They were afraid I might fall in one of the old pools . . . so they put about this notion that they were bottomless. They said it so often that I believed it, and in a different way I believe it still. As a child I used to imagine my helpless body whistling down a black shaft forever and ever.

180. See *Roget's Thesaurus*, section 345, Marsh.

181. The phrase derives from Kavanagh. See 'King of the Dark', art. cit., p. 181.

182. 'The Bog', *Seamus Heaney*, ed. Broadbridge, op. cit., p. 40.

183. Glob, op. cit., p. 180.

> "In the summer of 1961 Harald Andersen uncovered at Foerlev Nymlle three sacrificial sites . . . In one of these sites the stones were gathered up in a heap, and under this heap lay a cloven oak-branch nine feet in length – the goddess herself. The branch in itself possessed natural feminine form . . . Her significance as a goddess of fertility is underlined by the presence of a bunch of flax placed upon the heap of stones under which she was preserved in the bog water when not needed for feast days."

184. 'The Bog', *Seamus Heaney*, ed. Broadbridge, p. 40.

> "There was a summer migration to the peat face and a winter hibernation beside the peat blaze, the heat on the back of your neck as you handled it, the heat of the fire on your shins as you

burnt it. The opened hearth and the opened bog were the poles
of a whole domestic world."

185. Dylan Thomas, 'Fern Hill', Collected Poems, ed. cit., p. 159.
186. Glob, op. cit., p. 152 and pp. 159–162.

"At a time laid down in the distant past all peoples that are
related by blood meet through their delegations in a wood, which
the prophetic utterances of their ancestors, and inherited awe,
have rendered sacred. Here they celebrate the grim initiation
of their barbarous rites with a human sacrifice for the good
of the community . . . . . In an island of the ocean is a holy
grove, and in it a consecrated chariot, covered in robes. A single
priest is permitted to touch it:he interprets the presence of the
goddess in her shrine and follows with deep reverence as she
rides away drawn by cows: then come days of rejoicing and all
places keep holiday, as many as she thinks worthy to receive and
entertain her."

187. Seamus Deane, 'Seamus Heaney: The Timorous and the Bold', *Celtic
Revivals*, pp. 180–181.
188. Heaney is here adapting an analogy first used by John Hewitt in his
poem, 'The Colony', which compares the occupation of Ulster under
the English crown with colonisation under the Roman Empire.
189. Richard Murphy, 'Poetry and Terror', a review of *North*, *New York
Review of Books*, 30 September 1976, p. 39.
190. Louis MacNeice, *Autumn Journal*, XVI, London: Faber, 1939, p. 61.
191. Sean O Tuama and Thomas Kinsella, introduction to *An Duanaire
1600–1900: Poems of the Dispossessed*, Portlaoise: Dolmen, 1981,
p. xxvii.
192. Daniel Corkery, op. cit., p. 173. In the poem, 'Brightness most
bright', one of the first *aisling* poems ever written, 6 Rathaille
laments that Ireland should be forced to marry a ruffian, instead
of the handsome Scots prince – Bonnie Prince Charlie – whom she
deserves.
193. Blake Morrison provides the whole quotation from Aubrey used by
Heaney in the first part of 'Ocean's Love to Ireland'. The title, he
informs the reader, echoes that of Ralegh's poem to Queen Elizabeth,
'Ocean's Love to Cynthia'. See *Seamus Heaney*, London: Methuen,
1982, pp. 64–65.
194. Seamus Heaney, interview with John Haffenden, art. cit., p. 61.
195. See Arthur E. McGuinness, 'The Craft of Diction: Revision in Seamus
Heaney's Poems', art. cit., p. 88.

me unlearning so complacently
the rights of conquest,
preferring gradually
your geography to politics . . .
a field worker

in love with soil-creeps,
rain wash and gullying.

196. Ibid. Unwelcome 'advances' in the reign of Elizabeth are succeeded, following James's accession, by the determined embraces of the Planters, who "came determined upon occupation" (stage II, l. 19). The rather smugly confident narrator provides a nice line in understatement when he mentions how the resistance to English 'possession' over the seventeenth and eighteenth centuries took the form of 'skirmishes', until one memorable 'row' – the 1798 Rebellion – convinced England that a more permanent relationship might be desirable. Apart from the obvious political consequences of the 1800 Act of Union, there was a linguistic consequence, "Your mouth is fluent with my language now" (Stage II, l. 33). Disappointed that his kindly withdrawal from Ireland should have resulted in "civil strife inside the compound/ That was reserved in you for my love's sake" (lines 37–38), the naive English narrator ends with the 'reasonable' expectation that *provided* Dublin and Westminster become 'hand in glove', and *provided* Protestant anxieties can be put to rest, 'the triangle of forces' on the island may be reconciled in a union of lasting 'love'. In his article on these drafts, McGuinness claims that the above speaker is "a sympathetic figure, aware of Ireland's suffering" (p. 69).
197. Philip Hobsbaum, letter to MRP, 24 April 1986.
198. 'At a Potato Digging', *DN*, p. 33. Perhaps only the reunification of Ireland might heal the sore. If attempted without Protestant consent, it would obviously open up more.
199. Seamus Heaney, an article for the *P.B.S Bulletin*, 85, Summer 1975, reprinted in *Thirty Years of the Poetry Book Society 1956–1986*, ed. Jonathan Barker, Hutchinson 1988, p. 128.
200. Seamus Heaney, interviewed by Edward Broadbridge, in *Seamus Heaney*, Danmarks Radio, 1977, p. 14.
201. Seamus Heaney, 'Celtic Fringe, Viking Fringe', art. cit., p. 254.
202. Having said that, it is hard not to admire the persistence of his faith in the assuaging power of art, his belief that poetry could obliterate the mean lines of 'bigotry' and 'sham' that divide the communities, 'Given the right line, *aere perennius*', verses 'more lasting than bronze'. *Aere perennius* is a quotation from Horace's *Odes*, Book III, XXX. The Latin poet is referring to the immortality of his art. In successive lines, Heaney reconciles three of the tongues of his education, Ulster dialect ('drouth' means an unquenchable thirst), standard English, and classical Latin.
203. A reference to the Williamite settlement following the Battle of the Boyne which resulted in the dispossession of the Catholic supporters of James II. Heaney delights in making James his namesake.
204. Seamus Heaney, 'The Poet as a Christian', art. cit., p. 605.
205. Ibid., p. 603.
206. State priests, magistrates, and censors in Ancient Rome wore purple-edged togas. On Ash Wednesday, Catholic priests don purple

vestments. His reference to 'lampreys' may be connected with one Vedius Pollio, a freedman himself, and friend of Augustus, who fed unsatisfactory slaves to his lampreys. (I am grateful to Mrs Sandra Cameron of Holy Cross College, Bury, for illuminating the classical details in this poem).

207. *The Power and the Glory* follows the hunt and execution of a Catholic priest in Mexico during an anti-clerical purge. The priest's adversary is a lieutenant, whose every appearance necessitates a reference to his 'polished holster' and gun. In Chapter IV he runs into a boy called Luis.

> "He had his eye on the holster.
> 'Would you like to see my gun?' the lieutenant asked. He pulled his heavy automatic from the holster and held it out . . . . . ' This is the safety-catch. Lift it. So. Now it's ready to fire.
> 'Is it loaded?' Luis asked.
> 'It's always loaded.'
> The tip of the boy's tongue appeared: he swallowed. Saliva came from the glands as if he smelt food."
>
> (Graham Greene, *The Power and the Glory*,
> Harmondsworth: Penguin, 1972, pp. 57–58)

208. Kenneth Neill, op. cit., p. 22.
209. Seamus Heaney, Introduction to *Collected Short Stories of Michael McLaverty*, ed. cit., p. 7. Several of McLaverty's phrases in 'Foster-age' first appeared in an unpublished poem entitled 'An Evening in Killard' which is also dedicated to the novelist. 210.
210. Seamus Heaney, interviewed by Caroline Walsh, art. cit., p. 5.
211. Heaney alludes here to *Tristia*, a book of elegiac complaints by the Roman poet, Ovid, written following his banishment to the shores of the Black Sea in A.D. 8 – a work displaying the poet's "bewilder-ment, self-pity, and sense of guilt" (Horace Gregory, Preface to *Love Poems of Ovid*, New York: Mentor, 1964, p. xvi). Osip Mandelstam's second collection also bears the title, *Tristia*. In her memoir, *Hope against Hope*, Nadezhda Mandelstam recalls her husband reading a poem by Pushkin called *The Gypsies* containing a 'description of Ovid's northern exile' which 'affected him greatly' (220) since he too was on his way into exile. The selection from *Tristia* with which Heaney was familiar begins on a note of self-recrimination,

> "How these veils and these shining robes
> weigh me down in my shame"

and the title poem, like 'Exposure', is heavy with the grief of partings:

> "I have studied the science of goodbyes,

the bare-headed laments of night."
(Osip Mandelstam, *Selected Poems*, translated by Clarence
Brown and W. S. Merwin, Harmondsworth: Penguin,
1977, pp. 35 and 46).

212. Nadezhda Mandelstam, *Hope against Hope*, first published in the U.S.A. in 1971. Quotation from Harmondsworth: Penguin edition, 1975, p. 205.
213. Ciaran Carson, 'Escaped from the Massacre?', *The Honest Ulsterman*, No. 50, art. cit., p. 150.
214. Edna Longley, '*North*: "Inner Emigré" or "Artful Voyeur"?,' in *The Art of Seamus Heaney*, ed. Curtis, Bridgend: Poetry Wales Press, 1982, p. 85.
215. Conor Cruise O'Brien, 'A Slow North East Wind', *The Listener*, 25 September 1975, p. 404.
216. Seamus Heaney, interview in Monie Begley's *Rambles in Ireland*, Old Greenwich, Conn: Devin Adair, 1977, p. 169.

5: Quickenings, 1975–84: Notes to poems from *Field Work* and *Station Island*

1. William Wordsworth, *The Prelude*, Book X, lines 919–926, ed. cit., p. 202.
2. Seamus Heaney, interview with Bel Mooney, *Turning Points*, BBC Radio 4, 15 November 1988. Heaney's comments on Dove Cottage and its significance in Wordsworth's poetic development could equally apply to Glanmore and its 'assuaging influence' on him.

> Secluded, integrated with the ground, battened down for action, it suggests to me the incubating mind, the dedicated retreat of that decade when Wordsworth founded his Romantic vision. In the poetic acts which engendered that vision, coupled the childhood years of glad animal movement with those later years that bring the philosophic mind.
> (*William Wordsworth Lived Here*, BBC 1974)

3. Whereas in the interview with Caroline Walsh in December 1975, he describes his thrill at 'embracing teaching again', a decade later, in conversation with Neil Corcoran, he regretted having succumbed to the safety of 'a salaried position'.
4. Seamus Heaney, interview with John Haffenden, art. cit., p. 59.
5. Seamus Heaney, interview with Bel Mooney, *Turning Points*.
6. Seamus Heaney, interview with John Haffenden, art. cit., p. 69.
7. *GT*, p. xi. In this recent collection of essays, the poet recalls one evening in 1972 when he and David Hammond set off for the BBC studios in Belfast to record a tape of poems and songs for a friend in

Michigan. Their journey was accompanied by explosions and sirens. All too soon came the news of casualties. On arriving at the studios, Hammond took his guitar out of its case, but didn't have the heart to 'raise his voice at that cast-down moment.'

8.   Bobby Sands (1954–81) was the first of ten hunger strikers who died in the 1981 H-Blocks protest. He had fasted for sixty-six days in the cause of political status for I.R.A. prisoners.

9.   The subject of an excellent poem by Michael Longley, in *The Echo Gate*, London: Secker and Warburg, 1979, p. 13. It is reprinted in *Poems 1963–83*, Edinburgh: Salamander Press, 1985, p. 149.

10.   Quoted in *The Provisional I.R.A.*, Bishop and Mallie, London: Corgi, 1988, pp. 289–290.

11.   *GT*, p. xii.

12.   Ibid., p. xvii. His longing to be quickened into 'verb, pure verb' recalls the resolution and independence of the final tercet of 'Digging', from some fourteen years earlier.

13.   Like the one just man sought after in 'From the Canton of Expectation', *HL*, p. 47.

14.   *GT*, p. xxii. Tony Curtis is surely mistaken when he suggests that the 'mould' is intended to be 'ambiguous'. Though obviously mould has associations with death, the whole of the final picture stresses fertility. (See 'A More Social Voice: *Field Work*', in *The Art of Seamus Heaney*, p. 107).

15.   In Jungian terms, the wounds on the tree indicate the individual's failure to achieve the conscious realization of Self, his individuation.

16.   Initially in *Door into the Dark* it served as a symbol of fertility in 'Rite of Spring' and as an additional cause for exhaustion in 'Mother'. It is only with the assistance of the opening section of *Preoccupations* that one is able to identify the omphalos and to discover a particular occasion which gave rise to poem.

> I would begin with the Greek word, *omphalos*, meaning the navel, and hence the stone that marked the centre of the world, and repeat it, *omphalos, omphalos, omphalos*, until its blunt and falling music becomes the music of somebody pumping water at the pump outside our door. It is Co. Derry in the early 1940s. The American bombers groan towards the aerodrome at Toomebridge, the American troops manoeuvre in the fields along the road, but all of that great historical action does not disturb the rhythms of the yard. There the pump stands, a slender, iron idol, snouted, helmeted, . . . marking the centre of another world. (*P*, p. 17)

In the aftermath of Internment, Bloody Sunday, the Newry march, the collapse of power-sharing, it is hardly surprising that Heaney should be thinking about routes being blocked.

17.   One of the most famous leaders of the 1798 Rebellion, Roddy McCorley, was hanged at Toomebridge not far from Mossbawn.

18. It is not until *Station Island* that Heaney's dead contemporaries reply to his questioning.

19. Dante, *The Divine Comedy: Purgatory*, I, ll. 94–97, translated by Dorothy L. Sayers, Hardmondsworth: Penguin, 1955, p. 75.

20. *SA*, p. 69.

21. *P*, p. 19. Close to Lough Beg lies Grandfather Toner's bog.

22. The name of one of Heaney's uncles was Hugh Scullion. He is celebrated in 'Kinship'.

23. *SI*, p. 82.

24. Seamus Heaney, interview with James Randall, art. cit., p. 21.

25. O'Neill reminds one of the tight-lipped experts from *Death of a Naturalist* and *Door into the Dark*.

26. The other 'thin lines' consist of no man's land and the 'cold zinc' peace lines dividing Catholic and Protestant districts of Belfast, and the ultimate in separation, the source of the conflict, the border. In her notes to *Purgatory*, Canto I – the source for several images in 'The Strand at Lough Beg' – Dorothy L. Sayers refers back to the rope-girdle "thrown over the Great Barrier between Upper and Nether Hell" in *Hell*, Canto XVI (ed. cit., p. 78). It is possible that this may have prompted Heaney's decision to begin 'A Postcard from North Antrim' with Carrick-a-Rede. Throughout *Field Work*, he enjoys *ulsterizing* Dante.

27. *The Ballad of William Bloat* can be found in *The Ulster Reciter*, ed. Joe McPartland, Belfast: Blackstaff Press, 1984, pp. 4–5.

28. *SI*, p. 94.

29. Blake Morrison, *Seamus Heaney*, op. cit., pp. 79–80. Neil Corcoran, *Seamus Heaney*, op. cit., p. 138.

30. Blake Morrison informs us that, "'Swad' used to mean 'mass' or 'clump', and 'swaddish' means 'loutish'", and implies that the mourners consist largely of the *Lumpen-proletariat*.

31. Nahum Tate, 'While Shepherds Watched Their Flocks By Night', verse 4,

> "The heavenly babe you there shall find
> To human view displayed,
> All meanly wrapped in swaddling bands
> And in a manger laid."

The phrase appears in Luke, Chapter 2, verse 12.

32. 'Viking Dublin', *N*, p. 24.

33. Balachandra Rajan, *W. B. Yeats*, London: Hutchinson, 1965, p. 112.

34. W. B. Yeats, 'Ego Dominus Tuus', *Collected Poems*, ed. cit., p. 182.

35. Yeats's mysterious angler, according to T. R. Henn, may have been partly based upon John Millington Synge, the playwright, since he was a 'keen fisherman, and a great rambler in the Wicklow glens' – the new Heaney country. See T. R. Henn, *The Lonely Tower: Studies in the Poetry of W. B. Yeats*, London: Methuen, 1965, p. 74.

36. 'The Guttural Muse', *F*, p. 28.

37. Gospel According to St Mark, R.S.V. version, Chapter 9, verse 50.

38. Both places are the subjects of well-known folk-songs.
39. *GT*, p. xx.
40. W. B. Yeats, 'The Second Coming', *Collected Poems*, ed. cit., p. 211.
41. *N*, 'North', p. 19.
42. *DN*, 'Follower', p. 24.
43. Two of O'Riada's most popular compositions are *Saoirse?* (Freedom?) and *Mise Eire* (I am Ireland).
44. Seamus Heaney, interviewed by Bel Mooney for *Turning Points*, BBC 1988.
45. In 1974 Heaney made a documentary for the BBC entitled *William Wordsworth Lived Here.*
46. Seamus Heaney, interviewed by Bel Mooney for *Turning Points*, BBC 1988.
47. Ibid. Freed from the self-imposed role of being 'bridegroom to the Goddess' – the awesome, ruthless, mythic Nerthus – Heaney learnt more of what it meant to be a husband to a real woman.
48. 'Gifts of Rain', *WO*, p. 24.
49. T. S. Eliot, *Little Gidding, The Complete Poems and Plays of T. S. Eliot*, ed. cit., p. 191. Eliot's poem, the last of the *Four Quartets*, was also written in the middle of a war, and depicts a place of spiritual retreat and renewal, where 'the soul's sap quivers'. Here we find also images of 'sempiternal' spring-time, including the 'transitory blossom/ Of snow', anticipating the haws of summer. The last unifying image of the poem is of a rose, a symbol of beauty, mercy and love.
50. Boris Pasternak, 'Hamlet', *translated by Richard McKane, in Post-War Russian Poetry*, edited by Daniel Weissbort, Harmondsworth: Penguin 1974, p. 33.
51. One of the finest dramatizations of this concept is 'The Thought-Fox' by Ted Hughes.
52. Seamus Heaney, interview with Frank Kinahan, art. cit., p. 412.
53. Deborah McLoughlin has suggested in her excellent article, "'An Ear to the Line':Modes of Receptivity in Seamus Heaney's 'Glanmore Sonnets'", *Papers in Language and Literature*, Spring/Summer 1989, pp. 201–215, that "the 'iron tune' may carry metaphoric connotations of sectarian fanaticism." Although in 'A Constable Calls' we are conscious of the contemporary resonances of his childhood experience of *fear*, the allusion to the railway in Sonnet IV and in *Preoccupations*, p. 20, serves simply to highlight the variety of the young Heaney's *aural/ sensual* experiences and his consciousness of small-town urban realities.
54. As Brian Friel does in Translations. See Seamus Deane's Introduction to *Selected Plays of Brian Friel*, op. cit, p. 22.
55. *P*, p. 18.
56. While Heaney was engaged on the poems which formed *Field Work*, his friend, Brian Friel, was examining the theme of linguistic dispossession in *Translations*. The play became the first ever production from Field Day.
57. Brian Friel, *Translations*, in *Selected Plays of Brian Friel*, p. 445.

58. *SI*, p. 80.
59. *P*, p. 45.
60. For Deborah McLoughlin, art. cit., p. 210, these gales possess a political significance.
61. 'Personal Helicon', *DN*, p. 57. Rats feature in 'The Barn' (p. 17) and 'An Advancement of Learning' (p. 18), while the 'infected fruit' reminds one of 'Blackberry Picking' (p. 20).
62. One of the Border Ballads. The two crows in the poem are about to feast on a 'new slain knight', hence Heaney's thoughts about 'armour and carrion'. In folklore, it is said of magpies 'One brings sorrow, two bring joy'.
63. Having cast himself as Hamlet in *North*, in *Field Work* Heaney becomes Macbeth for a moment. The phrase 'blood-bolter'd', meaning 'matted with blood', comes from *Macbeth*, Act IV, scene i, line 138, and refers to Banquo's ghost who ruins the King's coronation banquet. Ghosts from Heaney's Ulster past continue to trouble him in *Station Island*, of course.
64. Seamus Deane, in 'Seamus Heaney: The Timorous and the Bold', *Celtic Revivals*, op. cit., p. 175. According to Deane, each of the Glanmore Sonnets 'records a liberation of feeling after stress or, more exactly, of feeling which has absorbed stress and is the more feeling.'
65. Sir Thomas Wyatt, 'They flee from me', *The London Book of English Verse*, pp. 166–167.
66. John Fowles, *The French Lieutenant's Woman*, Jonathan Cape, 1969.
67. In both 'The Otter' and 'The Skunk' he describes her as 'beyond me'.
68. Dante, *The Divine Comedy: Hell*, trans. Dorothy L. Sayers, ed. cit., p. 271.

> *"The Ninth Circle is the frozen Lake of Cocytus. In the outermost region, Caina, are the betrayers of their own kindred, plunged to the neck in ice."*

Cantos XXXII and XXXIII contain the story of Archbishop Roger and Count Ugolino. The Archbishop imprisoned Ugolino, his former ally – along with two of his sons, Gaddo and Hugh, and two of his grandsons, Brigata and Anselm – in a tower subsequently known as 'the Tower Of Famine'. There all five starved to death. See also note 85.

69. The last line of 'An Afterwards' suggests that he has outgrown that phase. The experience of Glanmore, and his discovery of exemplary lives and lines – such as those of Dante and Mandelstam – provided him with a renewed faith in Art and a 'door into the light'.
70. Shakespeare, *The Winter's Tale*, Act IV, scene iv, ll. 87–88.
71. The others include 'Digging', 'Follower', 'Ancestral Photographs' (*Death of a Naturalist*), 'A Constable Calls' (*North*), 'The Stone Verdict' and 'Clearances VII' (*The Haw Lantern*).

72. From E. Estyn Evans's Irish Folk Ways, pp. 208–209, one discovers that

   > Harvest knots, twisted out of the ripe straw of the harvest, seem formerly to have been in truth love tokens, though now worn merely as buttonholes for the harvest fair.

73. The old bed referred to belonged to Henry MacWilliams, a 'childless widower', and neighbour of the Heaneys. His bedhead served as 'a gate for our back garden', according to 'Obituary', an unpublished poem from Groupsheet 1.

74. Francis Ledwidge, 'June', *The Faber Book of Irish Verse*, ed. John Montague, Faber and Faber, 1978, p. 257. Perhaps coincidentally this poem includes within its second stanza two images found in 'The Harvest Bow'. Both 'loop' and 'snares' are used as verbs, however.

75. See 'Broagh', *WO*, p. 27.

76. Ulick O'Connor, *Oliver St John Gogarty*, Granada 1981, p. 143. Ledwidge was born in the village of Slane, Co. Meath, in the Boyne valley, some nine miles from Drogheda. He worked from the age of twelve as a labourer on an estate, where his talent for poetry came to the attention of the landowner, Lord Dunsany, whose protégé he became. It was Dunsany who subsequently selected the fifty poems for Ledwidge's first publication, *Songs of the Fields* (1915).

77. Francis Ledwidge quoted in A. Norman Jeffares, *Anglo-Irish Literature*, Macmillan, 1982, p. 184.

78. Ibid. MacDonagh, a poet, was one of the leaders of the Rising, executed by the British.

79. Seamus Heaney, interview with Seamus Deane, 'Unhappy and at home', art. cit., p. 62.

80. In order to concentrate on Ledwidge the soldier, rather than Ledwidge the lover, Heaney does not mention the great love of Ledwidge's life, Ellie Vaughey, broke off their relationship during the summer of 1913 on the grounds that 'her family owned land', while 'he was merely a road-ganger' (Jeffares, op. cit., p. 183). Two years later after her marriage to someone else, she died suddenly. Ledwidge mourned her loss in many poems, perhaps including this one.

> TO ONE DEAD
> A blackbird singing
> On a moss-upholstered stone,
> Bluebells swinging,
> Shadows wildly blown,
> A song in the wood,
> A ship on the sea.
> The song was for you
> And the ship was for me.
>
> A blackbird singing

I hear in my troubled mind,
Bluebells swinging
I see a distant wind.
But sorrow and silence
Are the wood's threnody.
The silence for you,
And the sorrow for me.

81.   *P*, p. 183. The month of May has intense Marian associations. 'On May Eve', in Ireland, 'buttercups and ladysmock appeared on the windowsills in obedience to some primeval midsummer rite', and 'May flowers had to be gathered for her [the Virgin Mary's] altar on the chest of drawers in the bedroom'. (Seamus Heaney, *The Poet as a Christian*, art. cit., p. 605). During the Easter Vigil, water is blessed and sprinkled over the congregation as a purification rite, and presumably in rural areas the custom is extended to farm buildings to ensure a 'good year'. 'Mass-rocks' were places where open-air services were held in the time of the Penal Laws, while 'hill-top raths' were forts or circular enclosures from the pre-Christian era, the most famous being the one at Tara in Ledwidge's native County Meath. The word 'dolorous' is associated with the Virgin Mary, since she is referred to sometimes referred as *Mater Dolorosa*. The month, 'May', is named after from Maia, a Greek nymph, who in Roman times was elevated from the status of 'a minor fertility deity' and

> "identified with the *Bona Dea*, an earth goddess of plenty . . . Romans pelted each other with flowers during the licentious *Ludi Floreales* from April 23 to May 3 in honour of Flora, a Roman goddess of harvest and of fruitfulness whose cult was particularly associated with the heady flower of the hawthorn tree – mayblossom." (Marina Warner, *Alone of All her Sex: The Myth and Cult of the Virgin Mary*, London: Weidenfeld and Nicolson, 1976. Reissued by Picador Books, 1985, p. 282)

82.   It reminds me of the white 'wreath and spray' given to the troops in Wilfred Owen's 'The Send-Off'.

83.   Francis Ledwidge, 'A Twilight in Middle March'. This poem was perhaps a source for several of the images of 'In Memoriam'. Ledwidge's title links in with Heaney's phrase 'the twilit note'. Twice he employs the image of a flute. The 'summer wood' becomes an Aeolian harp, played upon by the wind, while in the Heaney poem the wind 'tunes through the bronze'. The blackbird's song is sweeter than any music heard under 'the *blue* domes of London'.

84.   According to *The Oxford Companion to English Literature*, ed. Margaret Drabble, Oxford University Press, 1985, Ugolino "twice made himself master of Pisa by treachery" before being betrayed by the Ghibelline leader, Ruggieri degli Ubaldini.

Notes to poems from *Station Island*

85. Shyama Perera, 'Displaced Poet puts a Border in Order',*The Guardian*, 1983.
86. Seamus Heaney, *An Open Letter*, reprinted in *Ireland's Field Day*, Hutchinson, 1985.
87. Barry White, *John Hume: Statesman of the Troubles*, op. cit., p. 208.
88. Special status had been introduced in 1972 by William Whitelaw following a hunger strike in Belfast prison, and allowed prisoners from paramilitary groups to wear their own clothes, to receive extra visits and food parcels, and freed them from the obligation to work.
89. Bishop and Mallie, *The Provisional I.R.A.*, op. cit., p. 350.
90. Ibid. pp. 350–351. Eighteen were murdered between 1976 and 1980.
91. Ibid., p. 351.
92. Ibid., p. 351–352.
93. "One would hardly allow an animal to remain in such conditions, let alone a human being. The nearest approach to it that I have seen was the spectacle of homeless people living in the sewer pipes in the slums of Calcutta" (ibid., pp. 352–353).
94. For an excellent account of the sacrifice and the 'endurance' strategy in Republican mythology and history, see Richard Kearney, *Transitions*, Chapters 10 and 11, 'Myth and Martyrdom', pp. 209–236.
95. Barry White, op. cit., p. 220. According to White, the prison management demanded that protesters should first replace their blankets with prison clothes, while Bishop and Mallie refer to an occasion when families arrived at the prison gates with the prisoners' own clothes but 'the authorities would not pass them on' (op. cit., p. 362).
96. Quoted in Barry White, op. cit., p. 221.
97. Terence Brown, *Ireland: A Social and Cultural History 1922–1985*, p. 337.

> "Black flags were displayed in most towns and villages . . . These expressions of solidarity with the republican hunger strikers culminated in a mass demonstration to the British Embassy in Dublin on July 18 at which large scale rioting broke out."

98. In the Irish General Election which took place in June, two other strikers, Kieron Doherty and Paddy Agnew, won seats in the Dáil as representatives of Provisional Sinn Féin, the political counterpart of the P.I.R.A. When a second by-election was held in the Fermanagh and South Tyrone constituency in August, Sands's former election agent, PSF member, Owen Carron, retained the seat with an increased majority. Ironically, back in January, the Provisional Sinn Féin leadership had cautioned against a strike.
99. Vincent Buckley in *Memory Ireland* recalls visiting the Heaneys during the hunger strikes, and describes how Heaney "opened the

paper and said to his wife, 'Francis Hughes is weakening.' His tone was tense and wondering" (p. 118).

100. The words are from a report by the European Commission on Human Rights from the previous summer which exonerated the British Government from blame over their handling of the dirty protest and the first hunger strike, but criticised the "inflexible approach of the state authorities which has been more concerned to punish offenders against prison discipline than to explore ways of resolving such as serious deadlock" (Quoted in White, op. cit., p. 218 and Boyle and Hadden, op. cit., p. 68). Certainly British policy inadvertently boosted Provisional Sinn Fein as a political force, which delayed the chances of any political breakthrough for a considerable time. In the General Election of 1979 they won 8 per cent of the first preference votes. In the 1983 Election this rose to 13 per cent.

101. Kevin Boyle and Tom Hadden, *Ireland: A Positive Proposal*, op. cit., p. 69. In the two years following the ending of the strikes, the increasing use of 'supergrasses' – informers – and the alleged 'shoot to kill' policy of the security forces caused further outrage within the Nationalist community.

102. A quotation from Stephen Gill's *William Wordsworth: A Life*, Oxford University Press, 1990, p. 68, which refers to the effect on Wordsworth of political crisis in France and political repression at home.

103. Seamus Heaney, 'Envies and Identifications: Dante and the Modern Poet', *Irish University Review*, 15:1, Spring 1985.

104. 'Chekhov on Sakhalin', *SI*, p. 18.

105. 'A Kite for Michael and Christopher', *SI*, p. 44.

106. 'Old Smoothing Iron' from 'Shelf Life', *SI*, p. 22. Images of weight and lightening have become increasingly prevalent in Heaney's work from 'Westering' (*Wintering Out*) onwards.

107. In an earlier version of SI, XII, entitled 'Leaving the Island' – it appeared in *James Joyce and Modern Literature*, ed. W. J. McCormack, Routledge, Kegan and Paul, 1982, pp. 74–75 – Joyce contrasts his open break with the Church with Heaney's timorous attitude.

> When I refused to take the sacrament
> I made my life an instrument of grace
> . . . I was at nobody's service
> The way you are at theirs.

108. Introduction to *SA*, p. ii. See also Heaney's essays, 'The God in the Tree' (1978), in *P*, pp. 181–189, and 'The Government of the Tongue' (1986), in *GT*, pp. 91–108.

109. Seamus Heaney, interview with Randy Brandes, art. cit., p. 8.

110. In the title essay from *The Government of the Tongue*, he compares the Vatican's repressive influence with that operating in Plato's 'ideal republic', in the Bible-belt of the United States and the Soviet republics of the pre-Gorbachev era. In such states

"it is a common expectation that the writer will sign over his or her individual, venturesome and potentially disruptive activity into the keeping of an official doctrine, a traditional system, a party line." (*GT*, p. 96)

It is possible that some of his negative feelings towards the Church may have been partly influenced by the conservative pronouncements and policies of Pope John Paul II, or indeed by working in a Catholic educational institution.

111. Sydney Bolt, *A Preface to James Joyce*, Longman: London, 1981, p. 95.

112. *SI*, 'On the Road', p. 121.

113. Seamus Heaney 'A Tale of Two Islands', *Irish Studies*, I, Cambridge University Press, 1980, p. 9.

114. Tom O'Dea, 'Pleasant Purgatory', *Irish Independent*, 25 May 1990, p. 6. My main sources of information about Station Island have been *Lough Derg Guide*, by Joseph Duffy, revised edition 1978, and Deirdre Purcell's *On Lough Derg*, Veritas: Dublin, 1988, which includes an introduction by Joseph Duffy.

115. Thousands journeyed to Lough Derg during the Penal years, despite the fines that this incurred. Not surprisingly numbers declined after the Great Famine. In 1870, three years after the failure of the Fenian rising, and one year after the disestablishment of the Church of Ireland, a new St Mary's chapel was built, and for the next thirty years an average of 3,000 pilgrims would visit the island each summer. What Joseph Duffy terms as 'the modern resurgence' of Lough Derg began in 1909, at a time when the Nationalist drive towards Home Rule accelerated dramatically, and by 1921, when the modern Troubles were approaching their second climax, the outbreak of the Civil War, the number had reached 8,000 pilgrims a year. Another peak was reached in 1942, when 14,000 visitors came, including Patrick Kavanagh.

116. See R. F. Foster, *Modern Ireland 1600–1972*, Hardmonsworth: Penguin, 1990, p. 571.

117. *A Sense of Wonder*, produced and directed by Barnaby Thompson and George Case, Mark Forstater Productions, 1986.

118. The six 'beds' are the remains of beehive cells, remnants of an ancient monastery. Joseph Duffy, op. cit., p. 8.

119. *SA*, p. 40.

120. *On Lough Derg*, op. cit., p. 12.

121. Each of them gave their lives in the service of a sacred, mythic Ireland. Schoolmaster and poet, Padraic Pearse led the 1916 Rising and was executed by the British on May 3, 1916. In many of his poems he identifies his sacrifice with that of Christ. In 'The Fool' he speaks of 'taking Christ at His word', while in 'Renunciation', he smothers personal desire, and resolutely turns his face 'To this road before me/ . . . And the death I shall die.' (See *The 1916 Poets*, edited by Desmond Ryan, Allen Figgis: Dublin, 1963, pp. 18 and 27). Terence McSwiney was the Mayor of Cork at the time of

the Partition. He was arrested on 12 August 1920, and imprisoned in Brixton Prison. On 25 October 1920, after a fast that lasted seventy-four days, he died; he was the first Republican activist to die as a result of a hunger strike.

In justifying his fast to the priest, Father Denis Faul, Bobby Sands cited Christ's words, "Greater love hath no man than this, that he lay down his life for his friends" (see Bishop and Mallie, op. cit., p. 364).

122. Seamus Heaney, 'Envies and Identifications: Dante and the Modern Poet', *Irish University Review*, Vol. 15, Part 1, 1985, p. 19.

123. William Carleton, *Lough Derg Pilgrim*, quoted by Heaney in 'A Tale of Two Islands', art. cit., p. 11. Patrick Kavanagh, in the seventh lecture of a series entitled *Studies in the Technique of Poetry*, delivered in 1956 at University College, Dublin, said, "For all Carleton's stupid tirades he is like Stephen Daedalus saturated with that Catholicism in which he says he disbelieves" (see Peter Kavanagh, *Sacred Keeper*, Goldsmith Press, 1979).

124. Patrick Kavanagh, *Lough Derg*, in *November Haggard: The Uncollected Prose and Verse of Patrick Kavanagh*, edited by Peter Kavanagh, The Peter Kavanagh Hand Press, New York, 1971, pp. 119, 120.

125. 'Station Island', section VI, *SI*, pp. 75–76.

126. Seamus Heaney, interview with Frank Kinahan, art. cit., p. 411.

127. Seamus Heaney, 'Envies and Identifications: Dante and the Modern Poet', art. cit., p. 18. Heaney's emphasis in this article on Dante the *lyric* poet illustrates his own contention that "when poets turn to the great masters of the past, they turn to an image of their own creation, one which is likely to be a reflection of their own imaginative needs, their own artistic inclinations and procedures" (p. 5). Heaney's Dante is much influenced by Mandelstam, who sees the Italian poet "not as a mouthpiece of orthodoxy, but rather as the apotheosis of free, natural, biological process, as a hive of bees, a process of crystallization, a hurry of pigeon flights, a focus for all the impulsive, instinctive, non-utilitarian elements in the creative life" (p. 18). Such a Dante is clearly kin to Sweeney/Heaney.

128. A phrase from the third line of the first Canto of *The Divine Comedy*, ed. cit., p. 71.

129. Seamus Heaney, 'Envies and Identifications: Dante and the Modern Poet', art. cit., p. 18.

130. The pursuit ended with his 'loss' of Syrinx, but resulted in the creation of music.

> "When Pan thought he had at last caught hold of Syrinx, he found that instead of the nymph's body he held a handful of marsh reeds. As he stood sighing, the wind blew through the reeds and produced a thin plaintive sound. The god was enchanted by the new device and by the sweetness of the music.' You and I shall always talk together so!", he cried; then he took reeds of unequal length, and fastened them together with wax." (Ovid, *Metamorphoses*, trans. Mary Innes, Penguin 1955, pp. 47–48)

131. Sweeney is clearly seen by Heaney as a kind of Orpheus figure, attempting to assuage himself 'by his utterance' (*SA*, Introduction, p. ii). His anguish separated from his wife, Eorann, is beautifully rendered in *SA*, pp. 26–28.

132. Heaney uses this word in reference to himself in a relatively recent interview with Clive Wilmer, BBC Radio 3, 2 September 1990. My reservations about this poem are shared by Douglas Dunn in his essay 'Heaney Agonistes', originally published in *London Magazine*, 24, No. 8, November 1984, reprinted in *Modern Critical Views: Seamus Heaney*, ed. Bloom, op. cit, pp. 153–154.

133. Seamus Deane, *Celtic Revivals*, op. cit., p. 181.

134. *GT*, p. xvii. For Heaney the drinking of the cognac and smashing of the glass constituted:

> an emblematic moment: the writer taking his pleasure in the amber cognac, savouring a fume of intoxication and a waft of luxury in the stink of oppression and the music of cruelty . . . Let the cognac represent not just the gift of his friends but the gift of his art, and here we have an image of the poet appeased; justified and unabashed by the suffering which surrounds him because unflinchingly responsible to it.

135. Amongst the condemned on Sakhalin were 'the sweepings of Russian society' including 'political prisoners and agitators' (*GT*, p. xvii). Heaney had already referred to Long Kesh, without naming it, in the dedicatory poem to *Wintering Out*. This poem was later incorporated in 'Whatever You Say, Say Nothing' (*North*, p. 60).

136. Seamus Heaney talking on *Kaleidoscope*, BBC Radio 4, 11 October 1984.

137. Zbigniew Herbert, 'A Pebble', translated by Czeslaw Milosz and Peter Dale Scott, in *East European Poets*, Edwin Morgan, Milton Keynes: Open University Press, 1976, p. 23.

138. Ibid. The word 'lifted' illustrates Heaney's double voice, his ability to be 'adept and be dialect' ('Making Strange', *SI*, p. 32.) In Standard English, 'lifted' means 'picked up' in a physical sense; colloquially it can mean 'stolen'; in Ulster dialect, however, it means 'to be arrested'.

139. 'Lord I am not worthy'. It is recited three times in the Latin Mass immediately before Communion.

140. 'Freedman', *N*, p. 61.

141. Zbigniew Herbert, 'The Pebble', see above, notes 136–7.

142. It is interesting to compare Heaney's objects with the glamorous ones with which Yeats surrounded his desk. See 'Meditations in Time of Civil War', III, 'My Table', *Collected Poems*, ed. cit., pp. 227–228.

143. Edna Longley, 'Old Pewter', a review of *Station Island*, *The Honest Ulsterman*, Winter 1984, No. 77, p. 54. Philip Hobsbaum rates the poem as amongst Heaney's very finest.

144. Interestingly, when Oliver St John Gogarty took up the tenancy of

the Martello Tower, he envisaged it becoming "the Irish equivalent of the earth's navel-stone at Delphi", and pictured himself "as the Oracle" (see Frank Delaney, *James Joyce's Odyssey: A Guide to the Dublin of Ulysses*, Hodder and Stoughton, 1981, p. 17). Perhaps for Heaney, as for many Irish writers, because of its associations with Joyce, the Tower has become a kind of shrine, a new *omphalos* from which to take his bearings.

145. Seamus Heaney at a reading at Glasgow University, 25 November 1989.

146. William Wordsworth, *Michael, Poetical Works*, ed. cit., 1.414, p. 109. The final two couplets of Heaney's poem are reminiscent of the shepherd Michael's exhortations to Luke, his only son, about to set forth for 'the dissolute', rather than the 'empty city'.

147. W. B. Yeats, 'Meditations in Time of Civil War', IV, 'My Descendants', *Collected Poems*, ed. cit., pp. 228–229.

148. William Wordsworth, *Michael*, l. 448. On my visit to the Heaney family home in Bellaghy in the summer of 1985, Mr Patrick Heaney kindly showed me the pump and its latest occupant, 'the very same' as his son 'had written them' ('The Birthplace', *SI*, p. 35).

149. William Wordsworth, *The Prelude*, quoted in *P*, p. 41.

150. See T. W. Rolleston, *Myths and Legends of the Celtic Race*, op. cit., p. 256. 'An ancient sage and Druid named Finegas, who dwelt on the river Boyne' tells Finn of 'Fintan the Salmon of Knowledge' whom he must capture and eat.'

151. Before its inclusion in *Station Island*, 'A Kite for Michael and Christopher' was privately circulated along with a poem, entitled 'A Toy for Catherine'.

> "Aren't poems your toys, Daddy?
> Catherine said,
> "And didn't you and mammy make me
> And God made the thread?"

152. *The Gospel according to St Matthew*, Chapter 19, verse 24. "Again I tell you, it is easier for a camel to go through the eye of a needle than for a rich man to enter the kingdom of God."

153. Another allusion to the bedhead belonging to Henry MacWilliams, first mentioned in 'Obituary', Groupsheet 1. See Chapter 3, the analysis of 'Mother', and note 79.

154. 'King of the Ditchbacks', *SI*, p. 57.

155. At the beginning of the Latin Mass, the priest used to announce *'Introibo ad altare Dei'*, 'I will go up to the altar of God'. The word 'beseech' is frequently used in Catholic prayer. On Human Rights Day, 1985, Heaney published a poem in support of Amnesty International, 'From the Republic of Conscience', *HL*, p. 12. Although there is no evidence to suggest this last quatrain is linked with the fate of the hunger strikers, in *Biting at the Grave: The Irish Hunger Strikes and the Politics of Despair*, Blackstaff, 1990, Padraig O Malley writes that all of the strikers had previously been

arrested, held, interned, detained, interrogated, or physically maltreated by the security forces. Two, Hughes and Lynch, were beaten – Hughes severely so – by British soldiers. (p. 103)

156. Anthony Storr, *Jung*, op. cit., p. 13.
157. *SA*, p. ii. At the start of *Sweeney Astray*, the King is infuriated by 'the clink of Ronan's bell', a sign, he is informed, that the cleric 'is marking out a church in your territory' (p. 3).
158. In both Old and New Testaments encounters with God generally occur in high places, such as mountains. See, for example, *Exodus*, 19, v.20, or Christ's transfiguration in *Matthew*, 17, v.1.
159. 'Station Island', II, stanza 10. One might argue that the results of today's atrocities are equally as horrific as Carleton's description of "hanged bodies rotting on the gibbets/ . . . . their looped slime gleaming from the sacks".
160. James Joyce, *Ulysses*, Chapter III, ed. cit., p. 31.
161. The imagery of wounds generally has political associations in Heaney's work. See, for example, the 'running sore' of 'At a potato digging' (*DN*, p. 32), the 'raw . . . opened ground' of 'Act of Union' (*N*, p. 50), or, more recently, *The Cure at Troy*, in which it is a key symbol and image for the Ulster condition.
162. *SI*, p. 101.
163. Perhaps each time he heard *Agnus Dei* ('Lamb of God, who takest away the sins of the world, spare us O Lord'), he would picture 'Agnes Dei', 'Agnes of God'.
164. Walking the strand, Stephen Daedalus is similarly disturbed in hislyric phrase-making when he encounters 'the bloated carcass of a dog'. It leads him also to meditate on the 'one great goal' man and dog achieve. See James Joyce, *Ulysses*, ed. cit., Chapter III, pp. 37–39.
165. In *SI*, XII, Joyce identifies this as a tendency of Heaney's.
166. Seamus Heaney talking on *Kaleidoscope*, BBC Radio 4, 11 October 1984.
167. Seamus Heaney, 'Pilgrim's Journey', *Poetry Book Society Bulletin*, 123, Winter 1984, p. 3. Like Heaney, Kavanagh is appalled by the spiritually destructive elements in Catholic teaching, the way "The sharp knife of Jansen/ Cut all the green branches/ No sunlight comes in/ But the hot-iron sin" (*November Haggard*, op. cit., p. 133).
168. Immediately after this moment which Heaney has translated from the *Inferno*, Dante re-commences his journey on the 'savage path' to hell. Like Dante, the poet cannot take 'the short road' to Purgatory and lasting release; 'he is obliged to go by the long road – i.e. through Hell' (see Dante's *Hell*, translated by Dorothy L. Sayers, *note to line 120*, p. 83).
169. Joseph Duffy, *Lough Derg Guide*, op. cit., p. 24. This phase of the sequence might be equated with the vigil on Station Island, which itself has been described in narrative terms as 'a parable of all human life on this earth', during which the pilgrims reflect upon

'the mysteries of Passion, death and resurrection'. (See Joseph Duffy, *On Lough Derg*, op. cit., p. 13).

170. Wilfred Owen, 'Disabled' in *First World War Poetry*, ed. Jon Silkin, Penguin, 1979, p. 184. "One time he liked a bloodsmear down his leg/ After the matches, carried shoulder high."
171. *SI*, 'Station Island' IV and XII, p. 70 and p. 93.
172. Edna Longley, 'Old Pewter', art. cit., p. 56.
173. Patrick Kavanagh, *Lough Derg*, in November Haggard, op. cit., p. 119.
174. The poet's sorrow generates numerous images of blackness. His harbinger is a solitary magpie ('One for sorrow, two for joy'). His pain is likened to a shower 'blackening/ already blackened stubble', and immediately after Delaney's final words, Heaney's mind runs to the black basalt axe heads in the Ulster Museum, the Malone hoard.
175. I am reminded of Elizabeth-Jane's reflections in the final paragraph of Thomas Hardy's *The Mayor of Casterbridge*. "Her strong sense that neither she nor any human being deserved less than was given, did not blind her to the fact that there were others receiving less who had deserved more" (Macmillan, 1972, p. 334).
176. See *A Personal Selection: Seamus Heaney*, 1982, a booklet from the Ulster Museum, written by Heaney, with a foreword by Ted Hickey.
177. *The Shell Guide to Ireland*, by Lord Killanin and Michael Duignan, revised and updated by Peter Harbison, Macmillan, 1989, p. 291.
178. See Ciaran Carson, 'Escaped from the Massacre', art. cit., p. 185, or James Liddy, 'Ulster Poets and the Catholic Muse', *Eire-Ireland* (1978), Vol. 13, part 4, p. 135.
179. Barry Goldensohn, 'The Recantation of Beauty', *Salmagundi*, No. 80, Fall, 1980, pp. 76–83.
180. The phrase, 'competing discourses', is used in a different context by Seamus Deane in his essay 'Civilians and Barbarians', in *Ireland's Field Day*, Hutchinson, 1985, p. 39. If Heaney really felt 'The Strand at Lough Beg' was deeply *morally* flawed, it is unlikely that he would have included it in his *New and Selected Poems*, published in 1990, or allowed it to be used in the BBC2 School's Programme, *New Approaches to Poetry*, which was broadcast in January 1991. Could he be simply saying what he says Zbigniew Herbert is saying in 'The Knocker', "Enjoy poetry as long as you don't use it to escape reality" (*GT*, p. xix).
181. I am grateful to Elmer Andrews's book, *The Poetry of Seamus Heaney: All the Realms of Whisper*, Macmillan, 1990, p. 169, for this piece of information.
182. See Padraig O'Malley's *Biting at the Grave*, op. cit., p. 116.

"Faced with the unacceptable realities of the present and the comforting allure of myth, they chose myth, to imagine themselves 'as sacrificial heroes taken from the old mythologies'".

At the funeral of Bobby Sands, Owen Carron praised Sands's mother "who had watched her son being daily crucified for sixty-six long days. Mrs Sands epitomizes the Irish mothers who in every generation watch their children go out to fight and die for freedom." (ibid., p. 119)

Martin McGuinness in his funeral oration for Francis Hughes similarly translated Mrs Hughes into Mother Ireland.

183. See the final line of 'The Tollund Man', Part One, *WO*, p. 47.
184. *Hans Andersen: His Classic Fairy Tales*, translated by Erik Haugaard, Gollancz, 1976. Opening with an image of brotherly solidarity, five and twenty soldiers made from the one old tin spoon, the story goes on to focus on the adventures of one unconventional figure. He is eventually thrown out of the house, placed in a paperboat, and carried by a 'raging torrent' along a gutter. On his way he is harried by a big water rat, who shouts, "He hasn't got a passport and won't pay duty!". After being swallowed by a fish, 'a ray of light' appears before him and he enjoys a brief kind of resurrection. Finally a child's whim consigns him to a fire where he melts. All that is left of him is his little tin heart; all that is left of the ballerina he loved was a spangle from her dress, which was 'burned as black as coal'.
185. 'Chekhov on Sakhalin', *SI*, p. 19.
186. T. S. Eliot, *Tradition and the Individual Talent*, in *Twentieth Century Poetry*, ed. Martin and Furbank, op. cit., p. 80.
187. John Keats, 'Ode to a Grecian Urn'.
188. See Patrick Buckland, *A History of Northern Ireland*, Gill and Macmillan, 2nd edition, 1989, pp. 66–67, p. 70, p. 96.
189. Seamus Heaney, *Among Schoolchildren, A John Malone Memorial Lecture*, 1983, pp. 14–15. The kaleidoscope was a Christmas present, whose glamour was eclipsed when Heaney saw his Protestant friend's present, a glorious red-white-and-blue battleship. Jealous, he tried floating his toy in the water-butt, but it soon sank. "Its insides had been robbed of their brilliant inner space, its marvellous and unpredictable visions were gone."
190. *St John of the Cross: Poems*, Penguin, 1968, introduction by M. C. D'Arcy, S.J., p. 22.
191. Seamus Heaney, *Among Schoolchildren*, op. cit., p. 11.
192. James Joyce, *A Portrait of the Artist as a Young Man*, ed. cit., p. 227.

"I looked it up and find in English and good old blunt English too. Damn the dean of studies and his funnel! What did he come here for to teach us his own language or to learn it from us?"

The references to April 13, Stephen's diary and the Feast of the Holy Tundish, have been removed from the revised version of this poem in *New Selected Poems 1968–87*, February, 1990, p. 193.

193. The language issue had been resurrected in Republican circles in the late seventies. Prisoners in Long Kesh, including the hunger strikers,

taught themselves Gaelic, regarding it as an essential means for expressing their Irish identity and opposition to the occupying powers.

194. See above, note 108.

195. Osip Mandelstam, *Selected Poems*, translated by Clarence Brown and W. S. Merwin, Penguin, 1977, p. 105.

196. Seamus Heaney, 'Leaving the Island', in *James Joyce and Modern Literature*, ed. W. J. McCormack and Alistair Stead, Routledge, Kegan and Paul, 1982, p. 75.

197. *SA*, introduction, p. ii.

198. Padraig O'Malley, *Biting at the Grave*, op. cit., p. 145.

199. Ibid.

200. *SA*, p. 9.

201. *P*, p. 17.

202. *P*, pp. 20–21.

203. *SA*, p. 41. Earlier – on p. 29 – we are informed that Sweeney had three favourite hide-outs, trees located at Rasharkin, Teach mic Ninnedha and Cluan Creaha.

204. Initially the tanks are American ones (see 'The Toome Road', *F*, p. 15, and *P*, p. 17).

205. *SA*, p. 25.

206. *SA*, pp. 10–13. After the battle of Moira, a kinsman of Sweeney's with a band of his followers goes in search of him, and surround him in his yew tree. The king flees to Tyrconnell only to find himself besieged again. Another flight gains him a place of 'natural asylum'. His Glanmore is Glen Bolcain, a place of pebbles, woods, berries, and wild garlic.

207. An allusion, no doubt, to a late-night parade of five hundred men, organised by the Rev. Ian Paisley in February 1981. It was followed by eleven 'Carson trail' rallies, including a gathering at Stormont on March 28 which attracted an audience of 30,000. The rallies coincided with the hunger strikes; one, held on a hillside at Gortin, Newry, took place during the late stages of the Fermanagh and South Tyrone by-election campaign, in which Bobby Sands was elected as an MP.

208. Derek Mahon, *Poems 1962–78*, Oxford University Press, 1979, pp. 64–65.

209. E. H. Gombrich, *The Story of Art*, twelfth edition, Phaidon Press, 1972, pp. 428–433. "In his youth Cézanne took part in the Impressionist exhibitions, but he was so disgusted by the reception accorded them that he withdrew to his native town of Aix, where he studied the problems of his art, undisturbed by the clamour of the critics." Financially secure, just as Heaney was by the early 1980s, he devoted "his whole life to the solution of the artistic problems he set himself, and could apply the most exacting standards to his own work."

210. Ibid., p. 428.

211. A phrase used by the journalist, Martin Decoud, to describe the politics of South America in Joseph Conrad's *Nostromo*, Penguin, 1969, p. 135.

212. The long vowel in 'splayed' endorses the size. One wonders whether

Heaney intends to create a quasi-sexual *frisson*, since 'splayed' is frequently applied to legs, and 'dangled' and 'silky' have suggestive associations. In the final stanza he emphasises the untempting quality of the stone wall.

213. In Matthew Arnold's 'Dover Beach', the moon and sea are the dominant symbols.

> "The Sea of Faith
> Was once, too, at the full, and round earth's shore
> Lay like the folds of a bright girdle furled.
> But now I only hear
> Its melancholy, long, withdrawing roar . . .
> And we are here as on a darkling plain
> Swept by confused alarms of struggle and flight,
> Where ignorant armies clash by night.

In *Station Island*, however, it is the sun which features prominently. In the title sequence it serves as a pagan, lyric presence, while in this poem it appears as a symbol of Catholic majesty.

214. 'The Sounds of Rain', *Seeing Things*, p. 49.
215. *GT*, p. 55.
216. Ibid., p. 70.
217. Zbigniew Herbert, *Barbarian in the Garden*, trans. Michael March and Jaroslaw Anders, San Diego/ New York: Harvest, Harcourt Brace Jovanovich, 1986, p. 10. The cave paintings of Lascaux, in the Dordogne region of France, were discovered in September 1940. They date from before 13,000 B.C. One of the Lascaux paintings depicts a hunter with a 'bird's head' and 'straight beak' (ibid., p. 11). Herbert speculates that the primitive painter may well have been 'longing for his forsaken animal family . . . He was ashamed of his face, a visible sign of his difference. He often wore masks, animal masks, as if trying to appease his own treason' (ibid., p. 12). A revised version of Heaney's *Parnassus* review of Herbert's book appears in *The Government of the Tongue*.
218. *SA*, p. 20. Here Sweeney is awed by the beauty of a stag. Later in the poem, admiration is transformed into identification. 'I am a timorous stag/ feathered by Ronan Finn' (ibid., p. 46).
219. Neil Corcoran, op. cit., p. 179.
220. Seamus Heaney, interview with Randy Brandes, art. cit., p. 6.
221. *Isaiah*, 35, v.6–7. These lines form the first reading for Twenty Third Sunday of the Year in the Catholic Church. The Communion Antiphon for that same day comes from Psalm 42, v.1, lines quoted by Heaney in 'Clearances', 6, in *The Haw Lantern*. In the Missal the translation runs "Like a deer that longs for running streams, my soul longs for you, my God."

**6: Space, 1984–91: Notes to poems from *The Haw Lantern* and
*Seeing Things***

1. John Montague, interviewed by Shirley Anders, *Verse*, Issue VI,
    Oxford, 1986, p. 34. The same issue contains four Heaney poems,
    including 'The Haw Lantern'.
2. Seamus Heaney talking to Blake Morrison, in 'Seamus Famous: Time
    to be dazzled', *The Independent on Sunday*, 19 May 1991, p. 26.
3. Richard Pine, 'Vertical Lift-Off at the Half-Century', *Irish Times*, 11
    April 1989.
4. Seamus Heaney, 'An Amicable and a Candid Child', *The Poetry
    Book Society Bulletin*, Summer 1987, 133, p. 4.
5. Seamus Heaney, interviewed for *Gown* magazine, Queen's Univers-
    ity, Belfast, Vol. 31, No. 4 (1985), p. 4.
6. 'Alphabets' was written in 1984, the year that *Station Island* appeared.
7. An allusion to a famous passage from Thomas Hardy's *Jude the
    Obscure*, Macmillan Papermac Edition, 1966, Part First, Chapter Two,
    p. 23.

> "As you got older, and felt yourself to be at the centre of your
> time, and not at a point in its circumference, as you had felt when
> you were little, you were seized with a sort of shuddering, he
> perceived. All around you there seemed to be something glaring,
> garish, rattling, and the noises and glares hit upon the little cell
> called your life, and shook it, and warped it."

8. Ibid., p. 18.
9. Joseph Brodsky, 'The Power of the Elements' in *Less than One:
    Selected Essays*, Harmonsdsworth: Penguin, 1986, p. 161.
10. The maiden flight of the American space shuttle, Challenger, took
    place in the April of 1983. In his 1988 interview with Randy Brandes,
    Heaney likens Czeslaw Milosz to a 'weightless astronaut walking
    out there', a condition he clearly aspires to (art. cit., p. 10).
11. *Seeing Things*, 'Squarings', viii, p. 62.
12. At the village of Knock in Co. Mayo in 1879, the Virgin Mary is
    said to have appeared on the gable end of the church. Heaney again
    alludes to Knock, later in the collection, in 'The Mud Vision'.
13. William Wordsworth, 'Ode:Intimations of Immortality from Recol-
    lections of Early Childhood', IX, ll. 135–156, *Poetical Works*, ed. cit.,
    p. 461.
14. *Stations*, p. 19.
15. Seamus Heaney, interviewed by Randy Brandes, art. cit., p. 8.
16. Ibid., p. 11.
17. The threat posed to Heaney's private space by endless demands for
    interviews, readings, photographs, comments on articles/books, and
    from being endlessly subjected to critical dissection, should not be
    underestimated. Richard Pine describes in his article, already cited,
    how his conversation with Heaney was punctuated by repeated

telephone calls, "and meanwhile every post diminishes the poet's sabbatical year from Harvard with its inroads on his time." For an interesting contrastive encounter between a poet and a soldier see Michael Longley's excellent poem, 'On Slieve Gullion', *Poems 1963–83*, p. 198. Longley, however, sees the soldier as a kindred spirit, both burdened by history, both guilty of having 'dried the lakes and streams'.

18. The analogy between driving a car and driving a poem occurs again in 'Hailstones' which ends with Heaney laying 'perfect tracks in the slush' *HL*, p. 15.

19. In his interview with Clive Wilmer, BBC Radio 3, 2 September 1990, Heaney explained that "the household where I grew up", "the culture of rural Ulster, indeed Ulster generally, is suspicious of speech. The declaration of an emotion immediately makes the emotion suspect . . . It was highly in place in our minds and in our dumb beings that the unspoken was the trustworthy."

20. The intensity of the relationship stems from the commingling of the sensual and the spiritual, as can be seen in sonnet VI. In sonnet III conventional pieties, represented by 'the others' attending Mass and by the priest going 'hammer and tongs', seem dull and crude in comparison with the subtle, silent intimacy achieved by mother and son.

21. There may be a faint, unconscious echo of Robert Frost's 'Out, Out' (*Selected Poems*, ed. cit., p. 90) in this highly charged, finely controlled scene:

> "   the watcher at his pulse took fright.
> No one believed. They listened at his heart.
> Little-less-nothing! – and that ended it."

Heaney ends his poem, however, stressing the solidarity between the survivors and the victim.

22. *GT*, pp. 3–4. The move from Mossbawn was in part prompted by the death of Christopher, Heaney's four-year-old brother.

23. Ibid., p. 3.

24. Seamus Heaney, interview with Randy Brandes, art. cit., p. 19.

25. *SI*, 'On the Road', p. 121.

26. *Seeing Things*, 'Squarings', xlviii, p. 108.

27. Ibid., 'The Golden Bough', p. 1.

28. Ibid., 'Casting and Gathering', p. 13.

Bibliography

A. Works by Heaney

Death of a Naturalist, London: Faber, 1966.
A Lough Neagh Sequence, Manchester: Phoenix Pamphlet Poets, 1966.
Door into the Dark, London: Faber, 1969.
Wintering Out, London: Faber, 1972.
Soundings, Belfast: Blackstaff Press, 1972.
Stations, Belfast: Ulsterman Publications, 1975.
North, London: Faber, 1975.
Field Work, London: Faber, 1978.
Preoccupations: Selected Prose 1968–1978, London: Faber, 1980.
Station Island, London: Faber, 1984.
Sweeney Astray, London: Faber, 1984.
Hailstones, Dublin: Gallery Press, 1985.
The Haw Lantern, London: Faber, 1987.
The Government of the Tongue, London: Faber, 1988.
The Cure of Troy, London: Faber, 1990.
Seeing Things, London: Faber, 1991.

B. Uncollected Articles

'Out of London: Ulster's Troubles', *New Statesman,* 1 July 1966, pp. 23–24.
'Writer at work', *St.Stephens: Literature and Opinions,* No. 11, Series II, University College Dublin, Hilary Term 1967.
'Irish Eyes', *The Listener,* 28 December 1967.
'Civil rights, not civic weeks', *Gown* Queen's University Belfast, 22 October, 1968.
'Old Derry Walls', *The Listener,* 24 October 1968, pp. 521–523.
'Seamus Heaney writes', *Poetry Book Society Bulletin,* No. 61, Summer 1969.
'Celtic Fringe, Viking Fringe', *The Listener,* 21 August 1969, pp. 254–255.
'Delirium of the Brave', *The Listener,* 27 November 1969, pp. 757–759.
'King of the Dark', *The Listener,* 5 February 1970, pp. 181–182.
'King Conchobor and his Knights', *The Listener,* 26 March 1970, pp. 416–417.
'Views', *The Listener,* 31 December 1970, p. 903.
'Seamus Heaney praises Lough Erne', *The Listener,* 4 February 1971, pp. 142–143.
'A Poet's Childhood', *The Listener,* 11 November 1971, pp. 660–661.
'After the Synge-song: Seamus Heaney on the writings of Patrick Kavanagh', *The Listener,* 13 January 1972 pp. 55–56.

'Mother Ireland', *The Listener,* 7 December 1972, p. 790.
'Lost Ulsterman', *The Listener,* 26 April 1973, pp. 550–551.
'Summoning Lazarus', *The Listener,* 6 June 1974, pp. 741–742.
Biographical comment in *Worlds,* ed. Geoffrey Summerfield, Penguin, 1974.
Introduction to *T. P. Flanagan, Paintings 1967–1977,* Arts Council N.I., 1977.
Introduction to *Collected Short Stories: Michael McLaverty,* Dublin: Poolbeg Press, 1978.
'The Poet as a Christian', *The Furrow,* 29:10, October 1978, pp. 603–606.
Ulster Museum: A Personal Selection by Seamus Heaney, Belfast, 1982.
'A Tale of Two Islands: Reflections on the Irish Literary Revival', *Irish Studies,* I, Cambridge University Press, 1980, pp. 1–20.
'*Among Schoolchildren*', *A John Malone Memorial Lecture,* Belfast University, June 1983.
'Pilgrim's Journey', *Poetry Book Society Bulletin,* 123, Winter 1984.

C. Interviews and Radio Broadcasts

'The Poet Speaks', with Peter Orr, *The British Council,* 1966.
'Turkeys made him a Poet', article by Ray Rosenfield, *Ulster Tatler* 1966.
'Le Clivage Traditionnel', anon, *Les Lettres Nouvelles,* March 1973, pp. 87–89.
'Poets on Poetry', with Patrick Garland, *The Listener,* 8 November, 1973, p. 629.
Interview with Harriet Cooke, *Irish Times,* 6 December 1973.
'The Saturday Interview', with Caroline Walsh, *Irish Times,* 6 December 1975, p. 5.
'Unhappy and at home', with Seamus Deane, *The Crane Bag,* 1,1, 1977, pp. 61–67.
'A Raindrop on a Thorn', with Robert Druce *Dutch Quarterly Review,* Vol. 9, 1978, pp. 24–37.
'An Interview with Seamus Heaney', James Randall, *Ploughshares,* 5,3, 1979, pp. 7–22.
'Talk with Seamus Heaney', Seamus Deane, *New York Times Review,* 84, No. 48, 1979, p. 79–81.
Interview with John Haffenden, *Viewpoints.* London: Faber, 1981, pp. 57–75.
Interview with Frank Kinahan, *Critical Inquiry,* 8:3, Spring 1982, pp. 405–414.
Comments in *Kaleidoscope,* BBC Radio 4, 11 October 1984.
Interview, *Gown,* Queen's University Belfast, Vol. 31, No. 4, 1985.
'A Common Language', a discussion with Seamus Heaney, Derek Walcott, Joseph Brodsky, Les Murray, *Kaleidoscope,* BBC Radio 4, 24 June 1988.
Interview with Bel Mooney, *Turning Points,* BBC Radio 4, 15 November 1988.
Interview with Hermione Lee, *Third Ear,* BBC Radio 3, 6 December 1988.
Interview with Randy Brandes, *Salmagundi,* No. 80, Skidmore College, New York, Fall 1988.

Interview with Richard Pine, 'Vertical lift-off at the half-century', *Irish Times*, 11 April 1989.
Interview with Clive Wilmer, BBC Radio 3, 2 September 1990.
Interview for *Kaleidoscope*, BBC Radio 4, 4 June 1991.

D. Radio and Television Scripts

Explorations, BBC Northern Ireland, Radio 4, 'Words working', 'Words fail me', 'The long garden', 'Bitter Honey', 'Fields of Praise','The Chilly Sun', broadcast January 17–February 28, 1974.
Explorations II', 'Poetry: Authority', broadcast 28 March 1984.
William Wordsworth lived here, BBC, 1974.
Poems in their places, 'Wild Swans at Coole', BBC.
Bogland, BBC Northern Ireland, 1975.
The Boyne Valley, BBC Northern Ireland, 1980.

E. Selected Criticism

Books
Andrews, Elmer, *The Poetry of Seamus Heaney: All the Realms of Whisper*, London: Macmillan, 1989.
Bloom, Harold (ed.), *Seamus Heaney*, Modern Critical Views series, New Haven- New York-Philadelphia: Chelsea House Publishers, 1986.
Broadbridge, Edward (ed.), *Seamus Heaney*, Copenhagen: Danmarks Radio, 1977.
Buttel, Robert, *Seamus Heaney*, Lewisburg, Pa: Bucknell University Press, 1975.
Corcoran, Neil, *Seamus Heaney*, London: Faber, 1986.
Curtis, Tony, *The Art of Seamus Heaney*, Bridgend: Poetry Wales Press, 2nd edition, 1985.
McGuinn, Nicholas, *Seamus Heaney: A Student's Guide to the Selected Poems 1965–75*, Leeds: Arnold Wheaton, 1986.
Maguire, Aisling, *Selected Poems of Seamus Heaney*, Longman York Press, 1986.
Morrison, Blake, *Seamus Heaney* London: Methuen, 1982.

Articles
Anon, 'Life in numbers', *The Times Literary Supplement*, 9 June 1966, p. 512.
Anon, 'Fear in a tinful of bait', *The Times Literary Supplement*, 17 July 1969, p. 770.
Allen, Michael, 'Provincialism and Recent Irish Poetry', *Two Decades of Irish Writing*, ed. Douglas Dunn, Manchester: Carcanet, 1975.
Alvarez, A., 'Homo Faber', *The Observer*, 22 June 1969.
Bayley, John, 'In an Irish Cloister', *The Observer*, 14 October 1984.
Bloom, Harold, 'The Voice of Kinship', *The Times Literary Supplement*, 8 February 1980, pp. 137–138.

Brown, Terence, 'Four New Voices: Poets of the Present' in *Northern Voices: Poets from Ulster*, Dublin: Gill and Macmillan, 1975.

Carey, John, 'The Joy of Heaney', *The Sunday Times*, 21 October 1984.

Carson, Ciaran, 'Escaped from the Massacre?' *The Honest Ulsterman* 50, Winter 1975, pp. 183–186.

Curtis, Simon, 'Seamus Heaney's *North*', *Critical Quarterly* 18, 1, Spring 1976, pp. 80–83.

Deane, Seamus, 'Seamus Heaney: the timorous and the bold', in *Celtic Revivals*, London: Faber, 1985, pp. 174–186.

——, 'Irish Poetry and Irish Nationalism' in *Two Decades of Irish Writing*, ed. Douglas Dunn, Manchester: Carcanet, 1975.

Donoghue, Denis, Review of *Field Work*, *New York Times Book Review* 2 December 1979 p. 1 & p. 45–46.

Dunn, Douglas, 'Manana is now', *Encounter*, November 1975, pp. 76–77.

Ehrenpreis, Irving, 'Digging In', *New York Review of Books*, 8 October 1981, pp. 45–46.

Foster, John Wilson, 'The Poetry of Seamus Heaney', *Critical Quarterly* 16, 1 Spring 1974, pp. 35–48.

——, 'Seamus Heaney's "A Lough Neagh Sequence": sources and motifs' *Eire-Ireland* 12:2 (Summer 1977), pp. 138–142.

Green, Carlanda, 'The Feminine Principle in Seamus Heaney's Poetry', *Ariel*, Vol. 14, No. 3, 1983, pp. 3–13.

Harmon, Maurice, *Irish Poetry after Yeats*, Introduction pp. 9–30, Portmarnock: Wolfhound Press, 1979.

Hederman, Mark, 'Seamus Heaney: The Reluctant Poet', *The Crane Bag*, Vol. 3, No. 2, pp. 61–70.

James, Clive, 'A slough of despond', *The Observer*, 26 November 1972.

Kiely, Benedict, 'A Raid into Dark Corners: The Poems of Seamus Heaney', *The Hollins Critic*, Vol. 4, 4 October 1970, pp. 1–12.

Liddy, James, 'Ulster Poets and the Catholic Muse', *Eire-Ireland* 13, 4 Winter 1978, pp. 126–137.

Lloyd, David, 'The Two Voices in Seamus Heaney's *North*', *Ariel*, Vol. 10, 6, 1979, pp. 5–13.

Longley, Edna, 'Heaney's Hidden Ireland', *Phoenix*, 10, July 1973, pp. 86–89.

——, 'Fire and Air', *The Honest Ulsterman*, 50, Winter 1975, pp. 179–183.

——, 'Old Pewter', *The Honest Ulsterman*, 77, Winter 1984, pp. 54–58.

——, 'Poetry and Politics in Northern Ireland', *The Crane Bag*, Vol. 9, 1 1985, pp. 26–40.

——, 'Stars and Horses, Pigs and Trees', *The Crane Bag* Vol. 3, 2 1979, pp. 54–60.

Longley, Michael, 'Poetry' in *Causeway: The Arts in Ulster*, pp. 95–109, Belfast: Arts Council of Northern Ireland, 1971.

Mahon, Derek, 'Poetry in Northern Ireland', *Twentieth Century Studies*, November 1970, pp. 89–93.

Martin, Graham, 'John Montague, Seamus Heaney and the Irish Past', *Penguin Guide to English Literature*, Vol. 8, pp. 380–395, Penguin 1984.

Maxwell, D. E. S., 'Contemporary Poetry in the North of Ireland', in *Two Decades of Irish Writing*, ed. Douglas Dunn, Manchester: Carcanet, 1975.

——, 'Imagining the North: Violence and the writers', *Eire: Ireland* Vol. 8, 2 1973.

McGuinness, Arthur, 'Hoarder of the Common Ground', *Eire:Ireland* Vol. 13, 2 1978.

——, 'The Craft of Diction: Revision in Seamus Heaney's Poems', *Irish University Review*, 9, No. 1, 1979, pp. .62–91.

Montague, John, 'Order in Donnybrook Fair', *The Times Literary Supplement*, 17 November 1972, p. 313.

Morrison, Blake, 'Speech and reticence in Seamus Heaney's *North*' in *British Poetry since 1970*, ed. Peter Jones and Michael Schmidt, Manchester: Carcanet, 1980, pp. 103–111.

——, 'Encounters with familiar ghosts', *The Times Literary Supplement*, 19 October 1984, pp. 1191–1192.

Muldoon, Paul, 'Sweaney Peregraine', *The London Review of Books*, 1–14 November 1984 pp. 20–21.

Murphy, Richard, 'Poetry and Terror', *New York Review of Books*, 30 September 1976, pp. 38–40.

O'Brien, Conor Cruise, 'A Slow North East Wind', *The Listener*, 25 September 1975, pp. 404–405.

Porter, Peter, 'Poets' places', *The Guardian*, 30 November 1972.

Redshaw, Thomas, '"Ri" as in Regional: Three Ulster Poets', *Eire: Ireland*, Vol. 9, 2 1974, pp. 41–64.

Ricks, Christopher, 'Growing Up', *New Statesman*, 27 May 1966, p. 778.

——, 'Lasting Things', *The Listener*, 26 June 1969, pp. 900–901.

Riordan, Maurice, 'Eros and History: On Contemporary Irish Poetry', *The Crane Bag*, Vol. 9, No. 1, 1985, pp. 49–55.

Schirmer, G. A., 'Seamus Heaney: Salvation in Surrender', *Eire-Ireland* 15, 4, Winter 1980, pp. 139–146.

Thwaite, Anthony, 'Neighbourly Murders', *The Times Literary Supplement*, 1 August 1975 p. 866.

F. Irish History and Literature

Beckett, J. C., *A Short History of Ireland*, London: Hutchinson, sixth edition, 1979.

Bishop, Patrick and Mallie, Eamonn *The Provisional I.R.A*, London: Corgi, 1988.

Boyle, Kevin and Hadden, Tom, *Ireland: A Positive Proposal*, Harmondsworth: Penguin 1985.

Brown, Terence, *Northern Voices: Poets from Ulster*, Dublin Gill and Macmillan, 1975.

Buckland, Patrick, *A History of Northern Ireland*, Dublin: Gill and Macmillan, 1981.

Buckley, Vincent, *Memory Ireland*, Penguin Books Australia, 1985.

Chadwick, Nora, *The Celts*, Harmondsworth: Penguin, 1970.

Coogan, Tim Pat, *I.R.A.*, Fontana, 1980.

Corkery, Daniel, *The Hidden Ireland*, Dublin: Gill and Macmillan, 1924.

Deane, Seamus, *Gradual Wars*, Shannon: Irish University Press, 1972.

——, *History Lessons*, Dublin: Gallery Press, 1983.

Devlin, Polly, *All of us There*, London: Pan Books, 1984.

Dunn, Douglas, *Two decades of Irish Writing*, Manchester: Carcanet 1975.

Evans, E. Estyn, *Irish Folk Ways*, London: Routledge, 1957.

Flackes, W. D., *Northern Ireland: A Political Directory*, London: Ariel Books, 1983.

Flanagan, Thomas, *The Year of the French*, London: Arrow Books 1979.

Friel, Brian, *The Diviner: and other stories*, Dublin: O'Brien Press, 1984.

——, *Selected Plays*, London: Faber, 1984.

Hewitt, John, *The Selected John Hewitt* ed. Alan Warner, Belfast: Blackstaff Press, 1981.

——, *Colin Middleton*, Arts Council Northern Ireland, 1976.

Jeffares, A. Norman, *Anglo Irish Literature*, Macmillan, 1982.

Joyce, James, *The Dubliners*, St Albans: Granada 1977.

——, *Portrait of the Artist as a Young Man*, St Albans: Granada, 1977.

——, *Ulysses*, Harmondsworth: Penguin, 1986.

Kavanagh, Patrick, *Collected Poems*, London: Martin Brian and O'Keeffe, 1972.

——, *November Haggard: The Uncollected Prose and Verse of Patrick Kavanagh*, selected, arranged and edited by Peter Kavanagh, The Peter Kavanagh Hand Press, New York, 1971.

——, *The Green Fool* London: Penguin, 1975.

——, *Tarry Flynn* London: Penguin, 1978.

Kavanagh, Peter, *Sacred Keeper: a biography of Patrick Kavanagh*, Goldsmith Press, Newbridge: Ireland, 1979.

Kernowski, Frank, *John Montague*, Bucknell University Press, 1975.

Kinsella, Thomas, *The Tain*, Oxford University Press, 1970.

Longley, Edna, *Poetry in the Wars*, Newcastle-upon-Tyne: Bloodaxe, 1986.

Longley, Michael, *Poems 1963–1983*, Dublin: Gallery Press, 1985.

Lucy, Sean, *Irish Poets in English*, Cork: Mercier Press, 1973.

MacNeice, Louis, *Collected Poems*, London: Faber, 1979.

Mahon, Derek, *Night Crossing*, Oxford University Press, 1968.

——, *Poems 1962–1978*, Oxford University Press, 1979.

Montague, John, *Poisoned Lands*, Dublin: Dolmen, 1977.

——, *The Rough Field*, Dublin: Dolmen, 1972.

——, *A Slow Dance*, Dublin: Dolmen, 1975.

Neill, Kenneth, *Illustrated History of the Irish People*, Dublin: Gill and Macmillan, 1979.

O'Brien, Edna, *Mother Ireland*, London: Weidenfeld and Nicholson, 1976.

O'Connor, Ulick, *Oliver St John Gogarty*, London: Granada, 1981.

O'Faolain, Sean, *The Irish*, Harmondsworth: Penguin, 1947.

O'Malley Padraig, *Biting at the Grave*, Belfast: Blackstaff Press, 1990.

Ormsby, Frank. ed., *Poets from the North of Ireland*, Belfast: Blackstaff, 1979.

Pakenham, Thomas, *The Year of Liberty*, London: Hodder and Stoughton, 1969.

Paulin, Tom, *Ireland and the English Crisis*, Newcastle-upon Tyne: Bloodaxe, 1984.

Rolleston, T. W., *The Myths and Legends of the Irish Race*, Harrap, 1911.

Ronsley, Joseph. ed., *Myth and Reality in Irish Literature,* Ontario: Wilfrid Laurier Press, 1977.

Skelton, Robin. ed., *Six Irish Poets,* Oxford University Press, 1962.

Trevor, William, *A Writer's Ireland,* Thames and Hudson, 1984.

White, Barry, *John Hume: Statesman of the Troubles,* Belfast: The Blackstaff Press, 1984.

Woodham Smith, Cecil, *The Great Hunger,* New English Library, 1968.

Yeats, W. B., *Collected Poems,* London: Macmillan, 1933.

——, *Selected Plays,* London: Macmillan, 1964.

——, *Selected Criticism,* London: Macmillan, 1964.

G. Other Works

Brodsky, Joseph, *Less Than One: Selected Essays,* Harmondsworth: Penguin, 1987.

Dante *The Divine Comedy,* translated by Dorothy L. Sayers, Harmondsworth: Penguin, 3 vols, 1968.

Frost, Robert, *Selected Poems* ed. Ian Hamilton, Harmondsworth: Penguin, 1973.

Hill, Geoffrey, *Collected Poems,* Harmondsworth: Penguin, 1985.

Hopkins, Gerard Manley, *Poems and Prose* ed. W. H. Gardner, Harmondsworth: Penguin, 1963.

Hughes, Ted, *The Hawk in the rain,* London: Faber, 1957.

——, *Lupercal,* London: Faber, 1960.

——, *Wodwo,* London: Faber, 1967.

Longley, Edna, ed., *A Language not to be betrayed: Selected Prose of Edward Thomas,* Manchester: Carcanet, 1981.

Lloyd, A. L., *Folk Song in England,* London: Panther, 1969.

Magnusson, Magnus and Palsson, Hermann (translators), *Njal's Saga,* Harmondsworth: Penguin, 1960.

Mandelstam, Nadezhda, *Hope against Hope,* Harmondsworth: Penguin, 1975.

Mandelstam, Osip, *Selected Poems,* trans. Clarence Brown and W. S. Merwin Harmondsworth: Penguin, 1977.

McCaig, Norman, *Old Maps and new: Selected Poems,* London: Hogarth Press, 1978.

Milosz, Czeslaw, *The Captive Mind,* Harmondsworth: Penguin, 1980.

Roethke, Theodore, *Collected Poems,* London: Faber, 1985.

Storey, Graham, *A Preface to Hopkins,* London: Longman, 1981.

Storr, Anthony, *Jung,* Glasgow: Fontana, 1973.

Thomas, Edward, *The Collected Poems* ed. R.George Thomas, Oxford University Press, 1981.

Thomas, R. S., *Song of the Year's Turning,* Hart Davis, 1955.

Wordsworth, William, *Poetical Works,* Oxford University Press, 1933.

Index of Poems, Collections and Essays

A Constable Calls 148–9, 260 n53
Act of Union 98, 125, 133, 142–4, 167, 254–5 n195, 255 n196
A Drink of Water 158
After a Killing 155–6
A Hazel Stick for Catherine Ann 190
A Kite for Michael and Christopher 188, 190, 269 n151
A Lough Neagh Sequence 81–4
Alphabets 14, 211
A Migration 189
Among Schoolchildren: A John Malone Memorial Lecture 21, 141, 203, 272 n189
An Advancement of Learning 49, 166
An Afterwards 172, 261 n69
Anahorish 97–9, 242 n48
An Artist 207
Ancestral Photograph 1, 41, 56, 62
A New Song 97
A Northern Hoard 103–5, 115
An Open Letter 177
Antaeus 129
A Pillowed Head 121
'A Poet's Childhood' 5, 66
A Postcard from North Antrim: In Memory of Sean Armstrong 159, 161–2, 176
Aran (unpublished poem) 25
A Royal Prospect 219
Ash Plant, The 218
An Ulster Twilight 180, 223 n22
At Ardboe Point 83
At a Potato Digging 43, 62, 69–71, 167
At the Water's Edge 157–8
Away from it All 185

Badgers, The 176
Barn, The 24, 38, 66, 75, 133, 235 n25
Belderg 129–30
Biretta, The 220
Birthplace, The 189–90, 269 n148
Blackberry Picking 35, 43, 56, 65, 67, 75
Bog Oak 95
Bog Queen 135–6, 201
Bogland 61, 85, 87–8, 99
Bone Dreams 129, 133–4
Boy Driving his Father to Confession (unpublished poem) 2
Broagh 97–9
Bye-Child 112–13, 115

Cana Revisited 81
Casting and Gathering 220
Casualty 159, 161–4, 176, 259 n25
Changes 190
Chekhov on Sakhalin 180, 185–6, 268 n134, n135
Churning Day 63–4
Clearances 3, 4, 178, 211, 215–17, 276 n20, n21
Come to the Bower 134–5, 251–2 n169
Crossings 221
Cure at Troy, The 211, 270 n161

Dawn Shoot 34, 45
Death of a Naturalist 32, 61–76, 79, 85, 102, 133, 151, 209, 213, 221, 237 n58
Death of a Naturalist 17, 24, 38, 45, 52, 56–7, 65–6, 75
Digging 28, 38, 41, 45, 49, 56, 62, 173, 202, 258 n12
Diviner, The 56, 73

Docker 40, 55, 62, 71–2, 102
Door into the Dark 47, 61, 76–88, 109, 128

Early Purges, The 35, 55, 65–7
Elegy 164, 166
Elegy for a Still-Born Child 81
'Englands of the Mind' 44
Exposure 148–51, 154, 167, 208

'Feelings into Words' 3, 20
Field Work 83, 122, 152–77, 195, 207
First Flight, The 180, 206
First Gloss, The 205
First Kingdom, The 206
Fodder 94
Follower 43, 49, 62–4, 173, 218
For the Commander of the 'Eliza' 69
Forge, The 81–2, 238 n82
Fosterage 29, 132, 256 n209
Freedman 145–6, 225 n61
From the Canton of Expectation 214, 258 n13
From the Land of the Unspoken 214
From the Frontier of Writing 146, 214
From the Republic of Conscience 269 n155
Funeral Rites 129, 130–2, 250 n153, n154, n155

Gifts of Rain 97, 99–101, 115
Glanmore Revisited 219–21
Glanmore Sonnets 83, 167–72
Goodnight 110
Government of the Tongue, The 257 n7, 268 n134
Grabaulle Man, The 123, 136
Granite Chip 180, 187–8
Gravities 72
Guttural Muse, The 164

Hailstones 276 n18
Harvest Bow, The 154, 172–4, 223 n22

Haw Lantern, The 38, 178, 207, 209, 211–17
Hedge-School 8
Homecomings 172
Honeymoon Flight 72–3

In Gallarus Oratory 84–5
In Illo Tempore 208, 273–4 n212
In Memoriam Francis Ledwidge 173, 174–6, 262–3 n74, n76, n80, n81, n83
In Memoriam Sean O'Riada 164–6
In the Beech 206

Kinship 139–41

Last Mummer, The 97, 115
La Toilette 185
Limbo 112–13, 115
Linen Town 243 n59
Loaning, The 180, 191–2, 205
Lovers on Aran 48–9, 72–3, 82

Making Strange 189
Man and Boy 211, 218
Markings 218–19
Mid Term Break 13, 23, 35, 38, 49, 55, 67–8, 223 n22, 231 n52
Ministry of Fear 12–13, 147
Mossbawn: Two Poems in Dedication 126–9, 158, 173
   Sunlight 126–8, 130, 249 n140
   Seedcutters, The 128–9, 249 n142
Mother 79–80, 223 n22, 237 n77, 258 n16
Mother of the Groom 109–10
Mud Vision, The 214

National Trust (unpublished poem) 40, 55
New Selected Poems 1966–87 211, 271 n180, 272 n192
North 61, 83, 88, 93, 96, 99, 117–151, 207, 224 n45
North 129, 132–3

Ocean's Love to Ireland 133, 142

October Thought (unpublished poem) 24
Old Icons, The 180, 207–8
On the Road 208
Orange Drums, Tyrone 1966 148–9
Other Side, The 6, 101–3, 115
Otter, The 172
Outlaw, The 55, 82
Oysters 154–5

Parable Island 214
Peninsula, The 85
Personal Helicon 17, 24, 38–9, 56, 73–4
Pitchfork, The 219
'Placeless Heaven, The' 31
Plantation, The 85
Polder 172
Preoccupations 7, 11, 18, 20, 44, 74, 177, 258 n16, 263 n81
Punishment 137–8

Railway Cildren, The 190–1
Reaping in Heat (unpublished poem) 24
Relic of Memory 83
Remebering Malibu 185–6
Requiem for the Croppies 62
Rite of Spring 81, 258 n16

Sandstone Keepsake 180, 185, 187
Scaffolding 58
Seedcutters, The *see under* Mossbawn: Two Poems in Dedication
Seeing Things 207, 209–11, 217–21
Seeing Things 211, 218–19, 253 n177
September Song 165
Servant Boy 96–7
Settle Bed, The 220
Shelf-Life 187–8, 265 n106
Shoreline 85
Sibyl 156–7
Singer's House, The 164–5
Singing School 29, 146–51
Skunk, The 172
Sloe Gin 185

Song of My Man Alive (unpublished poem) 25
Squarings 218–21
Station Island 83, 153, 177–210
Station Island 133, 180, 192–204, 270 n159
Stations 6, 8, 10, 224 n45, 226 n94
Stone Grinder, The 212
Stone Verdict, The 216
Storm on the Island 58
Strand at Lough Beg, The 159–61, 176, 200–1, 259 n26, 271 n180
Strange Fruit 138, 145
Summer Home 110–12, 115
Summer 1969 149
Sweeney Astray (Buile Suibhne) 120–1, 177, 181, 183–4, 192, 205, 206, 268 n131, 270 n157, 273 n206, 274 n218
Sweeney Redivivus 205

Taking Stock (unpublished poem) 55–6
Terminus 38, 213–4
This Morning from a Dewy Motorway 93–4, 268 n135
Three Drawings 220
Tinder 104
Tollund Man, The 91, 99, 105–9, 115, 123, 136, 141, 201
Toome 97
Toome Road, The 158–9
Traditions 97
Trout 45
Triptych 155–8
Twice Shy 72
Turkey's Observed 44, 49, 55

Ugolino 176–7, 263 n84
Unacknowledged Legislator's Dream, The 144
Underground, The 184–5, 208, 267 n130
Undine 81–2

Valediction 72
Veteran's Dream 105
Viking Dublin: Trial Pieces 129, 132–3, 251 n164

Wanderer, The 10
Wedding Day 109
Westering 113–15
'Whatever You Say, Say
    Nothing' 144–5
Wheels within Wheels 220

Whinlands 85
Wife's Tale, The 80–1, 237–8 n77
Wintering Out 34, 47, 61, 88,
    89–114, 126, 169
Writer and Teacher (unpublished
    poem) 58

Index of General References

Æ (George Russell) 174, 243 n60
Akhmatova, Anna 150
Alvarez, A. 47, 82, 232 n77
Anahorish 7, 8, 65, 147, 198, 212
Andersen, Hans Christian 82, 202, 272 n184
Ardboe 47–8, 161
Armstrong, Sean 159, 161–2
    see under poem index A Postcard from North Antrim
Arnold, Matthew 84, 274 n213
Auden, W. H. 37, 103

Barnes, William 78–9
Beckett, Samuel 42
Belfast 27, 34, 44, 51–3, 58, 60, 90, 92–3, 117–19, 124, 126, 153, 154, 161, 165, 174, 186
Bellaghy 2, 13–14, 81, 180, 200–1
Berkeley, California
    see under Heaney, Seamus in America
Blake, William 23, 163, 232 n77
'Bloody Sunday' 117–18, 157, 161, 163–4, 179, 205
Bly, Robert 93
Bog Poems 91, 105–9, 134–40, 201
Bog landscapes 7, 87–8, 91, 135, 253 n179, 253 n184
Boyle, Kevin 118, 244 n73
Boyne Valley 131, 175, 262 n76
Breughel, Pieter 63, 128–9, 235 n13
British Army 86, 90, 92, 115–18, 124, 126, 137, 141, 158–9, 164, 174–6
British Government policy in Northern Ireland 86–7, 92–4, 117–18, 124–6, 178–80, 187, 264 n88, 265 n100, n101
Brodsky, Joseph 151, 212
Brookeborough, Lord (Prime Minister of N. Ireland) 39,59

Brown, George Mackay 78
Burntollet Bridge, ambush at 59, 78
Buttel, Robert 24
Butter, Peter 26

Camus, Albert 66, 231
Carleton, William 183, 192–4, 197, 204, 264 n123, 270 n159
Carrickfergus 40, 165
Carson, Ciaran 128, 150–1
Carysfort Training College 152, 177
Castedawson 1, 81
Catholic Church 14, 21, 115–116, 145–7, 180–3, 193–7, 206–7
    see also under Heaney, Seamus: Catholicism and Catholic community
Cézanne, Paul 20, 207, 273 n209
Chambers, Harry 51, 82, 83
Chekhov, Anton 30, 155, 185–6, 268 n134, n135
Chichester-Clark, James (Prime Minister of N. Ireland) 7
Civil Rights Movement 18, 77–8, 115, 117, 157
    see also N.I.C.R.A.
Clare, John 22
Clarke, Austin 36
Coleridge, Samuel Taylor 103
Corkery, Daniel 22, 29, 39–41, 45, 58, 61–2, 79, 82, 96, 119, 142, 222 n1, 238 n82, 254 n192
Corcoran, Neil 49, 163
Corrigan, Mairead 154
Craig, William 77

Dante 79, 159–61, 172, 173, 176–7, 181, 183–4, 187, 192, 198, 200, 217, 259 n26, 261 n68, 267 n127, n128, 270 n168, 271 n180
Deane, Seamus 11, 13, 16–18,

21, 147–8, 185, 249 n143,
   261 n64
Delaney, Tom   123, 192, 200,
   271 n174
Derry (Londonderry)   11, 16,
   77–8, 90, 116–18, 174, 206
De Valera, Eamon   47
Devlin, Bernadette   77, 118, 154
Devlin, Denis   183
Devlin, Marie
  see under Heaney, Marie
Devlin, Polly   47–8, 109, 244 n77
Donegal   87–8, 91, 165, 181
Donne, John   114
Dublin   72, 118, 120, 126, 152–3,
   155, 264 n97,
Dunsany, Lord   174, 262 n76
Dun Scotus   19

Easter Rising (1916)   85
Eliot, T. S.   14, 18, 31, 85, 167, 251
   n162, 260 n49
Estyn Evans, E.   2, 65, 69, 71, 74,
   238 n85, 240 n110, 241 n26, 242
   n37, 250 n158, 262 n72
Ewart-Biggs, Christopher   155

Famine, the Great Irish   69–71,
   236 n32
Faulkner, Brian (Prime Minister of
   N. Ireland)   118, 125–6
Field Day   177
Fitt, Gerry   77, 125
Flanagan, T. P. (Terry)   29, 46–7,
   55, 85, 87–8, 91, 161, 241–2 n37
Flanagan, Thomas   93, 240–1 n22
Fowles, John   172
Friel, Brian   40, 177, 214, 248 n136
   Translations   40, 184–5, 241 n34,
    245 n81, 260 n54, n56
   Making History   214, 254 n174
Frost, Robert   23–4, 76, 80–1, 83,
   227 n118, 238 n79, 276 n21

G.A.A. (Gaelic Athletics Associa-
   tion)   22, 156
Gabbey, Alan   49
Gallagher, Raymond   13–14
Gallagher, Jack 'Rusty'   13–14

Glob, P. V. (author of *The Bog
   People*)   7, 91, 105–7, 123,
   135–8, 140, 243 n69, n71, 252
   n170, n175, 253 n183, 254 n186
Golding, William   105
Greene, Graham   146, 148,
   256 n207
Goya   90, 146

H-blocks *see under* Hunger Strikes
   and Long Kesh
Hammond, David   3, 13, 52–5, 77,
   93, 123, 165, 233 n108, 257 n7
Hardy, Thomas   7, 8, 16, 22, 42,
   46–7, 73, 79, 83, 87, 100, 110,
   113, 189–90, 242 n51, 243 n80,
   271 n175, 275 n7
Heaney, Agnes (poet's aunt)   192,
   195, 270 n163
Heaney, Ann (poet's sister)   12, 14
Heaney, Christopher (poet's
   brother)   13, 68
Heaney, Margaret Kathleen
   (née McCann – poet's
   mother)   2–4, 8, 21, 26, 68,
   79–81, 109–10, 178, 188, 211,
   215–17
Heaney, Marie (née Devlin – poet's
   wife)   29, 46–9, 51, 55, 58, 72,
   109–10, 117, 142–3, 152–3, 167,
   170–2, 184, 190, 220, 244–5 n78,
   260 n47, 261 n67
Heaney, Mary (poet's aunt)   3, 8,
   127, 223 n12
Heaney, Patrick (poet's father)
   1–6, 11, 26, 62–4, 68, 70, 173–4,
   188, 190, 211, 212, 216, 217–19,
   269 n67
Heaney, Seamus Justin
   birth of   1
   parents of *see* Heaney, Margaret
    Kathleen and Heaney,
    Patrick
   brothers and sisters   3 *see also*
    Heaney, Ann and Heaney,
    Christopher
   ancestry   4–5, 37, 61–4, 95,
    100–1, 121, 140, 186, 190
   homes: Mossbawn   6–7, 13–14,

24, 28, 33, 64–6, 78, 85, 94–5,
98–9, 113, 124, 126–8, 133,
147–9, 153, 158, 166–70, 173,
190, 202–3, 205–6, 212–13,
217, 276 n22; Glanmore   28,
119–21, 143, 149–150,
152–3, 166–72, 189, 207;
Dublin   152–3
Catholicism, Catholic community, Catholic identity   4–6,
8, 32–4, 39–41, 44, 47, 55,
59–60, 72–5, 84, 89, 91, 5,
111, 112–18, 120, 124–6,
130–2, 139–40, 145–7, 160–4,
175, 181–3, 191–7, 203, 207–9,
212–13, 221, 245 n87, 245
n90, 246 n96, 255–6 n206,
263 n81, 265 n107, n110, 269
n155, 270–1 n167, n169, 274
n213, 275 n12, 276 n20
Celtic/Gaelic/pre-Christian
images and influences   1,
14, 21, 29, 39, 44–6, 63, 69,
73–5, 79, 83, 87, 88, 95, 97,
113, 116, 131–2, 140–1, 150,
157–8, 169, 175–6, 181, 190,
193–4, 212, 234 n12, 237 n51,
269 n150
landscape   6–8, 46–7, 64, 84–5,
87–8, 135–6, 153, 205, 224
n36, n38
education: primary   8–11, 212;
secondary   10–17, 212 *see
also under* St Columb's College; Gaeltacht   14, 212–13;
university   17, 21–7 *see also*
Queen's University, Belfast
sense of exile   13–14, 28–30, 72,
79, 100, 113–14, 117, 119–20,
123–4, 149, 180
political consciousness   15–16,
18, 39–40, 59–60, 69–71,
77–9, 85–7, 89–94, 205–8,
247 n118, 248 n138, 257–8 n7,
265 n110
sectarianism   6, 8–10, 15, 39–41,
48, 55, 59–60, 71–2, 101–5,
107, 145, 153, 176, 193–4, 199
colonialism   4–5, 7, 9–10,

21–2, 32, 97–9, 123, 133–4,
141–6, 187
sexuality   6–7, 20, 21–2, 24, 25,
31, 48, 66, 72–3, 81–2, 87,
111–12, 134–6, 139, 142–3,
147, 171–2, 183
guilt   2, 5, 64, 68, 136–7, 170,
176, 180, 185–6, 200–1
teaching career   29, 46, 76–7, 92,
117, 119, 177, 212
poetry as vocation   3–6, 32,
45, 119, 195, 246–7 n112,
248 n135
function of Art   3–4, 17–20,
35–6, 88, 91–3, 154, 180,
185–6, 188, 198, 202 207
Incertus   2, 20, 24–5, 33, 55, 219
speechlessness   2, 13, 56, 155,
216, 276 n19
haecceitas   19, 34, 44, 84
parochialism and provincialism   33–8
Belfast Group   50–3, 55–6
Faber and Faber accepts DN   58
marriage   58, 72–3, 79–80, 109,
166–7 *see also* Heaney, Marie
birth of sons, Michael and
Christopher, 76, 77, 153
birth of daughter, Catherine
Ann   121
in America   92–3, 113–14, 117,
119, 177, 240 n17, 243 n54
attitude to Civil Rights   77–8
communal solidarity   115–16,
137–8, 162–4, 204–8
'Bloody Sunday'   118, 157, 204
Hunger Strikes   178–80, 186
Irish language   3, 7, 41, 97–9,
139, 169, 204, 272 n193
biblical allusion in poetry of   3,
4, 6, 8.   10, 83, 86, 94, 99,
101–4, 112–15, 122, 133, 138,
150, 163–5, 191, 209–10, 215,
221, 253 n177, 274 n221
classical allusion in poetry of   1,
6, 63–4, 74, 145–6, 155–6,
184, 192, 208, 217–18, 249
n147, 255–6 n206, 263 n81,
267 n130

Heath, Edward 117
Herbert, Zbigniew 151, 154, 187,
   209, 212, 217 n180, 274 n217
Hewitt, John 36, 254 n188
Hobsbaum, Philip 21, 46, 49–52,
   55, 58–9, 76, 143, 146, 230 n34
Holland, Mary 59
Holub, Miroslav 151, 154, 212
Honest Ulsterman, The 51, 89
Hopkins, Gerard Manley 17,
   19–21, 24, 30, 34, 44, 45, 47,
   73–6, 82, 133, 226 n94, n95,
   n98, 227 n101, 228 n121, 235
   n13, n25, 238 m82
Horace 167, 198, 255, 255 n202
Houlihan, Kathleen ni 106, 134
   see also Mother Ireland and
      Nerthus
Hughes, Francis 180, 192, 201–2,
   269–70 n155, 272 n182
Hughes, Ted 19, 21, 23, 34, 42,
   44–5, 49, 56–7, 62, 66, 72–3,
   82–4, 85, 100, 177, 207, 231
   n77, 234 n5, 239 n91, 242 n51
   Hawk in the Rain, The 23, 34, 44,
      49, 56, 62, 72, 100, 252 n172
   Lupercal 42, 44–5, 49, 82
   Poetry in the Making 45, 53
   Wodwo 57, 72, 84, 85
Hume, John 11, 12, 14
Hunger Strikes 178–80, 186, 205,
   264 n93, n95, n97, n98, n99,
   n100, 267 n121, 269–70 n155,
   272 n193, 273 n208
   see also Long Kesh

Inishowen 186
I.R.A. (Irish Republican Army)
   15–16, 59, 72, 155
   see also Provisional I.R.A.

Jamison, Kenneth 46
John XXIII, Pope 72
John Paul II, Pope 178
Joyce, James 22, 23, 29, 39, 41, 72,
   82, 94, 97–8, 120, 130, 132–3,
   146, 181, 183, 187, 188, 192, 194,
   195, 203–4, 248 n136, 265 n107,
   267 n123, 269 n144, 270 n165

Dubliners 130
*Portrait of the Artist as a Young
   Man* 22, 39, 41, 94, 204, 238
   n82, 272 n192
Ulysses 181, 195, 270 n164
Jung, Carl Gustav 116, 168, 246
   n103, 258 n15

Kavanagh, Patrick 24, 29, 30–6,
   39, 47, 62, 69–71, 74,.76, 79,
   88, 146, 167, 183, 192, 194, 198,
   204, 223 n22, 228 n1, 229 n12,
   n14, 230 n33, 234 n10, 267 n123,
   270 n167
   Great Hunger, The 31–2, 34,
      69–71, 236 n34
   Green Fool, The 31, 34–5, 74, 235
      n27, 243 n60
   Lough Derg 183, 193, 198, 199
   Soul for Sale, A 30, 33
   Tarry Flynn 31, 79
Keats, John 17, 20, 42, 202
Keenan, Terry 192, 196–8
Kell, Richard 36
Kiely, Benedict 83, 223 n3
Kinsella, Thomas 28, 35, 36,
   120–1, 242 n45

Lascaux, caves at 209, 274 n217
Lawrence, D. H. 21–2, 25, 110,
   245 n80
Leavis, F. R. 15, 49
Ledwidge, Francis 172, 174–6, 262
   n74, n76, n80, 263 n83
Lerner, Laurence 22, 76
Lloyd, A. L. 81
Long Kesh (the Maze prison)
   178–80, 186, 268 n135
   see also Hunger Strikes
Longley, Edna 43, 51–2, 71, 151,
   188, 251 n160
Longley, Michael 2, 51–3, 59,
   76–7, 93, 115, 118, 223 n6, 258
   n9, 276 n17
Lough Beg 8, 159–61
Lough Derg 181–3, 266 n115
   see also Station Island
Lowell, Robert 110, 122–3,
   156, 166

Loyola, Ignatius 19
Lucie-Smith, Edward 49, 50, 58

McBurney, Martin 161
McCaig, Norman 42–4, 231 n69
McCartney, Colum 153, 159–61,
192, 200–1
see also under poem index The
Strand at Lough Beg and
Station Island
McCorley, Roddy 7, 258 n17
McCracken, Henry Joy 5, 162,
243 n59
McFadden, Roy 60
McLaverty, Michael 19, 29–30, 46,
49, 54, 55, 132, 149
McSorley, Monsignor 182
McSwiney, Terence 182, 266–7
n121
McWhirter, George 21, 24–26
Mac Laverty, Bernard 51
MacNeice, Louis 26, 141, 250 n156
Magilligan strand 117, 187
Magnusson, Magnus 132
Maguire, Anne 154
Mahon, Derek 21, 53, 59, 76,
115, 207
Malone, John 54
Mandelstam, Nadezhda 122
Mandelstam, Osip 122, 147, 150,
151, 154, 192, 204, 256–7 n211,
267 n127
Mansfield, Katherine 146
Marlowe, Christopher 22
Merriman, Brian 40, 238 n85
Milosz, Czeslaw 89, 151, 185, 212,
275 n10
Monteith, Charles 58
Montague, John 29, 36–9, 68,
121–2, 127–8, 211, 230 n45,
231 n52
Poisoned Lands 36–7,
Rough Field, The 121–2, 127–8,
231 n50, 247 n126, 248 n140
Morrison, Blake 163–4, 177, 229
n12, 254 n193, 259 n30
Mother Ireland 106, 134
see under Kathleen ni Houlihan
and Nerthus

Motion, Andrew 177
Mountbatten, Earl 178
Moyola, River 8, 100–1, 170
Muir, Edwin 29, 78
Murphy, Bernard 10, 192, 197–8,
224 n44
Murphy, Richard 36, 150

Nationalist Party of Northern
Ireland 14,160
Nerthus 106–7, 135–41
Newry 15, 118, 157
N.I.C.R.A. (Northern Ireland Civil
Rights Association) 77–8, 117
see under Civil Rights Movement
Northern Ireland Education Act
(1947) 11, 21, 48, 145
Nugent, Ciaran 178
Njal's Saga 132, 251 n160

O'Brien, Conor Cruise 93, 150,
151, 241 n22
O'Casey, Sean 204
O'Faolain, Sean 29, 183
O Fiaich, Archbishop Tomas 179,
264 n93
Oisin 8, 44, 88, 116, 181
O'Kelly, J. B. S. (Sean B.) 16–17,
19, 22, 30, 49
O'Malley, Padraig 205, 271 n182
O'Neill, Louis 159, 161–4
see poem index Casualty
O'Neill, Terence 59, 78, 90
O Rathaille, Aodhagan 40, 142,
254 n192
O'Riada, Sean 165–6, 260 n43
O Suilleabhain, Eoghan Ruadh
40–1, 61–2
Ormsby, Frank 37
Ovid 256 n211, 267 n130
Owen, Wilfred 154, 176, 191, 199,
263 n82, 271 n170
Oxford University 26,46

Paisley, Rev. Ian 59–60, 72, 78,
120, 125, 263 n82, 273 n207
Pakenham, Thomas 86–7,90–1
Parker, Stewart 51, 52, 58
Pasternak, Boris 167

Peace Movement   154
Pearse, Padraic   182, 266 n121
Planters   7, 98–9, 130
   see also Protestants and
      Protestantism
Plath, Sylvia   23, 57, 110, 244 n75,
   245 n88
Porter, Peter   50
Protestants, and Protestantism   5,
   6, 7, 8–10, 11, 21, 32, 39–40, 48,
   52, 54–5, 59–60, 71–2, 85–6, 96,
   98–9, 101–3, 120, 125–6, 131,
   143–5, 148, 154, 183, 187, 207
Protestant paramilitary groups
   126, 144
   see also under U.D.A. and U.V.F.
Provisional I.R.A.   91–3, 115,
   124–5, 144, 155–6, 161–2, 176,
   178–9, 251 n160

Queen's University, Belfast   17,
   21–27, 46, 47, 76, 92, 117, 119,
   124, 130, 133, 161, 169

Ralegh, Sir Walter   142
Rea, Stephen   177
Rebellion, the Great (1798)   69,
   85–6
Republican Action Force   154
Redgrove, Peter   50
Roethke, Theodore   10, 56–7
R.U.C. (Royal Ulster Constabu-
   lary)   15, 93, 148–9

St Brigid (Bridget)   74, 98, 146,
   182, 195
St Columb's College, Derry
   10–17, 21, 39, 133, 147, 169,
   206, 216, 226 n82
St Columcille (Columba)   72,
   123–4
St John of the Cross   192, 203
St Joseph's College   27, 50, 53
St Patrick   8, 116, 134, 181–2, 195,
   239 n91
St Patrick's Purgatory
   see under Lough Derg and
      Station Island
Saddlemeyer, Anne   167

Sands, Bobby   154, 179–80, 182,
   258 n8, 267 n121, 271–2 n182,
   273 n207
Shakespeare, William   44, 51, 98
   Antony and Cleopatra   101,
      239 n91
   Hamlet   64, 133
   Henry V   98
   King Lear   42, 44, 111
   Macbeth   199, 261 n63
   Merchant of Venice   171
   Othello   223 n13
   Richard III   76, 90
   Romeo and Juliet   151
   The Tempest   157, 251 n167
   A Winter's Tale   110, 173
Shklovsky, Victor   189
Simmons, James   51
Simpson, Louis   189
Skelton, Robin   36
Snyder, Gary   93
Spenser, Edmund   40, 95–6, 142,
   241 n28
Station Island   181–3, 266 n115
Stevenson, Anne   143
Strathearn, William   192, 198–9
Sweeney, King   160, 185, 192,
   205–9, 267 n127, 268 n131
Sweeney, Simon   192–3
Synge, John Millington   26, 204,
   259 n35

Tacitus   141, 252 n35
Thatcher, Margaret   180
Thomas, Dylan   21, 25, 140
Thomas, Edward   x, 22
Thomas, R. S.   21, 42–3
Thwaite, Antony   150
The Twa Corbies   170

U.D.A. (Ulster Defence Associa-
   tion)   124
U.U.C. (Ulster Unionist Coun-
   cil)   125, 153–4
U.V.F. (Ulster Volunteer
   Force)   117, 153–4
Ulster Workers Council   125

Vergil   167, 217–18

Viking history and myth 123,
129–35, 249 n150
Vinegar Hill, battle of 86

Walcott, Derek 212
Webster, John 22
Wilde, Oscar 204
William III, King of England 40,
251 n167, 255 n203
Williams, Betty 154
Williams, William Carlos 93
Woodham Smith, Cecil 69–71
Wyatt, Sir Thomas 171

Wordsworth, William 6, 10,
17–18, 20, 42, 45, 46, 49, 51, 56,
71, 75–6, 99, 101, 147, 166, 168,
213, 242 n50, 257 n2, 265 n102,
269 n146, n148
The Prelude 8, 10, 17–18, 75–6,
101, 152, 225 n82
Yeats, W. B. 101, 103, 122–3,
130–1, 140–1, 142, 144, 145,
146–7, 154, 164–7, 190, 204, 242
n53, 243 n54, n61, 249 n147, 259
n35, 268 n142